The Origins of Dominant Parties

In many autocracies, regime leaders share power with a ruling party, which can help generate popular support and reduce conflict among key elites. Such ruling parties are often called dominant parties. In other regimes, leaders prefer to rule solely through some combination of charisma, patronage, and coercion, rather than sharing power with a dominant party. This book explains why dominant parties emerge in some nondemocratic regimes, but not in others. It offers a novel theory of dominant party emergence that centers on the balance of power between rulers and other elites. Drawing on extensive fieldwork in Russia, original data on Russian political elites, and cross-national statistical analysis, the book's findings shed new light on how modern autocracies work and why they break down. The analysis also provides new insights about the foundations of Vladimir Putin's regime and challenges several myths about the personalization of power under Putin.

Ora John Reuter is Assistant Professor of Political Science at the University of Wisconsin, Milwaukee and a Senior Researcher at the Higher School of Economics in Moscow. His articles on elections, authoritarianism, and political economy have appeared in leading social science journals, including the *Journal of Politics*, *World Politics*, the *British Journal of Political Science*, *Comparative Political Studies*, and *Post-Soviet Affairs*.

The Origins of Dominant Parties
Building Authoritarian Institutions in Post-Soviet Russia

Ora John Reuter
University of Wisconsin, Milwaukee

CAMBRIDGE
UNIVERSITY PRESS

University Printing House, Cambridge CB2 8BS, United Kingdom

One Liberty Plaza, 20th Floor, New York, NY 10006, USA

477 Williamstown Road, Port Melbourne, VIC 3207, Australia

4843/24, 2nd Floor, Ansari Road, Daryaganj, Delhi – 110002, India

79 Anson Road, #06-04/06, Singapore 079906

Cambridge University Press is part of the University of Cambridge.

It furthers the University's mission by disseminating knowledge in the pursuit of education, learning, and research at the highest international levels of excellence.

www.cambridge.org
Information on this title: www.cambridge.org/9781107171763
DOI: 10.1017/9781316761649

© Ora John Reuter 2017

This publication is in copyright. Subject to statutory exception and to the provisions of relevant collective licensing agreements, no reproduction of any part may take place without the written permission of Cambridge University Press.

First published 2017

A catalogue record for this publication is available from the British Library.

Library of Congress Cataloging-in-Publication Data
Names: Reuter, Ora John, author.
Title: The origins of dominant parties: building authoritarian institutions in post-soviet Russia / Ora John Reuter.
Description: Milwaukee: Cambridge University Press, 2017. | Includes bibliographical references and index.
Identifiers: LCCN 2016051824 | ISBN 9781107171763 (hardback)
Subjects: LCSH: Political parties – Russia (Federation) | Authoritarianism – Russia (Federation) | Post-communism – Russia (Federation) | Russia (Federation) – Politics and goverment – 1991– | BISAC: POLITICAL SCIENCE / Government / International.
Classification: LCC JN6699.A795 R48 2017 | DDC 324.247–dc23
LC record available at https://lccn.loc.gov/2016051824

ISBN 978-1-107-17176-3 Hardback

Cambridge University Press has no responsibility for the persistence or accuracy of URLs for external or third-party Internet Web sites referred to in this publication and does not guarantee that any content on such Web sites is, or will remain, accurate or appropriate.

Contents

	List of Figures	page vi
	List of Tables	vii
	Acknowledgments	ix
	List of Abbreviations	xiii
1	Introduction	1
2	A Theory of Dominant Party Formation	42
3	False Starts: The Failure of Pro-Presidential Parties under Yeltsin	74
4	The Emergence of a Dominant Party in Russia: United Russia, Putin, and Regional Elites, 2000–2010	107
5	United Russia as the Dominant Party	159
6	United Russia and Russia's Governors	202
7	Economic Elites and Dominant Party Affiliation	222
8	Dominant Party Emergence around the World	244
9	Conclusion	267
	References	283
	Index	301

Figures

1.1	Proportion of authoritarian regimes with dominant parties: 1946–2006	*page* 2
1.2	Dominant parties around the world in 2006	8
1.3	Conceptual map of terms	10
1.4	Balance of resources and dominant party emergence	24
4.1	Russia's governors in United Russia, 2003–2007	128
4.2	United Russia performance in regional legislative election cycles	128
4.3	Percentage of SMD seats won by UR in regional legislative elections	129
4.4	Backgrounds of United Russia regional secretaries	134
4.5	Oil prices and economic growth in post-Soviet Russia	138
4.6	Share of gubernatorial appointees who are UR members prior to appointment	147
5.1	Popularity ratings of major Russian political parties	174
6.1	Effect of key variables on hazard of joining United Russia	218
8.1	Marginal effects plots	261
8.2	Predicted probability of dominant party emergence across various distributions of resources between leaders and elites	263

Tables

4.1	United Russia in the legislative, regional, and local elite	page 130
4.2	United Russia in the Federal Executive Branch	132
5.1	Bills passed in Duma by initiator, December 2, 2007–July 29, 2010	164
5.2	Transitional partisanship in Russia (2012)	175
5.3	Defections from United Russia in Russian regional legislatures	180
5.4	Defections from United Russia in gubernatorial and mayoral races, 2009–2014	181
5.5	UR defectors among top opposition candidates in regional legislative elections, 2009–2014	182
6.1	Weibull model estimates of governor's hazard of joining United Russia	216
7.1	Convocations used in analysis	228
7.2	Professions of regional deputies	231
7.3	Logistic regression estimates for effect of sector on likelihood of being visited by tax authorities	232
7.4	Logit models of dominant party affiliation	235
7.5	Sector employment and United Russia faction membership	236
7.6	Differentiating between party affiliation strategies	240
8.1	Conceptual map of party organization under autocracy	245
8.2	Determinants of dominant party emergence	258
8.3	Predicted probability of dominant party emergence	262

Acknowledgments

The roots of this project go all the way back to my undergraduate years. In the early 2000s, Russia's political system was undergoing a transformation and those changes seemed worthy of study. The creation of a single dominant party was hard to ignore, and I entered graduate school with a desire to study Russia's new party system.

The task of turning those nebulous interests into a dissertation and then turning that dissertation into a book was not undertaken alone. Many have lent a hand along the way. The first word of thanks must be reserved for my dissertation adviser, Thomas Remington. Early on, he pushed me to transform my hunches into theories and my ideas into a dissertation. His professionalism, intellectual curiosity, and scholarly rigor set a powerful example. I have tried to follow that example.

I have also accrued debts to other members of my dissertation committee. Jennifer Gandhi's support and friendship have been unfailing. She always asked the tough questions that have forced me to clarify my argument. For this, I cannot thank her enough. Other faculty members at Emory gave useful input at various stages. Clifford Carrubba, Hubert Tworzecki, Eric Reinhardt, Jeffrey Staton, Alan Abramowitz, Dan Reiter, and Kyle Beardsley all deserve thanks for this.

At various conferences and presentations, I received helpful feedback from Vladimir Gel'man, Regina Smyth, Lucan Way, John Paul Goode, Gulnaz Sharafitudinova, Rostislav Turovsky, Grigorii Golosov, and Henry Hale. I would also like to thank the anonymous reviewers at Europe Asia Studies and Comparative Political Studies, as well as George Breslauer, for providing comments on drafts of articles that formed the basis for several chapters.

While I was writing the book manuscript, Tim Frye, Graeme Robertson, Jen Gandhi, Sam Greene, and Tom Remington provided invaluable advice and encouragement. Noah Buckley, Israel Marques, David Szakonyi, Michael Rochlitz, Guzel Garifullina, and the rest of the gang at the Center for the Study of Institutions and Development were kind enough to put up with me as I finished fieldwork during our stints in Moscow.

Fieldwork for this project has been supported by the International Research and Exchanges Board (IREX), American Councils (ACTR), the Department of Education's Fulbright–Hays Doctoral Dissertation Research Abroad Program, and Emory University's professional development grants.

In Russia, my debts are many. The fieldwork for this project would not have been possible without the selfless assistance of those who helped with contacts and advice. Rostislav Turosky deserves special thanks in this regard for sharing from his bottomless well of contacts in the regions. I would also like to thank Rostislav for sharing with me his profound knowledge of Russian regional politics. Alexander Kynev must also be thanked for helping me get my foot in the door in the regions. I also owe a deep debt to Andrey Yakovlev and the Center for the Study of Institutions and Development at the Higher School of Economics for providing me an institutional base for fieldwork carried out between 2011 and 2014.

In Moscow, many others gave of their time and expertise, including Mikhail Tulskii, Konstantin Gaaze, Boris Makarenko, Vyacheslav Igrunov, Sergei Ryzhenkov, and Nikolai Petrov.

In Yaroslavl, Alexander Sokolov shared his knowledge of the region with me and helped me gain access. Vladimir Khryashchev's wry sense of humor made doing research in Yaroslavl a joy. A number of others in Yaroslavl deserve thanks for administrative, moral, and professional support, including Albina Egorova, Alexander Prokhorov, Pavel Isayev, Tatyana Akopova, and Irina Vorobyova.

In Perm, Viktor Mokhov, Oleg Podvintsev, Pyotr Panov, Vitalii Kovin, Nadezhda Borisova, Lyudmila Fadeeva, and Ilya Karnaukhov helped with contacts and counsel. In Ekaterinburg, it was Eduard Abelinskas, Maria Dronova, and Konstantin Kiselyov; in Kurgan, Pavel Ovsyannikov; in Marii El, Sergei Kiselyev; in Kirov, Tatyana Vitkovskaya; in Chelyabinsk, Andrei Koretskii and Alexei Tabalov; and in Samara, Olga Popova and Vladimir Zvonovskii. In addition, I would like to acknowledge the institutional support I received at Perm State University and Yaroslavl State University.

Finally, I must give thanks to all the regional officials and legislators who facilitated my interviews in Russia. Doing interviews in Russia requires building relationships and maintaining them. Out of respect for their anonymity, I cannot name many of the individuals who helped me string together contacts, but without their help, my fieldwork would have been much less fruitful. My thanks to them.

My biggest debts of gratitude are to my family. My late mother was my longest-standing supporter. Her love and guidance made everything possible. My partner, Terri, has been with me since the early stages of this project, and with a lawyer's eye for detail, she copy-edited several versions of the manuscript. I am forever grateful to her for putting up with my peripatetic lifestyle. She keeps the smile on my face and the spring in my step. For that, I owe her everything.

Abbreviations

BNP	Bangladesh National Party
CCP	Chinese Communist Party
CPSU	Communist Party of the Soviet Union
DIP	Department of Internal Politics
DPC	Dispersion per Capita
GOLKAR	Party of the Functional Groups (Indonesia)
KANU	Kenya Africa National Union
KMT	Kuomintang (Taiwan)
KPRF	Communist Party of the Russian Federation
LDPR	Liberal Democratic Party of Russia
NDR	Our Home Is Russia
NDP	National Democratic Party (Egypt)
OKS	All-Russian Coordination Council
ONF	All-Russian People's Front
OTAN	Fatherland (Kazakhstan)
OVR	Fatherland–All Russia
PDCI	Democratic Party of Cote d'Ivoire
PDP	People's Democratic Party (Nigeria)
PRES	Party of Russian Unity and Accord
PR	Proportional Representation
PRI	Institutional Revolutionary Party (Mexico)
SMD	Single Member District
SPS	Union of Right Forces
UMNO	United Malays National Organization (Malaysia)
UR	United Russia

1 Introduction

1.1 Overview

Many contemporary autocracies display all the institutional trappings of democracy – parties, legislatures, elections, and courts – but these institutions often fail to serve as mechanisms of representation and accountability. Under dictatorship, institutions of majority rule can become institutions of authoritarian rule. In fact, many authoritarian regimes fail to democratize, at least in part, because their leaders appropriate nominally democratic institutions and use them to entrench their rule. Elections provide dictators with much-needed information about opponents and allies. Legislatures provide forums for co-optation. Pliant courts legitimate arbitrary political decisions.

But the nominally democratic institution that many autocrats find most useful is the political party. In many non-democracies, regime leaders share power with a ruling party, which can help generate popular support and reduce conflict among key elites. Such ruling parties are often called dominant parties. In other authoritarian regimes, leaders prefer to rule solely through some combination of charisma, patronage, and coercion, rather than sharing power with a dominant party. This book explains why dominant parties emerge in some non-democratic regimes, but not in others.

Regimes that rule with the aid of a dominant party are now the most common type of authoritarian polity. As Figure 1.1 shows, they have existed consistently in about half of all non-democracies since 1946.

The Partido Revolucionario Institucional (PRI) in Mexico, the United Malays National Organization (UMNO) in Malaysia, the National Democratic Party (NDP) in Egypt, the National Resistance Movement (NRM) in Uganda, the People's Democratic Party (PDP) in Nigeria, and United Russia in Russia are just a few of the 128 dominant parties that have existed since 1946 in 96 countries.

Yet, the puzzling thing about dominant parties is not their prevalence but rather their nonexistence in so many non-democracies. After all,

2 Introduction

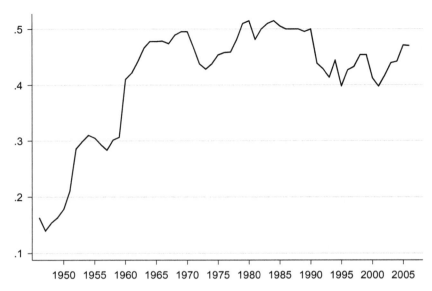

Figure 1.1 Proportion of authoritarian regimes with dominant parties: 1946–2006.

dominant parties are institutions – bundles of rules and norms – that reduce elite conflict by institutionalizing the distribution of careers and spoils among elites. In regimes with dominant parties, the distribution of spoils is determined, at least in part, by regularized norms and procedures embedded within the party. If party cadres remain loyal and serve the party, they have good reason to believe that they will continue to share in the benefits of office. This gives party cadres a vested interest in the regime. Indeed, many political scientists believe that dominant parties extend the life span of authoritarian regimes (Geddes 1999b, Brownlee 2007, Magaloni 2008, Levitsky and Way 2010, Svolik 2012). And yet, in a little more than half of all authoritarian regimes – in settings as diverse as Libya under Muamar Gadaffi, Belarus under Aleksandr Lukashenko, Brazil under Getulio Vargas, and Ukraine under Leonid Kuchma – regime leaders fail to construct dominant parties. If dominant parties fortify authoritarian rule, why do many leaders eschew building them? Why do dominant parties emerge in some non-democracies, but not in others?

Dominant party formation is often stymied by a series of commitment problems between leaders and elites. In non-democracies, leaders – i.e. dictators, presidents, prime ministers, juntas, and the like – would like

1.1 Overview

to keep important elites loyal. Such elites may include powerful regional governors, caciques, warlords, strongmen, nobles, chiefs, bosses, landlords, or the directors of economic enterprises, among others. Leaders could achieve this goal by promising elites some share of the spoils from governing, but they have no way to make those promises credible. Leaders may announce that they will promote certain cadres or give elites special privileges, but dictatorships lack third-party institutions that can enforce these promises. Without a constraint on the arbitrary authority of dictators, elites can never be certain that leaders will not abuse them.

Elites face a similar commitment problem vis-à-vis leaders. Elites want to gain dependable access to spoils and career advancement. Leaders might be persuaded to give them these if elites pledged their loyalty to the regime, but elites have no way of making this pledge credible. Elites may promise to support the regime's policy initiatives, mobilize votes for the regime, or quell social protest, but without a third-party institution that can monitor and enforce these commitments to the regime, leaders can never be sure that elites will remain loyal.

Mutual investment in a dominant party, with its institutional mechanisms for governing the distribution of spoils and monitoring behavior, could help ameliorate these commitment problems. But it is only part of the explanation for why dominant parties emerge, because it still does not explain why actors would choose to solve their commitment problem with a dominant party institution in some settings, but not in others. After all, these commitment problems are ubiquitous, but dominant parties are not.

To explain why dominant parties emerge in some settings but not others, I focus on how the relative balance of political resources between leaders and elites affects each side's incentives to cooperate with the other and invest in an institutional solution to the commitment problem. When leaders are very strong in resources – relative to elites – their incentives to seek the cooperation of elites are diminished and they are tempted to defect from any bargain with elites that would limit their freedom of maneuver. On the other hand, if elites are strong in autonomous resources – relative to leaders – they may be able to achieve their political goals on their own, and they will have strong incentives to defect from any agreement that would require them to relinquish their own autonomy. *Thus, dominant parties are most likely when elites hold enough independent political resources that leaders need to co-opt them, but not so many autonomous resources that they themselves are reluctant to commit to any dominant party project.*

Much of the book examines this argument and its implications in the context of post-Soviet Russia. In a span of just more than twenty years, post-Soviet Russia has witnessed the failure of two ruling party projects and the emergence of a dominant party. In the 1990s, Russia's powerful regional elites – in particular, governors – eschewed any real commitments to the various pro-presidential parties of the time, preferring instead to focus on the cultivation of their own political machines. In turn, apparently fearing the costs of supporting a party that could not be sustained, President Boris Yeltsin undermined his own pro-presidential parties.

By contrast, in the early 2000s rising oil revenues, sustained economic growth, and the attendant popularity of Yeltsin's successor, Vladimir Putin, changed the balance of power between the Kremlin and regional elites. This readjustment in the balance of resources gave elites more incentive to cooperate with the Kremlin than they had in the 1990s. And yet, regional elites were still strong enough that the Kremlin would need to co-opt them if it wanted to win elections, pass legislation, maintain social quiescence, and govern cost-effectively. After all, the political machines that elites had built in the first post-communist decade still provided them with ample levers of influence over other elites and society. Because the Kremlin needed to co-opt these elites and elites were no longer so strong that they would necessarily be unfaithful partners, Putin could feel comfortable investing his own resources in a dominant party that could be used to co-opt them. In turn, the signals of commitment sent by the Kremlin emboldened elites to make their own commitments. This dynamic led both sides to invest their resources in a dominant party, United Russia.

Through an analysis of United Russia's rise, this book tells the story of how the current regime in Russia was built. It addresses questions such as why elites affiliate with the regime, what keeps elites loyal, and how the regime wins elections. I argue that United Russia has been an important, and often overlooked, pillar of regime stability. And by demonstrating the party's institutional role in perpetuating the regime, this study demonstrates some of the limits of personalism in contemporary Russia. In turn, by identifying the conditions that lead to the creation of such dominant parties this book enriches our understanding of why some countries transition to democracy, but others do not.

1.2 What Are Dominant Parties?

A dominant party is a political institution that has a leading role in determining access to many important political offices, shares powers over policy making and patronage distribution, and uses privileged access to

1.2 What Are Dominant Parties?

state resources to maintain its position in power. Indeed, during elections dominant parties exploit state resources to such an egregious extent that one cannot speak of free and fair political competition. This distinguishes these regimes from democracies in which one party governs for long periods – such as Japan under the Liberal Democratic Party (LDP), Italy under the Christian Democrats, or Sweden under the Social Democrats – regimes that Pempel (1990) calls "uncommon" democracies. Thus, dominant parties are institutions that exist in *non-democratic* regimes.

Of course, long-lived governing parties in democracies often bolster their position with patronage distributed via clientelist linkage mechanisms (cf. Scheiner 2006). Indeed, the disbursement of state resources in order to forestall alternation in office places these regimes in a true "gray area" between democracy and authoritarianism. The list of states that complicate efforts to code regime type is full of such one-party dominant anomalies: Botswana under the Botswanan Democratic Party (BDP), South Africa under the African National Congress (ANC), Namibia under the Southwest Africa People's Organization (SWAPO), India under Congress, and Guyana under the People's National Congress (PNC) are only a few. The best one can do in discriminating between one-party dominant democracies and dominant party regimes is to assess the degree to which state resources are used to create an unbalanced playing field in elections. In well-known dominant party regimes the state places severe constraints on the ability of opposition parties to challenge the dominant party. Opponents may be jailed or repressed. Electoral fraud may be employed. State-controlled media determine the type of information that voters receive. State resources (contracts, subsidies, favors, and the like) are illegally deployed to favor incumbent politicians.

Dominant parties serve as institutions that organize political exchange among elites. The dominant party also regularizes the flow of patronage, careers, and spoils that runs from leaders to elites. Importantly, dominant party institutions ensure that these goods are distributed in a regularized fashion that is, at least to some degree, determined by norms or rules. Party loyalty is, more often than not, dependably rewarded with career advancement. A classic example of this can be found in the world's communist regimes, where career advancement was determined by the nomenklatura, system in which prospective candidates to political office were ranked according to seniority, qualifications, and ideology (Harasmyiw 1984). In personalist regimes, by contrast, dictators are not constrained by any rules or norms embedded within party institutions; rather, spoils and careers are distributed arbitrarily at the behest of the leader.

Dominant parties serve as forums where leaders can broker policy compromises with prominent elites and the opposition (Gandhi 2008). As institutions with some control over policy, dominant parties can promise influence over the national agenda. For example, Brownlee (2007, 130–137) describes how elite conflict in Mubarak era Egypt was mitigated because the ruling NDP could credibly promise policy access to potential defectors. In 2000, when prominent business leaders led by President Hosni Mubarak's own son, Gemal, threatened to start their own party, the NDP placated them with plum positions in parliament. While rewarding a group of upstarts left party stalwarts dissatisfied, the party successfully ameliorated potential conflict by informally increasing the number of candidates that would be elected to parliament with regime support.

Dominant parties also help the regime generate political support in society. As the site of coordination for many important elites, dominant parties join power holders and opinion leaders with the resources necessary to drum up support for the regime, whether at the ballot box or on the streets. Elites lend the party the use of their organizations, political machines, clientelist networks, economic leverage, and/or traditional authority. In electoral authoritarian regimes, a primary function of the dominant party is to coordinate the resources of elites toward the goal of winning elections.

In such regimes, dominant parties also help serve the vital function of coordinating expectations on the part of voters and candidates. Much of the literature on electoral coordination failures under authoritarianism focuses on the opposition; when two or more opposition candidates with similar political positions run against one another, they risk dividing the anti-regime vote and losing a contest that they might have won had they remained united. Authoritarian incumbents also confront such problems and must ensure that pro-regime candidates do not compete and risk dividing the pro-regime vote. In Russia's 1993 and 1995 parliamentary elections, pro-regime candidates from competing pro-presidential parties often divided the vote between them, opening space for Communist Party candidates to win in districts that they would not otherwise win. Dominant parties solve such coordination problems by coordinating elite and voter expectations about which pro-regime candidate or party will receive state support.

This definition of dominant party does not require that the party oversee an all-encompassing party-state, in which all, or even most, political decisions are made collectively by the party. Such an ideal type is approximated by few if any dominant parties in world history. Dominant parties exert some modicum of institutional influence. The extent

1.2 What Are Dominant Parties?

of their institutional influence is a matter of degree, such that some parties exhibit more institutional control over policy, patronage, and careers than others. In Chapter 2 of this book, I discuss in greater detail the ways that dominant parties exert institutional control over these spheres, and, in Chapter 5, I discuss the extent of United Russia's role in Russian politics.

Nor does this definition require that dominant parties persist in power for long periods (Greene 2010). While institutional strength and duration may often be correlated, strong dominant parties may be short-lived for reasons that are unrelated to their organizational capacity, just as weak dominant parties may be long-lived for reasons that are unrelated to their institutional weakness. After all, the factors that lead to the formation of dominant parties may not be the same as the factors that cause their failure. Party strength and party duration are different concepts. Moreover, even if duration were a perfect indicator of dominant party strength, selecting a long duration criterion for defining dominance effectively truncates the dependent variable, preventing the analyst from utilizing (or analyzing) variation in the duration of one-party dominance. Studies that posit a link between authoritarian regime survival and the presence of dominant parties should not make party duration a criterion for identifying dominant parties. If they do, their models will be biased in favor of finding that dominant party regimes are more durable. All this is not to mention the fact that such a rule would disallow analysis of dominant parties that have emerged recently.

To be sure, many of the world's most prominent dominant parties have been long-lived. In Central America, the PRI ruled Mexico from 1929 to 2000. In South America, the Colorado Party helped Alfredo Stroessner govern Paraguay from 1954 until his death in 1989. In East Asia, the KMT led Taiwan from the state's inception in 1947 until 2000. In the Middle East, the Ba'ath Party has ruled Syria since 1963, much of that time in conjunction with the Assad political dynasty. In Africa, the Kenya African National Union ruled Kenya from independence in 1963 until the defeat of its candidate, Uhuru Kenyatta, in the 2002 presidential elections. One-quarter of all the world's dominant parties survived in power for more than 28 years.

At the same time, a little less than 24 percent persisted for fewer than 10 years including the Democratic Party (DP) in Turkey, which ruled that country from 1950 until it was dislodged by a coup in 1960; the Citizens Union of Georgia (CUG), which served as President Eduard Shevardnadze's ruling party from 1995 until 2003, when it collapsed amid massive elite defections; and the Socialist Party of Yugoslavia, which served as Slobodan Milosevic's electoral vehicle until he was dislodged

Introduction

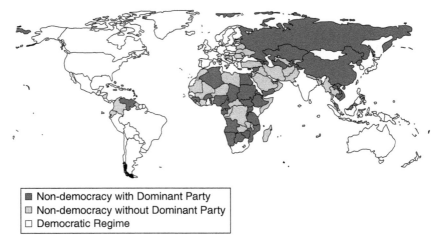

Figure 1.2 Dominant parties around the world in 2006.

amid anti-regime protests in 2000. As of 2006, there were 22 dominant parties in existence that emerged after 1990. Examples of recently emerged dominant parties include the PDP in Nigeria (1999), the Rwandan Patriotic Front (FPR) (2003), and Fatherland (Nur-OTAN) in Kazakhstan (1999).[1] Figure 1.2 shows the distribution of dominant parties in the world as of 2006.

The dominant party concept, as I have described it here, subsumes what scholars call hegemonic parties (e.g. Sartori 1976, Magaloni 2006, Reuter and Gandhi 2011). Hegemonic party regimes are regimes in which a dominant party competes in elections against opposition parties. Historically, 53 percent of the dominant parties existing in any given year have been hegemonic parties. Hegemonic parties have been key institutions in some of the 20th century's most prominent authoritarian regimes. In Latin America, the world's most studied hegemonic party, Mexico's PRI, won regular, semicompetitive elections for almost 70 years (Magaloni 2006, Greene 2007). In North Africa, the NDP helped Egypt's presidents win elections for nearly four decades (Blaydes 2011). In Southeast Asia, the United Malays National Organization (UMNO) has dominated Malaysia's multiparty parliamentary elections since independence in 1957.

---

[1] All facts and figures on dominant parties in this chapter are derived from an original operationalization of dominant parties that is discussed in more detail in Chapter 8.

1.2 What Are Dominant Parties?

More recent examples can be found across the world as well. In Africa, the Ethiopian People's Democratic Revolutionary Front (EPRDF) has won elections for Ethiopia's ruling elite since 1995 and facilitated the transfer of power to Prime Minister Hailemariam Desalegnhas after the death of long-serving Prime Minister Menes Zelawi in 2012. In the Middle East, Yemen's presidents have relied, until recently, upon the General People's Congress (GPC) to help them win elections and manage elite conflict since unification in 1990. In Southeast Asia, Cambodia's former Communist Party reformed itself into the Cambodian People's Party (CPP) and has handily won all elections in that country since 1998. In post-communist Europe, Russian Presidents Vladimir Putin and Dmitry Medvedev have depended on the United Russia (2001–) party to help manage relations with elites. These are just a few of the 37 hegemonic parties existing in the world as of 2006. This represents 84 percent of the world's dominant parties.

The dominant party concept also subsumes what some call single parties: ruling parties in regimes that only allow one party to exist and/or compete in elections. Such parties are now rare. As of 2006, only six single-party regimes existed in the world – the Communist Parties in Laos, Cuba, North Korea, China, and Vietnam, and the Democratic Party in Turkmenistan – and since 1980, only one new single-party regime has emerged in the entire world (the Democratic Party in Turkmenistan after the fall of the Soviet Union). Well-known historical examples of single-party regimes include KANU in Kenya, which barred all opposition parties from 1969 until 1992; the National Liberation Front (FLN) in Algeria from 1962 to 1991; and the Communist Party of the Soviet Union (CPSU), which ruled that country from 1917 until 1991.

Figure 1.3 lays out the terms and classifications used in the book.

I use the term "ruling party" somewhat loosely, to refer to the largest pro-regime party in an autocracy, dominant or otherwise. Thus, in my terminology, all dominant parties are ruling parties, but not all ruling parties are dominant. There are, of course, many authoritarian regimes without any ruling party. Saudi Arabia since independence, Chile under Augusto Pinochet, and Myanmar under the military junta are examples of regimes without any sort of ruling party. In many electoral authoritarian regimes, meanwhile, regime leaders support multiple or weak regime parties that never become dominant – e.g. Ukraine under Kuchma, Uzbekistan under Karimov, Pakistan under Musharraf, or Morocco since 1977. By examining the conditions under which dominant parties emerge, this book also seeks to understand why dominant parties do *not* emerge, both in regimes without any ruling party and in regimes that support nondominant, pro-regime parties.

10   Introduction

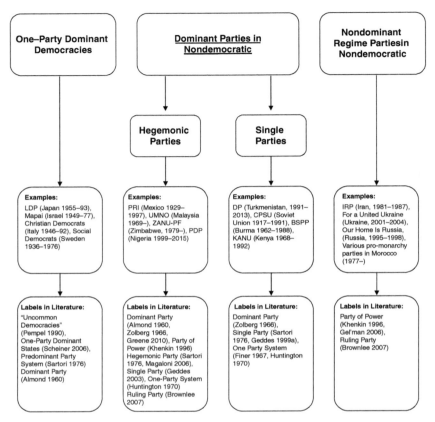

Figure 1.3 Conceptual map of terms.

1.3   Authoritarian Survival and the Puzzle of Dominant Party Formation

Dominant party regimes defy popular stereotypes of authoritarian regimes as highly personalized political systems. In contrast to personalist dictatorships, where all political decisions are subject to the arbitrary will of a single despot, dominant party regimes are characterized by the presence of party institutions that regulate certain types of political exchange. The first scholarship on dominant party regimes in political science described how these party institutions operated in equilibrium. Scholars of communist systems, to take but one world region, devoted enormous energy to understanding the workings of these parties. Through the nomenklatura system, communist parties routinized political recruitment

1.3 Dominant Party Formation

and advancement (on the Soviet Union, Hough 1969, Harasmyiw 1984; on China, Barnett 1968, Schurmann 1968, Burns 1989). Volumes of literature examined the Communist Party's other roles in mobilizing ideological support (Hough 1969, Remington 1988), socialization (e.g. White 1979), interest articulation (Hill and Frank 1981), and patronage distribution (e.g. Urban 1989). The party's central role in formulating and implementing policy, internal party decision-making processes, and the operative tenets of democratic centralism were also fleshed out in detail (e.g. Hough and Fainsod 1979).

Fewer in number, some works also detailed the workings of dominant parties in developing countries. Smith (1979) described how elections served to facilitate elite circulation in the PRI in Mexico. Others detailed the important role the PRI played in monitoring patronage exchanges (Ames 1970). Zolberg (1966) highlighted the role that West African dominant parties played in mobilizing support for incumbents, coordinating voters, and facilitating interethnic alliances. Party co-optation was also explored. Bienen (1978) outlined how the Tanganyikia African National Union (TANU) in Tanzania incorporated labor unions and business elites into its structures, buying off their support with institutionalized political privilege.

Much of this early literature on dominant parties, though rich in detail and immensely valuable for the amount of factual knowledge it generated, failed to develop a comparative, theoretical perspective on dominant party rule. In other words, early scholarship failed to transform observations about what dominant parties did into theories about why dominant parties did them. The lack of comparative perspective prevented scholars from pinpointing when and where such parties might flourish (see Kalyvas 1999)

Recognizing this lacuna, political scientists have recently begun the task of constructing testable theories about dominant party rule. Much of this work has been, implicitly or explicitly, situated within the theoretical framework that political scientists call neo-institutionalism – a school of thought that argues that institutions have effects on the behavior of actors. Scholars have argued persuasively that dominant party institutions entrench authoritarian rule by ensuring elite cohesion (Geddes 1999b, Brownlee 2007, Magaloni 2008, Levitsky and Way 2010, Svolik 2012). Party cadres in dominant party regimes are "anchored in an institutional setting that generates political power and long-term security" (Brownlee 2007, 33). Dominant parties reward loyal elites with spoils – policy influence, career advancement, or rents – in an institutionalized, rule-governed fashion. In dominant parties, senior cadres are retired and younger cadres are promoted through the ranks in a regularized manner (Svolik 2012, Reuter and Turovsky 2014). Party cadres have a vested interest in remaining loyal to the regime because norms and rules embedded within the party generate reasonable expectations that loyalty will be rewarded with spoils and career advancement in the future.

By contrast, elites in regimes without such institutionalized means of spoil distribution have no credible guarantees that they will receive access to spoils in the future. This reduces their time horizons and gives them more incentive to challenge the leader for control of spoils. Since elite defections are known to be one of the primary drivers of authoritarian breakdown (Haggard and Kauffman 1996, Reuter and Gandhi 2011), and dominant parties ensure elite cohesion, dominant parties are said to extend the life span of authoritarian rule.

These arguments are backed by an impressive array of empirical findings. Using slightly different measures, both Geddes (1999b) and Svolik (2012) find evidence that dominant party regimes are more durable than forms of authoritarian regimes. Gandhi and Przeworski (2007) show that autocrats who govern in the presence of partisan legislatures survive longer than those without such institutions.[2]

Qualitative studies reach similar conclusions. In an in-depth analysis of divergent democratization outcomes in four cases, Brownlee (2007) finds that strong ruling parties successfully mitigated elite dissention in Malaysia and Egypt, while weak party institutions contributed to factionalism in the Philippines and Iran. And, in a wide-ranging study of regime trajectories in 35 competitive authoritarian settings, Levitsky and Way (2010) find an association between robust authoritarianism and the presence of strong ruling parties.

These findings help explain the puzzle of why an autocrat might consider creating a parallel dominant party institution that constrains his arbitrary will. Leaders have an interest in creating dominant parties because these institutions generate elite cohesion and facilitate co-optation. Once a dominant party is established the dictator refrains from disrupting the regularized distribution of spoils to party elites, because such an infringement would lead to elite defections that could bring down the regime. Yet this begs a crucial question when viewed in light of the substantial variation in the formation of dominant parties: namely, that if dominant parties are known to entrench authoritarian rule, then why do so many authoritarian leaders eschew building them? More than half of authoritarian regimes do not feature dominant parties. Given that dominant parties can limit elite defections and stabilize the regime, why

---

[2] For a dissenting perspective see Wright and Escriba-Folch (2012).

1.4 Alternative Explanations of Dominant Party Emergence

would power-maximizing leaders refrain from building such a party? The remainder of this book attempts to solve this puzzle.

1.4 Alternative Explanations of Dominant Party Emergence

The most prominent theories of dominant party rule focus not on the origins of dominant parties but on the conditions that lead to their collapse. Some attribute dominant party survival to the monopoly on state resources that dominant parties enjoy (Greene 2007, 2010). Whether it is via patronage, unequal access to state-controlled media, or state resources available for campaigning and communicating with voters, dominant parties use their special advantages to marginalize opposition parties. When privatization removes patronage opportunities from the hands of incumbents, dominant parties lose their resource advantage and are prone to collapse (Greene 2007, 2010). Brownlee (2007) argues that long-lived dominant parties are those in which elite factionalism is decisively put to bed within the confines of the dominant party. In an influential study of the PRI hegemony in Mexico, Magaloni (2006) offers an account of party dominance that rests on three pillars: elite unity, opposition coordination dilemmas, and manufactured electoral support.[3]

These studies have advanced our understanding of dominant party regimes, but they all take the emergence of a dominant party as exogenous and proceed to examine the conditions that lead to the demise of already-established dominant parties. Thus, we know much more in political science about the equilibrium characteristics of dominant parties and the threats to that equilibrium than we do about how these equilibria come to be established in the first place.

Nonetheless, scholars operating in several research traditions have, implicitly or explicitly, addressed the question of dominant party emergence. In the 1950s, political historians devoted significant attention to analyzing the Bolshevik seizure of power in Russia (e.g. Fainsod 1953, Daniels 1960, Schapiro 1964). These studies focused primarily on gathering information on the period and described the unfolding of events in an atheoretical way. Influenced as they were by the "old institutionalism" and the prerogatives of the other subfields (primarily, history), these works refrained from developing or testing theory about the factors that contributed to the transformation of the revolutionary Bolshevik party into the Communist Party of the Soviet Union.

---

[3] Chapter 2 discusses the drawbacks of using society-based arguments to explain dominant party origins.

The first political theories about dominant party origins were developed to explain the proliferation of dominant parties in Africa after decolonization. These accounts were heavily influenced by the dominant paradigm in comparative politics at the time, modernization theory. According to these accounts, parties – including dominant parties – were necessary agents of mobilization and representation that emerged as society shed traditional authority structures and participation became mass-based (Schachter 1961, Lapalombara and Weiner 1963, Apter 1965). Just as parties were thought to be the only modern form of political organization in democratic societies, dominant parties were thought to be the only modern form of authoritarian government (Huntington and Moore 1970).

The national integrating functions of these parties were also trumpeted. Dominant parties, it was said, fostered national integration by reducing the "cultural and regional tensions and discontinuities" with the goal of "creating a homogeneous territorial political community" (Coleman and Rosberg 1966, 9). Dominant parties, it was thought, drew citizens of newly independent countries into the political process by fostering a participant political community (Schachter 1961, Weiner 1967).

Modernization-inspired accounts were intuitively appealing but ultimately fell short of convincingly explaining dominant party origins. First, modernization theorists were unsure about the direction of causality. Many thought that parties themselves were agents of modernization and national integration (Apter 1965, Coleman and Rosberg 1966). Second, by positing that dominant parties should exist and play certain roles because these roles needed to be filled, modernization-inspired theories were hobbled by a functionalist bias. Third, their focus on mobilization and linkage ignored the fact that most dominant parties in authoritarian regimes were crafted as authoritarian patronage machines, not linkage mechanisms (Bienen 1978). Finally, as Smith (2005) has noted and the data in Chapter 8 show, dominant parties have emerged across countries with similar levels of development and ethnic diversity.

A slightly different modernization-inspired account of dominant party origins was offered by Huntington (1968, 1970). According to Huntington, one-party systems grow out of processes of modernization that open up cleavages and conflict in society. Societies that produce complex patterns of cross-cutting cleavages, so the argument went, tend to develop into multiparty democratic systems, whereas "one-party systems tend to be the product of either the accumulation of cleavages leading to sharply differentiated groups within society or of the ascendancy

1.4 Alternative Explanations of Dominant Party Emergence

in importance of one line of cleavage over all others. A one-party system is, in effect, the product of the efforts of a political elite to organize and to legitimate rule by one social force over another in a bifurcated society" (1970, 11). Ruling parties were thus created when conflict – especially revolutionary conflict – erupted between opposing forces in a bifurcated, modern society (Huntington 1968).

Huntington's insights were groundbreaking, but they suffered from several faults. First, as Huntington himself acknowledged – and Lenin averred – political leaders could foster antagonistic group consciousness through agitation. In other words, social bifurcation was endogenous. Second, arguing that dominant parties emerge when a dominant social force organizes to repress another social force does not explain how a party would come to be constituted as the instrument of that repression. Organization may be called for by a competitive threat, but it may not always be possible. Internecine struggles among leaders of one ethnic group, recalcitrant regional elites, or a rebellious military may stymie efforts to organize a party on behalf of a class or ethnic group.

Third, as Chapter 2 and Chapter 8 make clear, most of the world's dominant parties emerged in situations that could hardly be described as revolutionary or as arising from a process of social bifurcation resulting in the repression of one social class by another. Most contemporary dominant parties – including many of those with origins in the mid-20th century – were not Leninist-style parties engaged in thoroughgoing social transformation via coercion, but rather were tools of authoritarian cooptation.

For nearly 35 years after Huntington, there was little effort to build a comparative theory of dominant party emergence. Only with the recent emergence of neo-institutional approaches to authoritarianism has the topic received some attention. The most general of these is Gandhi's (2008) model of institutional genesis under dictatorship, which posits a set of costs and benefits that face a ruler deciding whether to grant policy concessions to an opposition. Concessions take the form of access to policy influence and rents, both of which can be provided through legislatures and parties. Dictators who have the financial means necessary to make side payments to supporters on an ad hoc basis – e.g. significant rent revenues – and/or those who face a weak opposition are expected to make fewer concessions to the opposition. The model recognizes that there are costs from sharing control over policy and spoils. Dictators will only share when they must, i.e., when they face a tight fiscal situation that precludes ad hoc patronage distribution and/or when they face a strong opposition.

Smith (2005) takes a similar tack on the problem, arguing that robust dominant parties emerge when incumbent leaders face a social opposition that needs to be co opted or confronted with organization or lack resource rents that can be used to buy off supporters. Leaders have no need to broaden party coalitions when there are no demands for policy influence from an organized opposition. Smith also argues that leaders with ready access to rents can buy off potential supporters rather than sharing access to policy with a party organization.

1.5 The Setting of the Argument: Leaders and Elites

This scholarship on dominant parties has advanced our understanding of their origins, but these recent accounts suffer from several shortcomings. First, these explanations focus only on the incentives that *leaders* face in deciding over whether to invest in a dominant party. These accounts mostly discount other elite actors as conscious political actors who choose whether to cast their lot with a dominant party project. In existing accounts, elites may benefit from a dominant party, but this is typically a post hoc assertion, dependent on the existence of the party in the first place.

By elites I mean individual actors outside the central leadership of a country who exercise influence over and demand loyalty from other political actors. They may be landowners, caciques, kulaks, bosses, chiefs, local warlords, nobles, clan leaders, firm managers, regional governors, influential politicians, opinion leaders in society, or, as Joel Migdal calls them, strongmen (1988). Such elites control important political resources, such as political machines, clientelist networks, hard-to-tax economic assets, or positions of traditional authority. Elites may be capable of mobilizing citizens in elections, on the street, or on the battlefield. They may command the loyalties of important subelites, such as military officers, landowners, administrators, or enterprise directors. Elites are strong to the extent that they control such resources because these resources give them power over citizens that central rulers covet.[4] Indeed, leaders must sometimes gain the acquiescence of these elites in order to extract revenue, mobilize votes, and implement policy – in short, to govern.

---

[4] See Kern and Dolkart 1973, Schmidt 1980, Duncan Baretta and Markoff 1987, and Hagopian 1996, on Latin America; Powell 1970, Lemerchand 1972, Clapham 1982, Herbst 2000, and Koter 2013 on Africa; Van Dam 1979 on the Middle East; Chubb 1982 on Southern Europe; Cappelli 1988, Matsuzato 2001, Hale 2003, and Alina-Pisano 2010 on the Soviet Union and the post-Soviet states; Weiner 1967 on South Asia; Geertz 1965, Scott 1972 and Sidel 1999 on Southeast Asia.

1.5 The Setting of the Argument: Leaders and Elites

Introducing elite incentives to the equation helps make sense of many instances of dominant party emergence that appear puzzling in light of existing explanations. Take, for example, the case of contemporary Russia. In the mid-2000s, the Kremlin was awash in oil revenues and, with a growing economy, the Communist opposition had lost much of its vim and vigor. In this setting, some of the theories cited previously predict that Putin would have little reason to build a dominant party and would instead use rent revenues to buy cooperation in society (e.g. Smith 2005, Boix and Svolik 2013). Indeed, Putin employed rent revenues to buy cooperation, but contrary to some existing predictions, he also invested in the creation of a dominant party, United Russia.

This decision contrasted sharply with the mid- to late 1990s, when the Russian economy was in a state of decay and oil prices were at record lows. Partially as a result of these economic dislocations, a strong and well-organized Communist opposition emerged to challenge the Kremlin in the 1995 parliamentary elections and 1996 presidential elections. Some existing theory predicts that this competitive threat would force the Kremlin to invest in a pro-presidential party that could be used to co-opt important elites and create a united front against the Communist opposition (e.g. Gandhi 2008, Huntington 1968). Instead, however, Yeltsin had difficulty securing the commitments of important elite actors, and regional governors opted instead to pursue individual strategies of self-promotion. Fearing the costs of supporting a pro-presidential party when such a party could not be sustained, Yeltsin undermined his own party and opted to employ a divide-and-rule strategy against the country's powerful regional governors.

Other important historical and contemporary examples of dominant parties emerging despite impuissant social opposition and ample rent revenues include the PDP in Nigeria, the Botswanan Democratic Party in Botswana, and OTAN in Kazakhstan are prominent examples. Similarly, dominant parties have failed to emerge in countries with relatively strong social oppositions and few rent revenues (e.g. Ukraine under Kuchma, Brazil under Vargas, Madagascar in the 1990s). How can we make sense of United Russia and other such puzzling cases? I argue that we must consider elite incentives, particularly the incentives of regional elites, when building an explanation of dominant party emergence. As I elaborate below, elites must have an incentive to cast their lot with a dominant party, just as leaders must have an incentive to invest in a dominant party.

To be sure, not all accounts of ruling parties omit elites from the equation. Brownlee (2007) suggests that dominant parties emerge and thrive when elite factionalism is put to bed within the confines of the party. This is an important observation, but such an account begs the question of why elite factionalism was put to bed within the confines of the party. Slater (2010) also highlights the importance of elite collective action in the construction of a ruling party and further posits that elites will engage in this party-based collective action when they feel threatened by endemic contentious politics.

The account offered here shares this emphasis on elites, but also differs in important ways. Namely, I cast the problem of dominant party formation as a two-sided commitment problem whereby elites are engaged in a strategic interaction with regime leaders. In addition, I specify the incentives that elites have to invest in a dominant party and argue that these incentives emanate from elites' relative strength vis-à-vis leaders. Importantly, I theorize both the factors that make elites important in the decision over whether to form a dominant party and the factors that make them more likely to cast their lot with an emergent dominant party.

A second shortcoming of many existing explanations is their lack of attention to the commitment problems inherent in the process of spoil distribution under autocracy (e.g. see Magaloni 2008 and Svolik 2012). Such transfers involve time-consistent exchanges whereby elite loyalty is rewarded with spoils. But after a given elite actor demonstrates his/her loyalty, what is to prevent the dictator from reneging on his/her offer of spoils? In a dictatorship without institutions, there is nothing to constrain a leader to fulfill his past promises. Magaloni (2008) proposes that by delegating these appointments to a parallel, independent party organization, leaders place constraints on their ability to abuse the terms of the spoil-sharing bargain.

Unfortunately, this insight about how dominant parties constrain leaders in equilibrium is not an answer to the question of how such parties come to be established in the first place. In fact, this observation makes variation in dominant party formation all the more puzzling; dominant parties can help dictators commit to not abusing elites, and yet, they emerge in some settings, but not others. Thus, a theory of dominant party formation must move beyond demonstrating that dominant parties *can* solve the leader's commitment problem and posit the conditions under which leaders (and elites) *will choose* to solve their commitment problem by investing in a dominant party.

On the other side of the coin, no existing work addresses the commitment problem of elites. If the dictator offers spoils to elites in exchange for loyalty in a later period, what prevents elites from reneging on their promise of loyalty by running their own candidates in elections, voting against regime-sponsored bills in legislatures, undermining government policy initiatives, appointed non-approved cadres, or otherwise working against the regime. In Chapter 2, I lay out a theory of dominant party formation that 1) incorporates the incentives of elites (as well as leaders), 2) considers the commitment problem facing elites and leaders as they decide whether to invest in a new dominant party, and 3) identifies the conditions under which the two sides will seek to overcome their commitment problem through investment in a dominant party.

1.6 The Argument in Brief

In contrast to most existing works, I argue that dominant parties are the product of conscious decisions by *both* leaders *and* other elites in a strategic setting. Leaders are chief executives. They are presidents, dictators, monarchs, military leaders, or, sometimes, prime ministers. Elites are the aforementioned opinion leaders in society: landowners, chiefs, warlords, governors, bosses, and so on.

In non-democracies, leaders and elites face a series of commitment problems when it comes to cooperating with each other over the distribution of spoils, policy, and careers. The essence of this commitment problem is similar to commitment problems in many other political settings (e.g. North and Weingast 1989, Shepsle 1991, Greif, Milgrom, and Weingast 1994, Sanchez-Cuenca 1998, Myerson 2008): mutually beneficial cooperation depends on promises about future actions, but the inability of actors to make credible promises to each other stymies such cooperation.

Leaders would like to secure the loyalty of elites and ensure their support in various governing tasks, such as winning elections, managing legislatures, or controlling social unrest. Elites can help with these tasks because they control autonomous resources – e.g. political machines, clientelist networks, traditional authority – that give them power over citizens. This approach assumes that repression of elites is costly and that the cost of repression varies with the power of those elites. Leaders could secure the assistance of elites if they could credibly promise elites a fair share of spoils. But such an agreement entails that leaders relinquish some of their decision-making autonomy; leaders must support agreed-upon bills, distribute rents in a pre-determined way, and promote pre-agreed cadres. But leaders value their autonomy and given the absence of a third-party institution that can monitor and enforce this agreement, they may be tempted to defect from the bargain by shirking their promises and ruling arbitrarily. Due to their short-sightedness, they may defect from any agreement ex post. Examples of such defections might include decisions to support a different policy, withhold perks, pass over certain elites for promotion, or support an alternative candidate for office. In sum, they cannot make credible promises to reliably distribute spoils to elites.

For their part, elites would prefer to receive guarantees that leaders will channel careers, perks, and policy to them now and in the future. They could achieve this if they could credibly pledge their loyalty to a leader through an ex ante agreement that required them to prioritize the political goals of the regime over their own – e.g. supporting regime candidates in elections, mobilizing voters on behalf of the regime, supporting regime legislative initiatives, extracting revenue for the regime, quelling anti-regime protest and the like. But elites value their autonomy to bargain with opponents, make side payments to supporters, and control their own clientelist networks. Thus, short-sighted elites may be tempted to defect ex post from any ex ante agreement, and without a third-party institution to enforce and monitor their commitments, their promises to cooperate may not be credible.

For leaders and elites, the benefits of cooperation are only realized if both sides sign on to the collusive agreement. The ruler is unwilling to commit himself to any such agreement unless he can be sure that other elites will be loyal. For their part, elites will not tie their fates to the party project unless they can be sure that the leader will make it a mechanism for guaranteeing the supply of careers and resources. In sum, each side would be better off if it were to collude in the division of spoils, perks, and policy, but neither can credibly assure the other that it will be a faithful partner in this collusion.

Leaders and elites might be able to ameliorate their bilateral commitment problem through mutual investment in a parallel party organization – a dominant party – that governs and monitors the distribution of spoils (Magaloni 2008). A dominant party can help mitigate the leader's commitment problem if it is granted some modicum of independence to make decisions about the distribution of policy, perks, and privileges; that is, if leaders limit their ability to interfere in the party or increase the costs of doing so. One way that leaders can increase the costs of abusing the dominant party bargain is by relinquishing to the dominant party their ability to gather information on key political decisions. In this way, the creation of dominant party institutions increases the costs of reneging on the bargain.

Another way that a leader can use the dominant party as a commitment device is by linking his name, reputation, and/or personal brand to the party. To the extent that the leader's own authority is tied to a reputation for resolve the leader can tie his hands by making verbal commitments to or investments of symbolic resource in the party – e.g. include public endorsements, speaking at party functions, allowing one's image to be used on campaign materials. Moreover, the linkage between a leader's

1.6 The Argument in Brief

personal brand and the party is likely to be sticky, such that it is difficult to quickly decouple the two in the minds of voters.

Dominant party institutions can also solve elite collective action problems vis-a-vis the leader. Gehlbach and Keefer (2012) argue that authoritarian legislatures can enforce bargains between leaders and elites by providing an institutional forum that helps elite coordinate to defend their interests. A similar argument may be applied to dominant party institutions.

Finally, the party helps elites monitor agreements and thus reduces the temptation of the leader to sporadically abuse them (e.g. see Svolik 2012). Enshrined in the party arrangement are rules, parchment or implicit, specifying what constitutes compliance on the part of the leader (e.g. only supporting party candidates in elections, granting preference to party supporters in personnel, granting the party control over nominations, and certain areas of policy formulation). When the terms of the spoil-sharing agreement are formalized, then a transgression against the party's sphere of authority is easier to identify and punish (via defection, perhaps).

The dominant party can make elite commitments credible if elites give it the power to sanction them for reneging. The dominant party leadership is given the authority to punish individual elites with exclusion from benefit streams. Elite commitments are also made credible if elites place their own machines, political parties, legislative organizations, and/or lobbying networks under the control of the party leadership. By transferring these resources, elites tie their hands. In addition, much like leaders, elites make a symbolic transfer of reputational resources when they make a public commitment to one political party – the dominant party. Finally, dominant party institutions establish clear rules about the nature of the spoil-sharing bargain, which helps elites monitor the leader's level of commitment.

Unfortunately, positing an institutional solution to this commitment problem does not help us explain why dominant parties exist in some authoritarian regimes, but not in others. Such commitment problems are likely present in almost all authoritarian regimes, but we only observe dominant parties in some of those regimes. Scholars of political institutions know that efficient institutions are not always created, even if their creation would benefit both contracting parties (Moe 1990, Knight 1992). Any theory of dominant parties that seeks to explain variance in the emergence of those institutions across countries must move beyond simply describing the institutional solution to the commitment problem.

The argument here focuses on how the relative balance of political resources between leaders and elites affects each side's incentives to cooperate and invest in an institutional solution to the commitment problem. When leaders are very strong in resources (relative to elites) their incentives to defect from any bargain are high and thus it is particularly difficult for them to commit to cooperating with elites. Strong leaders have less incentive to coopt weak elites. And any change in circumstances or the balance of resources might leave them with no rational incentive to cooperate. Thus, credible commitments are infeasible. In addition, because nascent dominant party institutions will have trouble keeping leaders from reneging when their commitment problem is severe, elites will be unlikely to trust the institutional commitments of leaders when leaders are strong in resources. This can make elites less willing to cooperate. Indeed, the limited ability of nascent dominant party institutions to place binding constraints on leaders underscores the need for the commitment problem to be mitigated before it can be solved. As Sanchez-Cuenca (1998) puts it, "the more you need a commitment, the less useful it is to solve your problem (85)."

On the other side of the equation, when elites are strong relative to leaders they have especially strong incentives to defect from any agreement and find it hard to commit to cooperation with leaders. Elites are strong when they sit atop networks that embed the loyalty of sub-elites and citizens. When elite networks form the basis of social control and/or economic management in a polity, then elites have significant bargaining power vis-a-vis leaders.[5] I assume that leaders can, at some cost, repress any given elite at any given time. But, importantly, repressing all elites collectively may be cost-prohibitive if it undermines the ability of leaders to achieve key governing tasks such as controlling unrest, winning elections, passing legislation, and collecting revenue. When elites are strong, their political machines allow elites to achieve many of their political goals without relying on the leader. Thus, they have strong incentives to shirk, which they will often do, and the smallest shift in resources could leave them with no rational incentive to cooperate. Moreover, when elites are strong, leaders will not trust elites to be constrained by nascent dominant party institutions, so they will be reluctant to relinquish their own autonomy to a dominant party.

---

[5] When elites are strong relative to leaders, there is the danger that elites will capture the state, but this frequently does not happen because elites face collective action and coordination problems among themselves (e.g. Solnick 2000, Shvetsova 2003). Thus, an authoritarian state with strong elites and weak leaders is not necessarily an oxymoron (Migdal 1988).

1.6 The Argument in Brief

Thus, dominant parties are unlikely to emerge when the commitment problem of leaders is severe. But they are also unlikely when the commitment problem of elites is severe. In this way, these predictions concord with a tradition of work in political science which argues that commitment problems are less likely to be solved when they are severe (e.g. North and Weingast 1989, Sanchez-Cuenca 1998, Svolik 2012).[6] The two sides are more likely to invest in a dominant party when both see that there are significant gains to be made from cooperating and when each side has less incentive to defect. Incentives to defect from the ex ante agreement are hard to eliminate, but they can be reduced. Neither side can ever be sure that the other will hold up its end of the bargain, but they will be more likely to risk cooperation when they need that cooperation more and when there is common knowledge that mutual incentives to renege are reduced. Or, as I frame it, the commitment problem can be mitigated.

Nascent dominant party institutions are still necessary at this point in order to monitor commitments and enforce the bargain. But when the commitment problem is attenuated because neither side holds a preponderance of resources, leaders and elites are more likely to trust these nascent institutions to help constrain both sides. A solution to the commitment problem becomes feasible. Put simply, dominant parties emerge when elites hold enough independent political resources that leaders need to coopt them, but not so many autonomous resources that they themselves are reluctant to commit themselves to cooperation by investing in a dominant party.

The argument is depicted graphically in Figure 1.4. On the left side of the figure, elites are weak relative to leaders and a dominant party is unlikely because leaders have less reason to coopt elites. On the right side of the figure elites are very strong in resources and have little reason to relinquish their autonomy to a dominant party. Thus, leaders will not

---

[6] Svolik (2012) convincingly argues that authoritarian power sharing is more likely when there is a balance of power within the ruling coalition. Svolik's work, which became available after this project was under way (Reuter and Remington 2009, Reuter 2010), is concordant with the approach offered here, but also differs significantly. As I discuss in Chapter 2, Svolik's model addresses power sharing as a general phenomenon, while I focus on the specific dilemmas of forming a dominant party. This leads to differences in how the commitment problem is specified and, potentially, solved. I also focus on elites, and in particular, regional elites who are not part of the "ruling coalition". In contrast to Svolik, I argue that elites can threaten not just armed rebellion, but also defection or noncooperation. I show how institutionalized power sharing in a dominant party may be unattainable when dictators are weak because elites refuse to place themselves under the control of the party. By contrast, Boix and Svolik (2013) predict that institutions (legislatures) become more likely as the dictator weakens (e.g. loses access to rent revenues).

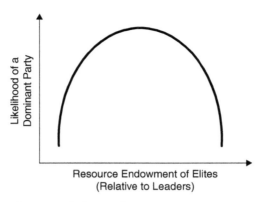

Figure 1.4 Balance of resources and dominant party emergence.

risk investment in a party and a dominant party is unlikely. In the middle of the figure, when the resources of elites and leaders are relatively balanced, a dominant party is more likely.

1.7 Why Russia? The Origins of United Russia

Much of this book examines the implications of the above argument in the context of contemporary Russia, one of the world's most prominent autocracies. One of the main reasons that Russia is a good case for studying dominant party emergence is that there is significant variation in the dependent variable over a short span of time. In the 1990s, then Russian president Boris Yeltsin eschewed investment in a powerful pro-presidential party. But in the 2000s, Vladimir Putin chose to sanction the creation of a dominant party, United Russia. Importantly, this variation in the dependent variable is puzzling in light of some existing explanations, and it unfolded recently, which permits the collection of data on the dominant party formation process.

For over 70 years, the Soviet Union was ruled by the Communist Party of the Soviet Union. In 1991, one-party rule ended and was replaced by its opposite – a hyper-fractious political system in which parties played little role and powerful elites pursued uncoordinated strategies of political advancement. The size of Russia, the dispersion of economic production within its borders, its decentralized state structure, ethnic divisions, and the political imperatives of the transition combined to make regional elites especially strong in post-Soviet Russia (e.g. Treisman 1999, Stoner-Weiss 1999, Slider 1994, Hale 2003). By the mid-late 1990s, the strength of regional elites vis-a-vis the Kremlin had been amplified by

Yeltsin's unpopularity, weak state capacity, historically low oil prices, and economic crisis. In this setting, Yeltsin (and, for some time after taking office, his immediate successor, Vladimir Putin) looked upon other elites as a threat. For their part, Russia's regional elites had little incentive to link their fates to a Kremlin-controlled ruling party and opted instead to pursue individual strategies of self-promotion. Regional elites built powerful local political machines, created their own parties, and clashed with Yeltsin over legislation. Russia's presidents feared the costs of supporting a pro-presidential party that could not be sustained, or worse, that could unite powerful elites against them. Thus, even though faced with a strong Communist opposition and a paucity of rent revenues – which existing theories predict would compel the construction of a dominant party – the Kremlin opted for a divide and rule strategy with respect to regional elites, securing their cooperation through ad hoc deal-making and bilateral accommodation. The result was that Russia's first 'party of power,' Our Home is Russia, never became a major political force.[7] In Chapter 3, I describe this process and show how the decisions made by actors were motivated by the balance of resources between leaders and elites and the two-sided commitment problem.

In 1999, regional elites reached the apex of their power. In this setting, the Kremlin allowed Our Home to whither and, by mid-1999, had still not identified a party of power that it would back in the December 1999 parliamentary elections. The Kremlin played a divide and rule strategy by sending mixed signals about which, if any, of several parties it would support and, then, at the last moment, endorsing its own skeletal movement, Unity, to secure the support of a plurality of unaffiliated governors.

But Unity was a campaign strategy, not a party. After the elections, elites continued to rely on their own autonomous resources to win elections and bargain for spoils with the Kremlin. They showed no interest in linking their fates to a centralized ruling party. And, as a result, the Kremlin did not make serious commitments to it. The 1999 elections had demonstrated just how powerful Russia's governors were, and the Kremlin feared these elites. In particular, Putin feared that a strong party could become a platform for challenges from either Moscow Mayor Yury Luzhkov or former Prime Minister Yevgenii Primakov. And if elites were not already wary enough, President Putin's reluctance to turn Unity into a dependable arena for securing access to spoils and careers left them with even less reason to make their own commitments.

---

[7] "Party of power" is a term used by post-Soviet area specialists to describe pro-presidential parties (Khenkin 1996).

Only after 2002 did United Russia, Unity's organizational successor, become a dominant party by attracting the unequivocal support of the Kremlin and across the board commitments from regional elites. United Russia's emergence as a dominant party occurred precisely because the resource balance had shifted in favor of the Kremlin. Sustained economic growth, windfall oil revenues, and the precipitous rise of President Putin's approval ratings all combined to strengthen the Kremlin's bargaining position with regional elites. This allowed Putin to push through centralizing reforms, such as the cancellation of gubernatorial elections that weakened – but did not eliminate – elites' political machines. The Kremlin had wanted to centralize authority since the mid-1990s, but powerful regional elites used their formal and informal resources to prevent the passage of such reforms.

This readjustment in the balance of power gave elites more reason to cooperate with the center than they had had in the 1990s. And yet elites were not so weak that the Kremlin could ignore or purge them. It needed to work with them in order to win elections, pass legislation, and maintain social quiescence. The political machines they had built over the past decade still provided them with ample levers of political influence. Supplanting these machines would be exceedingly costly. Rather, it was more cost-effective to coopt and govern through these political machines. Indeed, the regime's electoral strategy in the 2000s was predicated on coopting powerful elite governors, who then put their political machines to work for United Russia and the Kremlin.

Because elites were not so strong that they would shirk any obligations laid out for them in a dominant party arrangement, Putin could feel comfortable investing his own resources in such a party. By publicly endorsing the party, speaking at party conferences, heading the party list, and eventually becoming party chairman, Putin associated himself much more closely with the party than Yeltsin had ever done with his parties of power. In turn, Putin's signals of support emboldened elites to make their own investments. This dynamic led both sides to invest more in the ruling party than ever before. The result was a dominant party. In Chapter 4, I expand on this discussion, describing United Russia's emergence and situating its rise as a dominant party within the leader-elite commitment framework.

1.8 United Russia as a Dominant Party

United Russia's role as a dominant party is surprisingly understudied. Its control over elections and legislatures is well-known (Gel'man 2008, Smyth, Lowry, and Wilkening 2007, Ivanov 2008, Colton and Hale

2009, Reuter and Remington 2009, Makarenko 2011, Golosov 2011, Roberts 2012a, Reuter 2013), but theory-driven studies of its political role are lacking (see Gill 2012 and Roberts 2012b for exceptions). Since 2003, the party has held a majority in the State Duma, Russia's lower house, and by 2010 it controlled 75 percent of the seats in the Federation Council, Russia's upper house. The party dominated regional legislative elections in the 2000s, and by 2010 it held majorities in 82 of 83 regional legislatures. Almost all of Russia's governors had joined the party by 2007 (78 of 83 gubernatorial posts were held by United Russia in 2011). Most of Russia's mayors also joined the party over the course of the 2000s. In 2012, United Russia members held mayoral posts in 86 percent of Russia's 186 largest cities, and majorities in 92 percent of the city councils in Russia's 186 largest cities.[8] The party also built a hegemonic presence in organs of local government, and, with 56,330 regional, local, and primary branches, the party's organizational reach is extensive.[9] The party's domination of legislatures means that spoils and rents distributed in those forums are channeled by the party to its members. Particularly in the regions, the party has been a forum for rent distribution and the making of careers over the last decade.

However, the party did not come to exert collective control over the federal executive branch. Neither President Putin nor President Medvedev worked their way up through the party to become president. President Putin did not formally join the party in the 2000s, although he did tightly link himself to the party by heading its party list in the 2007 parliamentary elections and becoming party-chairman. In 2012, then-Prime Minister Dmitry Medvedev formally joined the party, but only 29 percent of his government were formal members of the party. Party penetration also appears to be low in the federal bureaucracy, military, and security services.

Given its lack of direct control over the executive branch, many descriptive studies of the party downplay its role as a political institution and seek to treat it as a *sui generis* phenomenon that should not be compared to other dominant parties (e.g. Bader 2011, Roberts 2012b, Isaacs and Whitmore 2014). To be sure, United Russia's state supervisory role pales in significance to that of the CPSU. In the Soviet Union, decisions on policy formulation and, often, implementation were made in autonomous party organs and formally enacted by state structures. United Russia does not do this, except perhaps in legislatures. Nor does

---

[8] Author's database.
[9] Accessed on UR Web site, November 8, 2010. www.edinros.ru/rubr.shtml?110103#2.

the party control careers at the top levels of the executive branch or in the federal bureaucracy.

Nonetheless, even though United Russia never approximated the 'ideal-type' state party with direct control over all political decisions, it has been something more than an institutional shell and has much in common with other dominant parties. Chapter 5 uses a combination of interviews with federal and regional elites, primary and secondary sources, and original quantitative data to show how United Russia has shaped actors' behavior and had substantive effects on political outcomes in Russia. Importantly, the party has served as a credible commitment device for both the Kremlin and regional elites, allowing them to enjoy the benefits of mutual cooperation. In turn, once United Russia was created, it became a 'sticky' institution because dismantling it would have been costly to both the Kremlin, regional elites, and party cadres. Russia's presidents and elites adapted their expectations about how the other side would behave and both preferred to continue reaping the benefits of mutual cooperation under the aegis of the dominant party.

Elites made a number of investments in the new party that constituted credible commitments. Regional governors relinquished their control over their own regionally based parties and instead linked them to the ruling party. This hand-tying move made it difficult for them retract their commitment and, for instance, run their own slates of candidates in regional elections. Elites also delegated to the party leadership the ability to sanction them for indiscipline. Indeed, the creation of United Russia party organizations in legislatures significantly increased the level of voting discipline among pro-Kremlin legislators.

In return, United Russia membership provides elites with a number of significant benefits, including access to rents, policy influence, and career advancement opportunities. From 2003 onward, almost all legislative bargaining has run through United Russia legislative factions. Legislative seats also provide party members with immunity from criminal prosecution and a platform for lobbying their own business interests. In elections, United Russia membership provides access to a valuable party brand, ballot access, and state administrative support.

Importantly, the party also reduces uncertainty about how the benefits of cooperating with the regime will be distributed. In legislative arenas, for example, the party has a near monopoly on legislative advancement opportunities, and appointment to these positions is based in large part on loyalty to the party.

The creation of United Russia also helped elites monitor the commitment of Russia's presidents to share spoils with elites, and, thus, reduced the temptation of the Kremlin to abuse those elites. Enshrined in the

1.8 United Russia as a Dominant Party

party arrangement are rules and norms, specifying what constitutes compliance on the part of the Kremlin (e.g. only supporting party candidates in elections, granting preference to party supporters in appointments, granting the party control over legislative nominations, and certain areas of policy formulation). If all elites contracted with the Kremlin via some unwritten agreement, then violations of those agreements could easily go unnoticed, especially if it is not clear what constitutes violation of the agreement. Under a dominant party system, it is clear that legislative spoils should be channeled, first and foremost, to members of the dominant party. Breaches of this norm are easy to observe. Thus, for example, when Russian governors were appointed (2005–2012), the largest party in regional parliaments was, according to the letter of the law, given the authority to nominate candidates for regional governor. When the Kremlin intervened in this process and asked the party leadership to nominate non-partisans, these deviations from the spoil sharing bargain could be easily identified by other United Russia partisans, because the new appointee lacked a ruling party affiliation. It did this rarely.

Investing in United Russia has also helped the Kremlin make its commitments to elites credible. Although he did not join the party, President Putin attached his name and reputation to the party by becoming party chairman, speaking at party events, and heading the party list. Prime Minister Medvedev joined the party and became its chairman. By delegating to the party some modicum of control over law-making in the legislative arena, the Kremlin limited its ability to deviate from the spoil-sharing bargain with elites. The Kremlin also delegated parts of the process of managing elections and candidate selection to United Russia. By relinquishing the ability to control the information necessary to making such key political decisions, the Kremlin limited its ability to micromanage politics in these spheres. If the Kremlin were to haphazardly dismantle United Russia, it would lack the organizational and informational resources necessary to manage these political tasks effectively.

United Russia also helps make Kremlin commitments to spoil-sharing with elites credible by solving collective action problems among Russia's key elite groups. The sanctioning mechanisms that rest in the hands of the party leadership give the party the ability to enforce discipline among its members. Should Russia's leaders attempt to abuse ruling elites (perhaps by initiating a purge or channeling privileges away from stakeholders) then elites could use the party to threaten the president. Such a scenario seems far-fetched in the environment that existed for much of the 2000s when Putin's personal brand was more popular than that of the party; United Russia would surely have been the loser in any confrontation with Putin. But this particular set of circumstances was not foreordained. If

Putin's popularity had fallen a rival might have sought to use UR as a platform to challenge Putin. Indeed, as I discuss in Chapters 3 and 4, the possibility that a rival might use the ruling party to challenge the leader was one of the primary reasons that Yeltsin eschewed investment in a dominant party in the 1990s and one of the reasons that Putin initially equivocated about the creation of United Russia in the early 2000s.

The mere act of creating the party also helped Russia's presidents monitor elite commitments to the spoil-sharing bargain. In legislative, regional, and local politics, membership in United Russia constitutes a dividing line between regime supporters and opponents. Leaving the dominant party constitutes defection. If a governor supports non-partisan candidates, this can be interpreted as a sign of disloyalty. Thus, the Kremlin knows whom to punish (or reward) and can clearly see when it is being abused by elites.

Finally, the role of United Russia as a commitment device for leaders and elites was strengthened because its place in the political system was nested in other institutional constraints. Fixed election cycles mean that United Russia majorities elected in one election would, at least according to the letter of the law, be stable until the next election. This stickiness was reinforced by imperative mandate laws, instituted in the 2000s, which forbade regional legislators from switching parliamentary parties. The introduction of proportional electoral rules for the 2007 elections made it impossible for the Kremlin or powerful governors to renege on support for the dominant party in order to support individual candidates and the introduction of high thresholds for representation removed the temptation to support multiple small parties.

In return for these investments, Russia's presidents have reaped significant benefits from the dominant party system. By dependably distributing spoils to elites, United Russia serves as a tool of cooptation that ensures elite loyalty to the regime. Although sporadic defections have occurred, the ruling elite in Russia has remained remarkably united through several major economic and political crises. The institutional bonds created by United Russia are one of the main reasons for this cohesion.

The party also reduces the transaction costs associated with forming stable legislative majorities. Before the creation of United Russia, Russia's presidents expended an inordinate amount of effort, time, and pork patching together ad hoc coalitions of legislators from various factions and groupings (Remington 2006). The creation of United Russia as a majority pro-presidential party helped the Kremlin pass legislation more easily.

United Russia also plays a key role in helping Russia's presidents win elections. The party brings together Russia's most important regional

1.8 United Russia as a Dominant Party

elites – governors, enterprise directors, mayors, prominent legislators, and other opinion leaders – who put their political machines to work for the regime at election time. The party also helps the regime coordinate pro-regime candidates. Russia's presidents, rather than having to bargain with thousands of individual elites to orchestrate strategic withdrawals in each election, can rely on United Russia to coordinate strategic withdrawals so that a single pro-regime candidate is put forward in each electoral contest.

Thus, mutual commitments made cooperation under the aegis of United Russia possible because they increased the credibility of each side's promises to cooperate. In turn, the pattern of mutual cooperation regulated by the dominant party provided significant benefits to both leaders and elites. United Russia helps leaders win elections, secure the loyalty of elites, and maintain stable legislative majorities. In turn, United Russia provides elites with access to patronage and reduces uncertainty about how that patronage will be provided.

Over the course of the 2000s, the Kremlin came to depend on United Russia for the maintenance of elite cohesion. Elites, meanwhile, came to rely on United Russia for the provision of spoils, especially in legislatures. The Kremlin did not want to provoke elite discord by dismantling the party, and elites did not want to jeopardize their access to spoils by defecting. And neither felt confident that one-time defections would go unpunished. Thus, both sides developed mutually shared expectations about how the other would behave under the dominant party system.

The extent of United Russia's institutional significance should not be overstated, however. As Chapters 5 and 9 demonstrate, United Russia's independence remains limited in many areas. It does not exert collective control over the executive branch, although advancement through the party ranks does represent one of several paths to power in the federal government. Moreover, to this point in history, Russia's presidents have not emerged from within the party ranks. President Putin remains Russia's most important political figure and is not directly subordinate to party decisions.

United Russia's institutional strength is also limited by the fact there still exist alternative paths to career advancement in Russia. Patron-client ties coexist alongside partisan ties as a means of political advancement. Moreover, the continued existence of a cadre reserve system within the executive branch, separate from the dominant party's own cadre reserve system, works to undermine elite beliefs in the role of United Russia as a purveyor of careers.

This does not mean that United Russia should not be studied as a dominant party. To be sure, United Russia does not oversee an all-encompassing party-state, in which all political decisions are made collectively by party organizations outside government structures. But, this is an ideal type that few, if any, dominant parties approximate. For example, even in the Soviet Union, personnel decisions were based as much on patron-client ties as they were on institutionalized performance criteria or party loyalty (e.g. Rigby and Harasmyiw 1980). Scholars of Mexican politics meanwhile have noted that the perceived overlap between the PRI and government was an "illusion" and that the party had little autonomous influence on policy-making in the executive branch (Rodriguez and Ward 1994). The Mexican presidency, it was argued, dominated all other political institutions in the country, leading scholars to characterize the PRI as "merely the electoral ministry of the presidency" (Weldon 1997, 226). Indeed, Castaneda's (2000) insider account of presidential succession in Mexico describes the process as a highly personalistic ritual in which the President selected his successor without consulting the party collective.

Still, the PRI and CPSU are dominant parties with high levels of institutional strength. It is peculiar, then, that most of our knowledge of dominant parties comes from studies of these parties, even though they are clear outliers in the extent to which they held a monopoly over political life. United Russia has less institutional significance than these paradigmatic dominant parties; rather, it is like most of the world's dominant parties in that it structures political exchange in some arenas, but not in others. Ultimately, United Russia's institutional significance should be judged not just against those rare examples of highly institutionalized dominant party regimes, but also against the weak or non-existent party organizations that exist, or do not exist, in many personalist autocracies. In the post-Soviet region, United Russia exhibits much more institutional significance than the fly-by-night parties of power that existed in Russia in the 1990s, Ukraine's weak parties of power under Kuchma, or the non-existent ruling party organizations in Belarus under Lukashenko.

Most dominant parties constrain key actors in some areas, but are still dependent on them in others. They share influence with other actors and institutions. United Russia falls into this category. Even while it constrained Putin in some areas, it remained dependent on him in others. It makes loyalty incentive compatible for elites in some areas, but sometimes fails to constrain elite discord in others.

1.9 Post-Soviet Russia and Authoritarian Institutions

Scholars of Russian political institutions have fruitfully engaged with debates in political science about economic reform (Shleifer and Treisman

2001, Frye 2010), party development (Hale 2006, Smyth 2006), electoral systems (Moser 2001), legislative organization (Smith and Remingon 2001) and democratization (McFaul 2001, Bunce 2003, Fish 2005, McMann 2006) to name just a few. Most of this work focused on Russia's post-communist development in the 1990s and viewed Russia through the lens of literature on emerging democracies. But as Russia became more autocratic in the 2000s, scholars were slow to apply recently developed theories of authoritarian institutions. Most analyses of Russia's Putin-era political institutions continue to compare these institutions to democratic institutions. Invariably, and unsurprisingly, these analyses conclude that Russia's elections, parties, and legislatures do not fulfill the same functions as their counterparts in democracies (e.g. March 2009, Whitmore 2010, Golosov 2011, White 2011).

But there are few studies analyzing Russia's political institutions as *authoritarian* institutions. Neo-institutional studies of elections, parties, and legislatures in modern authoritarian regimes have argued that these nominally democratic institutions help dictators gather information, coopt elites, and mitigate social opposition. To be sure, much recent scholarship views Russia's regime as a hybrid or authoritarian regime (e.g. Fish 2005, Ross 2005, Way 2005, Colton and Hale 2009, Kryshtanovskaya and White 2003), and post-Soviet area specialists have, in fact, contributed to the fine-tuning of those conceptual categories (Balzer 2003, Levitsky and Way 2010). But, we still know very little about how the Kremlin manages elites and gathers information through elections.[10] We also know little about how legislatures and parties are used for cooptation and spoil distribution.[11]

I do not deny that models of democratic institutions yield insights into the operation of Russia's political institutions. It is clear that they do. Rather, I simply argue that analyses of contemporary Russian politics can be improved by also considering Russia's parties, elections, and legislatures in light of the recent neo-institutional literature on authoritarian regimes. In turn, the study of Russia's authoritarian institutions can contribute to the appraisal and refinement of theory on the operation of institutions in modern authoritarian regimes. This study seeks to advance both those goals.

Studying United Russia's emergence also offers insights into the underpinnings of regime stability in Putin-era Russia. United Russia's primary function is to coopt and control Russia's traditionally unruly elites. In the early 2000s, President Putin initiated a series of federal reforms aimed

---

[10] See Treisman (1999) and Reuter and Robertson (2012) for exceptions.
[11] See Remington (2008), March (2009), and Reuter and Robertson (2015) for exceptions.

at recentralizing state authority and reducing the autonomy of powerful regional governors. These reforms culminated in the cancellation of direct gubernatorial elections in 2004. Yet, even after the cancellation of direct gubernatorial elections it was clear that Putin still depended on these elites to help him win elections and quell social unrest.

This balance of power resembles the situation that Migdal found to be characteristic of many African countries in the post-colonial period, where central state leaders could remove any one local strongman at any time, but "the pattern of social control" that they represented was difficult to displace (Migdal 1988, 141). Putin could deploy his resources to have any one governor removed, but he needed the totality of the governors' political machines in order win elections and govern cost-effectively.

Putin wanted to reduce the independence of Russia's regional elites. And so, he took measures, such as the cancellation of governors' elections, to chip away at their autonomous resources. But he also knew that weakening them too much would strip away the regime's ability to govern the country. This is an enduring dilemma for authoritarian leaders. How can a leader coopt the resources of an elite actor without destroying them? If the Kremlin were to remove all governors, the clientelist networks of the old governors would be disrupted and newly appointed officials would lack authority among voters and local elites. On the other hand, granting full independence to governors would maximize their vote-mobilizing ability, but then the Kremlin would not be able to depend on the support of those autonomous governors. The solution was to weaken them as much as possible and then coopt them with carrots – spoils and promises of career advancement – that could be distributed through the dominant party.

Putin needed the cooperation of Russia's elites just as those elites need his personal and political resources to maintain their careers. He was – and remains – dependent on them as much as they are dependent on him. There is no doubt that repression, coercion, fraud and patronage are common tactics that the regime employs to maintain control. But it is also clear that elite cohesion, facilitated by United Russia, both enables the regime to use these tactics and shores up regime stability on its own.

Thus, the picture of Russia's authoritarian regime that emerges in this book is one that is more institutionalized than what most existing accounts allow. Regime stability in Russia is founded not just on natural resource rents (Fish 2005), economic growth (Treisman 2011), coercion (Taylor 2011), or Putin's personality cult (Judah 2014). It also depends on elite cohesion, which is secured, in large part, by the dominant party institution, United Russia.

Between 1999 and 2015, Russia's authoritarian regime displayed more durability than many expected. After the 'colored' revolutions unseated long-serving incumbents in Ukraine and Georgia in 2003 and 2004, respectively, some observers thought Russia would be next.[12] But Russia somehow managed to avoid the large-scale elite defections that had precipitated regime change in those countries. In the wake of the 2008–09 global financial crisis observers again predicted that popular dissatisfaction with the regime would lead to elite defections, and yet these predictions proved incorrect as the ruling group remained remarkably cohesive during this period. Most recently, in 2011–13, as the regime's popularity declined and mass protests rocked large cities, many predicted the downfall of the regime. And yet, as Chapter 5 demonstrates, large-scale elite defections did not materialize and the regime persisted. I attribute much of this stability to the strength of Russia's dominant party institutions.[13] In sum, the story of United Russia's emergence tells us a lot about how the current regime was built.

1.10 Dominant Parties and the New Institutionalism

This book borrows from the new-institutionalism in political science and economics. In turn, it also seeks to contribute to that theoretical framework. In keeping with the main tenet of neo-institutionalism, this study holds to the notion that institutions influence actors' behavior. Dominant party institutions coordinate the expectations of leaders and elites, solve monitoring problems associated with power-sharing, and act as third-party enforcement mechanisms. But this study moves beyond illustrating how institutions influence actors' behavior to examine the conditions that lead actors to create the institutions that influence their behavior. In other words, this is a study of endogenous institutions.

In line with rational choices approaches to endogenous institutions, this study holds to the premise that institutions are the product of decisions by self-interested actors. Institutions emerge because they improve the welfare of individual actors. Much of the 'rational choice' literature on institutions sees institutions as solutions to problems of coordination or collective action. This book takes a similar approach. Dominant parties are solutions to problems of collective action and mutual commitment. In this way, this work shares much in common with rational choice works on the origins of parties in democracies, which tend to view

---

[12] See, for example, "The Cracks Appear" *Economist* 10 December 2011 and Judah (2014).
[13] See Levitsky and Way (2010) for a similar interpretation.

parties as solutions to a series of collective action problems (Schwartz 1986 Aldrich 1995).

Also in line with rational choice approaches to institutions, this study highlights the importance of strategic interaction between these self-interested actors. When deciding whether a dominant party is in their interest, leaders and elites not only consider their own preferences and constraints, but also the preferences and expected behavior of the other party.

But in contrast to much of the early work within "rational choice institutionalism," this study does not attribute the origins of institutions solely to the "value that institutions have for the actors affected by those institutions." (Hall and Taylor 1996, 945). Early works in the new institutionalism made major contributions by showing that institutions benefited actors by allowing them to cooperate, reap gains from trade, or reduce transaction costs. In turn, self-interested actors created institutions because those institutions helped them realize these benefits (e.g. Shepsle and Weingast 1981, Milgrom, North, and Weingast 1990). But these accounts of institutional origins were sometimes perceived as functionalist. Institutions emerged because they were called for. Accounts of institutional origins focused on stylized descriptions of the immediate decisions made by self-interested actors and the subsequent effects of the resultant institutions on actors' behavior.

Such accounts have difficulty explaining variation in institutional emergence. To say that actors would benefit from an institution does not explain why the institution is supplied in some cases, but not in others (Bates 1988, Ostrom 1990). Indeed, such approaches generate a puzzle: if institutions improve the welfare of actors, why do actors fail to create them in some settings (Bates 1988, Moe 1990)? Take for example Aldrich's (1995) account of why political parties emerge. Parties help solve collective action problems associated with voting.[14] They provide organizational and financial resources that help mobilize voters, which reduces the physical costs of voting, and a party label provides voters with information on candidates, which reduces the costs of acquiring information. The puzzle, then, is why parties remain so weak in much of the world; after all, if strong parties provide such benefits to candidates, then why do actors fail to create strong parties? In an analogous fashion, some of the best recent work on dominant parties suffer from a similar functionalist drawback. Dominant parties are viewed as institutions that

---

[14] Parties also solve collective action problems in legislatures where a centralized party leadership with the ability to sanction noncompliance helps legislators reduce uncertainty and achieve the public good of party discipline.

solve problems of credible commitment for leaders, allowing them to credibly promise spoils to elites which increases the chances that elites will remain loyal to the leader (Magaloni 2008). But again, this generates a puzzle: why is there variation in the emergence of dominant parties? If they generate such benefits then it seems strange that many authoritarian leaders would eschew building them.

The most illuminating recent work on party development in democracies embraces the rational choice view of parties as solutions to collective action problems and retains a focus on individual candidates as the key actors; but, crucially, this work seeks to identify the meso-level structural factors that affect the incentives of candidates to seek invest in party building. For example, Smyth (2006) shows that candidates with significant personal resources (such as wealth or a business that can serve as an organizational base) may eschew partisan affiliation because they have less need of the mobilizational resources that parties can provide. Hale (2006) highlights how candidates with ties to "party substitutes" such as regional political machines or prominent financial-industrial groups have less need to invest in party building, because these "substitutes" provide many of the same benefits that a party would provide.

My approach is similar in spirit. It melds a rational choice approach to endogenous institutions with social-structural variables that affect the incentives of actors to invest in dominant party institutions. Specifically, like rational choice approaches, I take dominant parties to be the immediate result of decisions made by individual actors, engaged in strategic interaction. Dominant party institutions help solve problems of commitment, coordination, and cooperation. But moving beyond 'shallow' rational choice accounts of institutions my theory focuses on how meso-level, socio-structural variables affect the extent to which actors demand solutions to these problems.

1.11 Dominant Parties and the Study of Democratization

This study helps explain why some countries democratize, but others do not. It does so by illuminating the origins of one institution – dominant parties – that fortifies authoritarian rule. In recent years, much of the research on democratization has focused on how characteristics of the authoritarian regime itself affect its propensity to break down. Transitologists and their heirs highlighted splits within the authoritarian regimes as a precipitating cause of authoritarian breakdown (Przeworski 1991, Burton, Gunther and Higley 1992). On its own, however, elite cohesion is of limited utility as an explanatory factor. Its proximity to the outcome of regime breakdown makes it border on tautology. To say that strong authoritarian regimes are those that command the support of those within the regime edges close to restating the definition of a strong regime. From an empirical standpoint, elite cohesion was often seen to melt in the face of contextual circumstances, which made it difficult to make predictions about regime trajectories on the basis of arguments about elite splits. Moreover, identifying periods of elite splits that are separate from their alleged effects on regime durability proved difficult.

Those who have endogenized elite cohesion are able to provide a more compelling account. Attempts to endogenize elite cohesion come in two varieties: structural and institutional. Those who take a structural approach posit economic and macro-social variables, such as economic growth (Haggard and Kaufman 1996) or social opposition (Acemoglu and Robinson 2006) as determinants of elite cohesion.

Those who take an institutionalist view argue that dominant parties foster elite cohesion by providing institutional guarantees about the benefits of regime loyalty and creating incentives for otherwise fractious elites to cooperate in the perpetuation of the regime. Geddes (1999) was the first to make this point and noted that regimes with party regimes survived for much longer than personalist or military dictatorships. This view of dominant parties as stabilizers of authoritarian rules has since been refined and extended in a number of works (Brownlee 2007, Levitsky and Way 2010, Slater 2010).

This literature advances the notion that dominant parties extend authoritarian rule by ensuring elite cohesion, but it does not provide a clear view of how that cohesion is established in the first place. Most starkly, these works fail to lay out the factors that make elites, both in the aggregate and at the individual level, more or less likely to commit themselves to dominant parties. This is important for causal inference. One of the key stumbling blocks in the new institutionalism is endogeneity. The primary difficulty is that institutions may be endogenous to a set of social conditions that abet the creation and maintenance of the institution (Rodden 2009, Przeworski 2004). Since we cannot randomly assign institutions to social settings, it is difficult to know whether institutions have causal effects or whether their existence masks the underlying social dynamics that actually determine outcomes.

In the case of dominant parties' effects on democratization, we cannot know for certain whether dominant party institutions stabilize authoritarian regimes or whether the social conditions that bring about and sustain these institutions actually forestall democratization (Pepinsky 2013). What is needed in order to improve causal claims about the

1.12 Research Design, Methodology, and the Plan of the Book

effects of dominant parties is an empirically robust explanation for dominant party emergence. Identifying the causes of dominant party emergence will help analysts sweep out the effects of social conditions in empirical analyses.

Concerns about causal inference have animated some of the most productive debates in comparative politics in recent years. But the question is not just about causal inference; it is also about what "makes a good cause" (Kitschelt 2003). Scholars have warned against constructing causal arguments on the basis of independent variables that are far-removed from outcomes of interest (Elster 1998). These scholars advocate specifying a chain of causal mechanisms explicitly linking cause and effect. On the other hand, scholars have also cautioned against "shallow" explanations, which focus on factors so proximate to the outcome of interest that they are not illuminating (Kitschelt 2003, Rodden 2009).

This book takes seriously issues of both causal inference and causal depth. My argument specifies both exogenous structural factors that affect the balance of resources between leaders and elites and a chain of reasoning linking those structural changes to changes in the behavior of actors. In turn, my argument specifies how individual, strategic actions taken by actors translate into the creation of a dominant party.

I then take a multi-method approach in order to examine both the internal and external validity of my arguments. Qualitative case studies excel at establishing internal validity. Case studies are also advantageous because they permit valid, low-level measurement of variables – elite and leader resources – that are difficult to measure for a large cross-national sample. At the same time, cross-national statistical analyses help to establish external validity. It is hoped that consistent results across multiple streams of evidence will prove more persuasive.

The empirical portions of the book begin with two qualitative case studies of dominant party emergence and non-emergence in Russia: Chapter 3 examines the non-emergence of strong ruling parties in Yeltsin era-Russia, while Chapter 4 examines the gradual rise of United Russia and its transformation into a dominant party. As noted above, the existence of a strong social opposition and a paucity of rent revenues would lead some existing theory to predict that Yeltsin would be forced to buy the cooperation of social forces by coopting (or confronting) them with a strong dominant party. But this is not what we observe. By contrast, my argument predicts that a dominant party would not emerge because elites were too strong. This is what we observe.

Chapter 4 is a least-likely "crucial" case (Eckstein 1975, Gerring 2007). A least-likely case is the obverse of a most-likely case. It is one that is predicted to *not* achieve a certain outcome on competing theoretical dimensions, but is expected to achieve the outcome on the theoretical dimension of interest (Gerring 2007). Some existing theory would predict that Putin would not invest in a dominant party in the mid-2000s, because windfall oil revenues would allow him to buy cooperation without institutions and a weak social opposition posed no threat that needed to be coopted (e.g. Smith 2005, Gandhi 2008). Again, this is not what we observe. My argument predicts that the relative balance of resources between the Kremlin and regional elites would lead to the creation of a dominant party, which is what happened.

Thus, as in Chapter 3, congruence between independent variables of interest and the dependent variable in Chapter 4 provides some evidence in favor of the argument. In addition, these paired, longitudinal case studies come from the same country, which permits us to hold constant some national-level macro-historical factors such as history (i.e. the legacy of the CPSU), culture, and levels of modernization.

Yet, demonstrating the congruence of independent and dependent variables in two-paired longitudinal case studies only takes us so far. So rather than conceive of these chapters purely as cross-case comparisons, I prefer to treat each of these chapters as within-case analyses. Within-case analysis is aided by the simple fact that the emergence of a dominant party is not a dichotomous event. These chapters endeavor to construct an analytic narrative that "identifies the actors, the decision points they faced, the choices they made, the paths taken and shunned, and the manner in which their choices generated events and outcomes" (Bates et al, 1998, 14). Recognizing the enormous variation in the actions and choices of both the Kremlin and regional elites as well as the variation in the final outcome of interest (dominant party formation), these chapters examine how the Kremlin and regional elites responded to shifts in the resource balance by reinforcing or undermining their own investments in the pro-regime party. In turn, the sum total of these decisions is related to the emergence or non-emergence of a dominant party. These chapters demonstrate the internal validity of the argument not just by demonstrating a correlation between within-case values of the independent variables (resource ownership) and dependent variables (individual commitment to the party project), but also by providing evidence that actors made their decisions for the reasons posited in the theory and that those decisions had real consequences for the success or failure of the

1.12 Research Design, Methodology, and the Plan of the Book 41

regime party. Chapter 5, with its emphasis on how United Russia structures actor incentives, also serves this role.

The empirical material in these chapters draws heavily on 18 months of fieldwork carried out in 10 Russian regions and Moscow. During this time, I conducted scores of interviews with regional elites, party leaders, legislators, and local experts. These interviews provided invaluable insight into the process of dominant party building and the role of United Russia in Russian politics.

Chapters 6 and 7 examine the individual-level causal mechanisms of the argument using quantitative data. Although my theory is ultimately concerned with the macro-outcome of dominant party emergence, its implications concern the behavior of individual actors. In these chapters, I endeavor to show that elites have interests in retaining their own autonomy and make dominant party affiliation decisions on the basis of those interests. If elites, as a whole, are less likely to join a dominant party when they control significant autonomous resources, then the same should hold true of individual elites in a dynamic process of dominant party formation. I test this hypothesis with original data on when 121 of Russia's regional governors joined United Russia from 2003–2007. Event history models are employed to show that governors with strong political machines were more likely to postpone joining United Russia. Chapter 7 extends testing of this hypothesis to another elite group in Russia: regional legislators. Using original data on the party affiliation of over 2,000 Russian regional legislators this chapter shows that legislators whose careers are built on the basis of business enterprises that are difficult to tax or control by the Kremlin were less likely to join United Russia.

Chapter 8 presents a series of cross-national statistical tests that probe the generalizability of my arguments. Are my arguments applicable outside post-Soviet Russia? In this chapter I develop an original, cross-national measure of elite strength based on historical patterns of political decentralization, geographic distributions of human population, and territorial concentrations of ethnic groups. I then use original data on 128 dominant parties and to test the main argument. I find that dominant parties are most likely to emerge in countries when resources are balanced between leaders and elites.

Chapter 9 concludes the book, highlighting both the comparative and Russia-specific implication of the study. I discuss the how the theoretical framework in the book can help us understand the evolution of United Russia and conclude by offering some thoughts on the future of the dominant party system in Russia.

2 A Theory of Dominant Party Formation

The purpose of this chapter is to provide a theory of dominant party formation. In Section 2.1, I define elites and discuss why their inclusion in a model of dominant party formation is necessary. In Section 2.2, I lay out the terms of a two-sided commitment problem between leaders and elites in non-democracies. This two-sided interaction forms the basis of my analysis of dominant party formation. In Section 2.3, I discuss how the commitment problem is overcome. Here I focus on how changes in the balance of resources between leaders and elites increase the likelihood that these actors will make investments in a dominant party institution that can help solve their commitment problem. Ultimately, I argue that dominant parties are most likely to emerge when elites hold enough autonomous political resources (relative to the resources of leaders) that co-opting them is necessary, but not so many autonomous resources that they themselves are reluctant to participate in any cooperative bargain.

2.1 The Actors: Building a Theory of Dominant Party Formation

An explanation of dominant party formation can be approached from several possible angles. One is to examine the interests and choices of regime leaders. By regime leader, I mean the individual who serves as the effective head of government in a non-democratic regime. In regimes with nominally democratic institutions this may be the president or the prime minister. In other regimes, generals, monarchs, or dictators serve as regime leaders. Regime leaders may or may not choose to invest in a dominant party. Explaining the choices of leaders in this regard is the approach pursued by much existing literature (e.g. Smith 2005, Gandhi 2008).

The second approach is to examine the interests of elites. By elites I mean those actors outside the central leadership of a country who exercise influence and demand loyalty from citizens and other political actors. In many cases, their elite status is conferred – or simply confirmed – by

2.1 Building a Theory of Dominant Party Formation

political office (regional governors, prominent legislators, ministers, administrators, and the like), while in other cases their influence is not manifested by a formal political position, but rather depends solely on informal stature, as in the case of political bosses, strongmen, caciques, or warlords. In many developing countries, important elite actors draw upon traditional modes of authority, with chiefs, nobles, and clan leaders being prominent examples. In still other cases, political influence derives from economic resources, as with employers, businessmen, oligarchs, and landlords. In practice, of course, informal modes of influence often translate into formal influence.

Understanding variation in the power of such elites is crucial to understanding politics in the developing world. A rich vein of literature in comparative politics studies such elites, giving particular attention to subnational elites.[1] Indeed, in the center–periphery conflicts that have wracked much of the developing world, regional elites are often the key actors. Such elites control important political resources, such as entrenched political machines, clientelist networks, hard-to-tax economic assets, or positions of traditional authority that are difficult for leaders to expropriate or control systematically. Subnational elites may be capable of mobilizing citizens in elections, on the street, or on the battlefield. They command the loyalties of important subelites. Elites in a country are strong to the extent that they control such resources because these resources give them power over citizens.

For their part, central leaders covet the resources of subnational elites, because these resources can help leaders extract revenue, win votes, implement policy, control social protest, and the like. Regional elites may be individually indispensable (i.e. difficult to repress) and control resources that give them bargaining leverage vis-à-vis the center, or, as Migdal (1988) argues, they may be embedded in a broader pattern of effective social control that is costly for leaders to subvert. Thus, leaders must often find accommodation with these elites in order to govern cost-effectively.[2]

---

[1] See Kern and Dolkart 1973, Schmidt 1980, and Duncan Baretta and Markoff 1987, and Hagopian 1996, on Latin America; Powell 1970, Lemerchand 1972, Clapham 1982, Herbst 2000, and Koter 2013 on Africa; Van Dam 1979 on the Middle East; Chubb 1982 on Southern Europe; Cappelli 1988, Matsuzato 2001, Hale 2003, and Alina-Pisano 2010 on the Soviet Union and the post-Soviet states; Weiner 1967 on South Asia; Geertz 1965, Scott 1972, and Sidel 1999 on Southeast Asia.

[2] For the elite resources to have meaning, it must be difficult or costly for regime leaders to expropriate those resources. Clearly, the respective powers of leaders and elites are often endogenous to one another, but as I discuss in Chapters 3, 4, 6, and 8, exogenous factors such as ethnicity, geography, historical legacies, and economic structure make it more likely that elites will develop the political machines and clientelist networks that are hard

When their interests lie in striking temporary bargains with the regime, elites may act as allies. When neutrality or opposition is the best means of protecting their interests, they may choose those options. Indeed, throughout history, subnational power brokers have often used their resources to stymie the efforts of state leaders to construct strong central states (e.g. Migdal 1988, Sidel 1999, Treisman 1999, Hale 2003).

An elite-centric approach to dominant party formation would place the emphasis on the incentives of elites to join a party. They may see no reason to affiliate with the party, or they may have an interest in tying their fates to the regime's party project. A third approach is to assume that both elites and leaders matter and examine the process of dominant party formation as a strategic interaction between these two sides. The argument here embraces the final approach.[3]

Elites, Society, and Dominant Party Formation

This section discusses why it is important to consider the role of elites in a study of dominant party origins. But first it is useful to clarify how an elite-based explanation might differ from a society-based explanation. Most literature attributes the longevity of dominant parties to their ability to retain mass support (e.g. Smith 2005, Magaloni 2006, Greene 2007). It is hard to argue with this perspective, especially in electoral authoritarian regimes; when dominant parties win a plurality of votes then, ipso facto, they do not lose.[4] But as proponents of society-based theories themselves have pointed out (e.g. Magaloni and Krichelli 2010), such theories provide less insight into dominant party *origins*. After all, if a dominant party does not exist in the first place, how can mass support for that nonexistent party explain its origins? Society-based explanations

---

for leaders to displace. In those chapters, I also discuss plausibly exogenous factors that may determine the autonomous resources of leaders.

[3] To be sure, I am not the first to focus on elites as central actors in the process of dominant party creation. Slater (2010) also highlights the importance of elite collective action and further posits that elites will engage in this party-based collective action when they feel threatened by endemic contentious politics. The account of hegemonic electoral performance offered here shares this emphasis on elites, but differs in two ways. First, as I outline in the next section, I cast the problem of dominant party formation as a two-sided commitment problem whereby elites are engaged in a strategic interaction with regime leaders. Second, the incentives that elites have to invest in a dominant party are different in my account, emanating from their relative strength vis-à-vis leaders. Importantly, I identify the factors that make elites important to the decision over whether to form a dominant party.

[4] The relevant question in this line of literature then becomes, How do party leaders attain and maintain social support? This topic is taken up by various authors (e.g. Magaloni 2006, Greene 2007, Blaydes 2011).

2.1 Building a Theory of Dominant Party Formation

often have a hard time explaining why leaders and elites would create a party that might then strive to attain mass support. A focus on leaders and elites can help us understand why actors would create such institutions.[5]

To be sure, important explanations of dominant party origins do focus on society-based variables (e.g. Huntington 1970). As discussed, both Smith (2005) and Gandhi (2008) argue persuasively that leaders create parties when they face puissant social oppositions that need to be co-opted. In many settings, such explanations help us understand key aspects of the dominant party formation process, especially those aspects that pertain to how policy influence is accorded to social groups. But by their very nature, such explanations tell us less about why and when leaders and elites would enter into power-sharing deals with each other under the aegis of a dominant party. Thus, explanations of dominant party origins that focus only on the co-optation of social forces are incomplete because they leave out the incentives of elites to commit to the dominant party.

Empirically, it is clear that elite coordination is a necessary condition for dominant party formation, but the same cannot be said about a strong social base. For while it is very difficult to locate examples of dominant parties that do not subsume a large portion of the elite, it is easier to locate examples of dominant parties that got their start as a collection of elites and either never developed or took some time to develop a strong grassroots presence (e.g. the PDP in Nigeria, the True Whig Party in Liberia, Iran Novin in Iran, OTAN in Kazakhstan, ARENA in Brazil, the Jatiya Party in Bangladesh, or United Russia in Russia). Indeed, as early as 1978, Bienen had argued that many of the ruling parties in Africa were not nationally integrating, mass-based organizations – as the literature then assumed – but rather were collections of elites organized around patronage-sharing agreements. Such dominant parties win elections by relying not just on programmatic appeals, but also on some combination of clientelism, repression, abuse of state resources, and local machine politics (e.g. Magaloni 2006, Greene 2007, Blaydes 2011, Koter 2013, Reuter 2013). As a result, their electoral support base may shift from election to election.

Thus, studying the incentives of *both* elites and leaders can improve our understanding of dominant party origins. Understanding such dynamics appears crucial to understanding the origins of those parties that got their start as elite-based organizations. But even where some impetus to

---

[5] None of this is to say that society does not play a role in the argument that this book pursues. As I will argue, the popularity of regime leaders is a factor in determining the relative strength of leaders and elite and, in turn, their incentives to invest in a dominant party.

formation arises from society, focusing on elites helps us understand the elite power-sharing elements of dominant party formation.

Here it might also be appropriate to address how my theory relates to those dominant parties that started as revolutionary organizations or anticolonial liberation movements. The CPSU, the Chinese Communist Party (CCP), and the Cuban Communist Party are prime examples of the former, while the Popular Movement for the Liberation of Angola (MPLA), the Mozambique Liberation Front (FRELIMO), and Tanganyika African National Union (TANU) are examples of the latter. In such cases, certain elements of the party organization predate the regime itself. On the one hand, my theory of dominant party formation is less applicable in situations where a leader attains power already constrained by a preexisting party. Still, I think that my argument offers some insight into the reasons that leaders and elites remain committed to investing in a dominant party at the point when the regime is constituted. After all, history shows that leaders and elites retain significant agency in such transitional periods and the decision to retain or jettison a dominant party at those crucial junctures is clearly a conscious one.[6]

It is also worth noting, however, that, contrary to much of the conventional wisdom, dominant parties with anticolonial or revolutionary origins are not the modal category of dominant party, especially in the post–Cold War era.[7] Of the 128 parties in my global sample of dominant parties (see Chapter 8), 9 were revolutionary movements that predated the authoritarian regime they established, and 38 were once anticolonial liberation movements or, at least, dominated politics in the colony prior to independence. Meanwhile, 60 parties (47 percent of the sample) were established by the authoritarian regime in power at the time. And, with the end of both colonialism and the Cold War, only 3 of the 41 dominant parties that emerged between 1980 and 2006 have their origins in revolutionary or anticolonial struggle. It seems clear that, in the future, very few newly emerged dominant parties will have revolutionary or anticolonial origins.

---

[6] Indeed, even the Bolsheviks, the paradigmatic example of a revolutionary dominant party, were so riven by doctrinal schisms and local conflicts in the first years after the revolution that the continued existence of the party was constantly in doubt (e.g. Service 1979, Rigby 1981). And as the present argument would suggest, the unruliness of local officials was one of the most often cited threats to the continued existence of the party.

[7] Misperceptions about the prevalence of revolutionary parties may be due to the geopolitical significance of some of the countries where revolutionary parties ruled (e.g. the Soviet Union and China). And misconceptions about the number of anticolonial parties are probably due to the fact that much of the early literature on dominant parties focused on Africa, where anticolonial parties were the modal variety of ruling party in the 1960s.

A final reason why an elite-based theory helps advance our understanding of dominant party origins relates to how regime support is generated. It is well known that public opinion in non-democratic regimes is heavily influenced by elites (e.g. Geddes and Zaller 1989). This is part of what makes them undemocratic. Propaganda is spread. Government censors restrict the free flow of information. Voters are coerced and votes are bought. And in many regimes elite opinion leaders outside the ruling group – patrons, strongmen, chiefs, governors, economic elites, warlords, landlords, and the like – exert a heavy influence on citizens' political preferences (e.g. Lemarchand 1972, Schmidt 1980, Sidel 1999, Hale 2003, Koter 2013, Sharafutdinova 2013). My own work on Russia has shown that vote totals for United Russia depended heavily on the ability of powerful governors to mobilize votes for the party (Reuter 2013). Thus, it is not difficult to see why elite coordination in a dominant party would help generate support for that party. Even if social support were taken as a prerequisite for dominant party formation, elite commitment is one key determinant of that support.

Elite Commitment and the Study of Political Parties

The literature on party formation in democracies pays close attention to the problem of securing elite commitments. Parties harness together the ambitions of rivalrous elites, solving commitment problems among them. John Aldrich's (1995) account of why parties emerged in the United States is the most well-known example of such rational choice work on party development. According to Aldrich, legislators share a long-term interest in collaborating on policy logrolls. But their own shortsightedness and the lack of a commitment device lead legislators to defect from these logrolls ex post by voting their preferences myopically. In this setting, legislators may feel compelled to tie their hands by delegating responsibility to third party institutions (parties) that can solve these commitment problems.

But Aldrich's is not a full-fledged theory of endogenous institutions because it is the party *institution* that constrains actors. This begs the question: why and when would elites join in the early rounds before the institution has enforcement power? In this sense, the argument is functionalist, for it assumes the emergence of institutions to meet a need felt by actors. Extending this objection to its logical conclusion, one might be compelled to ask whether we should always expect actors to have a long-term interest in cooperating. It sometimes might be true that actors would find it in their interest to go it alone, crafting their own platforms, expending their personal resources on campaigns, and making ad hoc bargains to achieve desired policies.

Recent work on party development in hybrid regimes has made just this argument. It has questioned whether all actors find it in their best interest to commit to nascent political parties. In a study of post-Soviet Russian party development, Henry Hale (2006) shows that candidates with the support of so-called party substitutes (financial industrial groups and powerful political machines) can avoid party affiliation and be successful in running and winning campaigns. In another study of post-Soviet party development, Regina Smyth (2006) demonstrates that candidates who have personal vote resources, such as a local reputation or business ties are less likely to affiliate with parties. The upshot of this work is that politicians may not always find it in their best interest to commit to a party, an insight that is also useful as we turn our attention to the origins of dominant parties.

In the study of dominant parties, we know more about how party institutions, once established, can solve elite commitment problems than we do about why elites make investments in the party in the first place. A primary research frontier is to determine the factors that make elites more likely to make these investments. Identifying these factors will help provide a more complete theory of dominant party formation for two reasons. First, it will provide insight into the conditions under which leaders will have an interest in investing in a dominant party. And, second, it will help explain the conditions under which elites tie their fates to a nascent dominant party. I argue that elite affiliation does not always follow automatically from a leader's decision to invest in a dominant party (although it may appear that way when we take into account a leader's ability to assess strategically other elites' propensity to invest in the party). There are times when elites do not have an interest in investing in a dominant party.

2.2 Dominant Party Formation as a Two-Sided Commitment Problem

In this section, I lay out a theory of dominant party formation that focuses on a set of commitment problems between a ruler and a body of elites. Broadly speaking, commitment problems arise when an individual (or individuals) cannot make credible promises to behave a certain way (Schelling 1960, Elster 1979, North and Weingast 1989, Shepsle 1991). This inability to commit can become "problematic" if an individual would be made better off by maintaining his/her commitments over time. In some of the most interesting social applications, such long-term benefits are only realized through the cooperation of other actors, but if these actors anticipate the potential for reneging by the first party and would be harmed by it, they will not cooperate.

2.2 A Two-Sided Commitment Problem

While most scholars agree that the inability to make credible commitments inhibits cooperation in a great many settings, the source of the credibility problem may differ (Moe 1990, Shepsle 1991, Sanchez-Cuenca 1998). One type of credibility problem emanates from a tension between ex ante incentives to *seek* cooperation and ex post incentives to defect. Sanchez-Cuenca (1998) sets up the problem in the following way: "A promises B at t that if B does something in A's favor at t = 1, then A will reciprocate at t = 2." But A's promise to reciprocate at t = 2 is not credible, because once A receives the benefit at t = 1, A has no incentive to reciprocate at t = 2, especially if there is no prospect of a repeated interaction or if time horizons are short. To use the jargon of social science, A's preferences are time inconsistent. Recognizing this, B may not believe A's promise and, as a result, may not offer the favor at t = 1.

To take but one prominent example, this type of credible commitment problem is often invoked in works that examine the effect of political institutions on economic growth. The inability of rulers to commit credibly to not expropriating the wealth of subjects creates a disincentive to investment. Thus, the ruler's inability to promise credibly that he will not expropriate wealth hinders long-run economic growth, which would benefit both society and the ruler (e.g. North and Weingast 1989, Olson 1993, Stasavage 2002, Gehlbach and Keefer 2012). This variety of commitment problem also features prominently in studies of clientelist exchange (Stokes 2005, Hicken 2011), democratization (Kalyvas 2000), common pool resource problems (Ostrom 1990), coalition government (Laver and Shepsle 1990), and many other topics. In the study of autocracy, both Myerson (2008) and Svolik (2012) describe the problems that dictators have making credible commitments to repay costly debts to past supporters.

Credibility problems may also emanate from temptations to free ride on the effort of others. An individual may benefit from cooperating with another actor, but if the provision of the benefits from cooperation does not depend on his/her individual effort, at least in the short term, then the individual will have an incentive to defect from the cooperative agreement and free ride on the efforts of others. If defections from the cooperative arrangement can remain undetected, an individual may be able to receive the benefits of cooperation without paying the costs. The temptation to defect and exploit other parties is always a barrier to commitment.

A classic metaphor for the bilateral case of this dynamic is the prisoner's dilemma. Many studies examine commitment problems in the framework of a repeated prisoner's dilemma when actors cannot commit over time to cooperative arrangements because they have one-time incentives to defect and seek the temptation payoff (e.g. Ostrom 1990,

Shepsle 1991, Greif, Milgrom and Weingast 1994). In these works, the problem of time inconsistent preferences and the problem of free riding are addressed as two elements of commitment problems.

A third source of credibility problems relates to concerns about future shifts in preferences. To use the jargon of game theory, cooperation may be a subgame perfect equilibrium in the present game, but one or more parties may be concerned that a future change in resources or circumstances will shift preferences in such a way that the other party will lose its incentive to continue cooperating. Thus, promises to cooperate may not be credible over the long term, especially if they are not robust to small shifts in preferences or if there is some expectation that circumstances will soon change drastically. Such concerns may be a problem even if cooperation is an equilibrium in the present, or they may complement the already-mentioned free-rider and moral hazard problems to create a set of credible commitment problems. Analyses of this type of credibility problem are most common in the international relations literature where rapid shifts in relative power are thought to deter peaceful cooperation in the present, because weaker states fear that they will be exploited in the future (Kim and Morrow 1992, Fearon 1995, Powell 2006).

These three types of commitment problems are not mutually exclusive; to the contrary, they may all act to stymie cooperation in a given social interaction. Indeed, as the next section points out, all three are liable to stymie the efforts of leaders and elites to cooperate in non-democracies. Nor must only one side in an interaction face a credible commitment problem. In the argument that follows, I describe how *both* leaders and elites may face credible commitment problems that can inhibit cooperation, even though both sides might benefit from mutual cooperation in the long term. In the next section, I discuss the long-term benefits that rulers and elites would like to achieve through mutual agreement on several issues. I then discuss the costs of cooperation and the associated incentives that rulers and elites may have to renege on any such ex ante agreement.

The Leader's Commitment Problem, Part 1: Benefits of Cooperating with Elites

Ensuring Loyalty to the Regime Leaders prefer to remain in office and to maximize their share of spoils and policy influence. Leaders in non-democratic regimes vary in the extent to which they require the cooperation of elites to achieve these goals, but all must rely upon an elite coalition of some size to stay in power. In many settings,

2.2 A Two-Sided Commitment Problem

elite schisms are the primary threat facing leaders. Leaders want to prevent coups, conspiracies, electoral defections, and the like. Leaders would very much like to find a way to bind elites to the regime. One way is by distributing spoils, policy, and careers through private transfers to these elites (Bueno De Mesquita et al. 2003). But as I elaborate later, elites have no way to be assured that leaders will continue providing them with these benefits now and in the future. This leaves elites with constant incentives to conspire, rebel, or shirk their duties before the leader. For co-optation to be effective in keeping elites loyal, the leader must offer guarantees that policy, spoils, and office will be dependably distributed to them now and in the future. If leaders can agree to distribute these spoils in a rule-governed and predictable manner, then elites will have a reason to remain loyal to the regime (Brownlee 2007, Magaloni 2008, Svolik 2012). In sum, leaders value effective co-optation.

Controlling Legislatures and Making Policy In many dictatorships, the legislature is a rubber stamp. And yet, the formal powers of the legislature are extensive in many autocracies. One such case is Russia, where the decree making powers of the president are relatively limited (Haspel, Remington, and Smith 2006). Thus, the legislature is only marginalized if it can be controlled by the executive.

In order to control the legislature, leaders can cobble together legislative majorities for each bill, trading individual favors and private goods for legislative votes. But such arrangements can be exceedingly costly and can generate uncertainty over the final content of legislation (e.g. Cox and Morgenstern 2002, Remington 2006). Leaders in nondemocracies are rarely excluded from influencing the majority coalition, but given the need to make side payments and concessions to shifting groups of legislators, the final outcome of legislation may deviate from the leader's ideal point. These logrolls are costly because leaders must expend time and effort winning over individual allies and gaining information on whom to court. Moreover, the private transfers or concessions that leaders must make to individual legislators or shifting coalitions of legislators are likely to exceed the amount of benefits they would have to offer if they could agree with elites on a long-term ex ante division of policy (see earlier discussion). After all, the uncertainty-reducing benefits that elites receive from knowing that spoils will be distributed according to the terms of some premade agreement are likely to offset some of the real value of spoils that they would require in on-the-spot transfers. Given these potential costs, leaders can benefit by making some agreement with elites to ensure that executive initiatives are adopted within the framework of a long-term deal. In Aldrich's (1995) terms, they would benefit from entering into a "long coalition' "with these elites.

Generating Regime Support and Winning Elections Elites are opinion leaders in society. The comparative politics literature is rich with studies of how strongmen, landlords, chiefs, clan leaders, bosses, local officials, and other such patrons use their resources to influence citizens' political preferences. In African elections, numerous scholars have described how traditional leaders draw on their authority to shape the vote (e.g. Lemarchand 1972, Clapham 1982, Koter 2013). In Indonesia, Scott (1972), drawing on the work of Geertz (1965), described the influence that *bupatis, wedanas, tjamats*, local military commanders, and clan leaders wielded over election outcomes in that country. Sidel (1999) has analyzed how political bosses play a similar role in the Philippines. In Latin America both political scientists (Kern 1973) and economists (Baland and Robinson 2008) have described how landlords have used their dominant position vis-à-vis tenants to influence their voting behavior. Hagopian (1996) provides a comprehensive review of the ways that Brazilian politics have been shaped by regional oligarchies and political machines. As detailed in Chapter 3, scholars of post-Soviet politics have outlined the various ways that regional governors use administrative resources to ensure favorable electoral outcomes (e.g. Matsuzato 2001, Hale 2003, Reuter 2013, Sharafutdinova 2013). Focusing on another type of post-Soviet political patron, Frye, Reuter, and Szakonyi (2014) have described how post-Soviet firm managers use economic coercion in the workplace to put political pressure on their employees at election time.

As these examples make clear, the resources that such elites draw upon to influence political behavior are varied. They may include fame, wealth, status, traditional authority, kinship and ethnic bonds, clan ties, norms of reciprocity, clientelist networks, patronage, and power asymmetries The methods they use include persuasion, agenda setting, material inducement, clientelist exchange, intimidation, and coercion. Elites also employ these methods and resources to influence the political positions of other subelites. This is the essence of the well-functioning political machine, in which asymmetric, mutually dependent ties between patrons and clients ensure both political support for the patron and the compliance of subelites (cf. Scott 1972).

Thus, it is not hard to see why central leaders would covet the resources of these subnational elites. Such resources can help leaders generate political support, whether at the ballot box or on the street. Cooperating with elites would help leaders gain access to these resources.

Coordinating Pro-regime Candidates during Elections When elections are held, leaders need tools for ensuring that pro-regime candidates are elected. Coordination failures among pro-regime candidates can lead to unexpected outcomes that are suboptimal for the ruler. Political scientists have devoted significant attention to the implications of coordination failures among opposition candidates in non-democracies (Howard and Roessler 2006, Van de Walle 2006), but the consequences of coordination failures among regime candidates remain understudied. Two pro-regime candidates may each calculate that they have a chance of winning an election. Both may seek to capitalize with voters on their support for the current regime and associate themselves with the ruler, while highlighting the differences between them. If they compete separately, there exists the possibility that they will split the regime vote and that an opposition candidate will win the seat or post. Such coordination failures are costly for a ruler trying to control elections.

The ruler may opt to ensure the election of loyal deputies by striking new bargains with powerful elites for every election. In other words, he can monitor each election and make side deals with ambitious candidates so that some will forgo running for office, perhaps in exchange for a preferred rent or the promise of future career advancement. However, the transaction costs associated with the constant revision of such ad hoc arrangements can be significant, especially when the regime hopes to see loyal candidates installed at several different levels of government. In addition, as with the division of legislative spoils, regime leaders will have to pay candidates less to coordinate if there is an agreement about how the payoff will be distributed in the future.

In sum, leaders can benefit from making an agreement with elite allies about how access to the ballot will be regulated. By allocating ballot access to some candidates and providing others with assurances that they will have their chance to run in the future, such an agreement would ensure that pro-regime candidates do not compete against one another.

Routinization of Political Appointment Processes Leaders in non-democracies typically make appointments to a great many offices. To the extent possible, they would like to reduce the costs associated with gathering information on cadres and determining who should receive promotions. As with legislative logrolls, this process is likely to involve costly negotiations and concessions. One way that leaders can avoid these costs is by making an ex ante agreement on the distribution of spoils. One clear example of this is the nomenklatura system operated by the CPSU in the Soviet Union. Such agreements ensure the efficient distribution of posts to loyal and talented supporters.

The Leader's Commitment Problem, Part 2: Costs of Cooperation and Incentives to Renege

As I elaborate later, elites will not relinquish control over their autonomous resources and cooperate with leaders unless they can be sure that leaders will share the spoils of governing with them in a predictable manner. If leaders want to co-opt these elites effectively, they will have to agree to some ex ante division of policy, rents, and influence. This may mean that the leader will support only agreed-upon candidates in elections. It may mean that he will promote only those whom he has promised to promote. Or it may mean that policy and rents will be distributed to elites according to the terms of some predetermined arrangement. Thus, in addition to the cost associated with spoil sharing, making an agreement with elites necessitates a loss of autonomy for the leader. This loss is all the more unsettling for rulers because elites may use these spoils and political positions to challenge or undermine them.

These costs create incentives to renege and make it difficult for the leader to commit to any such ex ante agreement. Leaders may make promises to distribute spoils in a certain way, but once the cooperation of elites is secured, they will be tempted to renege on their promises. To use the political science jargon, their promises are time inconsistent. And while cooperation might leave the leader better off in the long term, his shortsightedness may lead him to seek immediate gain by reneging on the terms of the agreement.

Alternatively, circumstances, resources, or preferences may change in such a way that the leader finds the original bargain unsatisfactory or obsolete and, thus, seeks to back out of the agreement. If circumstances change, the leader may want to support another candidate for office, craft a different piece of legislation, or promote another cadre. For example, a new oil discovery may increase the power of leaders vis-à-vis elites and reduce the leaders' need for cooperation with elites. Or if a policy failure harms the reputation of elites, the leader may want to distance himself from those tainted by the scandal. Elites may fear this potential for reneging and not cooperate as a result.

Strategic dilemmas of trust worsen the leader's commitment problem still further. After all, the leader's incentive to renege will be exacerbated if the leader believes that he can, unbeknown to elites, shirk his own responsibilities under the agreement and still secure the benefits of cooperation. Leaders may use state resources to back an alternative candidate during elections without the knowledge of insider elites. Or they may try to co-opt outsiders by channeling spoils to an elite group that is not part of the spoil-sharing agreement. In order to make an

2.2 A Two-Sided Commitment Problem

agreement attractive to elites, leaders must provide some assurance that they will abide by the terms of the bargain; otherwise elites would risk paying the costs of cooperation without assurances that they would be receiving the benefits.

It is worth noting that this ex ante "agreement" is just a fictitious construct presented here to highlight the cooperation problems between leaders and elites. But the implausibility of such an agreement only underscores the difficulty that a ruler has in refraining from abusing elites around him. In many countries around the world, leaders who cannot commit to such an informal co-optative arrangement are left to strike ad hoc, co-optative bargains with individual elites. Alternatively, under certain conditions that I outline later, they may seek out a way of assuring elites that they can be trusted to abide by the terms of the bargain.

The Elites' Commitment Problem, Part 1: Benefits of Reaching an Agreement with Leaders

Dependable Career Advancement   Career advancement is one of the primary goals that politicians pursue. In non-democracies, access to careers is at least partially controlled by the regime. Leaders make appointments, give promotions, and use their levers of administrative influence to support candidates for office. Elites may also reap electoral benefits from being associated with the leader, who may be popular among voters or carry weight among other elites. Thus, most elites would like to cooperate with leaders because such cooperation will help their careers.

Given the importance that elites place on career advancement, most are eager to reduce uncertainty about their future career prospects. Advancement opportunities may be distributed by leaders in an ad hoc manner on the basis of personal ties and clientelist networks, but elites would prefer to find an accommodation with the leader that gives them some sort of assurance that these goods could be provided on an ongoing basis into the future. They would like the peace of mind of knowing that they can retain their office and that career advancement will be possible in the future (e.g. Geddes 2003, Brownlee 2007, Magaloni 2008, Svolik 2012). Relatedly, elites would prefer that some stable criteria for career advancement exist and that these criteria are made known to them. Leaders will require loyalty from elites in order to grant such assurances, but elites can still benefit from such an agreement because it makes the price of promotion clear. Under such a deal, they can know that loyalty will be rewarded dependably with career advancement.

Securing Dependable Access to Spoils and Policy Influence A similar uncertainty-reducing benefit applies to access to spoils and policy. Leaders have the power to make policy concessions, as well as to grant personal privileges to elites – immunity from prosecution, career advancement for relatives, insider deals on government contracts, tax exemptions, real estate, government cars, preferential treatment in the procurement of permits and exemptions, and so on.

As with careers, some of these goods are distributed in an ad hoc bilateral fashion on the basis of personal ties. But elites would prefer an accommodation with the leader that gives them some sort of assurance that these goods could be provided on a predictable basis and into the future. Leaders may demand loyalty from elites in order to grant such assurances, but elites can still benefit from such an agreement because it makes the price of spoils clear. With it, elites can know that loyalty will be rewarded with perks, privileges, and rents. Elites value this reduction in uncertainty.

Reducing Transaction Costs Just as leaders would value the reduced transaction costs associated with reaching an agreement on the sharing of spoils, policy, and positions, elites would like to simplify the process of lobbying the regime for these benefits. Constant negotiation for policy concessions, perks, and career support is costly. Elites must pay for lobbyists in the capital, they must gather information about what perks and privileges are achievable, and they must expend time in the process of negotiation. Thus, elites not only value reduced uncertainty in its own right, they would also like to save time, effort, and resources on lobbying.

The Elites' Commitment Problem, Part 2: Costs of Cooperation and Incentives to Renege

Few studies of authoritarian politics emphasize the costs that elites pay when they cooperate with leaders. When elites enjoy autonomous control over political resources, they suffer the cost of losing that autonomy when they link their political fates to the regime. Reaching a cooperative arrangement with leaders would limit their ability to criticize the regime and to decide for themselves how and when they will run for office. Top-level elites would agree not to run their own lists of candidates in elections and to support regime appointments. Finally, elites would also be precluded from striking their own bargains on policy concessions outside the terms of the original agreement. These are costly restrictions on autonomy.

2.2 A Two-Sided Commitment Problem

Considering these costs, it is not hard to see how the elite commitment problem mirrors that of the leader. Elites would benefit, especially in the long term, from cooperating with leaders. They would like to know that they would receive their preferred policy, rent, or office in the future. Leaders might be willing to provide these assurances if elites could convince them that they would be dutiful followers, support regime sponsored legislative initiatives, back regime candidates for promotion and election, and put their political machines to work for the regime. But in making this commitment elites relinquish some of their political autonomy. This may give them incentives to defect, and they have no way of assuring leaders that they will not renege on these commitments.

While cooperation might leave elites better off in the long term, short-sightedness can lead them to seek immediate gain by reneging on the terms of the agreement ex post. For example, after receiving their own promotion, they may use their clientelist base to advance one of their own clients at the expense of regime-sponsored cadres. Or after receiving special legislative treatment for their own business interests, they may vote against a regime-sponsored bill. In sum, elites may have difficulty making their promises credible, and, as a result of this, they have difficulty ensuring the cooperation of leaders.

As with leaders, elite commitment problems can also arise from uncertainty about future preferences. Should circumstances change, elites may come to view the initial cooperative bargain with leaders as disadvantageous. For example, if a scandal taints a leader's reputation and popularity, elites may want to distance themselves from the regime. Or, if a fiscal crisis were to reduce the value of spoils flowing from the central government, elites will have fewer incentives to cooperate. Leaders are concerned about this potential for future reneging and may be dissuaded from cooperating as a result.

The temptation for elites to abandon their promises is likely to be especially strong if elites believe they can shirk their obligations without the regime's knowledge and, thus, continue to receive the benefits of cooperation. Elites may, unbeknownst to leaders, use their administrative resources to back oppositional candidates, or they may funnel corruption rents away from the regime and toward their own clients. More severely, they may criticize the regime in their localities and thus seek to undermine its popular support. In order for a cooperative agreement to be attractive to leaders, they must have some assurance that elites will abide by the terms of the bargain; otherwise leaders risk paying the costs of cooperation without knowing that they will receive the benefits.

Summing Up: A Two-Sided Commitment Problem

We can now put together the pieces from the foregoing section to provide a complete picture of the commitment problems that leaders and elites face. Leaders and elites would benefit over the long term by cooperating and supporting one another, but each side finds it difficult to assure the other that it will be a faithful partner in this collusion. Elites will not remain true to this bargain unless they can be sure that the leader will make it a mechanism for guaranteeing the supply of spoils and careers. The ruler is also unwilling to commit himself to the party unless he can be sure that other elites will be loyal to the party. The benefits of the bargain are only achieved when both players cooperate, but both have strong one-time incentives to defect, owing to their desire for autonomy. Each side would like to reach a mutually beneficial agreement, but is tempted to obtain short-term gains by defecting ex post, and shortsightedness may lead them to do just that.

The problem is complicated by the fact that each is tempted to try to exploit the other side and renege on the agreement while the other side continues to cooperate. Sporadic reneging by leaders, if unobserved by elites, can yield significant benefits because it allows the leader to gain the cooperation of elites, while he retains his autonomy. The same is true for elites; sporadic reneging while the leader remains true to the terms of the agreement can be very rewarding. In order to preclude being abused sporadically, the parties must find a mechanism for monitoring compliance.

2.3 Overcoming the Commitment Problem

Part 1: Dominant Party Institutions

Social scientists have sought solutions to commitment problems by looking for ways that commitments can be made credible in the eyes of other players. One way to solve commitment problems is through repeated play. If players can develop reputations of trustworthiness, then cooperation can be an equilibrium (Axelrod 1984, Ostrom 1990). However, as North and Weingast (1989), Greif, Milgrom, and Weingast (1994), Greif (1992), and others have pointed out, repeated play with reputation mechanisms is often insufficient, especially if actors discount the future heavily. As an alternative (or supplement), actors make seek to solve their commitment problems by delegating authority to third party institutions. For example, some of the most well-studied commitment problems in social science involve the inability of state leaders to commit

2.3 Overcoming the Commitment Problem

to not expropriating the wealth of subjects (e.g. North and Weingast 1989, Stasavage 2002, Frye 2004). A ruler's inability to commit creates a disincentive to contracting, investment, and other productive economic activity by subjects. In the past several decades, much of the literature has settled on institutions as the most effective solution to commitment problems of this sort. As Weingast puts it, "Appropriately specified political institutions are the principal way in which states create credible limits on their own authority" (1993, 288). In particular, independent judiciaries and parliaments have been touted as devices to constrain the arbitrary behavior of leaders (North and Weingast 1989, Gehlbach and Keefer 2012).

In the authoritarianism literature, Magaloni (2008) has argued that dominant parties help leaders commit to distributing perks and offices to elites. By delegating power to a parallel party organization that controls these appointments, leaders place constraints on their ability to abuse the terms of the spoil-sharing bargain. She offers the following: "By giving up his absolute powers to select members of the ruling clique into government positions, the dictator can more credibly guarantee a share of power and the spoils of office over the long run to those who invest in the existing institutions" (Magaloni 2008, 716). In Magaloni's account, dominant parties make leader commitments credible because the institution is somewhat independent of the leader. When elites know that they can count on the institution – and not just the leader – to deliver careers, perks, and policy, then they will be more inclined to make their own commitments to the bargain. Elites must know not only that the institution is independent of the leader, but also that it will survive into the future. Thus, leaders must give signals that they intend to continue to support the party. With time, it would become costly for the leader to renege on the bargain as leaders know that elite loyalty and, therefore, regime stability depend on the continued maintenance of the institution.

I agree with Magaloni that the key for leaders in making their commitment credible is to create an institution that has some modicum of independence. If a dominant party institution can be depended upon to control career advancement and spoil distribution, then elites will benefit from linking their fates to the party. Unfortunately, this is only a partial answer to the question of how new dominant party institutions solve the two-sided commitment problem described. It begs the question of how that reputation for reliable spoil distribution is established in the first place. What prevents the leader from impinging on the independence of the institution in its nascent phase, breaking the terms of the bargain, and promoting his preferred cadres or policy? In other words, how can a newly created dominant party institution with no reputation for binding actors constrain leaders? A second unanswered question is how the party can make *elite* commitments credible as well. In the following, I offer several propositions for how even new dominant party institutions can help to make elite and leader commitments credible. Because the commitment dilemmas sketched here are substantial, it is unlikely that any one institutional commitment device will be a silver bullet. Nor is it likely that the commitment devices be the same in every case. Thus, rather than focus on a single role that these institutions perform, I discuss a number of ways dominant party institutions can help mitigate commitment problems.

Dominant Parties and the Leader's Credible Commitments Perhaps the most common type of commitment device studied in comparative politics is delegation to political institutions. If steps are taken to delegate independent decision-making authority to the party, then the party can have a constraining effect on the leader. Leaders must take steps to ensure that promotions, policy, and privileges are at least partially distributed by the party itself. Of course, this is the difficult part. It is one thing to say that delegation to an independent institution can make commitments credible, but it is quite another to outline how this institution might acquire that independence in the first place (e.g. North 1993). What prevents the leader from impinging on the independence of the nascent institution? The answer may differ across settings, but there are several steps that leaders can take to increase the costs of infringement.

Institutional nesting is one way of raising these costs (cf. Tsebelis 1990). Leaders can link the powers of the dominant party to other institutional constraints such as the constitution. For example, article 6 of the Soviet Constitution stipulated the "leading role" of the CPSU in Soviet government and society. Leaders may change laws so that the dominant party is given explicit or implicit control over nominations in a specific sphere; or leaders can sanction other institutional changes, such as imperative mandate laws (laws that prohibit legislators from changing their party affiliation while in office) or fixed electoral cycles, to raise the costs of dismantling the dominant party at a moment's notice. To be sure, laws and constitutions are imperfect commitment devices, especially in autocracies, but by linking the preservation of the dominant party to these institutions, leaders increase the costs of dismantling or circumventing the dominant party.

Leaders may also take steps to ensure that the party receives its finances from an independent source. If the party is funded from state coffers, then it may be easy to cut off funding. But if the party has its own revenue streams, its independence is enhanced.

2.3 Overcoming the Commitment Problem

Leaders might also institute a norm of forbidding members of their inner circle to attend key party meetings and legislative faction gatherings. If the leader is able to refrain from interfering in the cadre selection and spoil distribution process for a short period, then costs to reneging are quickly built up as the party and its leadership, rather than the leader, become the patron of newly installed cadres. At the very least, cadres may develop dual loyalties. Even in the early stages, these nomenklaturist tendencies in the party create costs to reneging.

Of course, the ultimate commitment that a leader might make is to step down and let a party-nominated candidate take his spot. At the point when the leader owes both his career and position to the party, then the regime becomes a true party state. Of course, since leaders in all regimes have many avenues for cultivating their resource base outside the party, there are few examples of true party states in which there is no identifiable leader as distinct from the party. Even the general secretary of the Communist Party of the Soviet Union, who formally served at the pleasure of the Central Committee, was a formidable political figure in his own right with many formal and informal levers of influence at his disposal.

Another way that leaders can commit to granting some modicum of independence to the party is by relinquishing to the party their ability to gather information on key political decisions. If members of the ruling clique micromanage the party's affairs, then the dictator's commitment not to renege on the terms of the cooperative bargain is less credible. But if the leader takes steps to tie his hands in the gathering of information about which candidates to support, about how patronage should be distributed, and about how cadres should be appointed, then his commitment not to interfere is more credible. Leaders could do this by dismantling their own parallel mechanisms (parties, domestic politics directorates, coordinating councils, etc.) for managing elections, organizing legislative majorities, or appointing cadres.

To the extent that the ruler can grant the party independent authority for some period, elites change their expectations about how spoils and careers can be accessed. Likewise, the resources and skills necessary for achieving these goods change. Elites invest in these skills and jettison the resources that allowed them to access spoils and careers prior to the creation of the party. They invest in schemes to curry the favor of party leaders and promote the party's interests. In this way, they develop not only divided loyalties, but also strategies of political survival that are based on the continued existence of the party. By dismantling the party at this point, the leader risks backing elites into a corner and giving them no choice but to rebel. How long it would take for this to happen is difficult to say, but while the independence of the party institution is accumulating, other commitment mechanisms such as those described in this section are likely necessary.

A third way that dominant party institutions can help ameliorate commitment problems is by solving elite collective action problems vis-à-vis the leader. Gehlbach and Keefer (2012) argue that authoritarian legislatures can enforce bargains between leaders and elites by providing an institutional forum that helps elites coordinate to defend their interests. As they note, "Collectively organized supporters are better able to impose a variety of checks on leaders and to impose sanctions for predatory behavior that would not otherwise be possible" (622). A similar argument may be applied to dominant parties.

Indeed, in those countries where elites are very strong, they may be prevented from capturing the state only by their own collective action and coordination problems vis-à-vis one another. In 1990s and early 2000s, Russia's powerful governors could easily have won any presidential election if they had been able to unite their political machines, but divisions among the governors frequently stymied their efforts to put forward a single presidential candidate (Solnick 2000, Shvetsova 2003). The creation of a dominant party can give elites the institutional tools to keep themselves united. If leaders allow the creation of these institutional bonds within the elite, then there is always the chance that elites may use this newfound unity to challenge or constrain leaders.

Another way that a leader can use the dominant party as a commitment device is by linking his name, reputation, and/or personal brand to the party. By committing these personal resources, the leader is sending a signal to other elites that he is willing to accept part of the responsibility for policy failures or scandals that occur on the party's watch. Moreover, to the extent that the leader's own authority – and hence survival in office – is tied to a reputation for resolve, the leader can tie his hands by making verbal or symbolic commitments to the party.[8] Such commitments may include making public endorsements, speaking at party functions, allowing one's image to be used on campaign materials, and affiliating with the party. If a leader publicly associates himself with a party and then abandons the party soon after, he or she may appear irresolute and thus suffer reputational costs. Moreover, the linkage between a leader's personal brand and the party is likely to be sticky, such that it is difficult to decouple the two quickly in the minds of voters.

---

[8] Writing on how leaders communicate their foreign policy intentions, Fearon (1997) discusses how verbal commitments to certain courses of action can create "audience costs" that make it costly for leaders to renege.

Finally, the party helps elites monitor agreements and thus reduces the temptation of the leader to abuse them sporadically.[9] Enshrined in the party arrangement are rules – parchment or implicit – specifying what constitutes compliance on the part of the leader (e.g. supporting only party candidates in elections, granting preference to party supporters in appointments, or channeling spoils to party legislators). If all elites contracted with the regime via some unwritten agreement, then violations of those agreements could easily be unnoticed, especially if it is not clear what constitutes violation of the agreement. In this case, leaders would be tempted to defect and abuse elites. In contrast, when the terms of the agreement are set down on parchment, as they may be in a party's charter, then a transgression against the party's policy-making sphere of authority or its delegated authority over cadre decisions is easier to identify and punish (via defection, perhaps).

Dominant Parties and Elite Credible Commitments I now discuss how dominant party institutions can make elite commitments to the cooperative agreement credible. Elites grant the party the ability to sanction them for reneging. If they deviate from the party line in legislatures, they may be excluded from the party faction. If they criticize the party in election campaigns, they may be expelled from the party and lose its support in future campaigns. Elites can make such commitments more credible by linking commitment to the party to existing institutional rules. For instance, the regime can institute imperative mandate laws that state that if a deputy leaves his legislative group, he loses his legislative mandate. Or the party may institute laws that allow the party that nominates a candidate to withdraw his/her candidacy.

Elites can also make their commitments credible by dismantling or linking their political machines to the dominant party. By delegating to the party control over appointments and patronage distribution within their sphere of administrative control, elites give up some of the resources that made them independent. For example, many elites in Russia tied their hands by giving up their own regional political parties that had helped them win elections in the 1990s. If elites join the dominant party while maintaining their own political party on the side, then their commitment to the cooperative bargain with leaders is less credible. After all, they could always abandon the bargain and go back to using their own local party to help them win elections. This is exactly what happened in many Russian regions in the 1990s. Regional governors made tentative

---

[9] Svolik (2012) describes how institutions help alleviate monitoring problems in authoritarian coalitions.

statements of support for the various pro-presidential parties of the time, while using their own regional political parties to contest local elections.

A fourth way that elites can demonstrate the credibility of their commitment is simply by joining the party. Much like leaders, elites make a symbolic transfer of reputational resources when they make a public, verbal commitment to one political party. This demonstrates to the leader that elites are willing to pay the reputational costs of failures that may occur on the party's watch. What is more, it may be difficult to decouple their name and resources from the party's brand quickly.

Finally, the party makes it easier for leaders to monitor elite commitments and thus gives them reason to believe that elites are not shirking the responsibilities laid down in any such bargain. The dominant party establishes clear rules about the regime's accommodative arrangement and thus makes it easier for leaders to identify when they are being transgressed against. In most cases, the dominant party constitutes a clear dividing line between regime supporters and opponents. Leaving the dominant party constitutes defection from the regime. As Huntington noted (1970, 15), "The more important the party is in the system, the more difficult it is to become a member and the more frequent are the purges expelling members. If party membership becomes universal, it becomes meaningless." Leaders know whom to punish (or reward) and elites know what needs to be done in order to retain access to future spoils.

Summary Dominant parties are composed of a bundle of rules and norms that help leaders and elite solve problems of commitment. In turn, dominant party institutions allow leaders and elites to reap a number of benefits. They allow leaders to co-opt elites effectively, reduce the transaction costs associated with implementing cooptation, and win elections. For elites, dominant parties help them secure dependable access to spoils and career advancement. Thus, dominant parties are institutionalized manifestations of the mutually desirable agreements outlined in Section 2.2.

The exact configuration of commitment mechanisms is likely to differ across settings. Furthermore, because the rules are bundled under the aegis of an overarching institutional agreement, individual commitment devices are likely to work in tandem. I leave for future work to examine which of these commitment devices are most effective at constraining transgressions by leaders and elites.

As I describe later, dominant party regimes may evolve over time such that the institutional constraints become stronger and the equilibrium becomes more robust. Once elites begin to link their careers to the dominant party, leaders may refrain from impinging on the independence of the party not just because of the commitment devices sketched previously, but also because of their recognition that doing so will evoke elite defection and imperil regime stability.[10]

However, at their founding, dominant parties are likely to provide only very tenuous institutional constraints on leaders and elites. This makes investing in these institutions a real gamble. It is risky for actor A to make commitments to actor B when the institutional constraints on actor B are weak, leaving actor A vulnerable to abuse by actor B. As I discuss later, the frailty of nascent dominant party institutions only underscores the need for a theory of dominant party emergence that focuses not just on how institutions can help solve commitment problems, but also on how those commitment problems can be mitigated, such that there is much to gain and little to lose from cooperation.

Overcoming the Commitment Problem, Part 2: Changes in the Balance of Resources and the Likelihood of Dominant Party Emergence

Explaining Variation in the Emergence of Dominant Parties: The Limitations of Institutional Explanations Unfortunately, positing institutional solutions to commitment problems does not help us explain why dominant parties exist in some authoritarian regimes, but not in others. Commitment problems are likely to exist in all autocracies, but we only observe dominant parties in some regimes. Dictators almost always have incentives to keep elites loyal and thus should always invest in dominant party institutions, but dominant parties exist in only some regimes.

What distinguishes the most innovative recent work on institutions in comparative politics is that it moves beyond identifying the institutional solution to problems of cooperation and seeks to identify the conditions that generate the outcome in specific cases. For example, in the study of political parties, the problem of party formation has long been seen as a multilateral commitment problem. Legislators would prefer to agree on a long-term division of benefits, but they cannot credibly commit to voting according to the terms of that agreement. A party institution solves this commitment problem by changing the incentive structure.

The innovation of some recent literature on party development has been to identify the factors that make politicians more likely to participate in this long-term logroll. For example, Hale (2006) and Smyth

---

[10] In Magaloni's (2008) model, leaders do not impinge on the independence of the party because they know that doing so will undermine elite cohesion and endanger the regime.

(2006) have argued that if politicians have their own personal resources or access to party "substitutes" that can replace parties, they may feel less compelled to submit to party discipline. In other words, actors do not automatically seek out an institutional solution to their commitment problem when confronted with it. To say that there is a commitment problem and a potential institutional solution to that commitment problem does not tell us when that institutional solution will be employed.

Thus, the goal is to identify exogenous factors that determine the extent to which actors are willing and able to construct institutions that help solve their commitment problems. Frequently, such arguments consider the balance of power and/or resources among actors. Distributional theories of institutional origins argue that stronger actors use their resources to ensure that institutional configurations are designed in their favor (Moe 1990, Knight 1992). Important empirical studies of institutional origins highlight how the relative strength of actors affects their incentives to place themselves under institutional constraints and, relatedly, the likelihood that institutions will successfully constrain actors. For example, in North and Weingast's (1989) canonical account of how political institutions constrained predatory behavior by English kings after the Glorious Revolution, the creation of independent parliamentary institutions was only made possible by the Civil War, which reduced the power of the Crown vis-à-vis the opposition. In Svolik's (2012) account of power sharing under dictatorship, power-sharing deals are only credible (and thus possible) when they are backed by a credible threat of force, which occurs when there is a relative balance of power in the ruling coalition. In the study of Russian politics, Luong and Weinthal (2004) show that the emergence of an "effective" tax regime occurred only after the 1998 financial crisis created perceptions of mutual interdependence between Russian leaders and powerful business groups. In the argument that follows, I show how exogenous changes in the balance of resources between leaders and elites can help explain why and when the two sides will seek to invest in a dominant party to ameliorate their commitment problems.

Reducing the Severity of the Leader's Commitment Problem The leader's commitment problem can vary in its severity. When the gains from cooperation with elites are lower, the leader's commitment problem is more severe. This is because the benefits of co-opting elites are reduced, while the costs of relinquishing autonomy are increased. When leaders are strong *relative to elites*, they require less cooperation with elites in order to achieve their policy goals, generate support, and win elections. The strength of central state leaders is determined by the resources

2.3 Overcoming the Commitment Problem

at their disposal, which may include, among other things, personal popularity, strong central state capacity, and easy access to rent revenues.

When leaders are strong in such resources, they are more likely to defect from any arrangement that is reached with elites because the benefits of cooperation are reduced and, accordingly, there is less reason for leaders to relinquish autonomy by making a spoil-sharing agreement with elites.[11] Under these circumstances, the promises of leaders to share power and influence with elites are far from credible and it is less likely that leaders will delegate to a party that may constrain them.

The leader's commitment problem is mitigated as the potential benefits from cooperation with elites rise and the costs of relinquishing autonomy decrease. In turn, these costs and benefits are determined by the balance of political resources between leaders and elites. For leaders it becomes more necessary to co-opt elites as the balance of resources shifts toward elites. As leaders weaken or elites strengthen (or both), leaders may come to need access to the political machines of elites in order to win elections, generate support, and ensure regime stability. As it becomes more beneficial to find accommodation with elites, leaders will become more interested in finding an institutional arrangement that can ameliorate their commitment problem and will be more likely to invest in a dominant party that can help solve that problem.

The strategic calculations of elites also serve to reduce the chances of a dominant party's emerging when leaders are strong. The worst outcome for elites is for them to invest their resources in a dominant party, while the leader reneges on his commitments. When leaders are strong, elites will not trust the commitments of elites and, therefore, will be disinclined to invest their own resources in the party. Indeed, the weakness of nascent dominant party institutions only exacerbates this problem, as elites have few guarantees that strong leaders will be constrained by these institutions. However, if the resource balance were to shift toward elites, leaders will have more incentive to cooperate with elites and less incentive to defect. The leader's commitment problem will be mitigated and elites will be more likely to trust that nascent dominant party institutions will be able to make the commitments of leaders credible.

Reducing the Severity of the Elite's Commitment Problem If decisions about the creation of dominant parties depended only on leaders, then the probability of a dominant party's emerging would be increased, in a linear fashion, as the resources of elites grew. Yet leaders cannot

---

[11] Examples of such defections might include unwillingness to share spoils with elites (or at least not sharing spoils in a dependable fashion) or the promotion of nonparty cadres.

create a party whenever they want. Elites also have agency. They choose whether or not to conclude a cooperative bargain with leaders. Thus, we must not only consider the severity of the leader's commitment problem, but also that of elites' commitment problem.

When the gains from cooperation with leaders are lower, the commitment problem of elites is more severe. When elites are very strong *relative to leaders*, the resources they control provide them with the opportunity to achieve many of their political goals without the cooperation of leaders. Both between and within countries there is always variation in the extent to which elites hold or have access to some actual or latent base of resources that are autonomous from the regime. By autonomous from the regime I mean those resources that are costly for the regime to repress or expropriate systematically. As noted, such resources might include, but are not limited to, autonomous control over clientelist networks, de facto or de jure regional autonomy, hard-to-tax economic assets, traditional authority, and individual-specific ability to mobilize citizens.

When elites are strong in such resources, they will be more reluctant to relinquish their autonomy and link their political machines to the regime. Elites that are strong in resources find it difficult to make credible commitments to long-term cooperation with leaders because the costs of linking their fates to the regime are higher and the benefits are lower. Hence, they are highly prone to defect from any arrangement that is reached with leaders. In sum, as the balance of resources between leaders and elites shifts ever more in favor of elites, then it becomes increasingly likely that *elites* will want to forgo binding investments in a dominant party institution because they themselves see insufficient gains from reaching a cooperative bargain with leaders.

The elites' commitment problem is mitigated as the potential benefits of cooperation with leaders rise and the costs of relinquishing their autonomy go down. These costs and benefits are determined by the balance of resources between the two sides. It becomes more beneficial for elites to contract with leaders as the balance of resources shifts toward leaders. As central state leaders become stronger in resources relative to elites, elites have more interest in gaining dependable access to the spoils, perks, and privileges that the regime controls. In addition, as the ability of elites to achieve their political goals via their own autonomous resources decreases, they will have more interest in securing regime support. As it becomes more beneficial to contract with leaders, elites will become more interested in finding an institutional arrangement that can ameliorate their commitment problem and will be more likely to invest in a dominant party that can help solve their commitment problem.

2.3 Overcoming the Commitment Problem

The strategic considerations of leaders also may act to reduce the likelihood of a dominant party's emerging when elites are strong. After all, the strategic cooperation problem of leaders mirrors that of elites: the worst possible outcome is for leaders to invest their resources in a dominant party, while elites sporadically defect. When elites are strong, leaders will not trust elite commitments and will, therefore, be disinclined to make their own commitments to the cooperative arrangement. Strong elites cannot be counted on to deliver their side of the bargain, and since the gains from cooperation are only achieved when both sides participate, leaders will not be willing to invest either. What is more, since nascent dominant party institutions are limited in their ability to constrain, then leaders will be especially unlikely to trust the commitments of elites that are strong in resources. But if the balance of resources were to shift toward leaders, then the elites' commitment problem would be mitigated, and leaders would be more likely to believe that nascent dominant party institutions could make the commitments of elites credible.

When elites are strong relative to leaders, why do elites not simply capture the state and appoint one of their own as the new dictator? In some cases they do, but often as not, this does not happen because elites face collective action among themselves. While the collective power of elites may even be greater than that of leaders, each is much weaker than the leader and is individually dependent on him. This leaves the elite vulnerable to divide and rule tactics. And while there may be many among the elite who would like to become leader, none will want to challenge the leader without the support of other elites. Thus, an authoritarian state with strong elites and weak leaders is not necessarily an oxymoron and such polities are not necessarily democracies.

One might also ask why leaders do not simply confiscate the resources of strong elites and force them to relinquish their autonomy. To be sure, leaders would prefer this option, but the simple answer is that doing so may be exceedingly costly and may limit the ability of leaders to govern effectively. As noted, strong elites are those that control resources such as entrenched political machines, localized clientelist networks, hard-to-tax economic assets, or positions of traditional authority that are difficult for leaders to expropriate or control systematically. While leaders could certainly secure the ouster of any given elite at any given time, they may find it more difficult to undermine the *system* of social control that is maintained by elites (e.g. Migdal 1988, Voslensky 1984).

In many cases, they will find it hard to ignore elites because elites control resources that can help leaders win elections, control protest, collect tax revenue, pass legislation, and implement policy. Examples abound from the developing world; only a few will suffice here. In Brazil, for instance, leaders have long had to reach accommodation with powerful governors as a prerequisite for holding power (Hagopian 1996, Mainwaring 1999, Samuels and Abrucio 2000). In much of sub-Saharan Africa, state leaders, often following the lead of colonial authorities, have relied on traditional and ethnic leaders to help them exert state control into rural areas (e.g. Rothchild 1985, Bayart 1989, Van de Walle 2006). In the Philippines, Sidel (1999) describes how Philippine state leaders have had to make deals with local "bosses" in order to win elections and maintain control over the state's security services. In Putin era Russia, I and others have argued that the vote mobilizing capacity of the regime was heavily dependent on the political machines of regional governors (Golosov 2011, Reuter 2013). Thus, when elites are strong and prone to defect from agreements that require them to relinquish their autonomy, leaders may still find themselves having to co-opt elites on the basis of ad hoc deals.

Balanced Resources: Maximizing the Likelihood of a Dominant Party

I have argued that when leaders are strong in resources, their incentives to defect from any bargain are also strong. On the other side of the equation, when elites are strong, they have strong incentives to defect from any agreement. What then are the specific conditions that lead to creation of dominant parties and the solution of these commitment problems? Numerous scholars have pointed out that commitment problems are less likely to be solved when they are severe (e.g. North and Weingast 1989, Sanchez Cuenca 1998, Svolik 2012). We are more likely to see actors investing in institutional solutions to commitment problems when these commitment problems are less acute. There are two reasons for this. First, the gains from cooperation are higher and the benefits of defection are lower when the commitment problem is less severe. In other words, the stronger the incentives to defect, the less likely that credible commitment devices will be successful in constraining behavior (Sanchez-Cuenca 1998). Second, and relatedly, actors may not trust the nascent institution to perform the tasks assigned to it in its initial formation phase. The gains from cooperation must be high enough to offset this risk. Indeed, the very difficulty of believing that autocratic institutions can credibly constrain dictators illustrates why it is so unlikely that successful dominant parties will emerge when elites are weak. The limited ability of authoritarian institutions to constrain

2.3 Overcoming the Commitment Problem

actors only highlights the need for commitment problems to be mitigated if they are to be solved.

Turning to the specific case of dominant parties, leaders and elites are more likely to seek and secure a successful institutional solution to their commitment problems when the gains from cooperation are maximized. Incentives to defect from the ex ante agreement are hard to eliminate, but they can be reduced. In other words, the commitment problem can be mitigated for both sides. Thus, dominant parties are most likely to emerge when resources are balanced such that neither side has overwhelming incentives to defect from any bargain. In the language of institutional analysis, dominant parties become more likely as it becomes increasingly efficient for both sides to cooperate with one another. The commitment problem of the two sides is attenuated when neither side holds a preponderance of resources. When this happens, an institutional solution to the commitment problem is more feasible. Elites are strong enough that leaders benefit significantly from co-opting them, but weak enough that they themselves benefit from linking their fates to the regime. In other words, dominant parties are most likely to emerge when elites hold enough autonomous political resources (relative to the resources of leaders) that co-opting them is necessary, but not so many autonomous resources that they themselves are reluctant to participate in any cooperative bargain. This logic leads to the following hypothesis: *Dominant parties are more likely to emerge when resources between leaders and other elites are relatively balanced. They are less likely when leaders are disproportionately strong (relative to elites) or elites are disproportionately strong (relative to leaders).* This hypothesis is depicted in Figure 1.4 in the previous chapter.

On the left side of the figure, elites are weak relative to leaders and dominant parties are unlikely. On the right side the figure elites are very strong and a dominant party is also unlikely. In the middle of the figure, when the resources of elites and leaders are relatively balanced, a dominant party is more likely.

When resources are balanced, dominant party institutions are more likely to be created. But what role do these institutions – the bundles of rules and norms – play when resources are balanced like this? The short answer is that they help ameliorate commitment problems between the two sides. Delegation to institutions prevents leaders and elites from reneging and/or abusing the other side in the case when the balance of resources between the two sides is insufficient on its own to ensure stable commitments (i.e. the game is not an equilibrium, even when resources are balanced). Under such a view, the balance of resources still increases the feasibility of power sharing via a dominant party because it reduces the severity of the two-sided commitment dilemma. However, even if the balance of resources is sufficient to induce a cooperative arrangement between leaders and elites, institutions still play a role by 1) creating a focal point for coordination, 2) helping to monitor the commitments of the two sides, and 3) giving the two sides assurances that commitments will remain robust to future changes in the balance of resources.

Theory and Practice: Institutional Evolution in Nascent Dominant Party Systems The preceding argument has simplified reality by indicating that the process of dominant party formation is a single-stage process – a dichotomous choice over the creation of a full-fledged dominant party. This was done to facilitate exposition of the core elements of the argument. But these insights can easily be applied to the gradual processes of dominant party building that we observe in the real world.

Dominant parties are composed of bundles of rules and norms that govern political exchange in multiple spheres. Yet, dominant parties rarely emerge as full-fledged, dyed-in-the wool institutions. More often they are born of a gradual process by which leaders and subsets of elites make incremental commitments to sequentially layered institutional components.[12]

This view of dominant party formation moves us closer to the real world of dominant party formation, where leaders and elites typically give minimal structure and names to the "cooperative agreements" that I have discussed in the abstract. Often, they call them parties of some type. Political scientists may even call them ruling parties or "parties of power". These nascent ruling parties may contain some institutional devices that constrain leaders and elites, but leaders and elites often shirk many of their other commitments to the "party." In other words, ruling parties may emerge, but elites and leaders sometimes have difficulty committing to the initial agreements represented by those parties, and thus they may make additional investments in subsequent commitment devices to reap the benefits of more extensive cooperation. Indeed, leaders and elites may need not only additional commitment devices, but as per the preceding argument, additional shifts in the balance of resources to make it more likely that they will create these commitment devices.

Thus, dominant party *projects* transform into dominant parties when changes in the balance of resources further reduce the severity of the commitment problem and make it more likely that the two sides will

---

[12] Note that the net balance of resources between the two sides is what matters here and not the absolute strength of the two sides. If the two sides are both "strong" in resources, then I consider there to be a balance of resources between the two sides and a dominant party to be more likely. The same is true if both sides are weak in resources.

2.3 Overcoming the Commitment Problem

invest in new commitment devices that make their previous promises to the dominant party project credible. New institutional components of the dominant party layer upon one another to make previous commitments credible. Dominant parties link these layered commitments across multiple spheres of politics. Thus, for example, if a party member shirks his commitment by competing against the party leadership's preferred candidate in elections, then that member can be sanctioned in other arenas. He may be excluded from party logrolls or be passed over for a promotion. *By recognizing that the party is not a monolithic institution, but rather a bundled hierarchy of institutional commitment devices, we can talk about commitments to a party while still acknowledging that certain aspects of the emerging dominant party solve commitment problems between leaders and elites.*

Of course, this means that leaders and elites can make certain commitments and transfer some resources while refraining from making other commitments or transferring other resources. Thus, for example, the leader may delegate control over promotions in the legislative branch to the party, but refrain from giving it power over cadre politics in the executive branch. Or the leader may transfer some personal resources by lending the party his name and image for use in campaigns, but at the same time, refrain from dismantling parallel organizations that allow the ruler to manage cadres and policy without the party. For their part, elites may use their political machines to campaign for the party during national elections but still retain their own political parties for use in local elections.

The gradual nature of dominant party formation helps us to see why leaders might fear the "party" itself and how this can sometimes influence their decisions over whether to invest in one. The danger for the leader is that the party itself may grow so strong and independent that it comes to usurp policy, rents, and even office from the ruler (e.g. Kitschelt 2000). Alternatively, the party may groom a new leader who seeks to challenge the ruler (Hale 2006). This concern may grow as the strength of elites increases.

In sum, the gradual process of dominant party formation is marked by a set of commitment problems between leaders and subsets of elites. The speed with which actors make these commitments varies with the size of the shift in the resource balance between leaders and elites, and the process of dominant party formation can be arrested at any time if the distribution of resources ceases to shift toward a balance that favors mutual investment in the dominant party.

3 False Starts: The Failure of Pro-Presidential Parties under Yeltsin

I have argued that leaders and elites are most likely to invest in a dominant party when elites are strong enough that leaders need to co-opt them in order to govern, but not so strong that they themselves are inclined to eschew investment in the dominant party. In this chapter, I explore the second half of this hypothesis: are dominant parties less likely to emerge when elites are strong vis-à-vis state leaders?

In the pages that follow I present a narrative account that demonstrates how strong regional elites and a weak central state prevented the creation of a dominant party in 1990s era Russia. Russia's first "parties of power," Russia's Choice and Our Home Is Russia (NDR), failed to become dominant parties because Russia's elites, particularly regional elites, were unwilling to cede the significant autonomy they accumulated in the early 1990s to a centralized dominant party. In turn, knowing that elites would not invest in a party, Yeltsin was himself loath to waste resources and reputation investing in one. This stance only further undermined elites' incentives to link their fates to a pro-presidential party.

3.1 The Absence of a Ruling Party in the First Russian Republic: 1990–1993

The story of regime parties in post-Soviet Russia begins just before the fall of the Soviet Union. With the election of the Soviet Congress of People's Deputies in 1989, the Soviet Union witnessed its first competitive elections since before the Russian Revolution.[1] In March 1990, the Russian Republic followed suit and held elections to the Russian Congress of People's Deputies a part-time legislative body that selected a full-time Supreme Soviet from among its ranks. Formal parties were not permitted to nominate candidates, but loose groupings of like-minded deputies were identifiable soon after the election (Sobyanin 1994, 18; Hough

---

[1] This section draws on accounts in Andrews (2002), McFaul (2001), Hale (2006), and Hough (1998).

3.1 Absence of a Ruling Party in First Russian Republic

1998, 294–297; Remington 2001, 133). Approximately 40 percent of the seats were held by conservative communists, who advocated the preservation of the Soviet system. On the other side of the aisle, deputies from the democratic–reformist camp also held about 40 percent of seats. Many of these deputies were in some way affiliated with Democratic Russia, an umbrella political movement uniting anti-communist figures whose primary raison d'être was to mobilize street protest against the Soviet government.

The de facto leader of Democratic Russia was Boris Yeltsin, who was united with his allies primarily by their opposition to the Soviet government and their demands for Russian sovereignty. To a lesser degree, they were united around the push for deeper and more rapid market reforms.

In 1990 and 1991, Yeltsin enjoyed a precarious, but workable, majority in the Russian Congress. But Yeltsin's majority did not last long. With the collapse of the Soviet Union in December 1991, Yeltsin's motley crew of allies in parliament lost the antisystemic purpose that had united them. This, combined with the increasingly unpopular economic reforms initiated by the government, led to the crumbling of Yeltsin's legislative majority over the course of 1992. By the end of that year, the balance of power in Congress had shifted decisively against Yeltsin and his allies (Myagkov and Kiewet 1996).

Yeltsin's allies were divided on the direction of economic reform, the distribution of power between center and regions, and the proper scope of presidential power, among other issues (Remington et al. 1994, 168). In a parliament with multidimensional preferences and weak legislative institutions (e.g. political parties or strong committees), majority rule can be unstable (e.g. Aldrich 1995). And indeed, for most of its post-Soviet tenure, the Congress of People's Deputies was eviscerated by indecision. In order to pass his initiatives, Yeltsin had to expend inordinate amounts of energy recruiting centrist deputies, co-opting opponents, presiding over complicated logrolls, and identifying reliable allies (Remington 2001, 134–137). As 1992 progressed, Yeltsin increasingly was forced to rely on shifting coalitions to pass his reform initiatives.

Yeltsin's enemies capitalized on the chaos. As Josephine Andrews has shown, Supreme Soviet Chairman Ruslan Khasbulatov masterfully manipulated the legislative agenda to push through curbs on Yeltsin's presidential powers even when a majority in the hall likely opposed the final outcome of the bill (Andrews 2002, 236–245). Deadlock set in as parliament entered deliberations over a new constitution to replace the amended Soviet constitution that was then in force. Over the course of 1993, confrontation between Yeltsin and parliament intensified to such a point that Yeltsin deemed it necessary to take the constitutional drafting process out of parliament and place it in the hands of a specially convened constitutional assembly. The opposition quickly found that it could make little headway pressing its demands through this presidentially controlled constitutional assembly and decided to quit the forum. At this point, Khasbulatov began actively seeking alliances with powerful regional elites who were vying for increased sovereignty from Moscow (McFaul 2001, 194).

In the summer of 1993, parliament began making preparations to pass a constitution of its own, but it would never get its chance. On September 21, Yeltsin issued a decree disbanding the Congress and calling for popular ratification of a new constitution. The decree also called for new elections to a new bicameral parliament. These moves set off a bloody standoff between Yeltsin and supporters of Khasbulatov and the Supreme Soviet in which more than 100 people died. The standoff ended with parliament capitulating and the collapse of the First Russian Republic.

Multidimensional preferences and the extreme factionalism in parliament opened up possibilities for the cycling and deadlock that hindered policy compromise in the Russian Congress of People's Deputies. Disciplined political parties would have solved many of the cycling problems by institutionalizing stable logrolls, but such parties did not exist. Before its opening session, the Congress did authorize the creation of deputy factions within the body. But institutional rules allowing each deputy to belong to up to five groups and the lack of party affiliation at election time meant that the Congress quickly fragmented into more than 32 deputy groups (Hough 1998, Remington 2001, Andrews 2002). Changes in mid-1991 that limited the number of factions a deputy could join reduced the overall level of fragmentation, but the absence of any party labels or attachments and the lack of a party-based electoral connection ensured that party discipline in the Congress was minimal at best.

Yeltsin's position, in particular, could have been improved by the support of a pro-presidential party. While Yeltsin enjoyed the support of many individual deputies in Congress, his allies were notoriously undisciplined. Given its aim to unite all anti-Soviet forces, Democratic Russia tended toward extreme decentralization and intraparty democracy (McFaul and Markov 1993, 137). This decentralization transformed into disintegration over the course of 1992 and 1993 as faction after faction peeled off in order to pursue its own agenda. This process accelerated until only a rump group was left to compete in the 1993 Duma elections.

Democratic Russia's failure to transform into a potent political party was caused not only by the diffuse set of ideologies in its ranks and

3.1 Absence of a Ruling Party in First Russian Republic

unfavorable institutional design, but also by the fact that Yeltsin declined to lend his unequivocal support to it and turn it into a true pro-presidential party. McFaul (2001, 154–156) reports that this was a conscious "nondecision" made by Yeltsin. Yeltsin's closest adviser, Gennady Burbulis, counseled Yeltsin, as early as 1991, that Yeltsin's personal popularity would not last and that, therefore, an ideological, programmatic party was necessary. In Burbulis's view, the party could not only provide a link to society, but also simplify the process of passing reform legislation and serve as a mechanism for staffing political positions "until [such time as] there were stable state instruments run by well-trained personnel."[2]

Yeltsin, however, was reluctant to affiliate with any one party. According to Burbulis, his reluctance was based on two factors: (1) the belief that post-Soviet citizens had an antiparty allergy and had elected Yeltsin on a non-artisan basis to serve as president of all Russians and (2) the fear that a party would ultimately limit his autonomy (McFaul 2001, 155). Yeltsin's move to separate party and state went so far as to require appointees to the presidential administration to join the administration not as representatives of Democratic Russia, but as individuals (McFaul 2001, 175). Part of Yeltsin's aim, clearly, was to cultivate personal loyalty at the expense of partisan loyalty.

Yeltsin was a democrat, but also a pragmatist. He realized early on that he needed allies outside the democratic movement. Nowhere was this more evident than in his efforts to secure the loyalty of prominent regional leaders; in late 1992, Yeltsin met with them on two occasions and agreed to grant them more autonomy over taxation and made promises concerning the preservation of regional autonomy in the new constitution. These moves frustrated the Democratic Russia leadership, who, rather than compromising with regional nomenklaturists, wanted Yeltsin to disband the Congress and hold a referendum on a new constitution (Brudny 1993). Disregarding the wishes of his democratic allies, Yeltsin appointed, en masse, nearly all sitting chairmen of soviets to the newly created executive post of governor (Slider 1994). It appears that Yeltsin did this for two reasons. First, from a practical standpoint, there were very few experienced administrators in the democratic ranks who could be tapped to govern in the regions. Second, as a concession to the conservative opposition in parliament, Yeltsin had agreed to allow local soviets to confirm presidential appointees in the regions. Given the conservative composition of local Soviets, Yeltsin knew that he had to play ball when it came to appointing regional administrators.

---

[2] Quoted in McFaul (2001, 155).

Yeltsin's reluctance to associate himself closely with a party or link it to the state had clear consequences for how prominent elites related to the party. From 1991 to 1993, Democratic Russia suffered a string of debilitating defections. Prominent leaders from their heady days of street protest calculated that they were better off pursuing their political agendas independently. One of the coalition's founders, Moscow mayor Gavril Popov, created his own faction, Movement for Democratic Reforms. Popov feared that Democratic Russia had become too "populist and unprofessional" through its detachment from government (McFaul 2001, 175). Popov's strategy was to build a nonideological party that could curry favor with prominent regional leaders (Golosov 1999, 92). In November 1991, one of Democratic Russia's three coordinators, Nikolai Travkin, withdrew his Democratic Party of Russia. Travkin criticized Democratic Russia's overreliance on street tactics and its inability to build an effective governing structure.[3]

All this is not to downplay the role that policy differences played in Democratic Russia's demise. From the beginning, it united factions with markedly different views on the extent of Russian sovereignty, Yeltsin's leadership style, and the pace of market reforms. As the collapse of the Soviet Union became imminent in the fall of 1991, these policy differences led to numerous defections from the coalition (McFaul 2001, 174).

Summary: The First Russian Republic

Thus, the Russian Federation began its existence without a propresidential party. The failure of Democratic Russia was, in large part, preordained by the imperatives of the transition from communism. The evaporation of the Soviet Union removed the common banner around which Democratic Russia's broad coalition was organized. This exposed divisive policy disagreements that undoubtedly contributed to its demise.

But the failure of Democratic Russia to become a dominant party after the transition also illustrates some features of the commitment framework outlined in this book. Deadlock and chaos in the Russian Congress of People's Deputies revealed how costly policy making can be for a president who does not lead a well-disciplined party. But at the same time, the period 1991–1993 also demonstrated the premium that Yeltsin placed on autonomy even in the face of such costs. Yeltsin was not strong enough, even in 1991, to pass key reforms without building shifting majorities that depended upon diverse coalitions. And yet, Yeltsin feared that a party would limit his ability to play this game and, thus, inhibit his

---

[3] Interview with Nikolai Travkin, in McFaul and Markov (1993, 72).

ability to govern. For their part, many elites realized that if Yeltsin was not going to make Democratic Russia into a governing party that could help them gain access to power, then they were better off building their own parties or just cultivating personal relationships with Yeltsin. Elites were unwilling to subordinate their autonomy to Democratic Russia when the organization presented itself as little more than a protest movement with limited potential to influence policy.

3.2 Russia's Choice: The Failure of Russia's First Party of Power

In September 1993, Yeltsin decreed that elections would be held in December to choose a new parliament that would replace the Supreme Soviet as Russia's primary legislative body. Despite Yeltsin's reluctance to associate himself with Democratic Russia, members of his administration still recognized the need to organize some sort of political organization that could support the government. In June 1993, several prominent figures including the former presidential adviser Gennady Burbulis and former Democratic Russia leader Arkadii Murashev began negotiations with the remaining elements of Democratic Russia to create a new political bloc that would support the government (McFaul 1998, 117). Despite the misgivings of Democratic Russia's leadership, an agreement was reached and a new political organization called Russia's Choice was created. In addition to the rump elements of Democratic Russia, many prominent members of the government joined the new party including former Prime Minister Yegor Gaidar, Deputy Prime Minister Anatoly Chubais, and Foreign Minister Andrei Kozyrev. At the organization's founding congress in October 1993, it became clear that emphasis would be placed on recruiting well-placed members of the new Russian political elite. Democratic Russia leaders were unable to secure top spots on the federal list as 16 of these 19 spots went to members of the government. In the regions, the party leadership privileged pragmatism over ideology and chose to curry favor with powerful regional leaders, even if these former nomenklaturists were odious to liberal activists from Democratic Russia (Golosov 1999, 101).

The party's goal was to draw on the support of two groups: 1) liberal, market reformers and 2) members of the new political and economic elite who were benefiting from the status quo. This latter group was small in number but rich in the administrative and financial resources necessary to win votes. They included directors of newly privatized enterprises and newly created banks, government bureaucrats, and regional officials. On Election Day, the bloc boasted 13 members of the government and a number of regional administration heads. Yeltsin's chief of staff joined the bloc, but Yeltsin himself refused to endorse a particular party ahead of the elections (McFaul 1998, 119).

Going into the polls, most observers expected the party to do well. It combined a strong ideological appeal with significant access to administrative resources at the federal level. These expectations were not met. Although the party secured more party-list votes (15.5 percent) and more single member district (SMD) seats (25) than any other proreform party, it finished an embarrassing second to Vladimir Zhirinovsky's Far Right Liberal Democratic Party of Russia (LDPR) in the party-list vote. In 1994, only 73 of the State Duma's 450 deputies entered Russia's Choice's legislative faction.

In retrospect, it is clear why Russia's Choice failed to perform better. The contradiction between an ideological appeal to liberalism and an administrative reliance on the state and nomenklaturist elites was difficult to overcome. This conflict created friction within the party and undermined the credibility of the party's program. Second, the deteriorating state of the economy meant that pocketbook oriented voters would not be supporting the party.

Probably even more consequential than these factors, however, was the lack of commitment by Yeltsin and the reluctance of both federal and regional elites to coordinate within Russia's Choice. St. Petersburg mayor, Anatolii Sobchak, a former Yeltsin ally in the Soviet Congress of People's Deputies and one of Russia's most trusted politicians at the time, chose to run his own reformist party, the Russian Movement for Democratic Reforms. Sobchak organized the party in concert with former Moscow mayor Gavril Popov. Nikolai Travkin's Democratic Party of Russia also opted to contest the elections on his own. Another prominent member of the reformist camp, Grigory Yavlinsky, author of the 500 days program, which laid the groundwork for the Soviet Union's transition to a market economy, opted at the last minute to form his own liberal party in opposition to Russia's Choice.

But perhaps the most important nonparticipant in Russia's Choice was Sergei Shakhrai's Party for Russian Unity and Accord (PRES). In 1992 and 1993, Shakhrai was a deputy prime minister under Yeltsin. Arguably, he was Yeltsin's most powerful deputy prime minister because he chaired the committee on national politics within the government, which was responsible for relations with regional governments. This made Shakhrai the key figure for regional officials seeking to lobby Moscow. His control over subsidies and his influence over decisions that would grant writs of regional autonomy gave Shakhrai a great deal of influence with these leaders.

3.2 Russia's Choice: The Failure of Russia's First Party of Power 81

Shakhrai began by recruiting to his side top figures in Moscow, including Yeltsin adviser Sergei Stankevich, Deputy Prime Minister Alexandr Shokhin, Justice Minister Yurii Kalmykov, and Labor Minister Gennadii Melik'yan (Sakwa 1995). But what set Shakhrai's party apart from any other party of power at the time was the extent to which Shakhrai recognized how the political machines of regional leaders could be used to win votes. He thus intentionally crafted a party that eschewed specific ideological appeals in favor of a "pragmatic approach to solving Russia's problems" (Hale 2006, 49). Shakhrai used his cozy relationships with regional leaders to gain regional support for a "party of the provinces" (Treisman 1999, 145). Reports indicate that Shakhrai was open about his presidential ambitions and PRES was a first step toward realizing those ambitions (Sakwa 1995).

The failure of important liberal elites in Moscow to coordinate with Russia's Choice had serious consequences for the reform agenda. Together, reform oriented parties secured 47.8 percent of the party-list vote, but Russia's Choice on its own secured only 16 percent. In the SMD races, reformist parties competed against one another in a whopping 43 percent of districts, thus diminishing their overall seat total further.

The other important elite group that failed to coordinate with Russia's Choice was regional leaders (governors, enterprise directors, regional soviet speakers, etc.). To be sure, some regional leaders helped Russia's Choice mobilize votes. The most notable case of this was Moscow, where newly elected mayor Yurii Luzhkov, a key Yeltsin ally during the October events of 1993, put the powerful city bureaucracy to work for the party (Kullberg 1998, 321). In most other regions, however, regional leaders opted to steer clear of any affiliation with Russia's Choice.[4] Instead, they either threw the weight of their political machines behind independent candidates or supported other parties in the race. Thus, for example, in Bashkortostan, Bashkir Supreme Soviet Chairman Murtaza Rakhimov backed Shakhrai and PRES, openly undermining Russia's Choice's campaign in the region (Hale 1998).

For his part, Yeltsin refused to endorse Russia's Choice unequivocally. On several occasions he promised to speak at the bloc's convention or endorse its party list but failed to follow through. In retrospect, it was clear that Yeltsin never intended to support the party, but rather preferred to make his relationship with it appear ambiguous so that it could gather

---

[4] For evidence of this, see the series of regional case studies on the 1993 elections in Colton and Hough (1998). Of the 10 regions analyzed in that study, only 1 (Moscow) had a regional leader who put his machine to work for Russia's Choice.

votes as a pro-reform, pro-Yeltsin party, at the same time he would be able to make deals with other actors. Indeed, the clearest signal of Yeltsin's lack of support for Russia's Choice was the fact that he did not attempt to dissuade members of his government (or other reformist politicians) from joining competing parties of power (Colton 1998, 13).[5] During the campaign, Yeltsin made few comments about the parliamentary election, preferring instead to speak to voters about the constitutional referendum scheduled for Election Day.

Yeltsin's noncommittal stance cost Russia's Choice dearly. Days after the election, Burbulis blamed the bloc's poor performance on Yeltsin's ambiguous stance.[6] Some pro-Yeltsin voters were left unsure of whom to support and many regional elites, even if they were inclined to support a national party, did not intend to support one that could not help them lobby in Moscow.

Why Yeltsin Failed to Invest in Russia's Choice

Yeltsin repeatedly stated that he wished to remain "above" any party (Hough 1998, McFaul 2001, Hale 2006, Colton 2008, Baturin et al. 2001). In interviews with biographers, he expressed two justifications for this choice. One was personal: Yeltsin claimed to have an "allergy" to the word "party" after his experiences in the CPSU. Yeltsin felt that Russian voters shared the same distaste for parties and, therefore, the chief executive should "act as president of the entire population" (McFaul 2001, 155).[7]

Yeltsin's other reason for not wanting to nurture a pro-presidential party was more political. He reasoned that a party would "force him to coordinate his decisions with others and thereby limit his autonomy: (Colton 2008, 350). After interviewing Yeltsin and his aides, Timothy Colton concluded that "Yeltsin had seen Gorbachev labor to steer both the CPSU and the Soviet State, while he as an oppositionist had flexibility when he walked out of the party in 1990. He was not sure how agreeable Russia's untrammeled political elite would be to re-imposition of party discipline in any form" (Colton 2008, 350). Members of Yeltsin's inner circle echoed this sentiment. One Yeltsin adviser reported that he believed Gaidar and others were building Russia's Choice in order to become independent of Yeltsin and that the emergence of a strong party

---

[5] Six cabinet members were members of Russia's Choice, but five were members of other centrist parties.
[6] *Komsomolskaya Pravda*, December 15, 1993.
[7] Quoted from interview conducted with Gennady Burbulis by Michael McFaul.

would result in Yeltsin's allies' splitting their loyalty between the party and Yeltsin.[8] Yeltsin, noted the aide, agreed and actively sought to hinder the process of party building. Thus, in 1993, Yeltsin was put off not only by his own ideological misgivings, but also by doubts about how easy it would be to control Russian elites in the early 1990s. Instead, he found it preferable to cultivate personal relationships and employ divide and rule tactics.

Why Elites Failed to Invest in Russia's Choice

For Yeltsin's inner circle and advisers, the uncertainty of the transitional environment made presidential bids all the more attractive. At times, Yeltsin looked very beatable. Opinion polls found that several other prominent leaders were at least as well respected as Yeltsin – including Yavlinsky and Shakhrai. Thus, prominent members of the reformist camp sought to cultivate their own parties to serve as vehicles for their own presidential bids (Urban 1994, 147, Sakwa 1995, McFaul 2001).

Yeltsin's weakness made recruiting allies an easy task for potential challengers. Both Yavlinsky and Shakhrai were able to lure important members of the liberal coalition to their parties. As noted, Shakhrai was especially well positioned in this area as he used his position as minister for nationalities to curry favor with regional elites, a group whose status and influence were growing rapidly at that time.

For regional elites, the decision not to affiliate was motivated mostly by a simple cost–benefit analysis. In the early 1990s, their autonomy was such that they were not willing to put themselves under the yoke of a dominant party. Indeed, the autonomous resources of Russian regional elites form such an important part of the story that unfolds over the next two chapters that it is worth saying a few words about those resources here.

Regional elites in the early 1990s derived their autonomy both from the dislocations spawned by the collapse of the Soviet state and from the built-in impulses toward regionalism and clientelism that undergirded the Soviet system. Despite the fact that key decision making in the Soviet Union was highly centralized, the accumulation and perpetuation of power had always included a regional dimension. National party leaders constructed power by building clientelistic networks made up of provincial party leaders. In what was known as the circular flow of power, the general secretary of the CPSU was removable by the central

---

[8] This synopsis is taken from Hale (2006, 209). Hale conducted the interview with the Yeltsin aide.

committee, which in turn was elected at the party congress, delegates to which were selected at regional conferences that were controlled by regional party secretaries. In a practice initiated by Lenin and perfected by Stalin it became a norm that the general secretary would have the key role in nominating and removing regional party secretaries (Daniels 1971, Hough 1997). The regional secretaries thus became a support base for the general secretary, who was simultaneously under their collective control. Thus, under the old regime, power was both personalized around the general secretary and concentrated in the hands of regional party officials.

What is more, the specialized knowledge and expertise of regional party officials played a key role in lubricating the wheels of the Soviet command economy. Given the empire's size and diversity, Soviet leaders recognized a need for economic planning that could conform to local needs. Thus, local party officials were ceded the crucial task of coordinating economic production in their region (Hough 1969). This entailed managing relations among enterprises and branch ministries so that supply and demand of key goods were coordinated. This task involved informal bartering, off-plan exchanges, and, oftentimes, managing personnel at the enterprise level.

Thus, by the time of the transition, a pattern had emerged in the Russian regions whereby the functioning of the economy was highly dependent on the ability of political managers to solve practical problems and coordinate economic exchange. As Jerry Hough has pointed out, post-Soviet Russia's regional governors took on this management and coordination role (Hough 2001, 44). Indeed, already by 1992, regional governors were amassing immense informal authority due to their key role in stewarding the informal barter that oiled the early post-Soviet economy. In a pattern that would continue throughout the post-Soviet period, Russian central leaders would become dependent on the skill and clientelist networks of regional managers who could effectively solve political and economic problems on the ground.

The Soviet (and early post-Soviet) workplace also created a panoply of opportunities for regional elites to build political machines that would serve them as power bases when central control weakened. This is largely because Soviet enterprises, and especially collective farms, internalized so many social and economic services upon which citizens depended. Large enterprises often operated their own stores, health clinics, day care centers, vacation resorts, summer camps, and even farms. Families' lives thus revolved around the enterprise, giving their directors a high degree of political power (Hale 2003, Alina-Pisano 2010, Frye, Reuter, and Szakonyi 2014). As these enterprises were privatized and enterprise directors were removed from the ministry chain of command, this source of autonomous power only grew in many cases.

A further source of political resources for some regional elites in the early post-Soviet period was ethnicity. The Soviet Union institutionalized ethnicity by matching certain subnational administrative divisions to ethnic boundaries. In the Soviet Union, members of the titular ethnic groups in ethnic regions had been favored through various affirmative action–style programs in education and political advancement. In the post-Soviet period, members of these groups had a vested interest in the continuation of these privileges. The leaders of ethnic republics thus had a ready-made political base that they could use in negotiations for formal and informal autonomy from the center. At the extreme, leaders could threaten ethnic strife if their demands for sovereignty were not met.

By privileging members of the titular group for promotions in the regional state-administrative apparatus, regional leaders quickly built strong political machines that featured them at the top, their coethnic clients in the middle, and the ethnic populace at the bottom. As Hale (2003) notes, the most skillful republic leaders expanded their support among nontitular groups in the region by arguing that their ethnically based sovereignty claims were gaining benefits for the region as a whole.

As if these resources were not enough to make regional elites in early 1990s Russia sufficiently autonomous, the political imperatives of the transition only strengthened their hand. Russia inherited the Soviet Union's federal structure, so as soon as the Union collapsed, regional leaders found themselves sitting atop well-defined political entities – republics, oblasts, *krais*, autonomous *okrugs* – that could serve as administratively legitimate platforms from which to demand political and economic autonomy. In 1990 and 1991, Yeltsin recognized that regional leaders could be key allies in his struggle with the Soviet leadership. Their desire for more autonomy mirrored the Russian Federation's desire for sovereignty from the Soviet Union so Yeltsin actively courted these leaders in late 1990 and 1991, promising support for regional autonomy in exchange for opposing Gorbachev. In 1992 and 1993, when Yeltsin faced opposition in the Congress of People's Deputies, he again turned to regional leaders for support, even as their demands for greater sovereignty pushed the state to the brink of collapse.

Yeltsin understood that policy could not be implemented outside Moscow without the support of regional leaders. As regional leaders withheld tax revenue and ignored federal laws on everything from privatization to tax remittances to foreign trade, Yeltsin granted the regions even greater political autonomy.[9] The 1992 Federation Treaty granted the regions significant autonomy over areas related to taxation, education, historical preservation, and the environment, as well as significant residual powers over policy areas not specified in the treaty. The treaty also granted ethnic republics special rights, including the right to self-determination and the right to choose their own governmental structure (most chose to create presidencies). While the Federation Treaty was subsequently superseded in December 1993 by the new Russian constitution, which scaled back some of the republics' powers, significant regional autonomy was nonetheless enshrined in Russia's federal constitution. Furthermore, the powers of individual regions were expanded between 1994 and 1998 by a series of bilateral agreements between Moscow and some of the more powerful regions. In these ad hoc deals, 46 Russian regions secured extensive supplemental rights over taxation, budgets, natural resource revenues, and foreign economic relations.

This policy autonomy was matched by both de facto and de jure political autonomy. Between 1991 and 1994, direct elections for regional chief executives were held in 30 regions, including most of the ethnic republics. Even in those regions where governors were appointed, Yeltsin frequently was forced to compromise with hostile local soviets over appointments. In extreme cases, regional administrations simply ignored Yeltsin's attempts to fire governors (e.g. Novosibirsk and Irkutsk) or elections were held without Yeltsin's permission (see McFaul and Petrov 1998, 127, Ivanov 2013, 84).

The period 1990–1993 also saw the emergence of informal powers that regional elites would continue to wield well into the 2000s. In many cases, these powers were accumulated at the expense of the central state. It is well known that Russia was suffering through a cataclysmic economic crisis during the early years of transition. Estimates vary, but most agree that the Russian economy contracted by more than 40 percent from 1989 to 1994 (Åslund 2007). As the fiscal and organizational resources of the Russian central state withered in the early 1990s, regional governments carved out great swaths of de facto policy autonomy in a variety of policy areas including social services, budgets, privatization, judicial reform, foreign trade, landownership, and environmental protection. Regional authorities often used illiberal and illegal methods to extend control over civil society and the media. Where federal institutions failed

---

[9] For just a few of the many good discussions of how the center devolved authority to the regions in this period see Slider (1994), Lapidus and Walker (1995), Solnick (1998), and Treisman (1999), Stoner-Weiss (1999).

to provide services, regional and local governments stepped in to provide public goods and services as best they could. And as the federal government became increasingly impoverished, regional governments extended their control over law enforcement organs and the courts.

In many cases, regional elites were given authority over the conduct of privatization as well (Åslund 1995). Regional leaders used this power to give local clients an inside track in acquiring shares and property. In recognition of Russia's size and diversity, Gaidar admitted defeat in advancing a common price liberalization policy when he stated that "a common policy for subsidies [of basic consumer goods] was not only difficult, but perhaps impossible" (quoted in Slider 1997, 450). Thus, regional elites were left with extensive powers over prices and subsidies. In budgetary policy as well, the regions took great liberties. Although Russia has always had a relatively centralized tax system, many regions simply diverted federal transfers earmarked for one purpose (for instance, wages) to other purposes (Slider 1997).

Throughout the 1990s, regional authorities used these extensive resources to build political machines that could be used for controlling elections in their regions. In 1993, regional elites had just started to play this game, but clearly the learning curve was not very steep. In an in-depth study of six SMD races in Bashkortostan in 1993, Hale (1998) reports that the most decisive factor that determined electoral success was backing from the republic leadership. Slider (1996) found that enterprise directors and representatives of the local administration were more successful at winning seats in the 1993–1994 regional legislative elections than were candidates tied to national political parties. Similarly, Golosov (1997) showed that members of the managerial elite outperformed all other candidates in the 1993–1994 regional elections.[10]

Regional and local "bosses" translated their machines into votes through a mixture of clientelist and administrative tactics. Their control over local media, law enforcement, courts, tax inspectorates, licensing agencies, and prosecutors gave them ample coercive leverage over competitors. Through their control of utilities and social services, regional administrations could credibly threaten disloyal districts with punishment (e.g. Alina-Pisano 2010). Similarly, enterprise and collective farm directors could threaten their employees with reprisal, but more often than not, the possibility of such reprisal induced compliant voting behavior. Even without such implicit threats, the advantage these officials enjoyed in visibility, authority, and material resources was difficult to match.

---

[10] For further confirmation of the power regional elites wielded in the 1993 elections, see the collection of regional case studies presented in Colton and Hough (1998).

With such expansive autonomous resources under their control, it is not hard to see why regional elites in 1993 might be reluctant to surrender their autonomy to any party, much less one that would put them under the tutelage of the state. They were clearly able to secure their political survival and obtain concessions from Moscow without submitting to the discipline of a dominant party. As the former Orel governor Egor Stroev characterized it in an interview with the author:

> None of the existing parties [in the early 1990s] had any sort of authority. For me it was more advantageous to focus on maintaining popular support and to maintain relations with all parties. I was friends with all of them. I knew all the key figures, both in the region and at the federal level. Public opinion in that period determined more than political parties could.[11]

According to Stroev, joining Russia's Choice would only have been a "minus" since it was more advantageous to maintain his autonomy to negotiate with multiple parties and build his electoral coalition in the region.

Even Sergei Shakhrai's PRES party, whose campaign was based on securing regional support, had difficulty securing unequivocal commitments from governors. As Skhakhrai stated in an interview: "We could only ask them [governors] to do what was possible for them. A few of them joined the party, but there was no use in even asking most others. They were governors. They needed to work with PRES and Russia's Choice and Chernomyrdin and Yeltsin. If they joined just one, it would limit their ability to secure support from the others. So governors wouldn't join."[12]

But even in this setting, if Yeltsin had committed wholeheartedly to Russia's Choice, making it a clear governmental party through which governors could lobby their interests and policy could be distributed, it is possible that regional elites may have seized the opportunity. In choosing their party affiliation for the 1993 election, regional leaders were keen to find out what that party could do for them; how it could help them take tangible benefits back to their clients and constituents. But regional elites did not feel assured that any of the parties of power on offer in 1993 could help them achieve this. None had the unequivocal backing of Yeltsin. Indeed, press reports from the PRES congress reveal that Shakhrai's calls to develop a "conservative" party program were yelled down by specific demands from regional leaders for assurances on items as diverse

---

[11] Author's interview with Egor Stroev, former chairman of the Federation Council, June 6, 2013, Moscow.

[12] Author's interview with Sergei Shakhrai, former chairman of PRES and vice prime minister, May 27, 2014, Moscow.

as aluminum export regulations and logging licenses. Regional leaders in attendance were decidedly uninterested in becoming affiliated with a party ideology, especially if there were no guarantee that they would receive their preferred concessions from Moscow in exchange for this affiliation. As the prime minister of Buryatia put it at the party's founding conference, "Our platform should be flexible ... differentiated by region... And, in general, after I join the party, what will I get in return?"[13]

Summary: The Failure of Russia's Choice

Russia's Choice continued to wither after the elections. And while the party's failure clearly had several causes, the reluctance of both Yeltsin and other elites to commit themselves to it seems to have contributed to its failure. Each player's reluctance was based both on its own calculations about the benefits of investing in Russia's Choice and its estimation of what the other side would do. Yeltsin could not control elites so it was better to keep them divided. For elites, their political future seemed well secured by continuing to build their own political machines. They may have wanted to cooperate more closely with the Kremlin in order to reduce the uncertainty surrounding the procurement of federal rents, but they were receiving no clear signals from Yeltsin that he would support a party organization that could provide those benefits. And given their expanding personal resources, they were not so desperate for cooperation that they were willing to link their fate unilaterally to the party of power. Thus, even if Yeltsin had wanted to build a strong party, it is not clear that he would have been able to persuade elites to join it. These dynamics, which were only becoming perceptible in 1993, became more pronounced as the decade wore on.

3.3 Our Home Is Russia: Russia's Second Failed Party of Power

In the First Duma (1994–1995), Russia's Choice was the party most supportive of Yeltsin, and Yeltsin favored this party over others, but it was not a closed shop for lobbying in the Duma. Yeltsin was not going to invest any more political capital in the party. Just one month after the 1993 elections, claims emerged that the presidential administration was planning to construct a new presidential party (Hale 2006, 208). Russia's Choice, for its part, began opposing Yeltsin on some issues, including the war in Chechnya.

[13] *Segodnya*, October 19, 1993, p2.

In the Duma, Russia's Choice controlled only a plurality, and rather than trying to induce other parties or independents to join with Russia's Choice, Yeltsin settled into a routine of passing reforms with the aid of shifting coalitions (Haspel, Remington, and Smith 2006, Smith and Remington 2001, Huskey 2001, Troxel 2003). This routine of repeatedly building new coalitions was costly and time-consuming for Yeltsin. For deputies, it likely posed grave uncertainties.

In the 1994 regional legislative elections, very few legislators affiliated with any party, much less Russia's Choice. Between 1993 and 1995, a whopping 87.5 percent of all elected deputies were independents. Russia's Choice contested only 22.4 percent of the elections held in this period. In those regions where it did contest elections, it won on average a mere 11 percent of seats (Golosov 2003). In seven regional executive elections that Yeltsin permitted between October 1993 and June 1994, none of the incumbent governors or winning candidates took on a Russia's Choice affiliation. All were independents.

By early 1995, Russia's Choice was no longer the party of power. Still, recognizing the need for some sort of pro-presidential party, Yeltsin's inner circle set to work on creating a new party of power. But recalling the difficulty that Yeltsin's then-advisers had had in convincing the president to support a party of power in 1993, Yeltsin's election team opted for a different strategy. They proposed creating two "parties of power," one right of center and one left of center. According to Shakhrai, the initiator of this idea, the parties would "outwardly compete, but internally would constitute a joint, electoral movement" (Baturin et al. 2001, 536). Shakhrai thought that two blocs could provide the basis of a parliamentary majority in the Duma and siphon votes away from opposition parties on both sides of the political spectrum. Yeltsin gave his support to this idea and in April 1995, it was announced that Chernomyrdin would lead the right bloc, now called Our Home Is Russia. The Duma speaker, Ivan Rybkin, elected with the support of the main opposition groups in early 1994, was tapped to head the center–Left bloc.

Despite its designs as a Right–center party of power Our Home very quickly shed its ideological baggage. Its platform, which criticized the "shocks" and "experimentation" of the past, called for stability and professionalism in government (Golosov 1999). At Chernomyrdin's urging, several members of the government joined the party, which then sought to form alliances with regional leaders. Indeed, 36 governors joined the party's political council in May 1995.[14] In the Federation

[14] www.panorama.ru/works/vybory/party/ndr.html.

3.3 Our Home Is Russia

Council, where governors and the chairman of regional legislatures sat ex officio, 57 of 187 seats were occupied by supporters of Our Home (Belonuchkin 1997).

The designs for the center–Left bloc, now called Ivan Rybkin Bloc, never really got off the ground. The party had difficulty credibly positioning itself as an oppositionist party when it was so clearly in collusion with the Kremlin. It thus failed to co-opt any prominent figures from existing Left opposition parties. Even the Agrarian Party, on whose list Rybkin had been elected in 1993, refused to cooperate. In August, the bloc's fortunes appeared to be on the rise as it attracted the support of the popular general Boris Gromov. Unfortunately, Gromov deserted the bloc weeks later in order to run his own party in the elections (Belin and Orttung 1997, 37). By December, when the elections were scheduled, no one expected the party to do well. And indeed, On Election Day, the party collected a little more than 1 percent of the party list vote.

The expectations for Our Home Is Russia were different. With its potential to mobilize the vast political resources of both the Kremlin and regional administrations, the party looked poised for success. But these expectations were not borne out. On Election Day, the party managed to secure only 10.1 percent of the party-list vote and 10 SMD seats. In the regions, the party fared little better. Although reliable data from the period are scarce, most sources agree that only a handful of elected governors were party nominees (Hale 2006, Slider 2001, Solnick 1998, Belonuchkin 1997). The party fared no better among other regional elites. From 1995 to 1999, the party only managed to field candidates in 27 percent of regional legislative elections, and it averaged a dismal 4.2 percent of the seats in those contested elections (Golosov 2003). During this period the standard was for strong candidates to run as independents. And indeed, 79 percent of regional deputies were elected as independents during this period (Golosov 2003).

After the 1995 elections, the party quickly dwindled. While it retained branches in most regions up through the 1999 elections, regional governors paid it little attention, and, as I discuss later, those who did affiliate made very shallow commitments to the party. Needless to say, the party played no role in the selection of personnel at either the regional or national level. Its main organizational presence was its Duma faction, where it held 65 seats. Thus, in the Second Duma, just as in the First Duma, Yeltsin relied upon ad hoc logrolls and cross-factional bargaining to advance his legislative agenda, rather than securing support through the construction of a stable majority faction. Thus, like Russia's Choice before it, Our Home was a weak party of power.

The Immediate Causes of Our Home's Failure: Presidential and Regional Neglect

Our Home's failure to transform into a dominant party had several causes. First, being associated with the status quo was disadvantageous at the time. Bloodshed in Chechnya and economic collapse made Yeltsin and the policy course associated with him increasingly unpopular. But policy preference was likely not the most important factor.[15] After all, despite his lack of popularity, Yeltsin won reelection in 1996. Also, reformist parties more closely associated with the reform packages of the early 1990s (e.g. Russia's Choice and Yabloko) garnered just as many party-list votes as Our Home. In total, centrist and Right–centrist parties gathered more than 35 percent of the vote. In any case, as I discuss later, Our Home's low vote totals were determined as much by the hesitance of Russia's regional elites to put their political machines to work for the party as they were by the unadulterated preferences of Russian voters. Russia's increasingly powerful governors and financial industrial groups could have mobilized more votes for Our Home had they chosen to do so.

Rather, the proximate causes for Our Home's failure were 1) national political elites' failure to coordinate and invest in the party, 2) regional elites' failure to invest in Our Home, and 3) Yeltsin's failure to invest in the party. I discuss each of these in turn and the consequences they had for Our Home's prospects. Then I consider why each of these sets of actors opted to make only minimal commitments to Our Home.

National Elites and Our Home Is Russia

On paper, the lack of coordination by parties and elites in Our Home is clear. The ballot for the 1995 elections contained more than 40 parties. Divisions were particularly acute in the reformist camp. Gaidar's Russia's Choice refused to cooperate with Our Home, ostensibly over the war in Chechnya. A panoply of smaller centrist parties refrained from joining Our Home in order to pursue their own campaigns. Most of these small parties were vehicles designed to serve the larger ambitions of their leaders. For instance, in a replay of 1993, Sergei Shakhrai, who had come up with the idea to create Our Home, left the party in late 1995 to head the list for his PRES party again. In many single member districts, Our

---

[15] However, as I emphasize throughout, Yeltsin's popularity certainly influenced the calculations of elites about the relative value of affiliating with a party that was associated with Yeltsin.

Home failed to attract prominent local independents who it had hoped would run on its list. These coordination failures not only split the vote at the national level, but also meant that reformist and centrist candidates ended up competing against one another in numerous single member districts (Belin and Orttung 1997, 57–58). The result was a lower vote total for the party and confirmation of Yeltsin's suspicion that members of the political elite could not be counted on to submit to the control of a centralized party.

The business elite also chose to place its eggs in multiple baskets. Although several major banks did funnel support to Our Home and the party enjoyed the backing of the state-owned natural gas giant Gazprom, other parties had no difficulty securing major financing from large banks in Moscow (Johnson 2000). For example, the Stable Russia group, created in early 1995 as a pro-presidential faction in the Duma, was reportedly formed at the behest of prominent Moscow bankers (Johnson 2000, 119). In the December elections, this centrist party steered clear of affiliation with Our Home.

Regional Elites and Our Home Is Russia

Our Home's troubles with securing commitments from important regional elites began just months after its formation. In August, in its first major electoral contest, the Our Home–backed governor of Sverdlovsk Oblast lost heavily to the locally popular chairman of the regional parliament, Eduard Rossel.[16] Seeing that Our Home backing was not enough to ensure reelection, many sitting governors began distancing themselves from the party. In elections held in 1995 and 1996, the Kremlin circumvented Our Home by creating two umbrella organizations for coordinating campaigns in the gubernatorial races – the All-Russian Coordinating Council (OKS) led by Presidential Administration Chief of Staff Sergei Filatov and a parallel committee chaired by Deputy Chief of Staff Aleksandr Kazakov (McFaul and Petrov 1998, Solnick 1998). Our Home supported candidates in several races, and many governors proclaimed solidarity with the party, but the extent of Our Home's involvement in the races was minimal. Kremlin support was channeled through OKS and had few strings attached in terms of platform, personnel, or policy. Rather, the goal of these nonpartisan coordinating committees was to work to ensure that individuals Yeltsin deemed loyal were elected.

[16] *Russian Regional Report*, January 1, 1996

The extent to which governors relied upon any parties to secure election was limited (Solnick 1998, Slider 2001). Those who did make use of party support either were supported by the KPRF or created their own regionally based parties of power (see, for example, Makarenko 1998, Lapina and Chrikova 2000, Golosov 2003, Turovsky 2012).[17] Between 1994 and 1999, at least 39 governors created their own regionally based political parties, including 17 governors who sat on Our Home's political council.[18] According to Makarenko (1998), many such governors actively inhibited the formation of Our Home factions in regional legislatures. In turn, local Our Home branches were "captured" by governors and incorporated into their own political machines.

In the Federation Council, regional leaders also eschewed party affiliation, deciding that parliamentary work in the upper house would be conducted without the help of legislative factions. Our Home did not prevent governors, even those affiliated with it, from opposing Yeltsin initiatives. For instance, in July 1997, the Federation Council voted unanimously to appeal to the constitutional court to overturn two Yeltsin vetoes.[19] It also rejected a bill passed with presidential support that would require regional administrations to consult city mayors on certain budgetary matters.[20]

Many Our Home–affiliated governors distanced themselves from the party from the very beginning. Moscow Mayor Yurii Luzhkov and Tatarstan President Minitmer Shaimiyev declined to join the coordinating council, appointing representatives to sit in their place (Makarkin 1999). Egor Stroev, then-speaker of the Federation Council, sat on the party's political council but was adamant about not joining the party and explained that his main reason for sitting on the council was his personal relationship with Chernomyrdin, which dated back to their time together on the Central Committee of the CPSU.[21] The shallowness of governors' commitments is demonstrated most vividly by the fact that so many held

---

[17] Prominent examples included Eduard Rossel's Transformation of the Urals party, which was Sverdlovsk Oblast's regional party of power from 1994 until 2002; Petr Sumin's Ural Rebirth party in Chelyabinsk; and Mintimer Shaimiev's Unity and Progress movement. Even some strong mayors sought to establish their own political movements

[18] Of the mayors who got in on the act of spurning Our Home and creating their own parties, Ekaterinburg mayor Arkady Chernetsky's Our Home Is Our City movement was one of the most prominent examples.

[19] One relating to a law that would prohibit the return of valuables and art seized by the Soviet Union during World War II and another requiring the removal of the entire cabinet should the prime minister resign or be sacked. RFE/RL Newsline, July 7, 1997

[20] RFE/RL Newsline, July 8, 1997.

[21] Author's interview with Egor Stroev, June 2013, Moscow

dual affiliations with other political parties: in mid-1999, 26 of 30 governors known to be affiliated with Our Home also had public affiliations with other national or local political parties.[22] A standard practice was for governors on Our Home's political council to support candidates from other political parties openly in regional elections (Hale 2006, Ryabov 2006).[23]

Our Home's standing with regional governors only deteriorated over time. By 1997, just two years after its founding, the number of governors on the political council had dropped to 30. By early 1999, only 16 remained on the council. Throughout this period, governors took no active part in what little party work there was and very few were ever formal party members

Among the regional managerial elite, Our Home's position was no stronger. Regional business leaders diversified their investments rather than linking their fates solely to Our Home. As one representative of a Perm-based financial industrial group put it at the time, "Representatives of our group participate in the political councils (*politsovety*) of practically all parties and groups in the region. That way, we feel more confident."[24] Our Home's presence in regional legislatures (where most members of a region's economic elite are represented) was minimal. It contested only 27 percent of all regional elections held between 1995 and 1999, and won seats in only 11 percent of those elections (Golosov 2003). It won more than 10 percent of seats in only one very minor region, Koryak Autonomous Okrug (Golosov 2000).

The Kremlin and Our Home Is Russia

The final major reason that Our Home failed was the lack of real investment by the Kremlin. Yeltsin made only halfhearted commitments to Our Home. In April 1995, his advisers debated the relative merits of supporting a single party of power versus supporting several. As they discussed the options before them, Yeltsin surprised everyone by jumping the gun and publicly announcing that the Kremlin would be supporting two separate blocs during the elections – Our Home and the Ivan Rybkin Bloc mentioned earlier.

In the summer of 1995, Yeltsin did not campaign for Our Home or speak at its preelection congress. In September, he went a step further

---

[22] Based on data from Lussier (2002), Hale (2006), and author's own calculations.
[23] Golosov (2000) gives an example in which the governor of Rostov Oblast, a member of Our Home's central political council, supported loyal-to-him members of Yabloko in that region's regional elections.
[24] Interview cited in Lapina and Chirkova (2000).

by expressing doubts about the party's electoral chances in the upcoming elections, predicting that they would not be able to gather more than 15 percent of the vote. During the campaign, key Kremlin advisers and members of the government worked on Our Home's campaign, but the Kremlin also helped other independent candidates get elected. Two days before the election, Yeltsin gave a live televised address on the elections, but he had nothing positive (or negative) to say about Our Home and instead focused his speech on the communist threat.

Thus, in late 1995 and early 1996 Our Home could not credibly tell elites that it spoke for the president. For candidates, affiliation with Our Home did not offer any advantages over running independently. By undermining the party in 1995, Yeltsin sent no clear signal that a strong party of power would be supported in future elections (or even in the election in question).

In the Duma, the Our Home faction did not exercise a monopoly on lawmaking. Legislators from other parliamentary factions could lobby their interests directly with the Kremlin. Indeed, in the Second Duma, behind-the-scenes negotiation with multiple party factions and individual deputies was the core of the Kremlin's legislative strategy (e.g. Remington 2001). Because the party did not win anything close to a majority in the Duma, making it the sole basis for distributing legislative goods was not feasible. Although many SMD deputies joined Our Home, the Kremlin did not take significant steps to lure other deputies into the faction and turn it into a pro-government majority. Instead, Yeltsin played a divide and rule game in the Duma, making cross-faction alliances that shifted with each bill.

With respect to personnel, the party played no role in promoting cadres within either the executive or the legislative branch or in the regions. The chairman of the Duma was elected from the KPRF, while Our Home received one in five deputy chairmanships and only 10.7 percent of committee chairmanships. In the executive branch, the party played no role in selecting cadres in the Kremlin or in the government.

Why Yeltsin Did Not Invest in Our Home

Yeltsin's failure to associate himself with Our Home or seriously invest the Kremlin's resources in the party is puzzling in light of existing theory. Facing strong opposition from the communists, the literature predicts that Yeltsin should have invested in a strong party that could co-opt this opposition (Smith 2005) or confront it (Shefter 1994). In contrast to existing accounts (e.g. Huntington 1968), the regime's foundational crisis did not lead Yeltsin to create a strong regime party. What is more, historically low oil prices had left the Kremlin short on the rents that it could have used to buy off elites on an ad hoc basis. Thus, Yeltsin should have substituted for these fiscal shortcomings with an institution that could be used to co-opt elites (Gandhi 2008, Svolik 2012). But we observe the opposite type of behavior. Yeltsin undermined Our Home at every step. Why?

According to his aides, Yeltsin's advisers had repeatedly proposed the idea of creating and sustaining a party in order to create a pro-presidential majority in the Duma, but Yeltsin always refused.[25] Yeltsin made few public statements that explain this decision so it is hard to analyze his reasoning systemically, but the interviews he did give and the views of his advisers indicate that he had two motivations. The first was personal. Yeltsin stated on several occasions that the CPSU had left a bad impression on him. As he put it, "The CPSU had 'left a belch in the air.' [Therefore] I had an extreme reaction against the word party and an extreme reaction against all of this stuff" (quoted in Colton 2008, 349). This might explain Yeltsin's personal politics, but it does less to explain why he did not see utility in uniting his supporters around him through some sort of organization. In the same interview, Yeltsin repeated his oft-cited reasoning for remaining "above party politics":

[I] felt I should be above the interests of any party. I was the president. He should respect every registered party and every tendency in society; he should help them and listen to them… If I had been a member of one of the parties, I would have had to concern myself with lobbying for that party. That would have been incorrect… The president should be above all these things. (quoted in Colton 2008, 350)

It seems that Yeltsin was concerned that a party might limit his autonomy. Statements by Yeltsin's advisers help clarify this hesitancy to "lobby" for a particular party. In a collective memoir published in 2001, several of those advisers claimed that Yeltsin had been unwilling to commit himself to the party out of fear that the party's success would put Chernomyrdin in a position to challenge him in the coming presidential election (Baturin et al. 2001, 536–537). Chernomyrdin himself averred that the presidential administration withheld support for the party because they feared his ambitions in 1999 (Colton 2008, 350).

In an interview with the author, Sergei Filatov, head of the presidential administration in 1993–1996 and Our Home's coordinator in the Kremlin, also emphasized the difficulty of ensuring the loyalty of elites,

---

[25] Interview with former Yeltsin political adviser Georgi Satarov, June 24, 2009, Moscow, and interview with Vyazheslav Nikonov, June 18, 2012, Moscow.

especially regional governors. When asked whether Our Home's persistently low ratings were perceived by the presidential administration as being attributable to a lack of support from governors, Filatov responded:

> Of course. First of all, you need to remember that at that time there wasn't any unity among the regions on support for Yeltsin. Most regions voted as "wholes" and their voting was connected with the position of the leader there. There were pro-communist regions, there were national republics which absolutely didn't like Yeltsin... At that time, there just wasn't any special hope that we could secure the support of governors.[26]

When asked why the presidential administration did not decide to turn the OKS, which Filatov coordinated, into a party in 1996 after seeing that Our Home was dead in the water, Filatov noted:

> We didn't control the situation in the regions and even if we did control the situation, the parties [the pro-presidential forces that participated in the OKS] were always arguing with each other, they couldn't find a common language. If, in Moscow we would agree with the parties that we are going to support this or that candidate, in the regions they would say "No, we don't want to support that candidate." Of course, as we see now (referring to United Russia) that is possible, but at the time it was impossible.[27]

As the following excerpt from a May 2013 television interview indicates, Filatov also drew a direct connection between low oil prices in the 1990s and the government's inability to build a strong regime party:

> FILATOV: We couldn't go down that path [creating a pro-presidential party]. The creation of parties without financial support, without deciding the question of financing these parties ... you just couldn't create parties without this. Because, we would have either had to create parties controlled by oligarchs or create some parties that were financed by the government. And we just couldn't do the latter. We didn't have the possibility to fund parties.
>
> INTERVIEWER: So the main difference between your administration and Surkov's was that Surkov already had oil money and he could finance parties founded by him and you couldn't do that.
>
> FILATOV: I think yes. I think yes.

Note also the important point about oligarchs, which is consistent with the perspective offered in this book. In the view of the presidential administration, any party that they created would ultimately be controlled by oligarchs. Such a party would be difficult for the presidential administration to control. Yeltsin looked upon other elites as a threat, especially if they were organized and united at a time when they had

---

[26] Author's interview, May 20, 2013, Moscow.
[27] Ibid.

acquired so much de facto and de jure autonomy from the center. Yeltsin disliked working with a parliament that was filled with his opponents. He later expressed regret at supporting Our Home even in its watered-down form: Yeltsin thought that supporting a minority party in parliament undermined the authority of the government and the president.[28]

Yeltsin apparently reasoned a party might limit his freedom to maneuver and he would not be able to assure elite loyalty in any case. Inability to attract elite support for the party made sustaining it seem senseless. Thus, Yeltsin opted for a divide-and-rule strategy. He and his aides believed that the creation of two parties of power, one on the left and one on the right, would prevent these elites from setting up their own parties to challenge the Kremlin (Belin and Orttung 1997, 33). As it turned out, the creation of multiple parties of power only served to splinter elites further.

Why Elites Did Not Invest in Our Home Is Russia

For their part, regional elites were disinclined to affiliate with Our Home for two related reasons. First, their considerable autonomous political resources gave them little reason to limit their autonomy by linking their fates to a party of power. Second, since elites were so strong and Yeltsin's circle knew this, the Kremlin made no moves to invest in a dominant party. Without any signals from the Kremlin that it would be channeling policy, perks, and privilege through a single party, regional elites had even less reason to limit their freedom of maneuver by investing serious resources in Our Home. I discuss these points in turn.

As the 1990s progressed, the fiscal position of the Russian central state continued to deteriorate. This was in part due to the inefficiencies of stalled economic reform (Hellman 1998, Åslund 2007) and in part to historically low commodity prices, which the Soviet economy increasingly had come to rely upon (Gaidar 2003). In turn, regional elites used the resources accumulated in the early transition and the openings created by a weakened central state to entrench their political machines further.[29] Governors and mayors used control over regional regulatory schemes, local taxes, utilities, regional pension funds, and enterprise subsidies to construct elaborate clientelist networks among the economic elite that were predicated on the careful use of carrots and sticks. A particularly

[28] See Yeltsin's statements on Our Home Is Russia in *Presidentskii Marafon* (Moscow: Izdatelstvo AST, 2000).
[29] For several good treatments of the governors' machines during this period see Matsuzato (2001), Hale (2003), Sharafutdinova (2013).

relevant set of carrots were subsidies and government contracts. In the turbulent 1990s, when most Russian enterprises were experiencing losses, many regional businesses became dependent on subsidies and access to stable government contracts. Governors used these tools to exert control over regional businesses and accrue loyal clients among the economic elite. As sticks, regional and local authorities used their power to issue the myriad licenses, permits, and regulatory approvals that are required to operate any business or organization in Russia as leverage over economic and social actors. Indeed, one of the most common justifications for regional authorities to close an unfriendly business, newspaper, or social organization was a "failed" fire safety inspection. Regional leaders and enterprise directors also extended their machines into society. In the vacuum of power left by the weakening Russian central state, regional authorities took up the mantle of providing many social services that Moscow was unable to fund (see, for example, Stoner-Weiss 1997). They did this through formal budget allocations, as well as through informal off-budget programs funded by "voluntary" donations from regional businesses. And through a combination of economic and political pressure, regional leaders and financial industrial groups exercised control over many of those local media organs that they did not own outright. Social organizations, political parties, and interest groups were also often incorporated into governors' political machines.

Regional elites also accrued significant direct economic power. During the transition, two groups – business elites and regional executives – accumulated significant economic resources that could easily be converted into political resources. The most lucrative privatization auctions concentrated a large percentage of productive assets in the hands of relatively few well-positioned individuals. In turn, these newly minted oligarchs expanded their business empires into a variety of other spheres. These so-called financial industrial groups acquired vast swaths of Russia's productive economic assets and, in the process, a great deal of usable political resources.[30]

For their part, regional authorities had control over the privatization of small and medium-size enterprises, and receipts from the sale of these enterprises could be kept by regional governments (Shleifer and Treisman 2001). More significantly, the privatization of these enterprises could be used by governors to create or reward loyal clients. Regional authorities were also frequently allowed to take control of enterprises

---

[30] "Financial–industrial group" is a term used to describe the economic empires built out of privatized enterprises by major Russian businessmen and companies in the mid-1990s (see, for example, Johnson 1997, Orttung 2004, Zubarevich 2005, and Hale 2006). These financial–industrial groups usually began from some core privatized enterprise and expanded outward, so that they eventually held banks and diversified assets across several sectors. The most politically ambitious groups also acquired major media outlets.

in their regions, ostensibly for later privatization (Hale 2003, 241). This constituted a de facto transfer of property from the center to the regions, as these enterprises either became long-term regional government assets or were later privatized in auctions tightly controlled by regional elites. Furthermore, by the mid-1990s, Moscow's fiscal problems led it to transfer control over regional enterprises to local governments in lieu of budgetary transfers. In the late 1990s and early 2000s, governors continued to strengthen their economic hand by using cooperative courts to orchestrate takeovers of bankrupt private enterprises (Slider 2005). Naturally, this control over regional economic resources supplemented and was supplemented by the political resources and autonomy that regional authorities had accrued during the transition.[31]

Leaders of Russia's ethnic republics also perfected their political machines as the 1990s wore on. These governors (presidents, in most cases) initially leveraged on their ability to mobilize ethnic strife to win greater sovereignty from Moscow. As time wore on and their political machines became the source of stability in those regions, these leaders increasingly promoted themselves to Moscow as indispensable guarantors of ethnic and social harmony in their regions. As election results in the late 1990s and early 2000s showed, ethnic leaders were the most adept at using their political machines to garner voters for themselves or, if it suited their interests, the Kremlin.

The power of Russia's regional leaders was reflected in their confrontational stance toward Moscow. The gradual introduction of direct gubernatorial elections between 1991 and 1996 had codified and strengthened the political independence of regional governors. At the federal level, governors used their ex officio seats in the Federation Council to block attempts by Yeltsin to restructure the balance of power between Moscow and the regions (e.g. Solnick 2000, Remington 2001).[32] In their own regions, elites made a practice of adopting laws that contravened the

---

[31] The nature of the relationship between regional administrations and regional business was, and remains, of singular importance to Russian political economy. In some regions the relationship was characterized by cooperation between business and the authorities; in others there was open conflict. In many cases the regional administration was captured by business, while in others the state closely tutored business (Lapina and Chirikova 1999). Stoner-Weiss (1997) has stressed how the factors influencing cooperation between these groups contributed to public goods provision during the transition. Others have focused on the consequences of these relationships for electoral politics (Turovsky 2002, Hale 2006) and economic development (Lapina and Chirikova 1999, Remington 2010).

[32] In 1998, the Federation Council rejected a law unifying how systems of representative government were organized in the regions. When the law finally passed in 1999, its content was heavily influenced by regional leaders. In another example, the Federation Council rejected a bill in April 1997 that would have subjected all bilateral treaties to legislative ratification (Solnick 2000).

Russian Constitution or laws passed by the Federal Assembly. Some reports suggest that as many as 22,000 regional legal acts were in contravention of the Russian Constitution in 1996 (Stoner-Weiss 1999). In turn, opposition to Moscow often generated significant economic benefits for the regions, as, Moscow sought to buy back the support of oppositional regions with intergovernmental transfers (Treisman 1998). In sum, by the late 1990s, Russia was seemingly trapped in a vicious decentralizing cycle whereby the considerable informal resources of regional elites allowed them to make demands for more formal autonomy from the center, which, in turn, gave them additional resources to strengthen their political machines.

With such expansive resources in their possession, regional elites were in a very strong position to influence election outcomes. Regional leaders used control over local media, law enforcement, courts, tax inspectorates, licensing agencies, public utilities, appointments, budgets, and prosecutors to support preferred candidates and frustrate those who opposed them. Taken together, these resources are sometimes referred to as *administrative resources*, and regional leaders used them to attract armies of loyal clients, who, in turn, helped them win elections.

Observers disagree on the exact role regional leaders played in Yeltsin's reelection campaign. Some such as McFaul (1997) highlight the electoral importance of Yeltsin's alliances with key regional leaders. Of 89 heads of regional administrations 77 ended up endorsing Yeltsin. Others, such as Brudny (1996), however, have pointed out that Yeltsin changed course in his campaign after the December 1995 parliamentary elections. In those elections, regional governors demonstrated that, while they could certainly generate votes, they were undependable in their support for the Kremlin. According to Brudny, Yeltsin's advisers abandoned the idea of trying to force regional leaders to generate votes for Yeltsin when it became apparent that many governors were either cutting deals on the side with the communist candidate, Zyuganov, or hedging their bets. Whether they were important to Yeltsin's victory or not, the issue was not whether regional leaders controlled the resources to secure votes, but rather, whether they could be controlled by the Kremlin in doing so. In the end, some governors put their machines to work for Yeltsin, while others equivocated or supported Zyuganov.

Regional economic elites gained significant political power during this period as well. Powerful enterprises and newly created financial–industrial groups penetrated and captured regional legislatures. Enterprise and collective farm directors continued to enjoy the same advantages in visibility, authority, and administrative resources that they had enjoyed in the 1990s. Beginning in the mid-1990s large financial–industrial groups with vast material and organizational resources began to field lists of candidates and support independents in regional elections. Golosov (2003) reports that 41.2 percent of all regional deputies in the period 1995–1999 were businessmen. This is an increase from the 23.5 percent who Darrell Slider (1996) reported were "enterprise managers" in the regional parliaments elected in 1994.

At the national level, the power of major financial–industrial groups was famously demonstrated in Yeltsin's reelection campaign when the Russia's two main television networks, belonging to Vladimir Gusinsky's Most group and Boris Berozovsky's LogoVaz group, provided wholly positive coverage of Yeltsin's reelection campaign. Financial–industrial groups also financed the Duma campaigns of most political parties and many independents (Hale 2006).

Thus, already by 1996, the Kremlin had learned that winning elections depended, in large part, on gaining the support of powerful regional leaders. Despite the fact that the regions were financially dependent on Moscow and that the Russian presidency was the single most powerful political institution in the country, the political machines of regional leaders were increasingly becoming the de facto basis of political stability in Russia. While the Kremlin could take on any individual regional elite or oligarch (even in the 1990s) it was in no position to undermine them as a whole. Their ability to secure votes and maintain stability in the regions forced the central government to grant them further autonomy, which regional elites then used to strengthen their political machines further. All that prevented regional elites from capturing the state during this period were their own collective action problems (Solnick 2000).

When positioned against the continuing weakness of central state institutions, Yeltsin's faltering health and poll numbers, and sustained economic crisis, the substantial autonomous resources of Russia's regional and business elites were even more significant. They could use these resources to achieve many of their most important political goals, such as retaining office and expanding their spheres of influence. Thus, elites had little motivation to relinquish these resources to a party institution that could limit their freedom of maneuver.

Indeed, it is telling that 46 percent of appointed governors joined the Our Home political council in May 1995, while only 33 percent of elected governors did. Those who were more dependent on Moscow were more likely to join. This conclusion is further supported by the fact that the average margin of victory for those elected governors who joined Our Home's political council was 32 percent, while the average margin of victory for those who did not was 47 percent. Moreover, only four presidents of Russia's 21 ethnic republics joined Our Home. In sum, those with autonomous electoral or ethnic resources were more likely to eschew making even shallow commitments to Our Home. As I show in Chapters 4, 6, and 7, this pattern, whereby strong governors with autonomous resources were the most likely to eschew affiliating with the party of power, was repeated during the creation of Unity and United Russia.

Qualitative evidence paints a similar picture. When asked about his party affiliation choices in 1999, then–Perm governor, Gennady Igumnov, said:

I consciously avoid talking about the fact that I am a member of NDR. I am Chernomyrdin's deputy in NDR. No one can accuse me of paying special attention to NDR in Perm. I never publicize the fact that I am in the NDR leadership. If I lean toward just one party, then I will be closed to others. Then when KPRF leaders come to me in order to discuss some situation (and they are always coming to me; I just recently sat with them for an hour). It is totally reasonable that oblast leaders don't talk about their party affiliations, because this would push them away from others. (quoted in Lapina and Chirikova 2000, 160–161)

Much like Yeltsin, Russian governors placed a high priority on being autonomous from party influence. In a rich study of "regional parties of power" during the 1990s, the Russian political analyst Boris Makarenko (1998) demonstrated that the most powerful Russian governors were most likely to create their own political parties. His study led him to conclude that "when it came to building parties, governors clearly consider autonomy from the center to be a more important goal than cozying up to the center through party channels" (15).

Kremlin Signals and Elites' Reluctance to Invest in Our Home

For Our Home to have become a dominant party, regional elites would have had to invest their resources in it and the Kremlin would have had to make the party an avenue for accessing patronage, careers, and policy. Even if regional elites had been inclined to cooperate with the Kremlin under the aegies of Our Home, they would have to have had some assurance from the Kremlin that it was going to channel these spoils through Our Home. As we have seen, Yeltsin and the presidential administration gave no such signals. The administration took no steps to build a legislative coalition around Our Home, supported all manner of candidates in national and regional elections, made appointments without regard to potential appointees' partisan affiliation, and, eventually, abused key members of the party.

Yeltsin's initial decision to support more than one party of power in the 1995 elections made regional elites unsure of the Kremlin's intentions. In an interview with one of Yeltsin's biographers, Chernomyrdin reported having difficulty rounding up the support of regional elites because they could not "figure out" whether the Kremlin was "together" or not (Colton 2008, 350).

Indeed, the Kremlin's lack of support for Our Home became especially clear as the bloc unraveled in 1998. In March of that year, Yeltsin removed the party leader, Chernomyrdin, from the post of prime minister, a move that alarmed many leaders of Our Home. In May, the appointment of a nonpartisan junior member of the government, Georgii Gabuniya, to the post of minister for industry sparked an angry reaction from Our Home's parliamentary faction leader, Alexander Shokhin, who had expressed interest in the position. Shortly after, Shokhin announced that, since no one from Our Home had been recruited into the new government, Our Home would no longer support the government.[33] That same month, the powerful governor of Samara Oblast, once one of Our Home's most vocal supporters, left the party, saying that the bloc's decision to declare its support for Chernomyrdin in the 2000 presidential ballot was ill conceived, since Chernomyrdin was "just a former prime-minister."[34] This move occurred just as Kabardino-Balkaria President Valery Kokov refused to accept the post of deputy leader in Our Home and Saratov Governor Dmitry Ayatskov decide to desert the movement in order to set up his own party.[35] In the months that followed, the stream of defections only grew.

3.4 Conclusion

Several factors undermined the construction of a dominant party in Yeltsin era Russia. Yeltsin's personal aversion to the CPSU and the complexities of the transition period likely militated against the construction of a dominant party, but this chapter has argued that commitment problems between Yeltsin and powerful elites further undermined party-building efforts. Indeed, the story of Our Home Is Russia illustrates how strong elites can undermine the formation of a dominant party even

---

[33] "Our Home Is Russia Outraged over New Appointment" *NUPI Chronology of Events*, May 11, 1998. www2.nupi.no/cgi-win//Russland/krono.exe?2192
[34] *Moskovsky Komsomolets*, May 8, 1998.
[35] Ibid.

better than the case of Russia's Choice. In the 1990s, elites had accumulated significant autonomous resources that were used to construct powerful political machines. The resources of regional elites were so significant that many observers doubted Russia's future as a single state. Collectively the governors were more powerful than the Kremlin. And while collective action problems prevented governors from capturing the state – as they would again in 1999 – their machines gave governors the resources to achieve many of their political goals autonomously. Cooperation with the Kremlin could still be useful to individual elites, but elites wanted to enjoy the support and resources of the Kremlin without actually giving up their autonomy to conduct their own campaigns as they saw fit, support their preferred candidates, and appoint whomever they wanted. Despite all this, Yeltsin might still have induced elites to join a dominant party if he had been able to commit himself to sustaining one. But the high possibility of elite defections and the very real possibility that such a party could be used against him led Yeltsin to conclude that supporting a party was too risky. The irony, of course, was that by neglecting his own pro-presidential party, Yeltsin ensured that this fear would become a self-fulfilling prophecy.

Thus, Our Home Is Russia was not a dominant party. It did not keep elites loyal, it did not reduce the transaction costs that Yeltsin faced in bargaining with the Duma, and it was not an effective tool for coordinating pro-regime candidates in elections. For elites, membership in the party did not significantly reduce the costs associated with lobbying the Kremlin for spoils. Yeltsin did not link his reputation to the party, sanction institutional changes that privileged Our Home Is Russia, or take steps to relinquish parallel institutions for dealing with elites. Nor did he give Our Home any control over policy, rents, or careers. Elites did not link their reputations to the party, and they retained their own political machines and parties outside the party. Thus, Our Home was not in a position to solve commitment problems for the two sides.

4 The Emergence of a Dominant Party in Russia: United Russia, Putin, and Regional Elites, 2000–2010

I have argued that leaders and elites are most likely to build a dominant party when elites are strong enough that leaders need to co-opt them in order to govern the country, but not so strong that they themselves are inclined to eschew investment in the dominant party. In this chapter, I explore this hypothesis by examining Russia's experience with ruling parties in the late 1990s and 2000s.

As the 1999–2000 election season approached, the Kremlin had no ruling party. A last ditch effort was made to create a new party of power, Unity. But, as with previous parties of power, this project failed to attract serious commitments from either the Kremlin or elites. In 1999, governors were collectively stronger than the president. The only thing stopping them from capturing the presidency was their own inability to coordinate. Given their substantial resources, few were inclined to link their fates to a centralized dominant party. For its part, the Kremlin feared that it could not control a ruling party composed of these powerful elites. Thus, the Kremlin refrained from making serious investments in Unity. In turn, the Kremlin's reluctance to commit to Unity – and only Unity – gave elites even less reason to invest in the party.

However, in the early 2000s circumstances began to change. A surge in oil prices, a growing economy, and Putin's high popularity ratings strengthened the federal center vis-à-vis regional elites. Elites were still very powerful and the Kremlin needed to co-opt them if it wanted to win elections and govern the regions. But as the federal center strengthened, elites became more inclined to cooperate with it. Because these elites were no longer so strong that they would shirk any obligations laid out for them in a dominant party, Putin felt comfortable investing his own resources in such a party. By publicly endorsing the party, speaking at party conferences, heading the party list, and eventually becoming party chairman, Putin associated himself much more closely with his pro-presidential party than Yeltsin had ever done. In turn, Putin's signals of support emboldened elites to make their own investments. This dynamic led both sides to invest more in the ruling party than ever before. The result was United Russia.

This chapter draws heavily upon my interviews with political elites conducted in Moscow, Yaroslavl, Rybinsk, Perm, Kurgan, Kirov, Chelyabinsk, Ekaterinburg, and Yoshkar-Ola between 2007 and 2014. Because my primary interest is in the formation of United Russia, I include only limited discussion of events after the 2011–2012 election cycle. Some of those developments are addressed in Chapter 5 and in Chapter 9.

4.1 Initial Failures: The Story of Unity, 1999–2001

From Our Home Is Russia to Unity

By early 1999, Our Home was a rump organization. Its parliamentary leader, Alexander Shokhin, had deserted it, and most governors had declared their intention to leave, begun to build their own political parties, or signed up with competing parties.[1] It retained a faction in the Duma, and its leadership prepared to run in the 1999 parliamentary election, but the party could no longer claim special ties to the Kremlin.

To understand the Kremlin's next steps in this situation, we must first understand the position that regional elites found themselves in during the run-up to the 2000 presidential election.[2] With Yeltsin still ailing, it was clear that he would not be running for a third term, but no successor was yet apparent. Governors, for their part, wanted good relations with the president. For all the formal and informal autonomy that regional leaders accumulated in the 1990s, the Russian presidency, which was vested with extensive formal powers and direct control over a massive state apparatus, remained the strongest single office in the country.

Every governor wanted to support the winning candidate, but it was not clear which candidate this might be. The governors' dilemma was made worse by the fact that no institution (e.g. a party) existed to help them coordinate any such endorsement. Collectively, the governors (or a majority of governors) could put their political machines to work and

---

[1] In the end, six governors were included in Our Home's 1999 party list.
[2] The following draws heavily on accounts in Makarkin (1999), McFaul and Colton (2003), Hale (2004a), (2006), and the collection of essays in Hesli and Reissinger (2003).

4.1 Initial Failures: The Story of Unity, 1999–2001

have almost any candidate elected, but, for an individual governor, it was not clear which of many possible candidates should be supported. The timing of the Russian electoral cycle, in which parliamentary elections are held four months before presidential ones, meant that the leader(s) of the best showing noncommunist party in the December 1999 parliamentary elections would be well positioned for presidential elections scheduled in March 2000.

In this setting, some of Russia's strongest and most ambitious governors began forming their own political movements to contest the December 1999 parliamentary elections. The first to move in this direction was Moscow Mayor Yurii Luzhkov, who, in December 1998, launched a political movement called Otechestvo (Fatherland), that drew together 11 governors in support of the bloc's demands for more federal attention to "regional matters." To all, however, it was apparent that Fatherland would be a vehicle for Luzhkov's own presidential ambitions. In January of 1999, another governors' party emerged with the creation of Konstantin Titov's (Samara Oblast) Golos Rossii. This grouping, which Titov initiated to further his own presidential campaign, attracted the support of 20 governors. In April 1999, another major governors' party, Vsya Rossii (All Russia), was created by Tatarstan President Mintimer Shaimiyev and St. Petersburg Governor Vladimir Yakovlev. Seventeen governors participated in this effort. Several smaller governors' parties were also started in early 1999 including, Aman Tuleev's (Kemerovo Oblast) Vozrozhdeniye (Revival) and Edinstvo (Unity) bloc, but these efforts were less successful in attracting regional leaders.

At first, the flurry of organization did not trouble the presidential administration. Yeltsin's advisers believed that the governors would be unable to present a united front against the Kremlin. In fact, the Kremlin encouraged these divisions and, at various times, offered its tacit support to each of the governors' parties, seeking to fragment the field by airing the possibility that it might support each successive attempt to organize. Thus, by the summer of 1999, there was still no certainty about who would be the most likely presidential successor and the governors had divided into several camps in nascent support of several prospective presidential hopefuls.

As Olga Shvetsova (2003) has usefully pointed out, the governors during this period were facing an electoral coordination dilemma. Individual governors wanted to back the candidate/party that a majority of other governors backed. After all, this candidate/party would surely win. The problem for each governor lay in knowing how other governors would behave. What was needed was a signal or focal point to coordinate actors' behavior on one of several possible equilibria. An existing party of power and/or an incumbent president might have created such a focal point, but neither was on hand in early 1999.

On August 4, 1999, the governors seemed to have found their focal point when Luzhkov's Fatherland formed an alliance with All-Russia. The new bloc announced its intention to support the presidential candidacy of one of Russia's most popular politicians at the time, Yevgeny Primakov. Primakov was well respected, since, as foreign minister, he had stood up to the West over NATO expansion and, as prime minister, had presided over Russia's first months of economic recovery following the 1998 financial crisis. Fatherland–All Russia's (OVR, hereafter) imminent endorsement of Primakov seemed to cement a focal point for the governors to rally around his candidacy.

The Kremlin was startled to action by the OVR alliance and its support of Primakov. Yeltsin's circle was characterized by a coterie of political and business elites whose wealth and power depended crucially on their access to the president.[3] Indeed, Yeltsin and his coterie had reason to believe that they might be subject to criminal investigation under a Primakov presidency. If they did not control presidential succession, Yeltsin insiders risked losing access to the power and privilege they enjoyed.

The Kremlin recognized the importance of the governors and devised a plan to counter OVR, which depended on the governors' coordination dilemmas and their enormous political resources. It centered on the creation of an alternative governors' bloc that would be given the tacit backing of the Kremlin and newly appointed prime minister, Vladimir Putin. The goal of creating the bloc was to divide the governors and ensure that a majority did not line up behind one of the governors' parties existing at the time. The bloc's symbolic leader would be the popular Emergency Situations Minister Sergei Shoigu. At the September 1999 session of the Federation Council, the Kremlin circulated a vague open letter calling for "Clean and Honorable Elections." The letter was perceived by observers as a statement by the signatories to coordinate their efforts in favor of the Kremlin's candidate. Thirty-nine governors

---

[3] Members of this circle included the oligarchs Boris Berozovsky and Roman Abramovich; Yeltsin's daughter, Tatyana Dyachenko; Presidential Administration Chief Alexander Voloshin; former Presidential Administration Chief Valentin Yumashev; Deputy Presidential Administration Chiefs Igor Shabdurasulov and Vladislav Surkov; and other members of the presidential administration.

4.1 Initial Failures: The Story of Unity, 1999–2001

signed the letter. Then, at the end of September, Putin invited a group of regional leaders to his office to assure them that the Kremlin would not be supporting Fatherland and that it approved of the new bloc, which did not yet have an official name. This meeting led to another letter signed by 32 governors agreeing to help Sergei Shoigu win the December parliamentary elections. On October 3 and 6, the bloc, now called the Mezhregionalnnoye Dvizheniye "Edinstvo" (Interregional Movement "Unity"), held its founding congress.

Unity's ratings were initially stagnant, hovering at around 5–8 percent throughout October and early November. But just before the elections Unity's rating skyrocketed and it finished with 23 percent of the party-list vote, ahead of the Kremlin's main rival, Fatherland–All Russia, and more than any other party except the KPRF.

Unity's meteoric rise was clearly linked to Putin's own rising star as a presidential candidate and, crucially, the signals that Putin then sent about his support for the movement. By late November, Putin's ratings had soared on the shoulders of Berezovsky's media empire and the prime minister's firm reaction to a series of terrorist attacks in August and September 1999. As Russia's most popular politician and the most likely candidate to be supported by the Kremlin in the upcoming election, Putin spoke before a gathering of governors on November 24, announcing that he would be "voting for Unity, as a citizen." As Shvetsova (2003) has emphasized, this endorsement from the Kremlin's popular favorite cemented the recoordination of a plurality of governors away from the "Primakov Equilibrium" to a "Putin Equilibrium." The best evidence of this was that while Putin's rating as presidential candidate had climbed to 42 percent in mid-November, Unity's support remained at 8 percent. But the week after Putin's address Unity's rating jumped by 10 percentage points (Shvetsova 2003, 226).

Putin would go on to win the March presidential elections in a landslide. For its part, Unity set up a parliamentary faction in the Duma that initially counted 81 deputies (18 percent of the chamber). This number included the 63 mandates it had won, as well as 18 independents and defectors from other parties. Thus, as Yeltsin had to do in the First and Second Dumas, Putin would need to build shifting and cross-factional majorities in the Third Duma.

Like its predecessors, Unity's position was weak in the regions. The party was not an attempt to co-opt Russia's regional elites into a dominant party, but rather a hastily constructed effort to keep them divided. Despite the fact that some 40-odd governors supported its campaign, Unity could claim no governors as party members. In 44 gubernatorial elections held in 2000, not a single winning candidate accepted a Unity nomination. Most governors hedged their bets by supporting multiple parties and continuing to nurture their own regional parties.

Among other regional elites Unity's position was no stronger. Regional parliamentary elections held after 1998 were even more nonpartisan than in the mid-1990s. On average, only 14 percent of regional legislative seats were won by party nominees between 1999 and 2003. And Unity won *zero* seats in 81 percent of the regional elections held between 1999 and July 2003.[4]

Unity's organization was minimal. The movement held a campaign rally for President Putin in February 2000, but it was not until May that the party had a founding congress that established Unity as a political party in the juridical sense. While it had branches in all regions, none of the political elite were members and branches had no permanent employees or fixed budgets. The incipient party played no role in the selection or advancement of cadres in the executive or legislative branch. And because its faction in the Duma did not hold a majority, it could not claim for its members unrivaled access to the president or the government.

By early 2001, it seemed that Unity, like its predecessors, would become just another discarded party of power. And, indeed, if we view Unity as an organizational entity, this is what happened. In early 2001 negotiations began for the creation of a new pro-presidential party that would be formed out of a merger between Unity and OVR. On December 1, 2001, the two parties formally merged to create the All-Russia Party "Unity and Fatherland – United Russia." But before I turn to discuss that new party, I first discuss how the Kremlin and elites related to Unity and how their actions prevented the party from becoming dominant in 1999 and 2000.

The Kremlin and Unity

From 1998 to 2001, the Kremlin was still very hesitant to invest unilaterally in a dominant party. Until Unity's last-minute creation in September 1999, the Kremlin made almost no moves to indicate that it would be investing in its own ruling party. Indeed, it was not until the fall of 1999 that the governors could even be sure that the Kremlin would not support OVR. According to one of OVR's leading figures, Bashkortostan President Murtaza Rakhimov, OVR's leaders had approached the Kremlin on several occasions to ask its blessing for the creation of a

---

[4] Golosov (2003). These data are for United Russia after 2001.

4.1 Initial Failures: The Story of Unity, 1999–2001

party of power but had never received a clear signal. Rakhimov claimed that the governors finally received tacit support for the creation of All Russia in 1998, but needless to say, the Kremlin did not follow up on that promise.[5]

The Kremlin instead preferred to keep elites guessing by extending its support to various parties so that elites would not coordinate on one party. Indeed, even after it sent signals that it would be supporting the Unity bloc, it continued to hedge its bets. During the campaign, the Kremlin also gave its support to Soyuz Pravykh Sil (Union of Right Forces), a Right–center party that included prominent liberal politicians from the 1990s as well as the rump of Titov's Golos Rossii movement. Putin even appeared on television with the bloc's leader one week before the election to express support for the party's platform.[6]

Putin did not speak at Unity's founding congress, but he did avow later in the campaign that he would vote for it as a citizen, and in March 2000, Putin spoke at a conference of the movement's supporters. This was the first time in history that a Russian president had officially participated in a party event.

Nonetheless, the idea of turning Unity into a dominant party was not yet on the Kremlin's mind in 2000. Unity was designed as a governors' bloc and was not intended to be positioned as a pro-Kremlin party (Ivanov 2008, 43). It held far less than a majority in the Duma, and, like his predecessor, Putin used patronage and policy concessions to build shifting coalitions that were composed of Unity and other factions (Remington 2006). Nonpartisan deputies from the single member districts were key to passing legislation. Presumably, the Kremlin could have invested resources in attracting SMD deputies to the party (e.g. the Kremlin could have started privileging Unity members above others for promotions and patronage), but the Kremlin did not do this. In fact, some sources indicate that Putin explicitly rejected his advisers' proposals to begin the process of merging Fatherland–All Russia and Unity in 2000 (Ivanov 2008, 76). Deputies not affiliated with the party of power felt secure in knowing that they could advance their interests outside the party.

In regional elections, the Kremlin continued to hedge its bets as well. In 1998 and 1999, the Kremlin devoted minimal attention to regional elections. It did not even organize a coordinating organization (the OKS) as it had in 1996. Regional leaders were left to their own devices. The

---

[5] "Putin – ne plokhoi paren" *Segodnya*, February 15, 2000.
[6] "Putin podderzhal SPS" *Vostochno-Sibirskaya Pravda*, December 17, 1999.

president's special envoys in the regions, who were, in part, charged with ensuring the election of suitable governors, gave no exclusive support to Unity-supported candidates. Hale (2004b) reports that the presidential envoys supported Unity (later United Russia) candidates in only 4 of the 24 gubernatorial elections when presidential envoys chose to endorse candidates between May 2000 and May 2003. In three cases, the presidential envoy even worked against the candidate endorsed by the party of power. The result was that multiple pro-Kremlin candidates competed with one another in many races. In a number of regions, this led to the victory of opposition candidates.

Elites and Unity

Before it joined with Fatherland–All Russia to create United Russia, Unity fared no better than Our Home at attracting investments from elites. The initial letter signed by regional leaders in support of honest elections was extremely vague, and many leaders later claimed that they did not realize it was a statement of support for the Unity bloc (Lussier 2002, 66). In the end, while 50 leaders signed one of the two letters of support for Unity, only 1 (Vladimir Platov of Tver) actually ran on the party list and only 8 appeared at a joint press conference in September announcing the formation of the bloc. Thirty-eight of the 50 governors who signed the letter ended up being affiliated with other parties during the election. Most governors were actively hostile to the party. The leader of the Unity branch in Samara provides a vivid example:

Relations with the [regional] authorities are very difficult. For a long time Titov [then-governor, and longtime Yeltsin ally] forbade everyone from participating in the party. And, of course, those who had something to lose were afraid to get close to us. He [Titov] pulled away a lot of key figures and we ended up in competition with the governor.[7]

The 1999 State Duma elections were the ultimate demonstration of how the post-Soviet elite sought to avoid exclusive affiliations with federal parties that would limit their autonomy. Their preferred strategy was to hedge their bets by making provisional commitments to multiple political forces. The pattern of gubernatorial affiliation on Election Day was a snarl of crisscrossing and overlapping attachments. Of Russia's 88 governors, 36 maintained dual affiliations with at least two national parties/blocs in 1999 (Our Home, Unity, Fatherland, All-Russia, Voice of

---

[7] Quoted in Lapina and Chirikova (2002, 247).

4.1 Initial Failures: The Story of Unity, 1999–2001

Russia, KPRF).[8] As an adviser to Yaroslavl Governor Anatoly Lysytsin in 1999 put it:

> When the presidential administration asked Lysytsin to assist in organizing a Unity branch in the region, he did not react in a positive manner. He had been a supporter of Otechestvo. So he didn't want to work seriously on it. At the same time, he didn't want to refuse outright… [Therefore] he asked Tonkov [head of the local tire factory, one of the region's largest enterprises] to organize the party. In turn, Tonkov asked one of his subordinates to head up the effort.[9]

In turn, Lysytsin was said to have advocated the principle of "a party for every oligarch," whereby he encouraged the main business figures in the region, most of whom were his clients, to support various parties (Lapina and Chirikova 2002, 258–259).

In the elections themselves, Unity was unable to attract strong candidates under its banner. Only nine candidates nominated by Unity were elected in SMD races. Incumbents and candidates with administrative resources accruing from their positions in regional and federal state administrative apparatuses overwhelmingly chose to run as independents.[10] In regional legislative elections, the party was almost nonexistent. As noted previously, Unity failed to have a single candidate elected in almost 80 percent of regional elections. Where it did win seats, it won, on average, only 21.6 percent of seats (Golosov 2003). Party legislative factions were rare during this period, but when they did form, they were most often created on the basis of regional parties or interest groups (see, for example, Slider 2001), and Unity factions emerged in only a handful of regions (Glubotskii and Kynev 2003).

In gubernatorial elections held between 1999 and 2001, governors eschewed entanglement with the new party of power nearly as much as they did with Our Home in the mid-1990s. Instead, as in the 1990s, they relied on their own regionally based parties and political machines to secure election or, in 66 percent of cases, reelection. Unity did not

---

[8] Author's calculations based on data presented in McFaul, Petrov, and Ryabov (1999). In fact, this number is only the tip of the dual-affiliation iceberg, because it does not count the regional parties and movements that many governors backed as well. Ten governors made three or more "commitments." Astrakhan Governor Anatolii Guzhvin was especially fond of electoral blocs; he signed the letter in support of the Voice of Russia group, joined All-Russia, signed the statement of 39 in tacit support of Unity, and simultaneously sat on the Political Council of Our Home.

[9] Author's interview with Alexander Prokhorov, Yaroslavl, June 11, 2009.

[10] Only 2 incumbents ran for reelection as Unity SMD candidates, as opposed to 91 who ran as independents. Unity attracted 2 candidates with high-ranking state administrative backgrounds, whereas 47 candidates with such backgrounds ran as independents (Golosov 2002).

officially nominate any candidates in these elections. When endorsements were issued, the party leadership often split and supported different candidates (Turovsky 2002, 25).

Russia's business elite kept its political investments diversified as well. Regional business was clearly not affiliated with Unity, as indicated by Unity's dismal representation in regional legislatures. Instead, major regional enterprise directors preferred to run as independent candidates and use their resources to support their own slates of candidates (Turovsky 2002, Hale 2006).

Why Elites Were Hesitant to Invest in Unity

The inability of elites to commit to Unity is explained by the same factors that prevented elites from making investments in Our Home Is Russia. In short, they were too strong in autonomous resources. The political machines of elites were at their strongest at the end of the 1990s. Even if a dominant party could have made them better off by reducing uncertainty over access to spoils, there was too much to risk in relinquishing even partial control over their political machines, and, for this very reason, signals from the Kremlin that it would begin investing in institutions to ameliorate this commitment problem were not forthcoming. Thus, because of the risks and the lack of party-building signals from the Kremlin, the governors sought to pursue their own individual, diversified strategies of political advancement.

By 1998, Russia's regional elites had grown extremely powerful at the expense of the central state. In 1998, oil prices reached $15.81/barrel, their lowest inflation-adjusted level since before the Second World War. The worsening fiscal position of Moscow culminated in the August 1998 financial crisis and debt default. The central state's capacity to provide social services, levy taxes, pay wages, and enforce the rule of law was at an all-time low. The crisis led to renewed calls for autonomy by regional leaders, who argued that the crisis demonstrated the necessity for the regions to have more fiscal autonomy in order to insulate themselves from crises that originated in Moscow. Not surprisingly, Yeltsin, who was in and out of the hospital during this period, had approval ratings in the single digits.

In Chapter 3, I outlined how regional governors took advantage of a weak central state to build powerful political machines. To a lesser degree, mayors, municipal administration heads, and other local politicians built similar machines at lower levels. The late 1990s gave regional elites extra time to entrench these machines and create stronger bonds of mutual support with subelites. By the late 1990s, these regionally based political

4.1 Initial Failures: The Story of Unity, 1999–2001

machines had become the primary channels of social control and, thus, political power in Russia.

I also have reviewed how enterprise directors used leverage over employees to build their own expansive political machines. Having won big through insider privatization in the mid-1990s, Russia's business elite began turning its sights on expansion in the regions by the end of the 1990s. Although the financial crisis had weakened many of the most prolific financial industrial groups, their immense material resources outmatched any other nonstate entity in the late 1990s. Moreover, as several scholars have noted, the financial crisis actually strengthened regional firms vis-à-vis Moscow-based firms, since the former were less tied up in the capital's banking sector (e.g. Turovsky 2002).

The political strength of Russia's regional elite was demonstrated clearly in the late 1990s. Their strategy of eschewing major party affiliation and building their own regionally based movements to contest regional elections paid dividends. From 1998 to 2001, the incumbency rate of governors was 66 percent (up from 54 percent in the 1996–1997 electoral cycle). In regional legislative elections, the governors successfully packed many regional legislatures with their own clients (e.g. Slider 2001)

In national elections, the power of governors was demonstrated just as clearly. The entire drama surrounding the 1999 elections centered on which party the governors would support. Indeed, Myagkov (2003) shows that Unity received 30.4 percent of the vote in regions led by governors who supported Unity, compared to 7.5 percent in those regions led by OVR governors (Unity received 23 percent nationwide). OVR received 36.9 percent of the vote in those regions led by OVR governors and 15.9 percent in regions headed by Unity governors (OVR won 13 percent nationwide).[11] Studies of the election results would later reveal that strong governors were exceptionally successful at having their clients elected in the single member district contests of the 1999 election.[12]

Business also flexed its electoral muscles during this period. The late 1990s and early 2000s were a period when business engaged in greater and more direct participation in politics (Turovsky 2002, Hale 2006). In

---

[11] That this correlation is not due to ideological congruence among voters' preferences, governor's bloc affiliation, and electoral results is demonstrated by the electoral blocs' self-professed lack of ideology. Unity's organizers consciously sought to avoid a programmatic ideology in its campaign (McFaul and Colton 2003). As one Unity-supporting governor stated, "The ideology of Unity is the lack of any kind of ideology" (quoted in Hale 2004a, 184).
[12] Russian Regional Report, December 22, 1999. See also Hale (2006).

the 1999 Duma elections, large financial industrial groups had significant success in getting their candidates elected to the Duma and placed on key committees (Hale 2006). In some regions, large companies attempted to capture the state by having their own executives elected to governorships.

In the late 1990s, regional legislatures transformed from representative arenas in which regional business was one of the main lobbying groups into institutional fora completely dominated by competing firms and financial–industrial groups. A sample of deputies in 43 regional legislatures collected by the author shows that this proportion had grown to 55 percent by the early 2000s.[13] But even this number likely understates the true extent of business influence in regional legislatures since many deputies were owners or major shareholders of enterprises even though they were not full-time employees of the enterprise while they served as deputies. In sum, by the late 1990s, regional legislatures usually contained all the most important economic elites in a region.

The primary goal of elites in this period was to preserve their autonomous resources. Joining a regime party would have placed limits on their autonomy. The presidential administration might have tried to force elites to join Unity, but it appears that the Kremlin was unwilling to force the issue. As Oryol Governor Egor Stroev stated in an interview with the author: "Of course, Unity asked me to join. Any party at that time would have liked to have me as a member. But I believed that by joining a party, I would just be joining a temporary sect. I think history proved me correct."[14] Stroev was a powerful and influential figure whom Unity would have liked to attract, but it was unable to do so.

Samara Governor Konstantin Titov, who had adopted an oppositional stance toward Unity from the beginning and maintained his own political party, Golos Rossii, reported that the Kremlin did not try to prevent him from running for reelection in 2000: "No one tried to stand in my way. Although, I, of course, understand that they could have… It would be so easy to find a 'mistake' in my signatures [voter signatures that candidates were required to collect in order to gain ballot access] and say, that's it, 'your signatures were improperly gathered.'"[15] Just after the elections, Putin visited Samara and Titov left with the impression that Putin supported him. When asked why he thought the Kremlin did not try to stop him from being reelected, Titov responded: "Everyone

---

[13] These data are discussed in more detail in Chapter 7.
[14] Author's interview June 6, 2013, Moscow.
[15] Author's interview June 14, 2012, Moscow.

4.1 Initial Failures: The Story of Unity, 1999–2001

was against it. The local elites and so on. They helped me with financial and organizational resources and so on." In other words, Titov was able to avoid being pushed around by the Kremlin because he could mobilize political support in his region. As this and subsequent chapters will soon show, this dynamic, by which the Kremlin refrained from coercing powerful governors because of the strength of their political machines, would become a central element of the story of dominant party formation in Russia.

The fact that the autonomous resources of elites led them to eschew close affiliation with Unity is demonstrated by several pieces of quantitative and qualitative evidence. A simple analysis of the party affiliation behavior of governors during 1999 suggests that Unity attracted Russia's weaker governors. Among those governors with some sort of party affiliation in the run-up to the 1999 Duma elections, Unity affiliated governors had an average margin of victory of 32 percent, while supporters of other parties averaged a 38 percent margin. Another operationalization of governors' machine strength during this period is provided by Henry Hale, who measures the strength of machines as the average percentage of the vote received by clients of the governor in the State Duma elections. According to these data, the clients of Unity governors won by an average margin of 24 percentage points, while the clients of other party supporters won by an average margin of 30 percentage points.

The bloc did not attract leaders of any prominent ethnic republics. Its most eager first joiners were governors who were having legal problems or who were up for reelection and were in danger of being defeated (Petrov and Makarkin 1999, Sakwa 2003). In an interview after retirement, the primary architect of the Unity campaign and then–First Deputy Head of the Presidential Administration Igor Shabdurasulov stated quite plainly:

> The task was to create a counterweight to OVR. And, we created one; although it was created from governors that were considered weak, lacking in influence; roughly speaking, we gathered up all the leftovers. But at the same time, there began the struggle for those who were oscillating ... this struggle was over those that feared placing all their eggs in one basket... Since I knew many of the governors, I traveled to the regions, and I frequently met with such a situation. This or that governor or president would say something like "we'll support you, and our own guys, and somebody else." They did this so they wouldn't make a mistake.[16]

Those governors with the strongest resources (i.e. those who had strong electoral machines or ran powerful ethnic republics) were either OVR leaders or independents. As Shabdurasulov stated in a 2009 interview, "We had a massive problem with the regional lists. In those places that

---

[16] Author's interview, May 17, 2010, Moscow.

were close to OVR, we had to choose among the second and third echelons of the elite. People were frightened, didn't believe, and were afraid of being discredited."[17]

Governors in this period continued to favor individual strategies of political advancement over commitments to Unity. For this reason, the bloc was intentionally designed so as to require a minimum amount of effort or commitment from governors. The bloc had no organizational power or ideology that could restrict a governor's freedom of maneuver. The initial letter signed by the governors in the Federation Council bound them to nothing except "supporting honest candidates for election to the Duma." Many governors later claimed that they were "surprised" to learn that the letter was perceived as a statement of support for the Unity bloc (Lussier 2002, 66). Bloc leaders emphasized that the bloc was not an exclusive organization and that participation did not preclude them from being members of other movements (Markov 1999, Shvetsova 2003).

After the elections, elites continued to eschew even shallow commitments to Unity. In April 2000, at the founding congress of Unity, prominent Duma veteran and Regions of Russia faction leader Oleg Morozov balked at joining the new movement because of its ban on simultaneous membership in other political parties.[18] Most elites continued to criticize the Kremlin when it suited their needs, ran their own lists of candidates in elections, and did not submit to the party in their regional legislatures. They retained their own political parties, continued to cultivate reputations for independence, and refused to cede the party any authority in their regions.

Russian leaders knew that Russia's elites were so strong that they would balk at any attempt to impose constraints upon them. So rather than try to create a centralized ruling party and force governors into it, the Kremlin sought to build a weak party of power – one without an ideology, policy platform, formal membership requirements, or rules governing the behavior of cadres – that could coordinate the governors around the Kremlin's preferred candidate without requiring much from them in the way of commitment. Indeed, the Kremlin's halting and uncertain commitments to Unity further deterred elites from investing in that party, for if elites were to take the risk of relinquishing some of their autonomy, especially when they were so strong vis-à-vis the Kremlin, then they needed clear guarantees from the Kremlin that it would be

---

[17] "Edinstvo Protivopolozhnostei" *Profil*, October 5, 2009.
[18] From Morozov's biography at http://history.peoples.ru/state/politics/morozov/index.html

4.1 Initial Failures: The Story of Unity, 1999–2001   121

supporting Unity and only Unity. These guarantees were not forthcoming. When asked how the Kremlin provided guarantees to governors that Unity would continue to be supported after the elections, the main coordinator of Unity's campaign, Igor Shabdurasulov, replied simply, "There were no such guarantees."[19] And yet, consistent with the framework outlined here, the minimal signals of support that the Kremlin *did* send produced changes in the behavior of elites. Indeed, Putin's November speech to announce that he would be voting for Unity "as a citizen" was directed at an audience of governors, and in the week after that speech, governors began, for the first time, to announce their support for Unity publicly.[20]

Why the Kremlin Was Hesitant to Invest in Unity

Yeltsin's hesitancy to invest in a dominant party when elites were strong was elaborated in Chapter 3. Given the statements of Yelsin's advisers, it appears that Yeltsin feared investing in Our Home when elites could not be counted on to live up to their commitments and indeed, might even use the party to challenge the president. In 1998–1999, when regional elites were at their strongest, this consideration could only have been elevated in the president's mind. Requiring dominant party commitments from elites at such a time was unrealistic.

Perhaps the best circumstantial evidence of the Kremlin's motives for refraining from making investments in a party of power is that the absolute nadir of the Kremlin's involvement in party-of-power politics coincided with their weakest moment vis-à-vis regional elites in 1998. In that year, the Kremlin had withdrawn all support for Our Home and had no plans for creating a new party of power. The presidential administration and government were even less involved in party politics than they were in 1995. Meanwhile, oil prices had reached their lowest level in December 1998 and remained low until May 1999. The fiscal position of the central state was abysmal and state capacity was weak.

In the summer of 1999, oil prices began to climb steeply, reaching their highest level in 10 years in November 1999. Moreover, the fall of 1999 witnessed strong economic growth – a first since the Soviet collapse – and Prime Minister Putin's meteoric rise in popularity. And,

---

[19] Author's interview May 17, 2010, Moscow.
[20] A handful of governors declared their public support for Unity prior to that – including those on its coordinating council and Platov of Tver, who was on its party list – but it was not until these few weeks before the election that the other governors who signed Unity's initial letter of support began to associate with the party's campaign. See, for example, "Putin bankyuet po-Uralski" *Kommersant*, November 30, 1999.

as we have seen, the fall of 1999 was when the Kremlin made its first tentative steps toward creating Unity. Of course, such a correlation must be taken with a large grain of salt, since the fall of 1999 was the height of the Duma election campaign, but the correlation is still informative, because the Kremlin made its first tentative commitments to Unity only three months before Election Day and embarked on a crash campaign thereafter. The Kremlin's weakness and the governors' strength tell us why the commitment was so tentative and why they equivocated on supporting a party of power until the last moment.

Those close to Yeltsin in late 1998 and early 1999 were divided on the issue of whether to support a party of power in 1999. Most advisers thought that a pro-Kremlin party would not have "the slightest chance of success, and, therefore, why expend the effort, people, and money on it."[21] Since it was clear at the time that a successful campaign depended crucially on the support of regional leaders, Kremlin insiders feared investing in a party that could not hope to attract the support of Russia's regional elites. As Sergei Popov, vice-chairman of Edinstvo's election campaign, noted in an interview with the author, "We tried to attract as many governors as possible, but in such a process it is impossible to force people. Moreover, the movement was new and unknown."[22] Indeed, by early 1999, it seemed so apparent that OVR would win that many in Yeltsin's circle were secretly negotiating with OVR's leaders about their futures in a Primakov administration. Such insiders, therefore, thought that helping to build a party to compete with OVR would only damage their future career prospects.[23] Thus, the Kremlin was reluctant to invest in a strong party of power in the run-up to the 1999 election because they thought that such a party could not hope to draw the support of powerful governors. The strength of Russia's governors had reached such heights that many Kremlin insiders were worried more about their careers after the governors' party, OVR, won the election, than they were about figuring out a way to co-opt and control the governors in order to win the election.

The reasons for the Kremlin's hesitancy to rush headlong into building Unity into a dominant party after the elections were similar. Indeed, it has been suggested by those close to the presidential administration at the time that Putin was skeptical of transforming Unity into a party

---

[21] Author's interview with Igor Shabdurasulov, first deputy head of presidential administration 1999–2000, May 17, 2010, Moscow.
[22] Author's interview with Sergei Popov, June 8, 2012, Moscow.
[23] Author's Interview with Igor Shabdurasulov, first deputy head of presidential administration 1999–2000, May 17, 2010, Moscow.

in 2000, because of the fear that it would be "taken over by Luzhkovites and it would slip out from under the Kremlin's control" (Ivanov 2008, 76). Governors (and other elites) were still extremely strong in the early 2000s. Their support was needed to pass legislation in both houses and govern the regions. Putin appears to have been initially unwilling to sanction a strong party when governors could not make the most basic commitment that a dominant party requires – refraining from directly challenging the leader for office and authority.

Summary

Regional elites reached the apex of their power in 1999. Their own inability to coordinate was the only obstacle that prevented them from capturing the state. Although the Kremlin could have used a dominant party to manage presidential succession, it still feared the power of regional elites at this time and was reluctant to invest in one. Instead, it adopted a divide-and-rule strategy, which consisted of sending conflicting signals about which party it would support and then a last-minute effort to draw a plurality of weak governors into its own haphazardly assembled movement. Since the Kremlin was not willing to offer any clear signals about which party it would support, elites were not willing to relinquish their significant resources and place themselves under their suzerainty of a regime party. Indeed, the Kremlin had to craft expectations about which party it would support just to draw the weakest governors to its side.

Some view Unity as the first stage in the creation of Russia's now-dominant party, United Russia (Hale 2004). And, indeed, it is true that Unity is one of the organizational predecessors of United Russia, but Unity in 1999 had little in common with United Russia in the mid-2000s. Unity was the culmination of divide-and-rule politics, not an institution intended for the co-optation of elites. It was a campaign strategy, not a political party. The decision to create United Russia as a dominant party was a separate one made under different political circumstances. The remainder of this chapter discusses those circumstances.

4.2 The Formation of a Dominant Party in Post-Soviet Russia: The Story of United Russia, 2001–2010

All previous parties of power in Russia were created as instruments to contest national parliamentary elections and then left to decay after the election was over. In late 2000–early 2001, it appeared that Unity would suffer the same fate. Putin declined to attend the party's founding congress in May, the party was languishing in regional elections, and the regional elite continued to place its eggs in multiple baskets. Yet, the period between the 1999–2000 and 2003–2004 election cycles turned out to be different from previous ones. In early 2001, negotiations began for the creation of a coalition among four centrist factions in the State Duma – Unity, OVR, and two factions composed mostly of SMD deputies, Regions of Russia and People's Deputies. In July, that coalition was given some institutional form with the creation of a coordinating council to help synchronize the voting behavior of its members. When created, the coalition controlled 234 votes, a simple majority.[24] Yet, intrafaction cohesion was low, especially among SMD deputies. Around that same time, negotiations began for the creation of a new political party that would join the Unity organization and what was left of the Fatherland and All-Russia party organizations. In December 2001, a merger of the parties was sealed, and a founding congress was held for the All-Russian Party "Unity and Fatherland – United Russia (UR)."

The idea for the alliance was that of then–First Deputy Head of the Presidential Administration Vladislav Surkov. Surkov, Putin's closest political adviser at the time, convinced the president and key figures in the two parties to support the alliance. Though he did not join the party, Putin spoke at its founding congress, the first time a Russian head of state had attended a party congress. It was also the first time that a party of power had been created more than a year before the beginning of a national election cycle. Despite the merger, the two parties retained separate parliamentary factions for the remainder of the Third Duma.

At its founding congress, the party created a nesting doll style leadership structure that included a congress, with delegates chosen by regional branches, to be held at least once every two years; a 100-member Central Political Council meeting several times a year and selected by the congress; a General Council that comprised 13 Central Political Council members, meeting as circumstances required between Central Political Council sessions; and a Central Executive Committee that would serve as the everyday organizational arm of the party. The primary political organs of the party were the Central Political Council and the General Council.[25] Former Putin adviser Alexander Bespalov was named chairman of the General Council and, simultaneously, head of the Central Executive Committee. These positions made Bespalov the public face of the party in its first year.

---

[24] For more on the centrist coalition, see Smyth (2002), Remington (2006)

[25] The former was staffed with Duma deputies and some regional legislative leaders. The latter was composed almost entirely of prominent Duma deputies. In the first General Council, Edinstvo's party leaders received five spots; Fatherland and All-Russia received four each.

4.2 Formation of a Dominant Party in Post-Soviet Russia

At its congress, the party also created a parallel organ to house prominent figures who wanted to be associated with the party but not incur the commitments of party leadership (or membership). This Higher Council, as it was called, met infrequently and had an ambiguous role in the party. At the first congress, several prominent governors joined the council, including Moscow Mayor Yurii Luzhkov, Tatarstan President Mintimer Shaimiyev, Tyumen Governor Sergei Sobyanin, and Bashkortorstan President Murtaza Rakhimov.

In spring 2002, the party began creating its own branches in the regions, contesting regional elections, and forming factions in regional legislatures. By the beginning of 2003, UR had established factions in 45 of Russia's 89 regional legislatures. But this was still a time when regional legislatures were dominated by independents and almost all were elected in single member districts. Consistent with the framework offered here, United Russia had difficulty attracting these independent deputies. On average UR controlled just 26 percent of seats in regional legislatures in early 2003, and it held a majority in only seven regions (Glubotskii and Kynev 2003). Nonetheless, UR's penetration into regional legislatures was by this time already more extensive than NDR's had ever been.

In the 36 gubernatorial elections held between 2002 and early 2003, the party did not play a major role, nominating only two candidates (one on its own and one as part of an electoral bloc with other parties). Of course, the custom was for Russian governors to run as independents even if they were actively supported by a political party, so this statistic is not especially informative. More informative as an indicator of party activity during these elections is the number of elections in which the party publicly endorsed a candidate. Between January 2002 and May 2003, United Russia did this in 9 of 15 elections.[26] But, since gubernatorial candidates were not official party nominees, the party had no control over the governors it supported, and sitting governors could, and did, decline party support if they thought it might harm their electoral chances.

The party was torn by infighting over leadership posts and often clashed with governors during this period. In some regions, the party leadership chose regional secretaries from the ranks of the governors' enemies (often the chairman of a local legislature, a local mayor, or State Duma deputy). In the 15 gubernatorial elections that took place between January 2002 and May 2003, the party supported non-incumbents in five contests and lost two of those races. The party also opposed governors' regional

---

[26] Data on party support for gubernatorial candidates in this period are from Ivanov (2008).

parties in several regional legislative elections (notably Sverdlovsk) and lost. Meanwhile, some of Russia's most powerful governors simply captured the party organization in their region, subordinating it to their own regionally based organizations.[27] Thus, by early 2003, it was clear that while the Kremlin could use the party and Putin's growing authority to help it weaken weak governors, stronger governors could still marshal the resources to keep the party at arm's length, and the strongest governors could simply capture the regional party apparatus.

Hence, in early 2003, the party shifted strategy and opted to focus on co-opting existing governors. Bespalov, who was blamed for adopting a counterproductive strategy vis-à-vis regional elites, was removed from his post as chairman of the General Council and replaced by Duma Deputy Valerii Bogomolov.[28] At the same time, the party introduced a new position, chairman of the Higher Council, headed by then–Minister for Internal Affairs Boris Gryzlov. Although the Higher Council was not a leadership organ – it could only make nonbinding recommendations to the Central Political Council on issues of cadres and strategy – the chairman's post was vested with significant informal importance. Throughout 2003 and early 2004, Gryzlov served as leader of the party even though his position gave him less formal authority within the party. This is indicated by the fact that Gryzlov delivered the key address on the status of the party at the March 2003 congress and all subsequent ones until then–Prime Minister Dmitry Medvedev became chairman in 2012.

By March 2003, United Russia, with 400,000 members, was the second largest party in Russia.[29] In the Duma, 151 deputies were members of the party and 41 Federation Council senators had joined. The party had set up regional branches in all regions and more than 2,400 local branches. But the party was still underperforming in regional elections and the 2003 State Duma elections were approaching in December. Therefore, the Kremlin redoubled its efforts to secure the support of powerful regional leaders. United Russia became the forum for such a co-optative arrangement. In 1999, regional leaders and financial industrial groups had advanced their clients into the Duma primarily through the single member districts. This practice continued in 2003, but the United Russia list also appeared as an attractive avenue through which regional leaders could, if they played their cards right, advance their clients into the Duma. Thus, to a greater extent than those of any party of power before it, United Russia's party lists were populated with the

---

[27] This was clearly the case in Bashkortorstan and Mordovia.
[28] The position was also renamed, becoming the "secretary of the Political Council."
[29] The KPRF remained larger by membership.

4.2 Formation of a Dominant Party in Post-Soviet Russia 127

representatives of regional leaders. Twenty-nine regional leaders also agreed to have their names listed on United Russia's party list and, by December 2003, 17 governors had joined the party's Higher Council.

At the Third Party Congress in September, Putin delivered an address reaffirming his support for United Russia. In December, the party's rating sat at 31 percent, higher than that of any party of power in post-Soviet history. In the election, the party received 37.5 percent of the party list vote and won 103 (45 percent) of the SMD seats (223 seats in total), the best ever electoral performance by a post-Soviet party of power.

When the new Duma convened, a further 55 deputies joined the United Russia faction, making the total 298. By the end of January 2004, the faction had grown to 310, a two-thirds majority. Gryzlov was named faction leader and speaker of the Duma. The party expanded the number of committees in parliament from 16 to 29 and kept for itself all chairmanships. Over the course of the next four years, United Russia served as a stable and loyal voting bloc for the passage of President Putin's legislative initiatives.

On other fronts as well the party continued to grow. As Figure 4.1 shows, governors joined at a gradual pace over this period. By October 2005 more than half of Russia's governors had joined the party, and by November 2007, all but eight of Russia's governors had. Between January 2004 and February 2005, 23 gubernatorial elections were held. UR nominated only four candidates but endorsed candidates in all races. The party made it a point to endorse the likely winner in almost all cases, losing only four contests in which it endorsed a candidate.

Other regional elites also gradually joined the party over this period. Russian regional legislatures in the early 2000s contained the most prominent social and economic leaders in a given region. The directors of major enterprises and collective farms, local state-run television anchors, rectors of universities, and heads of local hospitals could all be found in an average regional legislature. Thus, they provide a useful window into the political affiliations of Russia's economic and social elite.

After mid-2003, all regional legislatures were required by federal law to elect at least half their deputies on the basis of party lists. This reform helped United Russia (and all other parties) achieve higher levels of penetration in regional legislatures. As Figure 4.2 shows, the party's regional performance in the latter half of 2003 was much improved over its previous years, when it rarely managed to win any more than a handful of SMD seats.

Nonetheless, as the argument in this book would predict, the party continued to face challenges in attracting single member district deputies who commanded independent electoral resources (see Figure 4.3).

128   The Emergence of a Dominant Party in Russia

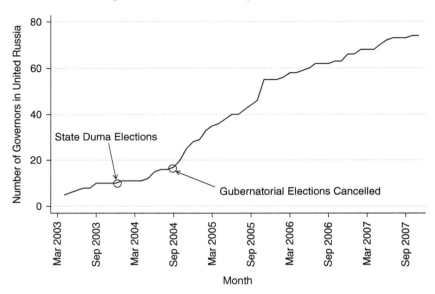

Figure 4.1 Russia's governors in United Russia, 2003–2007.

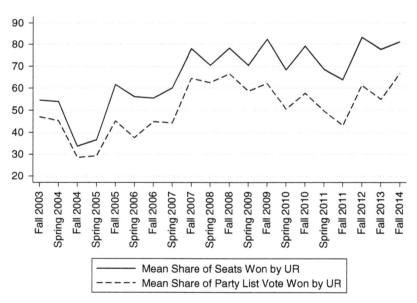

Figure 4.2 United Russia performance in regional legislative election cycles.

4.2 Formation of a Dominant Party in Post-Soviet Russia

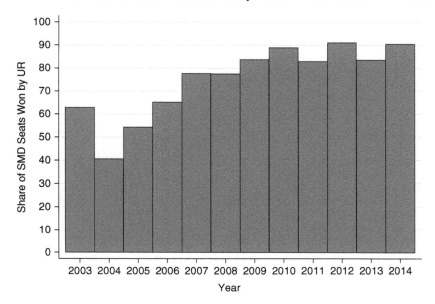

Figure 4.3 Percentage of SMD seats won by UR in regional legislative elections.

Between 2003 and 2005, the party was winning, on average, only about half the SMD seats in regional legislatures. In this period independents won, on average, more than 37 percent of all SMD seats, and despite the inherent disproportionality that favors large parties in majoritarian electoral contests, the party often won more seats on party lists than it did in single member districts.

As the decade passed, however, more and more single member deputies sought affiliation with the dominant party, and by the end of the decade the party was consistently winning more than 80 percent of SMD seats.[30] Capitalizing on disproportionality, UR's performance in those contests began to outstrip its performance on the party list. Between 2006 and 2014, UR consistently won majorities and usually supermajorities in almost all regional legislative elections. By 2010, the party controlled majorities in 82 of 83 regional legislatures and supermajorities in 68.

The orientation of Russia's national business elite toward United Russia is more difficult to assess. On the one hand, big business eagerly

---

[30] The early to mid-2000s was also a period when UR factions were created in regional legislatures and many previously independent deputies were joining those factions. Thus, many regional legislatures acquired UR majorities several years before elections were held under the new electoral system.

Table 4.1 *United Russia in the legislative, regional, and local elite*

	Number of positions	Number in UR	UR members, %
Governors (2008)	83	78	94
State Duma deputies (2010)	450	314	70
Federation Council senators (2011)	166	125	75
Chairmen of regional legislatures (2010)	83	83	100
Legislatures with UR majorities (2011)	83	82	99
Mayors of cities >75K (2011)	221	191	86
City council majorities in cities > 75K (2011)	217[a]	199	92
Municipal council deputies elected in October 2010	49,902	35,685	71.5
Heads of municipal administrations elected in October 2010	2512	1696	67.5

[a] As of the 2002 census, there were 221 Russian cities with populations above 75,000, but data are missing on 4 of these cities.

funded United Russia's campaign in 2003 and continued to fund the party's activities thereafter. In return, representatives of Russia's largest enterprises (e.g. Sibneft, Yukos, Lukoil, Severstal, Gazprom, Renovo, Norilsk Nikel, Basovyi Element) received Duma seats on United Russia's party list. Moreover, several of Russia's most politically active tycoons, including Russian Railways President Vladimir Yakunin, RosOboron Export Chief Viktor Chemezov, VTB Bank President Andrei Kostin, and prominent investor Suleiman Kerimov joined the party between 2003 and 2006.[31] The party's Higher Council frequently features the vice presidents of major Russian corporations, and the president of the Russian Union of Industrialists and Entrepreneurs, Russia's largest business lobbying group, took a seat on the Presidium of the General Council in 2008. United Russia frequently "taps" business to fund its special party projects or recruits business leaders to serve as special party emissaries in exchange for seats in the Duma.[32] On the other hand, many in the upper echelons of big business (figures such as Roman Abramovich, Viktor Vekselberg, Alexei Miller, Oleg Deripaska) have eschewed involvement in party politics.

[31] "Partiya Vlasti Podtyanula biznes-resursy" *Kommersant*, November 27, 2006.
[32] '"Partiya Vlasti' Torguyet Mestami" *Novaya Politika*, October 16, 2006 www.novopol.ru/–partiya-vlasti-torguet-mestami-text12342.html

4.2 Formation of a Dominant Party in Post-Soviet Russia

At the local level, the party initially had difficulty making inroads, but in the mid-2000s it became dominant there as well. Between 2004 and 2007, the mayors of most of Russia's large cities joined the party.[33] By 2011, 87 percent were members.[34]

At lower levels of local self-government (city, local, and district councils and municipal district heads) the party began making inroads after 2004, when the party leadership instructed regional branches to step up efforts to increase the party's penetration in local government.[35] Local administration heads are key vote brokers in the Russian countryside, so co-opting them was a priority for the party. By September 2007, 51.6 percent of Russia's 12,369 municipal regions, city districts, city settlements, and rural settlements were headed by a UR party member. In elections held in fall of 2010, the party won 68 percent of elections for municipal district heads.

And while nationwide figures are not available, reports and interviews with United Russia officials in the regions indicate that regional party branches expended significant effort between 2004 and 2007 on establishing party majorities in Russia's previously nonpartisan municipal and local councils.[36] As Table 4.1 shows, this effort paid off. By 2011, the party held majorities in 92 percent of the city councils in Russia's large cities, and in elections held in October 2010, the party captured 72 percent of the seats in local councils.[37] The party's penetration of local self-government is particularly striking given the organizational resources required to recruit and field candidates in the thousands of elections that take place during each election cycle.

The party has also made significant inroads into other segments of Russian society. Although figures are not available, reports indicate that the rectors of most major universities are party members and use their positions to drum up votes during elections.[38] Famous actors, directors,

---

[33] See, for example, "Edinaya Rossiya goroda beryot" *Kommersant*, December 25, 2006.
[34] In 2007, 53 percent of elected mayors and 88 percent of appointed mayors were UR members. These and other data on the party affiliation of elites presented in this chapter are taken from the *Database of Russian Political Elites*, a database of elite biographies and career tenures compiled by the author.
[35] Author's interview with, Andrei Rusakov, deputy head of United Russia's Central Executive Committee in Sverdlovsk Oblast, July 3, 2007.
[36] By July 2007, the Sverdlovsk regional branch had established factions in 68 of 72 local councils. By July 2009, the Yaroslavl regional branch had established factions in 17 of 21 local councils. Other reports indicate that more than half of municipal council deputies were UR members by mid-2007: "Knut i Pryanika dlya Munitsipala" *Nezavisimaya Gazeta*, July 26, 2007.
[37] These data are not readily available for other years. Data for these elections were compiled by United Russia and provided to the author.
[38] At Yaroslavl State University, professors report that the rector met with heads of departments ahead of the presidential election and while he gave no specific instructions stressed the importance of the election result to the governor.

Table 4.2 *United Russia in the Federal Executive Branch*

	Number of positions	Number in UR	UR members, %
Presidential administration officials (2011)[a]	50	6	12
Security council (2011)	33	13	39
Vice prime ministers (2011)	10	4	40
Ministers (2011)	19	5	26

[a] Includes heads of departments, chief of staff, vice chiefs of staff, official representatives of president (including Polpredy), and official advisers listed on Kremlin homepage.

musicians, and athletes have all joined the party, and some are even Duma members. State employees and bureaucrats are the modal category among rank-and-file party members, but party membership is not a requirement for civil service advancement. In many regions, the editors of state-run print media and the directors of local state-run television networks are party members. Directors of prominent enterprises that are not represented in legislatures are usually invited to sit on the regional Political Council (*politsovet*), though their influence there is less than it would be if they held seats in the party's legislative faction.

However, two important institutions remained mostly nonpartisan in the mid-2000s: the government and the presidential administration. In 2007, only three members of the government and only a handful of Vladimir Putin's inner circle were party members. Rather than becoming part of the party, the presidential administration sought to keep its bilateral relationship with it intact. The only area in which this rule was breached was within the presidential administration's Department for Internal Politics (DIP), the arm of the presidential administration that deals with all matters relating to parties, interest groups, and elections. From 2002 onward, a permanent staff was assigned to work with United Russia. In 2010, 10 specialists worked in this department. Between this department and United Russia, a bridge of cadres was created such that DIP staff frequently transfer over to work in the party, and vice versa.[39]

As Table 4.2 shows, the share of executive branch officials that were UR members did increase significantly by the end of the decade and

---

[39] In 2003 and 2004, Deputy Head of the Department for Internal Politics Leonid Ivlev simultaneously held a position as deputy head of the United Russia Executive Committee. Oleg Govorun, DIP head between 2006 and 2011, was also a party member.

4.2 Formation of a Dominant Party in Post-Soviet Russia

several high profile government officials owed their seats to party work. Moreover, no other political parties had representatives in the federal executive branch. Nonetheless, most of that branch remained nonpartisan throughout the 2000s.

At its Fifth Congress in November 2004, the party shifted to the organizational structure that it has retained to the present day.[40] The Central Political Council was replaced by the General Council as the primary leadership organ, meeting several times between congresses. Within the General Council, a Presidium was created that would meet frequently and serve as the permanent political leadership organ. The nesting doll appointment scheme was retained, with local conferences selecting delegates to the yearly Congress, which chooses the General Council, which chooses the Presidium. The Presidium selects the Central Executive Committee.

In place of the old leadership posts, the party created the post of party chairman and secretary of the Presidium. Both offices are charged with directing and leading the work of the General Council and Presidium, though the former also is charged with directing the work of the Higher Council. The party chairman and the secretary of the Presidium are selected by the Congress.[41]

For its part, the Higher Council was retained as a symbolic institution that meets infrequently and does not participate directly in party decision making.[42] Within the Higher Council, a higher-level star chamber was created at this congress, the Bureau of the Higher Council. This organ contained the most prominent governors from the Higher Council as well as the head of the party executive committee, the party chairman, and the secretary of the Presidium and his deputies.

Gryzlov was chosen as party chairman, and Valery Bogomolov, vice chairman of United Russia's Duma faction, was chosen as secretary of the Presidium. Given his position as Duma speaker, his keynote addresses at the party congress, and his post as head of the Higher Council, Gryzlov was clearly first among equals in this setup. In the spring of 2005, Bogomolov resigned and was replaced by Vyacheslav Volodin, vice

---

[40] This discussion of personnel changes and intraparty intrigue draws on Ivanov (2008, 186–211).
[41] In 2012, the party introduced multi-candidate, intra-party elections with secret ballots for members of the General Council, the presidium, the secretary of the Presidium, and the party chairman. Delegates to the congress serve as electors for the General Council, the secretary of the Presidium, and the Party Chairman, while the General Council votes for members of the Presidium.
[42] At the 2005 party congress, the party changed its charter so that Higher Council candidates were required to have been members of the party for more than one year in order to be considered for membership.

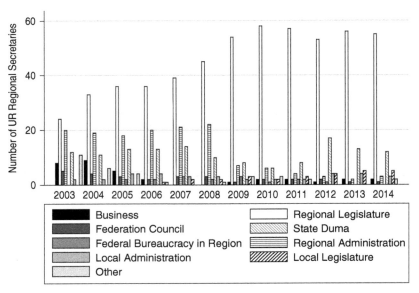

Figure 4.4 Backgrounds of United Russia regional secretaries.

speaker of the Duma and former OVR deputy from Saratov, as the new secretary of the Presidium.

The party's organizational reach expanded rapidly in the mid-2000s. By 2007, it had 83 regional branches, 2547 local branches (28 local branches per regional branch, on average), and 53,740 primary cells. Regional branches consist of a Political Council that contains a region's most prominent economic and political figures, a Presidium within that *politsovet* that meets monthly, and a Regional Executive Committee that serves as the permanent organizational arm of the regional branch and is staffed by anywhere from 10 to 50 employees. The secretary of the *politsovet* (who is always simultaneously the secretary of the Presidium) is the leading party figure in the region. These positions are not full-time positions, however. As Figure 4.4 shows, most regional secretaries are the speakers or vice speakers of regional legislatures, though some are also Duma deputies from the region, vice governors, or governors themselves. Like their federal counterparts, regional (and local) secretaries are selected by lower-level party institutions. The regional conference selects the regional secretary and the regional politsovet. The regional *politsovet* selects the presidium.[43]

---

[43] As at the federal level, intra-party elections for these posts were introduced in 2012.

4.2 Formation of a Dominant Party in Post-Soviet Russia

Local branches consist on average of 687 members, though branches tend not to be distributed evenly across the population, but, rather, are established to correspond to administrative divisions. So, large cities often have a single local branch while some rural branches correspond to an administrative division that contains only a few thousand people. Like the regional branch, the leading political organ of the local branch is the *politsovet* and its Presidium, which are headed by a secretary (usually a mayor, collective farm director, or local administration head). Local branches, as a rule, are staffed with at least two or three permanent employees, though the largest local branches can have up to 20 permanent employees. The local branch executive committees play an important role in making sure that local enterprises and interest groups support the party in elections and with a dependable stream of funding. The head of the local executive committee offers the carrots (access to municipal contracts, preferential utility rates) and sticks (threats of license revocation and utility disruption) that induce local businesses and elements of civil society to cooperate with the party. Although the executive committee head almost never has personal resources of his/her own (these officials are either hired hands from the regional capital or local civil servants), he/she can speak for the secretary of the *politsovet* and call upon the authority of that position. The same type of arm twisting and co-optation go on at the regional level as well, but in most regions, it is much more overt at the local level (especially in small and medium sized towns and rural areas).[44]

United Russia's primary party cells average 33 members per cell. Each primary cell is headed by a secretary, who is a not a full-time employee; rather, these are the party's activists. They are overwhelmingly public sector employees. Many are neighborhood opinion leaders – school principals, hospital directors, or factory production line supervisors – who have access to public meeting spaces. A majority are female.[45]

Whereas in the past the approval rating of regime parties had fallen after election campaigns (when administrative resources were not being deployed to drum up support), United Russia's rating only grew after the 2003 elections. According to the Levada Center, in March 2004, 33 percent of likely voters were prepared to vote for the party. By December

---

[44] This discussion was heavily informed by a series of interviews I conducted with local United Russia executive committee officials in Tutaev, Yaroslavl Oblast (February 2010) and Berezniki, Perm Krai, July 2008.

[45] I only have data on this for the Berezniki local branch, where 22 of 25 primary party cells are headed by women, of whom 14 are the directors of local schools. But my interviews with party officials in Yaroslavl Oblast and Kurgan Oblast tell me that this pattern of gender and occupational background is also evident in those oblasts.

2006, that figure had grown to 55 percent. The party's membership also climbed precipitously from 400,000 members in 2003 to 1.25 million in early 2007 to 1.75 million at the end of 2007. By 2014, it had 2.1 million members.

Putin continued to voice his support for the party in the interelection period. His most significant signal of support occurred in fall 2007, when he announced that he would head the federal component of United Russia's party list. With Putin's announcement, the party's election campaign became highly personalized around his image and a platform called "Putin's Plan," a vague, nonideological manifesto. The party also emphasized clientelist appeals, billing itself as the *partiya realnykh del* (the party of real deeds) and attaching its brand to tens of billions of dollars in public works and social spending – the National Projects – funded by oil revenues. It also secured billions of dollars in budgetary funds for its own so-called "party projects," which were managed directly by the party.

The other great resource for the party in the 2007 campaign was the support of regional governors, almost all of whom were now members. In contrast to previous Russian elections, almost all of Russia's governors put their machines to work for a single party. This, combined with Putin's popularity and lavish patronage spending, gave United Russia a landslide victory. On Election Day, the party raked in 64.2 percent of the vote, which translated into 310 mandates in the State Duma.[46]

After the election, United Russia endorsed the candidacy of Putin's handpicked successor to the presidency, Dmitry Medvedev, who subsequently won a landslide victory in the March presidential elections. Putin became prime minister under Medvedev and in April 2008, Putin accepted United Russia's invitation to become party chairman, though he did not become a party member.[47] Vladislav Surkov, United Russia's longtime advocate and coordinator in the Kremlin, stayed on in the presidential administration, but over time, the party began to coordinate its actions less with the presidential administration and more with the Prime Minister's office. Between 2008 and 2012, Putin met with party leaders monthly and organized all official meetings between the Kremlin and United Russia leaders.[48] Putin's chief of staff, Sergei Sobyanin, handled relations with United Russia for Putin, and the party leadership's biweekly meeting with Surkov was replaced by biweekly meetings with Sobyanin.[49]

---

[46] For the 2007 elections, the single member district portion of the electoral system had been removed and all deputies were elected on party lists.
[47] Gryzlov was demoted to Higher Council chairman.
[48] "Vladimir Putin vzyal partiyu v svoi ruki" *Kommersant*, June 5, 2008.
[49] See, for example, "Uravnenie s dvumya izvesnymi" *Russkii Newsweek*, May 31, 2010.

This process was gradual and incomplete, however. The presidential administration retained a staff whose sole task was coordinating with United Russia, and reports indicate that Surkov retained significant influence on relations between the executive branch and UR. After Putin's resumption of the presidency in March 2012, responsibility for coordinating with UR remained divided between the government and presidential administration. Medvedev, as Putin's prime minister, formally joined United Russia and became party chairman. At the same time, in the presidential administration, Vyacheslav Volodin, who was named as first deputy head of the presidential administration in December 2011, and Oleg Morozov, the new head of the DIP, became the primary points of contact for the party in the presidential administration.

In sum, compared to previous party of power projects, United Russia was a much more robust ruling party. It consistently won elections at all levels, had an extensive organizational structure, and penetrated politics at the national, regional, and local levels. Although the party did not exercise collective control over the federal executive branch, it controlled legislatures at all levels and was the primary vehicle facilitating the consolidation of regional and local elites. As Chapter 5 explores in more detail, the party became an important forum for the distribution of rents, spoils, policy influence, and career advancement. Unlike in previous party of power projects, strict party discipline was imposed. As an institutional tool for distributing careers and spoils, the party became an effective means of co-optation for the Kremlin and helped reduce uncertainty among elites about how these goods would be disbursed. In short, United Russia became a dominant party. The next section explores why the Kremlin, on the one hand, and elites, on the other, made the investments that led to United Russia's emergence as a dominant party.

The Kremlin and United Russia

Putin and his advisers in the presidential administration have exhibited a higher level of commitment to United Russia than the Kremlin had to any other party of power in post-Soviet history. But their commitments increased gradually, in response both to increases in the Kremlin's own strength vis-à-vis elites and to the Kremlin's perception of elites' level of commitment to the party.

By 2002, commodity prices had risen several times over from their all-time lows in 1998. And as Figure 4.5 shows, the economy was growing as well.

Though inflation was high, incomes were expanding at a breakneck pace over the period from 1999 to 2002. At the end of 2001, Putin's

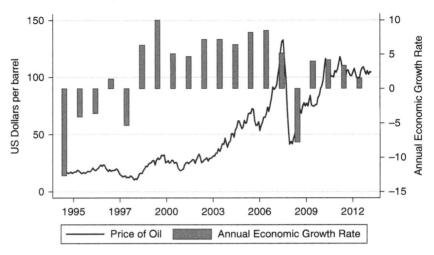

Figure 4.5 Oil prices and economic growth in post-Soviet Russia.

popularity rating exceeded 80 percent, the highest for a Russian leader since Yeltsin's in 1990. Putin wasted no time in spending part of this political capital. In 2000, he pushed through legislation eliminating the governors' (and regional parliamentary speakers') ex officio seats in the Federation Council. Henceforth, governors and regional parliaments would appoint senators to sit in the chamber. The reforms also divided the federation into seven districts, each headed by a federal appointee, who was charged with coordinating federal agencies in the district and working with governors there. The reforms were also accompanied by an invigorated effort to force regional governments to bring their legal acts into compliance with the federal law.

The balance of resources between center and regions had begun to change, and this allowed for formal changes to be made that reflected the new balance.[50] But the autonomous resources that regional leaders continued to wield meant that Putin's efforts to recentralize authority

---

[50] As noted in Chapter 2, the powers of leaders and elites are often endogenous to one another. In Russia in the early 2000s, however, it is clear that rising world oil prices were exogenous and contributed to several other changes that shifted the balance of resources, including renewed economic growth, improved state capacity, and Putin's rising popularity. Each of these factors also had some exogenous determinants of its own. Economic growth in 1999 and 2000 was partially the result of a rebound from the 1998 financial crisis. Putin's popularity meanwhile was determined by economic growth as well as idiosyncratic factors relating to his personality and governing style (Hale and Colton 2009, Treisman 2011).

4.2 Formation of a Dominant Party in Post-Soviet Russia

were still limited. Regional elites continued to be purveyors of stability and political authority in their regions and localities (e.g. Turovsky 2002, Hale 2003, and Goode 2007). Putin could undermine any single regional elite actor, but he still would need the collective support of these actors to govern Russia cost-effectively. The Kremlin learned this lesson in 1999 and again in 2002 when United Russia failed to make much headway at undermining regional governors.

So, the Kremlin would need to work with regional elites somehow. The only question was whether they were still strong enough that co-opting them into a dominant party would be dangerous or a waste of the Kremlin's resources. The Kremlin decided that it could afford to risk some commitments, but not yet others. So, Putin spoke at the founding congress, the first time a Russian president had spoken at a party congress, and let it become public knowledge that he approved of the merger between Unity and OVR. Thus, Putin devoted some of his personal resources to the party by attaching, if only partially, his name and reputation to it. Moreover, his top political adviser, Vladislav Surkov, made it public knowledge that the Kremlin was interested in exploring ways to make the political system more stable and less dependent on Putin. At a 2002 gathering of United Russia leaders and sympathetic governors, he said: "We need to look to 2008; we will survive until then somehow... The president may leave (we will not stop him) and then what will happen? Some extreme left or extreme right president may come to power... We could make a mistake and not win. We can't just be on artificial respiration and an I.V. all the time."[51] Finally, the Kremlin also sanctioned new legislation that elevated the role of political parties in elections. These reforms – which effectively banned regional and small parties, made it easier for party nominees to register, and mandated that at least half of the seats in regional legislatures be elected on party lists – reduced the ability of both the Kremlin and regional elites to diversify their electoral strategy across multiple small parties and independent candidates.[52]

But in the period 2001–2003, Putin was hesitant to make other commitments. At the founding congress, he asked delegates not to think of the new party as a "party of power."[53] He rejected United Russia's public proposal to form the new government on the basis of the parliamentary majority. The Kremlin also placed its eggs in multiple baskets in

---

[51] Quoted in "Odinokii Paravoz" *Ekspert*, February 25, 2002.
[52] For more on these reforms see Wilson (2006).
[53] See official stenogram at http://archive.kremlin.ru/text/news/2001/12/38100.shtml. Accessed June 14, 2014.

gubernatorial elections, tacitly supporting non-UR candidates in several races (Hale 2004). Moreover, the Kremlin did not immediately push for the creation of a single majority faction in the Duma that would be the analog of the newly formed political party outside it. Instead, it allowed the separate factions to persist and continued to bargain with each of them in order to pass legislation (see Remington 2006).

The Kremlin was thinking not just of its own preferences, but also of how elites, especially governors, might relate to a new ruling party. When asked why the presidential administration did not push more governors to become party members in 2002 and 2003, a top official in the Kremlin's Department of Internal Politics responded simply that the Kremlin had to take into account the "political will of governors" and their desire to "survive in politics" and did not think that it could force governors to join the party.[54] Similarly, Sergei Popov, head of Unity's central executive committee in 2000–2001, stated that he feared that powerful Moscow Mayor Yuri Luzhkov "would not want to participate any party project [because] he had his own political strength."[55] Thus, in 2001 and 2002 the party leadership harbored no illusions about its ability to secure the commitments of Russia's governors and did not attempt to force their hand.

And even if they could induce governors to join the party, the Kremlin feared that it might not be able to control them. In a 2000 interview, Surkov expressed frustration at the fact that most of Unity's regional branches had been captured by governors.[56] Indeed, advisers close to the source claim that Surkov was hesitant to allow the newly formed Unity-OVR bloc to acquire a constitutional majority in the Duma, for fear that the "monster" would be difficult to control (Ivanov 2008, 136).

The Kremlin was uncertain of whether regional elites would remain loyal and not use the party to challenge the Kremlin. Given the manifest inability of SMD deputies to vote cohesively with their factions in the Fourth Duma (Remington 2006) and the shifting factionalism that characterized most regional legislatures, the Kremlin had good reason to doubt the ability of elites to remain loyal to one party.

And, as it turned out, the Kremlin's fears were not baseless. For example, at the party's Sixth Congress in 2005 in Krasynoarysk, party leaders, led by Moscow Mayor Yurii Luzhkov, harshly criticized the government's implementation of an unpopular new law on the monetization of social

---

[54] Author's anonymous interview with former official in the presidential administration's Department for Internal Politics, June 1, 2010.
[55] Author's interview with Sergei Popov, June 8, 2012.
[56] "Tak vot, ya vam govoryu: demkratia neischerpaema," *Kommersant-Vlast*, July 18, 2000.

benefits.[57] And in the early and mid-2000s, party leaders periodically warned about the danger that the regional branches of UR were being captured by powerful regional elites. As General Council Secretary Valery Bogomolov put it in early 2004, "Oligarchs who can no longer bribe Duma deputies are moving out to the provinces and influencing local party organizations. It is important to us to build a system where leaders of regional party branches are subordinated only to the central party leadership and not to local business elites."[58]

This fear of not being able to control a party that contained powerful elites clearly motivated the Kremlin to resist United Russia's repeated calls to form the government on a partisan basis. Soon after its victory in the 2003 Duma elections, United Russia leaders began making public statements to this effect, but the Kremlin was and has been unwilling to make such an investment in a dominant party. In a 2006 press conference, Putin unequivocally voiced his opposition to a bill allowing the majority party in the Duma to name the government, calling such a law "irresponsible." Putin added, "It is my deep conviction that in the post-Soviet space, in the conditions of a developing economy, strengthening state capacity, and the definitive realization of federal principles, *we need firm presidential authority.*"[59] Nonetheless, United Russia leaders continued to state their desire to attain more influence in the government. Vyacheslav Volodin, then-secretary of UR's Presidium, described the formation of a party government as one of United Russia's "main objectives."[60] Another vocal advocate of a party government was Tatarstan President Mintimer Shaimyev, who repeatedly called for United Russia to "fulfill its duty as a party" and create a party government.[61] After Putin became party chairman and prime minister in early 2008, United Russia leaders made it known to the press that they expected the new government to be composed of United Russia members.[62] Putin clearly did not agree, however, and the Russian government remained largely nonpartisan.

As the 2003 Duma elections approached, however, the balance of resources continued to shift in favor of the Kremlin. Economic growth remained strong, oil prices continued to rise, central state capacity was

---

[57] See Makarkin, Aleksei and Tat'yana Stanova. "Edinaya Rossii: Ot partii vlasti k pravyashei partii" Politcom.ru, November 28, 2005. www.politcom.ru/article.php?id=1664
[58] "Power to the Powerful. United Russia's Success Will Depend on Effectiveness and Popularity of Its Leaders" *Rossiskaya Gazeta*, August 10, 2006 (Translated on Johnson's Russia List, August 11, 2006).
[59] "Edinaya Rossiya utochnyaet presidenta" *Nezavisimaya Gazeta*, March 2, 2006.
[60] Ibid.
[61] "Pravitelstvo i partiya ediny?" *Novaya Politika* www.novopol.ru, January 24, 2007.
[62] "Partiinoye pravitelstvo obkatayut k 2010 godu" *Kommersant*, April 16, 2008.

improving, and Putin's personal popularity was near an all-time high. As the relative position of regional elites weakened, the Kremlin increasingly calculated that they would be able to secure the commitments of elites. At the same time, the political machines of regional elites were crucial drivers of the vote, so the Kremlin needed to work with regional elites. In exchange for supporting the party, governors were given the chance to have their clients placed on United Russia's party list and have them elected in SMD races (see, for instance, Petrov 2003, Hale 2004a, Slider 2006).

Breaking with the past, the Kremlin made overt commitments to United Russia in the run-up to the 2003 campaign. Most notably, the Kremlin set as its task not just to have loyalists elected to the Duma, but to have them elected under United Russia's banner. The Kremlin did give its assent to the launch of several smaller parties – Motherland, the Party of Life, People's Party – but as 2003 wore on, it became increasingly clear that United Russia would be the Kremlin's primary vehicle. And indeed, Putin addressed the party's preelection congress, pledging his support for the party.

After the elections, the Kremlin's position vis-à-vis regional elites continued to strengthen. Commodity prices were climbing at an even faster rate than in the early 2000s, reaching historical highs by 2007. Revenues from the sale of commodities swelled the federal budget and allowed for the creation of massive social spending programs. This concentration of resources in the hands of the government gave regional elites even more reason to develop good relations with Moscow. Moreover, the improved fiscal position of the federal government strengthened central state capacity. As Moscow became more efficient at collecting taxes, paying salaries, providing social services, and enforcing laws, regional elites began to lose some of the informal influence they had accrued in the 1990s.

In large part as a result of persistently highly commodity prices, the Russian economy continued to grow apace. From 2003 until 2008, it grew at an average rate of 7 percent per year, an even faster rate than in the early 2000s. Whether this was enough to make Putin popular – according to the Levada Center, 87 percent of Russians approved of Putin's work as president in August 2006 – or whether his own personal characteristics added percentage points to his popularity rating is not important for our purposes; the bottom line is that Putin was a wildly popular politician, who sat atop a massive central state apparatus that was flush with oil revenues.

Putin capitalized on these advantages. In September 2004, a terrorist hostage taking at a primary school in North Ossetia left hundreds dead.

4.2 Formation of a Dominant Party in Post-Soviet Russia 143

After the tragedy, Putin announced the need for more centralized control over regional affairs and proposed canceling gubernatorial elections. The legislation was passed in the Duma, and the president was given the authority to appoint Russia's governors henceforth.[63] By depriving governors of their electoral bases, Putin removed one of their most significant autonomous resources. Another important, but underappreciated centralizing reform of this era was the reform that ended most of the regions' rights to determine how to use natural resources extracted from the substrate. The Kremlin's preferences for such changes had been constant since the mid-1990s, but these reforms could not be passed when regional elites were so strong. The shift in the balance of resources away from regional elites made these changes possible. In this way, the institutional changes that redistributed power between center and regions can be seen as a reflection of the change in the balance of resources, rather than a cause of it.

With all these resources concentrated in its hands, it is perhaps surprising that the Kremlin continued to invest in a ruling party. Some existing accounts predict that the Kremlin would eschew party building when it was so strong vis-à-vis the weakened communist opposition. But in fact, the Kremlin stepped up its commitments to United Russia after 2003. Why? The answer lies in the strength of regional elites and the Kremlin's need to co-opt them. Regional elites had weakened to the point that they were more willing to make investments in a dominant party, but they were not so weak that the Kremlin did not need to work with them in order to win elections, pass legislation, and maintain social quiescence.

Even after the cancellation of direct gubernatorial elections, regional elites remained essential for mobilizing votes. The Kremlin learned this the hard way in fall 2004 and spring 2005 when United Russia suffered several electoral defeats in regional elections (see Figure 4.2), brought about chiefly by elite factionalism and lack of dependable governor support. In the 10 regions where governors were UR members, the party managed to collect 57 percent of seats, but in those 24 regions where governors were not UR members, the party managed to win only 41 percent of them.

Supplanting elites' political machines would be politically costly, because few alternative mechanisms for exercising social control existed. Those at the top of these clientelist networks were politically indispensable. Removing them could lead to the dissipation of their clienteles, and

---

[63] More concretely, the president presented his choice to the regional legislature, which then confirmed the choice. If the regional legislature rejected the president's candidate, the president proposed another candidate. If the legislature rejected the second candidate, the president could disband the regional legislature and call new elections.

thus degrade the regime's ability to mobilize votes. Thus, it was more cost-effective to co-opt and govern through these political machines, and this is exactly what the Kremlin did. In the first two years of the appointment era, Putin replaced only 13 of Russia's 89 governors, leaving in office scores of independent and even moderately oppositional governors. Even as late as January 2009, only 34 of Russia's elected governors had been replaced. Governors with the strongest political machines were much less likely to be replaced, especially in the first three years after the reform (Reuter and Robertson 2012).[64] In fact, some have suggested that Russia's strongest governors were resigned to the reform because they could then be reappointed and avoid looming term limits (Goode 2007, Titkov 2007). In turn, as I discuss in Chapter 5, United Russia won more votes over the course of the 2000s in those regions where governors with strong political machines supported it (see also Golosov 2011 and Reuter 2013). And, as several studies have shown, the Kremlin evaluated governors on their ability to mobilize votes for the ruling party such that those who were successful at mobilizing voters for United Russia were more likely to be reappointed (Turovsky 2009, Reuter and Robertson 2012, Reisinger and Moraski 2013). Thus, rather than firing them en masse, the Kremlin decided to co-opt Russia's governors and enlist them in the task of mobilizing support for a dominant party.

Russia's elites were strong enough that they needed to be co-opted, but not so strong that they would be prone to shirk their commitments to the ruling party. As it became increasing clear that elites could make such commitments, the Kremlin stepped up its own investments in the party. After the 2003 elections, the Kremlin did not equivocate in its support for the party of power as had become customary for the Kremlin to do. In a February 2006 speech before United Russia leaders, Surkov suggested that UR could "dominate the political system for at least the next 10–15 years."[65] In a July 2006 speech, he informed activists from another pro-Kremlin party, Just Russia, that the political system would be "built around United Russia" for the foreseeable future.[66] In 2007, Putin gave an unprecedented signal of his willingness to invest in a regime party by agreeing to head the United Russia party list. Putin associated himself even more closely with UR at the party's Ninth Congress in 2008,

---

[64] And when strong governors were dismissed, they were often replaced with clients from within their own regional administrations (see Buckley et al 2014).
[65] Accessed on United Russia Web site www.edinros.ru/news.html?id=111148 March 21, 2007.
[66] Accessed on United Russia Web site www.edinros.ru/news.html?id=114850, March 21, 2007.

4.2 Formation of a Dominant Party in Post-Soviet Russia

when he agreed to become party chairman. As prime minister, Putin attended every party congress – including a series of policy-based mini-congresses between 2009 and 2011 – and met frequently in public with party leaders.[67]

In its relations with the Duma, the presidential administration clearly privileged United Russia over other parties (Tolstykh 2007, Remington 2008). The president's representative to the Duma attended United Russia's faction meetings, which became the primary means of lobbying in the Duma (Tolstykh 2007). By working closely with UR in the Duma, the Kremlin sent a signal to elites about how access to legislative pork, rents, and policy would be determined.

In the years following the 2003 elections, the Kremlin also sanctioned party-building institutional changes that both strengthened United Russia's position and demonstrated the regime's commitment to investing in a dominant party. First, the electoral law for the State Duma elections was changed to a fully proportional system in which all deputies would be elected on closed party lists. Although United Russia was projected to do well in SMD races –disproportionality in first-past-the-post contests inherently favors large parties – the Kremlin loathed spending time and resources on coordinating candidates in SMD races. Thus, as Regina Smyth and her colleagues have astutely observed, the Kremlin "traded seats for certainty" (Smyth et al 2007). New legislation also increased the barrier for gaining seats from 5 to 7 percent. Simultaneously, the Kremlin encouraged regional legislatures to increase their electoral thresholds for the party list component to a minimum of 7 percent. With most regional legislatures dominated by United Russia, the regional assemblies needed little active encouragement. All regional elections held after December 2005 occurred in regions that had raised the barrier to at least 7 percent, while some such as Moscow City had raised it to as high as 10 percent.

Several other electoral reforms in the mid-2000s further strengthened UR at the expense of smaller parties. New legislation adopted in 2005 also mandated that all regional and municipal elections be held on one of two specially designated "United Election Days," one in the fall and one in the spring.[68] This allowed United Russia to take advantage of economies of scale in the coordination of its electoral campaigns. Electoral blocs were banned from participating in regional elections. This removed the governors' final method of creating their own regional organizations

---

[67] See, for example, "Edinaya Rossiya Prishla k svoemu lideru" *Kommersant*, June 9, 2009 and "V polukruge pervom" *Kommersant*, April 10, 2010.
[68] In 2011, the number of unified Election Days was reduced to one per year.

to contest elections.[69] Finally, members of one party were prohibited from serving on the party lists of another party. This meant that United Russia members could not simultaneously run on the party list of another party without first renouncing their membership.

A further party-building reform adopted in 2005 was the introduction of an imperative mandate rule, which was implemented after the 2007 elections. Under the imperative mandate rule, deputies are prohibited from changing their faction affiliations once they take their seat in the Duma. This reform was later applied to regional legislatures as well.

By implementing these changes the Kremlin sought to cultivate a single dominant party that could win elections and reduce the costs associated with identifying, coordinating, and channeling resources to pro-regime candidates. Simultaneously, it made it harder, at least in the short term, for the Kremlin to renege on its investments in UR by supporting independents or multiple parties.

The Kremlin's increasing willingness to commit to United Russia was also demonstrated by its cadre politics. As Figure 4.6 shows, after 2006, most newly appointed governors were United Russia members.[70]

In March 2009, new legislation gave the party with the majority in a regional legislature the responsibility of drawing up a list of three candidates for the president to select from when nominating a governor.[71] This reform sent a clear signal to governors and potential governors that party loyalty was an important criterion for promotion. Although they might have preferred to be directly elected, their consolation prize was that they were now more certain about what it would take to secure promotion.

Elites and United Russia

As described in the previous section, the balance of resources between center and regions had begun to shift in favor of Moscow after 1999. This

---

[69] In 7 of the 10 elections in the second half of 2004 regional electoral blocs gained seats in the assembly. In the first half of 2005, regional electoral blocs won seats in 5 of 7 assembly elections and in Sakhalin, a regional bloc won the election.

[70] In 2005 and 2006, the Kremlin was forced to co-opt many strong, independent governors and, thus, reappointed many non-UR incumbents. I treat the elections held in 2012 and 2013 as appointments because even in the new era of Russian gubernatorial elections, the president retains the right to dismiss sitting governors and appoint interim governors. As recent history has shown, the president uses this prerogative to anoint the regime's preferred candidate, who invariably wins the election.

[71] The reform had been proposed four years earlier. "Strana Sovetov Edinoi Rossii" *Gazeta. ru*, October 3, 2005. United Russia first implemented this procedure in October 2006, when the party nominated Aslan Tkhakushinov to the post of president of the Republic of Adygea. Presidential envoy Dmitrii Kozak consulted the Federal Presidium of United Russia as well as party leaders in Adygea. President Putin then proposed Tkhakushinov, who was confirmed by the regional assembly. "Edinaya Rossiya odobrila vybor Dmitry Kozaka" *Kommersant*, October 11, 2006.

4.2 Formation of a Dominant Party in Post-Soviet Russia

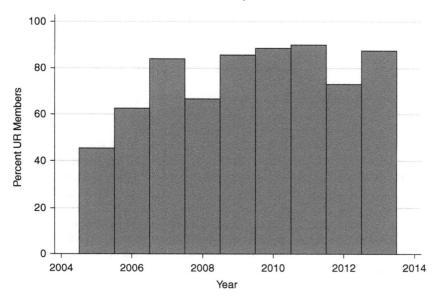

Figure 4.6 Share of gubernatorial appointees who are UR members prior to appointment.*

*Note: Figures for the latter half of 2012 and all of 2013 refer to direct elections.

shift made cooperation with the center more attractive to elites, who, as a result, grew more inclined to make some tentative commitments to a ruling party project. The first step in this direction was the formal merger of OVR with Unity in December 2001 and the decision of several prominent governors – i.e. Luzhkov, Shaimiev, Rakhimov, Merkushkin, Sobyanin – to allow their names to be associated with the new party. Several governors also allowed their clients to join newly formed United Russia factions in regional legislatures.

But much like the Kremlin, elites were at first hesitant to relinquish their autonomy and invest in United Russia.[72] Their first instinct was to retain their own political machines and make only superficial commitments to the party. Few governors joined it between 2001 and 2003, and those who did often did so in a limited way – for example, by joining the Higher Council, which did not require formal membership. In regional legislative elections, the party made little progress. UR found it difficult

---

[72] See "Edinaya Rossiya trebuyet ot Putina opredelennosti" *Nezavisimaya Gazeta*, July 2, 2003.

to attract independent candidates and by March 2003, the party had a majority in only 6 regional legislatures. It still held less than 20 percent of seats in 39 legislatures. Many governors remained overtly opposed to the party and ran their own regional parties or slates of candidates against the party.[73]

When regional elites did make promises to the new party of power, they often had a hard time keeping them. For example, Kemerovo Governor Aman Tuleev was a member of the party's Higher Council in 2003 and on United Russia's party list for the December 2003 elections, but he ran his own list of candidates, Sluzhu Kuzbassu (I Serve the Kuzbass), in the oblast regional election that same year. Several governors made a point to qualify their support for United Russia in the 2003 Duma election by noting that their future support was contingent on the party's future development (Slider 2006). Often governors who were members of United Russia demonstrated the shallowness of their commitment by using their administrative resources against the party even while they were formally affiliated with it. In the 2004 regional elections in Yaroslavl Oblast, the region's governor, Anatoly Lysytsin, who was by that time a party member, entered into a conflict with the head of the regional branch of United Russia and, allegedly, used administrative resources against the party in those elections. The party failed to win a majority of seats.[74] In other regions, governors joined the party, but tried to keep their decision secret.[75]

On policy debates, some party members had a hard time containing their criticism of government policy. For example, at the party's 2005 congress, held in the aftermath of controversial reforms that replaced a series of in-kind benefits to pensioners with monetary payments, tensions boiled over when Luzhkov gave a fiery speech criticizing the government for the reforms.[76]

Thus, in the early 2000s, many elites avoided affiliation with the party, while others made limited commitments. Regional elites were at first reluctant to invest in a dominant party because their independent resources were still significant. These resources afforded them

[73] A prominent example was Eduard Rossel, who was highly critical of Putin's centralizing reforms in the early 2000s and whose "For Our Native Ural" party beat United Russia in the regions's 2002 legislative elections.
[74] Author's interview with Alexander Prokhorov, head of United Russia's Regional Executive Committee in 2004, June 11, 2009, Yaroslavl.
[75] "Kurskii Gubernator Taino Vstupil v Edinuyu Rossiyu" *Kommersant*, March 13, 2005.
[76] For a good account of the debates between party and government leaders at this congress see "Edinaya Rossiya: ot partii vlasti k pravyashei partii" Politkom.ru. Center for Political Technologies, November 28, 2005. Accessed online www.politcom.ru/1664.html, June 20, 2014.

4.2 Formation of a Dominant Party in Post-Soviet Russia   149

the opportunity to achieve many of their political goals without relying on the Kremlin. Entering the cooperative bargain with the Kremlin was attractive, but still not yet attractive enough that elites were willing to relinquish their hard-earned autonomous resources. However, as noted, a surge in oil revenues, strong economic growth, and Putin's persistently high popularity rating were leading to a shift in the balance of resources away from the regions and toward Moscow. In turn, the Kremlin was using its newfound resources to reduce the autonomy of elites. As this balance of resources shifted, cooperation with the Kremlin became increasingly necessary in order to gain access to rents, policy, and career advancement. Thus, the incentives for elites to cooperate with the Kremlin grew over the course of the early and mid-2000s. And as a result, more and more elites found it in their best interest to seek cooperation with the Kremlin and make commitments to the emergent ruling party. Thus, after 2002 an increasing number of political elites began joining United Russia and serving in its leadership organs. Figure 4.1 shows this dynamic for governors. Similar dynamics were observed for regional legislators – by 2006, UR had majorities in 76 regional legislatures, up from just 6 in 2003 – mayors, local legislators, and businessmen. This trend persisted through the mid-2000s as the Kremlin continued to strengthen vis-à-vis elites.

That elites joined because of calculations about their own autonomy and resources is demonstrated by several pieces of qualitative and quantitative evidence. As discussed, United Russia initially performed better in the party list component of regional elections. Prominent single member district deputies with their own autonomous electoral resources eschewed joining the party and often beat United Russia candidates. Further quantitative evidence is presented in Chapters 6 and 7, where I analyze in detail why governors and regional legislators chose to affiliate with United Russia when they did and find that those regional elites strong in autonomous resources postponed joining United Russia longer than those without. If Putin could have created a dominant party whenever he desired, then it should not be the case that variation in resources determines the order of elites' entry into United Russia.

My interviews with regional legislators in Perm, Yaroslavl, Kurgan, Kirov, Chelyabinsk, Ekaterinburg, and Yoshkar-Ola are consistent with those findings. Deputies were unanimous in professing a desire to retain as much autonomy as possible. Even those who had joined United Russia quite early and occupied leadership positions in the regional branch lamented centralizing tendencies within the party. Deputies who had joined the party later and, therefore, did not have leadership positions in the regional branch tended to be more concerned about remaining autonomous of the regional party leadership. As the assistant to one deputy in the Perm Krai legislature put it, "People know XXXX in YYYY [the deputy's hometown]. He is respected and is authoritative as a manager. He could get elected without any sort of party affiliation. So he only linked up with United Russia at the last minute."[77]

In Chapter 7, I find that the characteristics of the firms that deputies represent help explain when they decided to give up their autonomy to United Russia. Deputies from state dependent enterprises (i.e. state owned, easily taxed, easily harassed, or dependent on government contracts) were more likely to join United Russia. In the interviews I have conducted, most deputies, for obvious reasons, were not forthright about how their firm's dependence on the state influenced their party affiliation decisions. However, there were some exceptions. One deputy in Yaroslavl explained that when he ran for city council in 2004, he and his investment partners calculated that United Russia affiliation was not necessary because they had already managed to obtain all the permits for the shopping center they were building.[78] Several other independent SMD deputies who only joined United Russia after being elected maintained that their polling showed that United Russia affiliation would have hurt their chances of winning in their districts. Of course, some deputies thought that being affiliated with Putin's party was a boon to their campaign and so joined. On the basis of these interviews, it is hard to sort out who had more personal resources, but the important point to conclude from such responses is that if a candidate believed that he/she could run and win without United Russia, he or she usually did so.

Few interview respondents reported being coerced into joining the party. In an interview with the author, former Samara governor Konstantin Titov claimed that he did not feel pressure from the center to join. Instead, he explained his decision to postpone joining in the following way: "I needed to think about the situation... I needed to see what the results would be. What kind of position it [UR] would take. How it would work. And when I saw that it was going to be something real, then I decided to join."

Moreover, the fact that many governors waited several years to join even after the decision to cancel elections was made in October 2004 indicates that coercion was not the only factor influencing the decision of elites to join. If Putin had the power to force all elites into the party, then it is hard to see why the party would exist: all elites would simply be

---

[77] This was an anonymous interview, so the deputy's name and hometown are obscured (XXXX and YYYY).
[78] Author's anonymous interview, March 3, 2010, Yaroslavl.

4.2 Formation of a Dominant Party in Post-Soviet Russia

purged and no resources would be expended on creating a party organization to manage relations with them.

The perspective that I develop also suggests that elites can reap benefits from party membership. When they are strong in political resources, these potential benefits are insufficient to induce dominant party affiliation, but as resources shift toward the center, the calculus of elites changes. Evidence from the Putin era suggests that these benefits existed and that elites considered them when making their affiliation decisions. Chapter 5 discusses in detail the benefits that United Russia provided to elites, so here I simply preview this discussion and relate these benefits to the affiliation calculus of elites.

To begin with, the Kremlin offered a number of explicit carrots to elites in order to secure their cooperation. In addition to allowing governors to avoid term limits by reappointing them, some have suggested that the centralizing reforms were also accompanied by several concessions to the regions such as allocating regional disbursements of national project funds and allowing regional governments discretion over the implementation of the new law on local self-government (Kynev 2006). Reports also indicated that United Russia directed extra budgetary funds to those regions where governors promised to support United Russia – and only United Russia – in elections.[79]

Governors also valued access to the party brand and, as the 2000s passed, were increasingly interested in making concessions to gain access to it. One example that grabbed headlines was a deal made between the UR leadership and Sverdlovsk Oblast Governor Eduard Rossel in 2003. In February of that year, a party delegation traveled to Ekaterinburg to hold negotiations with Rossel, whose "For Our Native Urals" party had just beaten UR handily in regional elections. After negotiations, the delegation's leader, Duma Deputy Vladislav Reznik, announced that "an understanding has been reached between the party and the Sverdlovsk governor about mutual support. United Russia asked Eduard Rossel to support its SMD candidates in the upcoming elections. And we will support Eduard Rossel if he runs for reelection with the same platform that he has now." By putting his machine to work for the party, Rossel was able to extract support from the center for reelection.

In exchange for their support, governors were often given the chance to have their clients placed on United Russia's party list. In contrast to 1999, when most governors advanced their clients as independents or through their own party vehicles, they did it also through the UR list in

---

[79] See, for example, "Gubernatoram vypisyvayut material'nuyu pomoshsch'" *Kommersant*, April 18, 2007.

2003 and almost exclusively through UR in 2007. In the Fourth Duma, 53 percent of UR deputies were from the regions. In the Fifth and Sixth Dumas, the shares were 59 percent and 56 percent, respectively. Thus, despite the centralizing tendencies of the 2000s, United Russia's faction remained mostly composed of deputies lobbying regional interests.

Putin's orientation toward the party also affected the calculations of elites. In interviews, several deputies mentioned their respect for President Putin as a reason for joining. As one early-joining deputy in Kurgan stated, "I respect Putin very much... I wanted to be a member of his party and I thought there was a future here."[80] Vyacheslav Volodin, then-secretary of the Presidium, explained his decision to join the party thus: "We joined the party because the President united us... After the 1990s, the country needed to be brought together – the territory, elites, all of society. The President did this... Vladimir Vladimirovich Putin is the moral leader of our party and we joined United Russia because this process of unification was occurring around him."[81]

In the regions, many elites closely followed signals from their governors in deciding whether to join. One deputy in Chelyabinsk said, "I have the deepest respect for Sumin [then-governor]. When he had his own party, I was a member. When he went over to United Russia, it was clear what I should do."[82] Thus, when making their affiliation decisions, elites not only considered how the balance of resources was changing or what concessions they could extract from the Kremlin, but also took cues from the Kremlin, and from their governors, to help them assess whether the party of power would be supported into the future. The signals that Putin and the governors gave in the early 2000s were sufficient to influence those legislators with insignificant or state dependent resources to join the party, while those with greater resources awaited deeper signals from the executive branch and more conclusive proof that they could not achieve their political goals while remaining independent.

Finally, when deciding to join, elites also took into consideration the institutional benefits of being a ruling party member. In my interviews with regional legislators, almost all cited a desire to lobby their interests from within the party's legislative faction. A commonly heard refrain,

---

[80] Author's interview with Alexander Luzin, leader of United Russia faction in Kurgan Oblast Duma, July 24, 2008.
[81] "Sekretar' presidiuma general'nogo soveta partii 'Edinoi Rossii' Vyacheslav Volodin" Osnova nashei ideologii – politika presidenta Vladimira Putina" *Izvestiya*, February 22, 2007.
[82] Author's interview with Semen Mitel'man, chairman of the Economic Politics Committee Chelyabinsk Oblast Legislative Assembly, July 5, 2007.

4.2 Formation of a Dominant Party in Post-Soviet Russia   153

especially from late-joining deputies, was that if you wanted to have influence in the legislature, you needed to be a UR member. There was an assumption that United Russia membership would translate into better legislative access. When Pavel Krashennikov, a prominent liberal Duma deputy and specialist on legal reform, was asked in 2003 why he had left SPS to join United Russia he responded:

We could, of course, all walk to the grave constantly talking about joining forces with Yabloko [another liberal party in Russia]. Maybe some parts of society would like that. But it seems to me that most want something different ... they want judicial reforms to proceed and so that there won't be counterjudicial reforms as there were 200 years ago. Therefore, I decided to build on what I've done and continue to work on judicial reform and on the new housing code. I understand that I will get more done on this if I will be persuading from inside the system, than if I were to persuade from outside the system. That's it.[83]

Businessmen in particular were frank about how joining the party could help them lobby for their businesses. As the leader of the United Russia faction in Yaroslavl Oblast told me:

There are lots of different people who joined our faction, many entrepreneurs ... and everyone wants everything all for themselves. Many entered parliament in order to defend their own interests and even joined our party in order to defend these interests, to lobby the interests of their own business, to get something for themselves ... and our role as the faction leadership was to keep in mind that old Soviet principle "Think about the motherland before you think about yourself."[84]

In addition to legislative goods, many regional elites viewed party membership as useful because it provided an elevated public platform or better access to the central government. One of Lapina and Chirikova's interviews with a Samara entrepreneur illustrates this viewpoint: "Business that wants to raise its profile, that wants to be involved in some sort of business-get together gets involved with the party [then-Unity]. This is mostly large business, which needs contacts with the center, which wants access to information and to participate in different programs" (Lapina and Chirikova 2002, 258).

In fact, it was not just politicians and legislators who cited the career benefits of being a party member as their motivation for joining. In 2010, the Russian edition of *Esquire* published a series of interviews with famous entertainers – actors, directors, musicians, ballerinas, television

---

[83] "Edinaya Rossiya slishkom mnogo prinyala" *Gazeta.ru*, December 18, 2003.
[84] Author's interview with Vladimir Savelev, March 1, 2010.

presenters, and so on – asking them why they had decided to join the ruling party. Russia's first openly gay recording artist, Boris Moiseev, explained his decision in simple terms:

A real artist shouldn't be involved in politics, but in order to live quietly and peacefully, every artist needs to be in a serious party. I used to be in another party – I won't name names – but I left that party because it wasn't providing me with, how to say, any sort of bunker, any sort of defense. After all, I am the type of person who has his own views, and I have expressed them publicly – that the world is not just black and white, but blue, orange, green, and many other colors. And therefore, I needed some type of bunker, some type of protection… Of course it is more peaceful for me to be a member of the ruling party. People need to do what they do – live, work, study, own something – and not be worried all the time. You know, I used to go on tour and half my shows were cancelled because someone there didn't like me, but now it's somehow uncomfortable to cancel my shows. After all, I'm a member of United Russia. I can go to some boss in Moscow and complain: "You know what they are doing to me, a party member? They are insulting me."[85]

Interviewed elites also recognized the uncertainty-reducing benefits of working within a dominant party. Even those who lamented the loss of autonomy suffered under United Russia admitted that they were able to have more influence on legislation because the legislative process had become more predictable under United Russia.[86] One leading member of the United Russia faction in Sverdlovsk Oblast (and an early joiner in that region) noted: "Several times each session we tell the leader of our faction which projects and initiatives are most important to us. Everyone does this and a fair division is then worked out. This way we all know that we can fulfill certain promises to our districts and our supporters… Personally, this arrangement lets me sleep better at night."[87]

Recognizing all these potential benefits and the increasing strength of Putin, elites began making more serious commitments to United Russia over the course of the decade. An increasing number, including many formerly independent SMD deputies in the regions, began linking their names and reputations to the party by becoming formal party members. In addition, more and more regional elites began relinquishing some of

---

[85] "Zachem baleriny i gei vstupayut v Edinuyu Rossiyu" Russian *Esquire*, March 24, 2010.
[86] Interviews with Yurii Yolokhov, United Russia faction member in Perm Krai Legislative Assembly, July 10, 2008; Evgenii Vyaznikov, vice chairman of the Perm Krai Legislative Assembly, July 12, 2008, Perm; Pavel Smirnov, chairman of the Committee on Agriculture, Ecology, and Natural Resources in Yaroslavl Oblast Duma, March 5, 2010, Yaroslavl; and Olga Khitrova, member of United Russia faction in Yaroslavl Oblast Duma, January 31, 2010, Yaroslavl.
[87] Author's interview with Nail Shairmardanov, vice chairman of Sverdlovsk Oblast Duma, July 2, 2007, Ekaterinburg.

their political authority to an increasingly centralized party. Aburamoto (2010), for example, shows how the local governor's party in Khabarovsk was melded into United Russia. Increasingly, over the course of the 2000s, regional secretaries who were governors' clients were replaced by party and legislative functionaries.

In turn, United Russia's leadership took an ever more active role in the management of regional elections. For example, in the run-up to the March 2007 regional elections in Murmansk, Andrei Vorob'ev, chairman of United Russia's Central Executive Committee, personally flew to Murmansk in order to iron out a conflict between the regions' two major financial industrial groups (the Kolsk Metallurgical Company, a daughter affiliate of Norilsk Nickel, and Apatit, a company controlling 85 percent of Russia's phosphate production) over spots on the party list.[88] In the past, the regional governor would have been given discretion over the allocation of these spots, but in this case, the United Russia central leadership decided the appropriate allocation of list spots.

The party also acquired the ability to sanction elites for lack of discipline. This was evident in the Duma, where party discipline among pro-presidential deputies increased markedly after the formation of the United Russia faction after the 2003 election (Remington 2006). Similar upticks in voting cohesion followed the creation of UR factions in regional legislatures. And, as Chapter 5 discusses in detail, breaches of party discipline were routinely punished.

4.3 Conclusion

This chapter demonstrated how the leader–elite commitment framework outlined in Chapter 2 illuminates Russia's experience with regime parties in the 2000s. Specifically, it illustrated how changes in the balance of resources between the Kremlin and elites as well as strategic calculations about each side's willingness to commit to a ruling party affected the process of dominant party formation. In 1999 and 2000, regional elites were near the peak of their power. Their political machines allowed them to hold an independent political line and made them reluctant to link their fates to a dominant party. With good reason, the Kremlin was skeptical of the ability of elites to remain committed to a ruling party and, therefore, did not want to pay the costs of sustaining such a party. In turn, the Kremlin's reluctance to invest seriously in Unity gave elites even less reason to make their own commitments.

---

[88] "Murmanskikh edinorossov pomirila rukha Moskvy." *Kommersant*, December 11, 2006.

In the early 2000s, elites remained hesitant to relinquish their autonomy to a centralized ruling party. But as the decade progressed, the balance of power between the Kremlin and regions changed as strong economic growth and treasury-filling oil revenues gave Putin enormous political capital. Given the already expansive formal powers of the Russian president and the region's persistent financial dependence on Moscow, these changes were enough to make cooperation with the center more attractive to elites, and, in turn, allowed Putin to push through centralizing reforms that weakened – but did not eliminate – elites' political machines. The Kremlin's preferences for such changes had been constant since the mid-1990s, but these reforms could not be passed when regional elites were so strong. These changes in the balance of resources also increased the incentives of elites to solve their own commitment problem vis-à-vis the center and find a way to cooperate with the Kremlin in the confines of a dominant party. Indeed, to the extent that rising oil prices and the attendant increase in rent revenues precipitated these shifts, this chapter demonstrates how natural resource wealth may not always lead autocrats to undermine their institutions. Rather, resource rents can abet the emergence of autocratic institutions if the primary impediment to institutional genesis is the hesitance of elites. In such cases, central state control over rents can make elites more inclined to cooperate with autocrats.

Importantly, however, elites were not so weak in the early to mid-2000s that the Kremlin could dispense with them entirely. The Kremlin needed access to the political machines of regional elites in order to win elections, maintain social quiescence, and implement policy. In this way, the balance of power in Russia in the 2000s resembles the balance that Migdal found to be characteristic of many African countries in the post-colonial period, when state leaders could remove any one strongman at any time, but "the pattern of social control" that they represented could not be undermined (Migdal 1988, 141). Putin could deploy his resources to have any one governor removed – an act that became simpler after the cancellation of gubernatorial elections in 2004 – but he still needed the collective support of the governors' political machines.

Putin wanted to increase his control over regional elites. And so, he took measures, such as the cancellation of governors' elections, to place them further under his control. But he also knew that eliminating their power bases entirely would strip away the regime's ability to mobilize votes and govern cost-effectively. This is an enduring dilemma for autocrats. How can an autocrat appropriate the political resources of elites without destroying those resources? If the Kremlin were to remove all

4.3 Conclusion

governors, the clientelist networks of the old governors would be disrupted and newly appointed outsiders might lack popularity among voters and local elites. On the other hand, granting full autonomy to governors would maximize their vote-getting ability, but then the Kremlin could not depend on being able to secure their support. The solution was to weaken them to a point and then co-opt them into the emergent dominant party.

Putin is hardly the first authoritarian leader to be faced with a need to control and draw upon the resources of elites simultaneously. In an earlier era, the first general secretary of the Communist Party of the Soviet Union faced a similar dilemma that he solved through the creation of a system that would outlive him by almost 40 years. Voslensky sums up Stalin's situation:

> Stalin's protégés were his creatures. But the converse was also true; he was their creature, for they were the social base of his dictatorship, and they certainly hoped he would ensure them collective dictatorship over the country. In servilely carrying out his orders, they counted on the fact that these were given in their interests. Stalin could of course at any moment liquidate any one of them (as he often did), but in no circumstances could he liquidate the nomenklaturist class as a whole. He showed zealous concern for his protégés' interests and the reinforcement of their power, authority, and privileges. He was the creature of his creatures, and he knew that they would scrupulously respect his wishes as long as he respected theirs. (1984, 51)

Putin found this approach attractive and, no doubt, familiar. Putin's power depended on his ability to keep elites loyal. In turn, elites needed access to Putin's personal and political resources to advance their careers. Putin's power was such that he could eliminate any one elite actor, but it was not sufficient to undermine fully the system of political control that regional elites commanded. And so, while fraud, repression, and patronage clearly have been important tools that the regime uses to maintain control, the successful co-optation of regional elites was a key intermediate factor that made these tactics successful and also contributed to regime stability on its own.

United Russia was the embodiment of this cooperative relationship. As elites joined the party and the balance of resources continued to shift in favor of the Kremlin, the Kremlin calculated that it could now risk its own investments in the emergent party. In turn, the signals of commitment that the Kremlin sent emboldened elites to make their own deeper commitments. And in return for giving up their autonomy, regional elites were granted access to spoils and the various benefits of party membership in United Russia. Thus, rather than being imposed from above, United Russia emerged out of a process of co-optation and cooperation between the Kremlin and regional elites. And as Chapter 5 shows, credible commitments associated with the dominant party system ensured that cooperation between the two sides would be stable.

5 United Russia as the Dominant Party

The goal of this chapter is to provide a theoretically driven assessment of the role that United Russia plays in Russia's authoritarian regime. Since the theory in Chapter 2 specifies that dominant parties help leaders and elites reap the gains from mutual cooperation, this chapter outlines the benefits that United Russia provides to both Putin and other elites. I outline how the party helps Russia's leaders maintain elite loyalty, control legislatures, win elections, and manage political appointments. For elites, the party provides access to spoils and lobbying opportunities and, importantly, reduces uncertainty over how those spoils are to be distributed. Following the commitment framework developed in previous chapters, I also discuss the ways that the dominant party system has helped the Kremlin and elites make their commitments to cooperate with one another credible. In particular, I highlight how Russia's leaders delegated political influence to the party, limited their ability to duplicate the party's functions, gave elites the institutional tools to solve their collective action problems, made public commitments to the party, and linked the maintenance of the dominant party system to other regime institutions. Elites made their commitments credible by linking their political machines to United Russia and giving the central party leadership the ability to sanction them for lack of discipline. In addition, I discuss how the party helps leaders and elites monitor each other. Ultimately, however, Russia's leaders stopped short of granting the party direct, collective control over the executive branch. In this way, United Russia differs significantly from the CPSU. Neither Putin, Medvedev, nor most important figures in the executive branch owe their careers to the party, and the executive branch sets the political course in Russia. This arrangement places limits on United Russia's autonomy.

Nonetheless, I argue that United Russia has more institutional weight than many accounts allow. Because of the commitments that both sides made and the benefits that the dominant party system provided, both the Kremlin and other elites developed an interest in the maintenance of that system. In particular, the Kremlin came to depend on United Russia for electoral support and the maintenance of elite cohesion, while many elites began to rely on United Russia for the provision of spoils, especially in legislatures. Thus, the Kremlin was loath to dismantle the dominant party system for fear of provoking elite discord, and elites were reluctant to defect for fear of losing access to patronage. In this way, the party came to serve as a bundle of rules, norms, and agreements that structure the incentives of both sides and, in turn, made Russia's authoritarian regime more stable. Indeed, as I will argue, United Russia became, over the course of the 2000s, one of the key pillars of regime stability in Putin's Russia.

5.1 United Russia's Role: Benefits to Elites

Access to Policy and Spoils

One of the primary benefits that United Russia provides elites is access to policy and spoils. The party does this primarily through its domination of legislatures at the national, regional, and local levels. Beginning in the Fourth Duma, United Russia supplanted the "zero-reading" – a consultative, prefloor logrolling mechanism whereby individual deputies bargained with the government – with meetings of its faction Presidium (Lyubimov 2005). Most legislative bargaining now runs through these Presidium meetings held every week when the Duma is in session. Deputies, ministries, and lobbying groups hammer out agreements in these sessions, such that the faction votes cohesively on the floor. In order to maximize their chances of influencing legislative output, deputies must be members of the faction and have a good relationship with United Russia's legislative leadership. This conclusion is supported by a number of analytic reports produced by the Center for the Study of Business–State Interactions, a Moscow-based think tank that businesses consult on how to lobby the Russian government.[1] These reports advise clients that the key points of legislative access in the Duma are the United Russia faction and the standing committees, the most important

[1] The various reports and studies issued by this group offer a rich source of advice for businesses on how to influence legislation and specific examples of successful lobbying efforts. See, for example, Tolstykh 2007. See also "Otraslevoye lobbirovanie v Rossii (naibolye aktualnyie ekonomicheskiye zakonoproekti na nachalo raboty Gosudarstvennoi Dumy FS RF V sozyva." Center for the Study of Business–State Interactions. Moscow. Accessed online: www.gr.ru/content/11. October 1, 2014. The center's yearly rankings of the Duma's top lobbyists regularly include only United Russia members. See Luchshie lobbisty Gosudarstvennoi Dumy FS RF IV sozyva, 2003–2007, special issue of Lobbying. ru journal, p. 65, available at: www.lobbying.ru.

5.1 United Russia's Role: Benefits to Elites

of which are chaired by United Russia members.[2] Indeed, according to data collected by the center, only 4.5 percent of the 334 deputy-initiated laws passed by the Fifth Duma between December 2, 2007, and July 29, 2010, lacked a cosponsor from United Russia.

This centrality of United Russia's role in the legislature is further demonstrated by academic case studies of the Russian legislative process, which tend to emphasize the patronage-distributing functions of the dominant party. Summarizing the conclusions of his study of rent distribution in the Fourth Duma, Thomas Remington writes:

> Less widely publicized, but of no less importance for Russian politics, however, is the activity of dominant party legislators off the floor, where they have created numerous opportunities to satisfy their appetites for money and influence. Once of piece of legislation has reached the floor for a vote, members of the dominant party rarely deviate from the party line, but in order to reach agreement on the final language of the legislation, deputies in the State Duma and members of the Federation Council act as entrepreneurs, championing the causes of the agencies, firms, and industries that sponsor them… This makes parliament an arena in which organized interests, both private and bureaucratic, compete for power over public policy by working through their allies in parliament. The result, however, is to make United Russia more at target of intensive lobbying than a source of unified and consistent policy direction for the country.

These same conclusions also apply to regional and local parliaments, where logrolling is carried out almost exclusively in United Russia faction meetings prior to plenary sessions. In most regional parliaments, the party has come to structure the lawmaking process in a way that was unthinkable in the early 2000s when almost all regional parliaments were composed of independent deputies (Glubotskii and Kynev 2003). In interviews with United Russia faction leaders and deputies from Perm Krai, Sverdlovsk Oblast, Kurgan Oblast, Chelyabinsk Oblast, Yaroslavl Oblast, and Kirov Oblast, nearly all respondents agreed that the key decisions on legislation were made during the faction meeting.[3] One deputy in Yaroslavl explained his decision to join United Russia in the following way: "I understood very well that the faction had a majority and that all important decisions that would be discussed in the Duma would be made by United Russia. If I weren't a member, I could still

---

[2] In the Fourth Duma, United Russia kept all leadership positions for itself. In the Fifth and Sixth Dumas, United Russia shared some leadership positions with opposition politicians in an attempt to co-opt opposition parties, but it kept the most important positions for itself (see Reuter and Turovsky 2014 and Reuter and Robertson 2015 for more discussion).

[3] See Chapter 4 for some excerpts from interviews with legislators discussing their desire to lobby inside the UR faction.

publicly announce my positions, but I couldn't have any influence on the decisions being made like I could behind closed doors at the fraction meetings."[4]

United Russia's control over legislation should not be overstated, however. In Putin era Russia, the executive branch, which is largely nonpartisan, sets policy direction in the Duma. The original drafts of many important bills are written by the presidential administration or the government, and representatives of both are present at United Russia faction meetings to ensure that the policy priorities of the executive are met. At the regional and local levels, party penetration of the executive branch is much higher, but nonpartisan representatives of regional and local administrations often set the policy direction at their respective levels as well.[5] Thus, those who argue that the independent influence of Russia's legislature has weakened since the 1990s, when it frequently clashed with Yeltsin, are surely correct (e.g. Fish 2005, Whitmore 2010).[6]

And yet, it would be a mistake to dismiss Russia's legislative organs entirely. As an increasing number of studies show, authoritarian legislatures can be important arenas for the distribution of spoils, patronage, rents, and policy influence, even if general policy direction is set by the chief executive (e.g. Gandhi 2008, Lust-Okar 2006, Blaydes 2011, Truex 2014).[7] And while legislatures in Putin era Russia may appear downright impotent when compared to most democratic parliaments – the implicit frame of comparison for many studies of Russian legislatures – they appear quite powerful when compared to most autocratic parliaments. For example, it seems clear that the State Duma has more institutional autonomy than the General People's Congress under Qaddafi, which met once a year for only two weeks, or Swaziland's National Assembly, which has no permanent staff and has one-fifth of its members appointed by the king.

---

[4] Author's interview with Ilya Osipov, Yaroslavl, March 3, 2010.
[5] The dominance of the regional executive branch over the legislature would not diminish United Russia's policy-making influence if the legislative initiatives of United Russia governors were formulated by nonstate party organs. But, as I discuss later, this is rare.
[6] Regional legislatures also frequently clashed with governors in the 1990s, but with the rise of United Russia, such conflicts were largely put to bed. However, in the 2000s, conflict between regional legislatures and governors was much more frequent than that between the president and the Duma.
[7] In Mubarak era Egypt, for example, Blaydes (2011) illustrates how parliamentary seats translated into protection of one's business interests, access to ministers, and preferential state loans. Lust-Okar (2006) discusses how Jordanian parliamentarians use their seats to secure patronage for their constituents. Truex (2014) shows how the businesses of Chinese legislators have higher profit margins than other businesses.

5.1 United Russia's Role: Benefits to Elites

Such impressions are confirmed by cross-national data. The Parliamentary Powers Index, a cross-national measure of parliamentary strength in 158 countries compiled by Steven Fish and Matthew Kroenig, ranked the State Duma as the 88th most powerful parliament in the world as of 2007. This put it well behind most democracies but also ahead of parliaments in countries such as Malaysia, Singapore, China, Zimbabwe, Zambia, Kazakhstan, and Algeria (Fish and Kroenig 2009). It is ranked as the 26th most powerful parliament among the 81 autocracies and hybrid regimes (regimes with Polity IV scores less than 7) in the data set.

Consistent with this view of Russia's parliaments as "typical" authoritarian legislatures, several recent studies highlight the ways that Russian legislatures serve as mechanisms of co-optation and rent distribution. Reuter and Robertson (2015) find that the co-optation of Communist politicians in regional legislatures significantly reduces protest by the KPRF. Remington (2008) and Chaisty (2013) analyze how the State Duma provides a forum where powerful business interests lobby and influence legislation. Indeed, the deep penetration of Russian parliaments by business interests is prima facie evidence that these organs act as fora for lobbying. For example, Chaisty (2006) calculates that 109 of 310 United Russia members in the Fourth Duma were direct representatives of big business. The representation of such economic interests sets the State Duma apart from the Supreme Soviet, where representation was based on class quotas and key economic interests were absent (Vannemen 1977).

As for regional parliaments, Chapter 7 of this book shows that most contained representatives of the region's major enterprises in the 2000s. Forty-eight percent of regional deputies between 2001 and 2010 were businessmen. And as Szakonyi (2015) shows, such representation translates into real benefits: businesses with representation in regional parliaments have significantly higher profits than those without direct legislative representation.

Studies by Russian analysts draw similar conclusions. Starodubtsev (2009) shows how in the Fourth Duma, SMD deputies used their legislative seats to extract budgetary concessions for their districts. An in-depth study carried out by the Center for the Study of Business–State Interactions concluded that lobbying the executive branch was necessary to "quickly decide a specific matter of an individual character while lobbying the legislative branch permitted groups to defend their general, long term interests" (Makhortov 2008, 4). The report concluded that lobbying via the executive branch was a top priority for businessmen, but at the same time, a "majority of respondents consider membership in a

Table 5.1 *Bills passed in Duma by initiator, December 2, 2007–July 29, 2010*

Initiator	Number of bills passed	% of all bills passed
President	127	13
Government	321	33
Federation Council deputies	72	7
State Duma deputies	334	34
Federation Council	6	1
Regional legislatures	104	11
Supreme Court	11	1
Arbitration court	3	0.30
Total	978	100.3

Note: Shares do not total 100 because of rounding.

party a key factor in the advancement of one's interests" (Makhortov 2008, 5). Naturally, United Russia was the most favored party among those interviewed.

Data from the State Duma indicate that deputies play a prominent role in initiating bills. As Table 5.1 shows, more than one-third of the laws passed during the first years of the Fifth Duma originated with Duma deputies.

All treaty and convention ratifications are included in the list of bills initiated by the president and government, so these numbers actually overstate the legislative activity of the executive branch. When ratifications are removed from the data, it turns out that the Duma and Federation Council together account for a larger share of initiated non-treaty bills than the executive branch.

My interviews with Duma deputies and officials in the presidential administration were concordant with the conclusions sketched previously. All recognized the substantial influence of the executive branch, but also pointed out the ways that deputies influence legislation by either initiating their own bills and or trying to influence the contents of legislation introduced by the executive branch. As Konstantin Kostin, former head of the presidential administration's Department of Internal Politics, characterized it in a 2014 interview:

Of course the Presidential Administration takes the lead in writing many bills. But we are all on the same team. There are so many examples where the Presidential Administration takes into consideration the opinions of United Russia deputies on its own bills. A lot of consultation with deputies is done before

5.1 United Russia's Role: Benefits to Elites

bills are introduced, and then after they are introduced a whole new process of consultation is begun.[8]

State Duma deputies whom I interviewed had a similar view of the matter. Many emphasized that even bills introduced by the executive branch could be influenced and amended in the committees and in faction meetings.[9] Prominent United Russia deputy Vladimir Pligin admitted that the Duma and the president coordinate their actions, an outcome that he viewed as natural in a situation where the majority party in parliament and the president are allies. He added, however, that

> it is probably true that the public, deliberative side of parliament hasn't been very prominent, or maybe even has become secondary, which has led society to take a fairly skeptical view of parliament. There has been fairly serious public criticism. And that criticism has probably been justified. There have been instances when parliament didn't serve its role as a public chamber for discussion. At the same time, it is also necessary to point out the behind the scenes work done by parliament on legislation. It has remained extremely significant. The texts of bills change significantly between the first reading and the final drafts, and we do serious substantive work on those bills in the committees.[10]

These sentiments were echoed by deputies in regional legislatures. No deputies reported that federal officials sought to influence legislation directly, but both regional deputies and regional administration officials recognized that the regional administration usually set the main policy priorities for the legislature. And yet, United Russia legislators believed that they could influence the content of legislation and even extract concessions from the governor when the opinions of legislators and the governor differed. One deputy in Yarolslavl Oblast offered the example of a controversial bill on regional privatization. Existing legislation had accorded privileges to the current renters of municipal property when it was privatized, but this privilege only applied to small and medium businesses. Businessmen from the United Russia faction agreed to eliminate the size requirements, but the governor objected and threatened to veto the bill. In the end, according to this legislator, an agreement was worked out that raised, but did not eliminate, the size requirements for the privilege.[11] This anecdote is a reminder that the absence of public conflict between legislators and the executive is insufficient evidence to conclude

---

[8] Author's interview with Konstantin Kostin, June 9, 2014, Moscow.
[9] Author's interview with Evgenii Trofimov, member of UR faction in Fourth Duma and vice chairman of United Russia's Executive Committee, June 11, 2013, Moscow.
[10] Author's interview with Vladimir Pligin, June 13, 2013, Moscow.
[11] Author's interview with Ilya Osipov, Yaroslavl, March 3, 2010.

that the former do not influence the content of legislation, since the final content of bills may be a product of bargaining between the two.

Aside from direct access to spoils via the legislative process, United Russia also offers its members an elevated platform from which to lobby their interests before other key political actors, particularly in the executive branch. Summarizing a study of lobbying by governors conducted by the Center for the Study of Business–State Interactions, Bogatyreva (2013) concludes:

> An analysis of expert commentary ... permits several conclusions about how partisanship affects the ability of governors to advance regional interests at the federal level. Among the main factors that affect their lobbying effectiveness are: good results for United Russia in federal and regional elections, successful participation of the governor in UR primaries, expansion of his influence in [United Russia's] regional *politsovet*, and his election to the party's Higher Council... Thus, the ability of governors to advance their interests can be severely undermined if there is conflict between him and the regional branch of United Russia, which would signify that the governor lacks the support of regional elites. (Bogatyreva 2013, 136)

I encountered similar sentiments in my interviews. In particular, governors who lacked strong connections in Moscow found it useful to lobby through the party. In Yaroslavl, one of the regional administration's top political advisers had this to say about why the then-governor Sergei Vakhrukov was not a party member, while the former governor Anatolii Lysytsin had worked more closely with the party:

> [Vakhrukov] had strong relations with Moscow. He had worked with several ministers. Therefore, he didn't any additional levers for strengthening his position in Moscow. He didn't need to lobby his interests through the party. By contrast, Lysytsin, who had fewer connections in Moscow worked more actively through the party in order to gain some sources of influence in Moscow.[12]

The party also helps legislators gain access to lobbying opportunities in the executive branch. Aleksander Sizov, a former deputy from Yaroslavl Oblast, provides an example: "In the Fourth Convocation, I went to the minister of Culture, Shvydkoi, several times to talk about the Volkov Theater [Yaroslavl's largest drama theater] and convinced him to renovate the building and support the holding of a drama festival in the oblast. As a deputy that was something I could do."[13] Such lobbying activities are also carried out by Federation Council senators, the vast majority of whom are United Russia members. In recent years, the Federation

---

[12] Author's interview with Pavel Isaev, June 11, 2009, Yaroslavl.
[13] Author's interview, April 3, 2010, Yaroslavl.

5.1 United Russia's Role: Benefits to Elites

Council's role in writing legislation has shrunk considerably, but senators remain important lobbyists for the regions they represent.

In the regions, the party's informal role as a mechanism for gaining access to lobbying opportunities and high-level officials is perhaps even greater. As Sergei Baburkin, head of UR's executive committee in Yaroslavl Oblast, told me: "[UR] members expect a certain level of support from and a certain relationship with the elite. Plus, they expect that those relations will continue in the future."[14] The Presidium of the regional *politsovet* includes top officials from the regional administration, the leadership of the regional legislature, the mayors of large cities, heads of important social organizations, and major enterprise directors. No other institution or gathering can claim such a concentration of regional political luminaries. Meetings of the *politsovet*, as well as party conferences, forums, clubs, and primaries, provide an opportunity for elites of different stripes to meet together, discuss regional politics, and make informal agreements. As one Russian political scientist describes it: "United Russia serves as a forum for the 'meshing' of the private interests of elite groups, who now feel compelled to make agreements among themselves in the framework of internal party interactions" (Panov 2008, 105).

The National Projects, and their successor, the Special Purpose Programs (Tselevyie Programmy), are one example of the type of spoils for which United Russia membership helps elites lobby. These oil-funded social development projects directed hundreds of billions of federal budget dollars to the Russian regions for the construction of social infrastructure such as schools, hospitals, and roads. In a January 2006 speech before United Russia Duma deputies, Putin set out the terms of the relationship between the national projects and United Russia: "The national projects are not something handed down from above – they are United Russia's projects… They were developed with your input taken into account. Your proposals and the proposals of the government form their basis… The realization of the national projects is strictly the work of the party."[15] In response, special party commissions were created to oversee allocation of National Project funds.[16] In turn, there developed fierce competition among UR deputies to see that project funds were directed toward their districts and clienteles.

---

[14] Author's interview February 21, 2010, Yaroslavl.
[15] Accessed at http://edinros.nov.ru/index.php?mmm=about&id=12 March 2, 2007.
[16] See the report on United Russia's Web site "Natsionalnyie Proekty vzyaty pod control 'Edinoi Rossii,'" December 27, 2005. http://old.edinros.ru/news.html?id=110023

Beginning in 2005, United Russia also developed its own, internally administered "Party Projects," a series of social and infrastructure projects funding primarily by the federal budget. As of 2014, there were 43 federal and 400 regional projects that channeled funds toward projects such as water purification plants, sports stadiums, school renovations, preschools, roads, swimming pools, drug treatment centers, libraries, church renovations, movie theaters, and libraries.[17] Completed infrastructure projects are emblazoned with the party's logo.

The total amount spent on these projects is difficult to calculate. Party officials do not make aggregate numbers public, perhaps because they are unwilling to publicize the large amounts of budget funds that are being spent for partisan purposes. However, my own rough calculations indicate that the party has earmarked tens of billions of dollars for these projects since 2006.[18] It is well known that loyalty to the party and the party's performance in elections play a key role in determining which regions receive funds.[19]

Several conclusions can be drawn from the preceding discussion. United Russia does not exercise singular and unrivaled collective control over policy making in Russia. The executive branch usually sets the general policy direction, but in exchange for delegating national policy direction to the executive branch, United Russia members receive significant benefits. United Russia's control over legislation allows members to influence the content of legislation, enabling them to secure policy concessions and spoils. In addition, United Russia membership provides elites a privileged position when seeking to lobby their interests outside legislatures.

Reducing Uncertainty and Securing Dependable Career Advancement Opportunities

United Russia not only provides access to spoils and policy influence but also reduces uncertainty over how those spoils are distributed. Prior

---

[17] Information on individual projects can be found at the Projects' Web site, https://proj.edinros.ru/.

[18] These calculations are based on numbers provided in party documents distributed at the party's Party Project Forum on May 17, 2013. In particular, see the booklet "Partinyie Proekty – Novoe Kachestvo Zhizni." Some numbers for individual projects are also given at the Party Project Web portal. For an example of a funding stream directed at an individual region, see SMS-golosovanie v tseni sem' milliardov" *Nezavisimaya Gazeta*. July 6, 2010. For more on funding see "Edinaya Rossiya otterla ot byudjeta 'chuzhie proekty.'" *Kommersant* May 20, 2013.

[19] "Krizisnyi razvorot partii vlasti" *Nezavisimaya Gazeta* August 21, 2009. "'Edinaya Rossiya' otblagodarit regiony rublyem" *Kommersant* October 14, 2010.

5.1 United Russia's Role: Benefits to Elites

to United Russia's emergence, regional elites could lobby for spoils on an ad hoc, bilateral basis, but the transaction costs and uncertainty associated with this method of accessing spoils were high. According to several regional legislators whom I interviewed, accessing policy through the UR faction was preferable to accessing it in a nonpartisan parliament (as many regional legislatures were until the early 2000s), because operating through the UR faction reduced uncertainty about how logrolls would be decided (see Chapter 4 for citations to these interviews). Faction members know that seniority in the party helps ensure better legislative access and toeing the party line will help them keep their place in line. Party membership makes clear the rules of the accommodative arrangement, and by accepting party membership, elites make a commitment to upholding that arrangement. In order to be granted access to spoils through the party, elites must agree to behave in certain ways. The author's interview respondents in regional legislatures recognized this clearly as they bemoaned the loss of autonomy they would suffer by joining the United Russia faction. At the same time, they viewed their chances of influencing policy to be contingent on the formal step of joining the party (or the faction) and maintaining party discipline.

Because United Russia regulates access to many political careers, elites may receive career advancement opportunities by joining the party. Importantly, the party also reduces uncertainty about how to secure such opportunities. Advancement through the United Russia party ranks, which is facilitated by party loyalty, seniority, and service to the party, can help make a political career in many political arenas. Elites value this reduction in uncertainty. They prefer clear expectations about the type of behavior that will be rewarded and the type of rewards that can be expected. In the absence of such guidelines, political advancement would be solely dependent on the whims of the dictator and local patrons.

The arena where UR regularizes career advancement opportunities the most is the legislative branch. The party's control over party lists and nominations gives it control over legislative careers. Within legislatures, leadership positions are determined by majority rule and allocated by United Russia's party organs. Seniority, loyalty, and a record of service to the party are important determinants of who receives these positions. Using data from regional legislatures in the 2000s, Reuter and Turovsky (2014) provide statistical evidence for this claim by showing that legislators who joined United Russia early in its existence, before the party had become assuredly dominant, had a higher probability of receiving legislative leadership posts than those who joined the party later. That study further demonstrates that party loyalty is a particularly important determinant of legislative advancement for those deputies who lack alternative personal resources and shows that these findings hold when controlling for several potentially confounding factors.

In the mid-2000s, United Russia began to pay serious attention to issues of party discipline in the regions. As discussed later in the chapter, this period was marked by a series of party "purges," in which hundreds of regional officials and candidates were expelled from the party for violating party discipline. As officials were purged for indiscipline and the criteria for party membership were stiffened, party cadres developed clearer expectations about the types of behavior that would be rewarded with advancement. In my interviews, regional legislators and party officials indicated that seniority, work on the aforementioned "party projects," adherence to the party line during election campaigns, and legislative voting discipline became important determinants of promotion to positions in both the regional party hierarchy and the legislature. In Chelyabinsk Oblast, an official on United Russia's executive committee reported that the regional party branch tries very hard to ensure that loyalty to the party is rewarded both in the legislative arena and at election time: "If a member works for the benefit of the party, then it is in the party's interest to ensure that he sees some future with the party. Therefore, we try to fill vacant list spots with party supporters who have not yet had their chance."[20] Thus, even if a cadre fails to achieve his or her preferred rent, policy, or career objective in the present, he or she has some reason to believe that continued loyalty and support for the party will result in access to these goods in the future.

To make room for upwardly mobile cadres, the party charter mandates 10 percent turnover in all regional *politsovets* each year. At the federal level 15 percent of the General Council is replaced at every congress. In recent years, an increasing number of top party posts have been occupied by individuals who got their start in the party's youth wing, *Molodaya Gvardia* (Youth Guard).

In the State Duma the party has also exercised a policy of rewarding loyalty. In 2007, UR's lists were notably more populated by United Russia functionaries than in 2003 (Ivanov 2008). For the 2011 elections, the party developed more precise criteria for granting list places on the basis of party work. According to then-Secretary of the Presidium Vyacheslav Volodin when deciding where State Duma deputies would be included on the party list for the 2011 elections, the party took into account "the deputy's successes in regional elections, their activity in the region, and their work in the party's constituent service branches."[21]

[20] Author's anonymous interview, July 6, 2007, Chelyabinsk.
[21] "Edinaya Rossiya Gotovitsya k vyboram v Gosdumu: partiitsam dana ustanovka uvelichit' rezul'taty. Also after next title, n. 22?]." *newsru.ru* April 29, 2010.

5.1 United Russia's Role: Benefits to Elites

For those older UR deputies who were replaced in the State Duma by younger party functionaries from the regions, a new law was passed allowing Duma deputies to take up positions in the Federation Council.[22] As of 2015, most of the party's top leadership in the Duma, including Sergei Neverov, Sergei Zheleznyak, Irina Yarovaya, and Andrei Isayev, owed their positions to advancement through the party ranks.

Press reports indicate that party loyalty can sometimes be an important factor in Federation Council appointments as well. News reports surfaced in 2009 and 2010 about how United Russia was pressuring newly appointed governors to appoint United Russia functionaries whom it deemed worthy of promotion to the Federation Council. One noteworthy example of this occurred in Chelyabinsk, where the new governor appointed the head of *Molodaya Gvardia*, 33-year old Ruslan Gattarov. According to press reports, the sitting senator in Chelyabinsk, Evgenii Eliseev, also a party member, had fallen out of favor with the party. Upon hearing that he was being replaced by Gattarov, Eliseev wrote a personal plea to Putin asking him to reverse the decision. Eliseev expressed hope that the prime minister would overturn the party leadership's decision, but weeks later, Gattarov was confirmed as senator by the Chelyabinsk regional legislature.[23]

In the executive branch, United Russia's control over careers is more limited. This is especially true in the federal government and presidential administration. Although about 20 percent of the government have been UR members since the mid-2000s, and several prominent government ministers hold (or have held) party membership – Prime Minister Medvedev being the most prominent – most important officials in the executive branch did not work their way up through the party to achieve their positions. Nonetheless, even here there are some important examples of high-ranking figures who did. The most prominent is Vyacheslav Volodin, who began his career as a Duma deputy and worked his way up to become secretary of the Presidium in 2005. In 2010, he became head of the government's apparat under Putin and then became first vice

---

[22] "Sovet Federatsii primyet na rabotu deputatov." *Kommersant* September 28, 2011.
[23] Vice Secretary of the United Russia Presidium Sergei Neverov stated: "Mr. Eliseev has the right to appeal to the party chairman... In any case, we did not notice much activity in Mr. Eliseev's work; therefore, we proposed to the governor Gattarov, who is an active party member." "K naznacheniyu chelyabinskogo gubernatora privekli Vladimira Putina" *Kommersant* April 28, 2010. For another example of United Russia pressuring governors to appoint party functionaries to the Federation Council see "Edinaya Rossiya formiruyet Sovet Federatsii" *Kommersant* May 6, 2010, and "Edinaya Rossiya perestavit funktsionerov." *Kommersant* March 5, 2009. For an earlier example, see "Astrakhanskii gubernator peremanil senator so svyazami iz Ryazanskoi oblasti" *Kommersant* February 14, 2005. "Ot polpreda k gubernatory" *Kommersant* August 27, 2010.

head of the presidential administration when Putin returned to the presidency. Other examples include Minister of Culture Vladimir Medinsky, who got his start in politics in United Russia's Executive Committee, and the current head of the Kremlin's Department of Internal Politics, Oleg Morozov, who made his name as one of UR's leaders in the Duma.

Party service has played a larger role in the selection of regional governors. Between 2009 and 2012, when governors were appointed by the president, the largest party in the regional legislature (United Russia in almost all cases) had the right to nominate the candidates whom the president would consider.[24] In 2012, direct elections were reintroduced, but given the fact that no regime-backed candidate has yet lost and United Russia was the nominating party for 91 percent of regime-backed candidates, United Russia's formal control over gubernatorial selection has remained unchanged.[25]

While insider reports suggest that the party leadership often takes its cues on whom to nominate from the presidential administration (Ivanov 2013), it appears that the Kremlin took party membership and service into account when making appointments.[26] Reuter and Robertson (2012) find that governors who were successful at mobilizing votes for United Russia were much more likely to be reappointed, and, as Figure 4.6 showed, almost all newly appointed governors were United Russia members. Thirty-eight percent of appointees between 2005 and 2010 worked in a legislature – federal, regional, or local – immediately prior to appointment, and, as we have already seen, these were arenas where United Russia exercised control over careers. Prominent examples of governors who owed their promotions to party work included Moscow Oblast Governor Andrei Vorobyov, who served as head of United Russia's Executive Committee in 2005–2012, and Pskov Governor Andrei Turchak, who gained political fame by coordinating United Russia's youth wing.

---

[24] The reform had been proposed four years earlier. "Strana Sovetov Edinoi Rossii" *Gazeta. ru* October 3, 2005. United Russia first implemented this procedure in October 2006, when the party nominated Aslan Tkhakushinov to the post of president of the Republic of Adygea. Presidential envoy Dmitrii Kozak consulted the Federal Presidium of United Russia as well as party leaders in Adygea. President Putin then proposed Tkhakushinov, who was confirmed by the regional assembly. "Edinaya Rossiya odobrila vybor Dmitry Kozaka" *Kommersant* Oct. 11, 2006.

[25] Of the 43 governor races held between 2012 and 2014, 39 of the winners were nominated by United Russia. One governor, Moscow Mayor Sergei Sobyanin, was a UR member but ran as an independent. Two governorships were given to in-system opposition parties and one governorship was given to an independent candidate.

[26] "Governors Appointed for Loyalty and Votes" *Moscow Times* January 26, 2007. "'Edinaya Rossiya'" poishet zamenu chetyryam gubernatoram" *Kommersant* May 14, 2009.

In sum, while the pool of eligibles for high government office in Russia does not consist only of United Russia members, advancement through the party ranks is one important path to power and influence. Early in its existence, party seniority could not provide a basis for promotion because all party cadres were new. In these early days, the party focused on co-opting new members (if they would join). As the 2000s progressed, however, the party would place more emphasis on discipline and loyalty-based promotions.

Electoral Benefits

Affiliation with the party also provides a number of benefits to elites seeking elected office. First, the party helps solve coordination problems for elites; such failures at the time of elections can be costly for candidates and elites, causing them to waste resources on futile races (Cox 1997, Shvetsova 2003). In the low-information environment that characterizes post-Soviet Russia, pro-regime politicians risk casting their lot with the wrong party. The need for information about the prospects of the multiple rival parties is acute. In the 1990s, the Kremlin extended fleeting and wavering support to multiple regime parties. In turn, competition among these parties led many otherwise viable pro-presidential candidates to lose. By sending a clear signal of support that United Russia would be the regime's main electoral vehicle, the Kremlin helped solve the coordination problem of pro-regime candidates. By affiliating with United Russia, candidates knew that they would be tying their fates to a viable pro-Kremlin electoral vehicle.

Second, affiliation with the party makes it easier to register for elections. The procedures for registering one's candidacy in Russia are onerous and complex. Capricious regional authorities use their informal influence over electoral officials to bar independent and opposition candidates from running. Such moves are often motivated by personal disputes or interclan conflicts. Carrying a United Russia affiliation eliminates the need to gather voter signatures – the most common method used to disqualify candidates – and provides some insurance against the unpredictable actions of regional authorities. As the former head of United Russia's Executive Committee in Yaroslavl stated: "In practical terms [affiliation] provides a certain guarantee that you'll be registered. If you are an independent, you have to gather signatures and there is no guarantee that they won't be found defective. Then you won't be able to register. That type of thing has become common now."[27]

[27] Author's interview with Sergei Baburkin, February 21, 2010, Yaroslavl.

174 United Russia as the Dominant Party

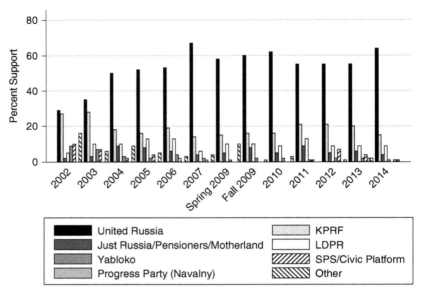

Figure 5.1 Popularity ratings of major Russian political parties.

Source: Levada Center Omnibus Surveys. The question is the following: "If elections to the State Duma were held this Sunday, would you vote and if so which of the following parties would you vote for?" Figures are given as the percentage of those who would vote and have chosen a party. Data are from November of each year, except 2008, for which data are not available.

Finally, United Russia provides candidates with a useful party brand and organizational resources. A United Russia nomination sends a signal to voters that the candidate is affiliated with the regime. And as Figure 5.1 shows, United Russia has been the most popular party in Russia since 2002.

Not only is the party popular; it also has the largest base of steady supporters. Using data from the Russian Election Studies, Hale and Colton (2009) have estimated that 30 percent of the Russian electorate were "transitional partisans" of United Russia in 2008.[28] In 2012 that number

---

[28] As they argue, transitional partisanship is an "instrument appropriate for societies new to party competition where one would not expect to find affinities as deep and time-test as those in the United States but where emerging attachments might exist" (Hale and Colton 2009, 14). To measure this concept, respondents are asked whether there is any party that they would call "my party." Those answering yes are asked to name that party without being presented with a list of parties. Those who do not name a party are then asked whether there is nevertheless a party that represents their "interests, views, and

5.1 United Russia's Role: Benefits to Elites

Table 5.2 *Transitional partisanship in Russia (2012)*

Party	Share of electorate (in percentage)
United Russia	32
KPRF	9
LDPR	3
Just Russia	3
All others	3

Source: Hale and Colton (2013).

had crept higher to 32 percent, which, as Table 5.2 shows is far higher than for any other party.

By 2014, many of these partisan attachments had become relatively long-lived (for a post-Soviet country). In a 2014 survey of 4200 respondents in 20 regions carried out by the author, 21 percent of United Russia's "transitional partisans" had been supporters for 10 years or more.[29] A further 26 percent had been supporters for more than 5 years. Thus, a sizable part of the Russian electorate are United Russia partisans and have been for some time. Affiliation with United Russia gives candidates access to the party brand and, hence, to those voters. Indeed, many legislators whom I interviewed cited access to the party brand as one of their motivations for joining.

In addition, United Russia gives candidates access to the extensive organizational resources of the party. With a membership of more than 2 million and more than 82,000 local and primary party cells, United Russia's organizational reach far outstrips that of other parties in Russia (see Roberts 2012a see also Chapter 4 of this volume).[30] Affiliation provides access to this army of agitators and local activists.

---

concerns" better than others. Those answering yes are asked to name that party without being presented with a list. Those naming a real party in response to either question are considered that party's "transitional partisans."

[29] Reuter, Ora John, Timothy Frye, and David Szakonyi. (2015) 2014 Russian Workplace Mobilization Surveys (data file and code book).

[30] These membership figures may seem small compared to some European democracies, but it is important to remember that party membership in Russia often "involves an elaborate application and approval process, sometimes including a probationary period, as well as expectations for dues payments and active participation in party events" (Hale and Colton 2009, 15). United Russia is no different in this regard. Becoming a party member has become more difficult over time. In the mid-2000s the party instituted a waiting period and more stringent requirements for retaining party membership. See "'Edinaya Rossia' zakreplyaet uspekh" *Kommersant* December 18, 2007. In 2008, the party initiated the first in a series of mass purges, excluding from its rolls tens of

5.2 United Russia's Role: Benefits to the Kremlin

Ensuring Elite Loyalty and Controlling Legislatures

United Russia not only provides benefits to the elites who join it, but to regime leaders. Importantly, the party serves as a mechanism for co-opting elites, turning neutrals and opponents into allies. As the previous sections indicated, United Russia incentivizes loyalty by dependably rewarding loyalty with rents, policy influence, and career advancement. The party thus reduces uncertainty about how spoils will be shared in the future and therefore lengthens the time horizons of elites. Senior cadres are retired, and younger loyal cadres are promoted through the ranks in a manner that incentivizes loyalty (Reuter and Turovsky 2014). In the jargon of social science, cadres have made sunk cost investments in service to the party that would be lost if the dominant party system were to collapse (Svolik 2012).

United Russia's role in generating elite loyalty is particularly important in legislatures. Since the early 2000s, United Russia has produced stable legislative majorities for the regime in most legislative organs. This is important, because, in Russia, rule by decree is more limited than commonly believed. The decree-making powers of the president are limited to the establishment of law where no existing law exists and to the resolution of inconsistencies in existing law (Haspel, Remington, and Smith 2006). There are also certain policy areas that must be governed by law rather than decree.

Therefore, presidents in Russia who have ambitious policy programs need to secure support in the legislative chamber, and a president whose margin of support in the legislature is insecure must bargain for support of his agenda, often trading off particularistic goods to build ad hoc majorities (Shugart 1998, Cox and Morgenstern 2002). Moreover, where pro-presidential parties in the legislature are weak, the opposition is in a good position to lure away disgruntled deputies, as happened in Ukraine under Kuchma (Way 2005, D'Anieri 2007).

President Putin understood this clearly. In the Third Duma (2000–2003), the Kremlin found it costly to buy a support coalition among SMD members and minority factions (Remington 2006). In addition to logrolls over specific legislation, package deals were struck over committee membership in order to forge a majority coalition (Smyth 2002). In the Fourth Duma, the Kremlin set about ensuring that it would not have to make these side payments. United Russia's majority faction has, in contrast to previous

---

thousands who had "lost contact" with the party. See "Partiya Vlasti snizhaet massu" *Kommersant* April 18, 2008, and "Volchii partbilet" *Kommersant* April 21, 2008.

5.2 United Russia's Role: Benefits to the Kremlin

party of power projects, exercised ironclad discipline over its members in support of the president's legislative agenda (Remington 2006). Perhaps the most noteworthy instance of this discipline was witnessed during voting on the 2004 bill to monetize social benefits. This reform was highly unpopular among voters – its passage sparked widespread street protests and led to a sharp drop in the regime's popularity ratings – but only five United Russia legislators voted against it. Thus, executive–legislative relations under Putin have resembled the situation that Jeffrey Weldon describes in Mexico, where the wide range of informal powers wielded by the Mexican president in the period of *presidencialismo* depended upon the PRI's maintenance of an absolute majority in both chambers of Congress and the ruling party's firm internal discipline (Weldon 1997).

In regional legislatures as well United Russia exercises strict voting discipline. Regional legislative clerks interviewed in five Russian regions all agreed that voting discipline increased sharply when United Russia factions were created after the third regional electoral cycle.[31] The abruptness of this increase in discipline indicates that it was not simply the preferences of the deputy groups or their loyalty to the regime that generated this cohesion but the institutional structure of the United Russia faction itself. Indeed, as one deputy in Yaroslavl put it:

> We have the faction charter. And it's written clearly there that everyone should have a voice in deliberations, but once a majority makes a decision to vote for or against, then it is also written there that every deputy has to vote that way. If you do vote against the faction, then, because it is written in the charter that every deputy should support the party position, it is clear that you have committed a violation of discipline; you have violated the charter. That makes a statement.[32]

Consistent with this emphasis on discipline, a number of regions took steps in the mid- to late 2000s to make roll-call voting compulsory.[33] Deputies also remarked on how party nomination in elections affected legislative discipline:

> In the current convocation, this situation [concerning party discipline] has become less of a problem. If you compare the situation with the last convocation, there were a lot of conflicts there, not just between parties, but within United Russia. Especially SMD deputies, and even party list deputies, there were conflicts and disagreements among them. I want to say, and all deputies I think would say this, that in this convocation there are many fewer such open conflicts. I link this with the fact that party lists and single member district nominations have been done differently. All the deputies who were nominated by United

---

[31] The regions were Perm Krai, Yaroslavl Oblast, Ryzan Oblast, Ivanovo Oblast, and Nizhegorodskaya Oblast.
[32] Author's interview with Olga Khitrova, March 11, 2010, Yaroslavl.
[33] For example, "Tyumen delayet tainoye poimennym" *Kommersant* May 28, 2010.

Russia now know well that they were nominated by United Russia... Therefore, all the deputies who are in the faction now know that they are members of the party. SMD deputies are now actively involved in party activity. They head projects and so on. So they feel their attachment to the party.[34]

Over the course of the 2000s, the party became increasingly concerned with ensuring discipline outside legislatures as well. In 2008 and 2009, the party publicized a purge of regional elites who had broken party discipline during elections. The most common reasons for expulsion included running against the party's official candidate, supporting nonparty candidates, or discrediting the party during campaigns.[35] In one of the most high-profile cases, the governor of Murmansk was forced out of office for publicly supporting a non-UR-sanctioned candidate in the capital's mayoral elections.[36] In a similar case, the party expelled the sitting mayor of Blagoveschensk for campaigning on behalf of non-UR city council candidates.[37] In other instances, United Russia members, attempting to appear autonomous and simultaneously enjoy the administrative backing of United Russia, were excluded for criticizing the party during their election campaigns.[38] These purges coincided with a decision at the party's December 2007 congress to increase the waiting period for attaining party membership and institute stringent party service requirements for nomination to leadership positions.[39] According to the party's Web site 4 percent of members had been excluded by February 2008.[40]

For the Kremlin, the upshot of all this is that the party has helped ensure elite cohesion. Since elite defections are known to be one of the primary drivers of authoritarian breakdown (Haggard and Kauffman, 1995, Reuter and Gandhi, 2011), the role of the dominant party in ensuring elite cohesion is crucial. When influential regime insiders join

---

[34] Author's interview with Olga Khitrova, March 11, 2010, Yaroslavl.
[35] For several discussions of the campaign see "Edinaya Rossiya Kompostiruyet Part Bilety" *Kommersant* August 18, 2008, "Chekisty 'Edinoi Rossii' Otpravilis' v problemniye regiony" *Nezavisimaya Gazeta* October 17, 2008, "Edinaya Rossiya obyavlyaet chistki postoyanno deistvuyuschim mekhanismom, v regionakh nachinayut ot nikh zaschischat'sya" *newsru.ru* www.newsru.ru September 18, 2008, "Edinaya Rossiya vozvodit chistku v sistemu" *Kommersant* January 29, 2009. For some more recent examples see "Chelyabinskogo edinorossa isklyuchili iz partii" *Kommersant* October 8, 2014, and "Vitse-premiera Gornogo-Altaiya isklyuchili iz ER za nepravil'nuyu agitatsiyu" *RIA-Novosti* September 19, 2013. Accessed online: http://ria.ru/politics/20130919/964223233.html
[36] "Pobedil, no proigral" *Gazeta.ru* March 16, 2009.
[37] "V blagoveshenske na zasedanii gorodskogo otdeleniya partii 'Edinaya Rossiya' prinyato resheniye isklyuchit iz ee ryadov mera Aleksandra Migulyu" *Rossisskaya Gazeta* July 15, 2008.
[38] See, for example, "Partiinaya Chistka" *Zvezda* July 1, 2008.
[39] "Edinaya Rossiya zakreplyaet uspekh" *Kommersant* December 18, 2007.
[40] Accessed on United Russia Web site, July 10, 2010. www.edinros.ru/rubr.shtml?110112.

5.2 United Russia's Role: Benefits to the Kremlin

the opposition or otherwise mobilize against the regime, the regime may find it difficult to maintain popular support or win elections.

The Putin regime has largely avoided such defections, even in the face of economic (2009) and political (2011–2012) crises. Very few high-level officials, governors, mayors, or prominent Duma deputies have defected from the regime.[41] In 2012–2013, the popularity ratings of Putin and United Russia were in steady decline and the fortunes of Russia's opposition were on the rise. This led many pundits to predict elite defections, especially in the regions.[42] And yet these predictions were not borne out in fact. There have been no cases of sitting governors defecting and I know of no cases in which a sitting mayor has defected from the regime. In regional legislative elections, United Russia continued to win by large margins.

To examine rates of defection among regional legislators more systematically, I gathered data on the share of incumbent candidates from United Russia who defected to the opposition (or ran as independents) in contests held between 2010 and 2014. To construct this measure, I first gathered data on the number of candidates in a given election who were members of the United Russia faction in the previous legislative convocation in that region. I then calculated the number of those candidates who ran either as independents or from an opposition party in that election. To calculate the percentage of incumbent candidates from United Russia who defected, I divided the second number by the first number.[43] As Table 5.3 shows, rates of defections have been quite low in the 2010s. The vast majority of incumbent UR candidates elected in convocations prior to the economic crisis stayed with the party in the next election (i.e. in 2010, 2011, and 2012). Consistent with news reports about defections in 2012–2013, there was an uptick in defections in 2013 as the regime's popularity waned, but the overall number of defections remained low. In 2014, the rate of defections decreased again.

---

[41] One important exception was the 2011 resignation of Finance Minister Alexei Kudrin. After his resignation, Kudrin repeatedly entertained offers to join the opposition. However, he had never been a member of the ruling party. The former Moscow mayor and high-ranking UR official Yurii Luzhkov came out against the regime in 2010, but this was after he was fired from his post.

[42] See "Regional Elites See United Russia's Stock Falling," *Moscow Times* August 26, 2013. "Kreml prozondiruyet region" Gazeta.ru March 1, 2013. "Aleksandr Kynev: Rushayetsya Traditzionniye Skhemy Politicheskogo Manipuliruvaniya" Golos Analytic Report. Accessed online at www.golos.org/news/5861 May 28, 2012.

[43] This figure likely overstates the number of defections because some former members were probably expelled from the party for various infractions. Furthermore, expulsions and defections are difficult to separate, because either can be strategic. Either way, this figure gives an upper bound to the number of defections.

Table 5.3 *Defections from United Russia in Russian regional legislatures*

Year	Regional elections	Number of incumbent candidates who were UR faction members in previous convocation	Number of defectors	Number of defectors elected	Share of incumbent candidates from UR who are defectors	Share of incumbent candidates from UR who are defectors and are elected
2010	14	248	13	2	0.05	0.01
2011	39	779	35	8	0.04	0.01
2012	7	172	7	3	0.04	0.02
2013	16	347	33	5	0.10	0.01
2014	11	249	13	4	0.05	0.02

Note: Data are from the Russian Central Election Commission (www.cikrf.ru) and the author's *Database of Russian Political Elites.*

Another way of examining rates of defection is by looking at the number of opposition candidates who are former members of the dominant party. Reuter and Gandhi (2011) develop a measure of defections from dominant parties based on the number of candidates in a presidential election who were former members of the dominant party. I adapt that approach here and apply it to the Russian regions. To construct this measure, research assistants examined the biographies (using online Web searches and *Panorama*'s Labyrinth Database of elite biographies) of opposition candidates to determine whether they were former members of United Russia. A candidacy was coded as a defection if that opposition candidate had been a member of United Russia (or held a post in the party that indicated membership) and then had left the party. Expulsions are not counted as defections.

Table 5.4 shows the frequency with which Russian gubernatorial and mayoral contests in the 2010s witnessed such defections. Rates of defection were quite low in gubernatorial contests. Reuter and Gandhi (2011) report that 19 percent of presidential elections in dominant party regimes witnessed such defections. Between 2012 and 2014, 5 percent of Russian gubernatorial elections had such defections.

The bottom rows of the table show the same data for mayoral elections in cities with populations greater than 100,000 in the period 2009–2013. With only limited information on the biographies of many mayoral candidates, we were only able to gather data on 60 races during this period, but the data tell a story similar to the gubernatorial data. Rates

Table 5.4 Defections from United Russia in gubernatorial and mayoral races, 2009–2014

Year	Number of elections	Number of opposition candidates	Number of opposition candidates that were former UR members	Share of all opposition candidates who were former UR members	Share of elections with a defection	Number of defectors who won an election	Number of elections with a defection won by opposition
			Governors				
2012	5	12	0	0	0	0	0
2013	8	32	2	0.6	25	0	0
2014	30	135	0	0	0	0	0
Totals	**43**	**181**	**2**	**0.1**	**4.6**	**0**	**0**
			Mayors				
2009	18	64	1	1.6	5.5	0	0
2010	10	26	1	3.8	1	0	0
2011	8	22	0	0	0	0	0
2012	19	85	3	3.5	15.7	1	1
2013	11	61	2	3.2	18.2	0	1
Totals	**66**	**258**	**7**	**2.7**	**10.6**	**1**	**2**

Table 5.5 *UR defectors among top opposition candidates in regional legislative elections, 2009–2014*

Year	Number of opposition candidates	Number of elections	Number of candidates in "top three" of opposition party list who are former UR Members	% of Candidates on in 'top three' of opposition party list that are former UR members
2009	99	12	1	1
2010	116	13	4	3.4
2011	351	39	10	2.85
2012	79	6	1	1.27
2013	193	16	11	5.7
2014	148	14	9	6
2015	96	11	2	2
Total:	1082	111	38	3.5

of defection were low, both in the postcrisis period (2009) and in the period when United Russia's ratings were falling (2012–2013). When defections did occur, they rarely contributed to the defeat of United Russia candidates.[44]

In Table 5.5 I extend this method to look at defectors among opposition candidates in regional legislative elections between 2009 and 2014. It is not feasible to examine the biographies of each of the tens of thousands of candidates who run for regional legislative office in Russia, so in Table 5.5 I focus only on high-level opposition candidates. Specifically, I look at candidates who occupied one of the top three spots on the regional party list of opposition parties that gained more than 2 percent of the vote. Since defectors in legislative elections may not be incumbents (they may be UR members in other political arenas), this table differs from Table 5.2. As the data show, this method for measuring defections also reveals a low incidence of defection: of the almost 1000 candidates who headed opposition party lists between 2009 and 2014, only 25 (about 2.6 percent) were former UR members.

In sum, United Russia has helped the regime maintain elite cohesion, especially in legislatures and in the regions. In turn, elite cohesion has

---

[44] There were two instances of this. One occurred in Yaroslavl in 2012, when the local opposition figure Evgenii Urlashov, who was himself a UR defector, won the election. The other possible instance occurred in Ekaterinburg, where the former Duma deputy and antidrug campaigner Evgenii Roizman won local mayoral elections in 2013 against a United Russia candidate. One other opposition candidate in that election, Evgenii Artyukh, was a former UR member and, as such, may have drawn votes away from the UR candidate.

5.2 United Russia's Role: Benefits to the Kremlin

been one of the fundaments of regime stability in Putin era Russia. In the face of economic crisis, widespread anti-regime protest, and flagging popularity, most political elites remained loyal to the regime. Hence, I conclude, as others have (Way 2008, Levitsky and Way 2010), that United Russia has made Russia's authoritarian regime more robust.

Winning Elections and Mobilizing Popular Support

Finally, one of the most important roles that United Russia performs for the regime is to help win elections. In the 2000s, it did this primarily by helping the regime co-opt powerful regional elites who put their political machines and personal authority to work for the regime at election time. Indeed, statistical analyses of United Russia's performance in regional elections show that the party has consistently performed best in those regions where governors have strong political machines and independent bases of personal popularity (Reuter 2013, Golosov 2011).[45] Regional elites use a range of tools to mobilize votes for the regime. Sitting at the top of complex patron–client networks, they induce their clients to deploy administrative resources against opponents, buy votes, put pressure on voters, and use their own political authority to campaign for the regime. One common tactic is to put pressure on local firms to mobilize their employees (Frye, Reuter, and Szakonyi 2014). Finally, many regional elites are intrinsically popular as elected politicians. This was especially true in the early to mid-2000s. The gubernatorial corpus in place at that time had cut its teeth on direct elections that were, at times, competitive. Those who survived these contests owed much of their success to political skill.

In addition to serving as a forum for co-optation, United Russia has proved instrumental in solving problems of electoral coordination. When pro-regime candidates compete against one another, opposition candidates stand a better chance of winning. Perhaps the most dramatic illustration of this occurred in the 1995 Duma elections, when as many as nine parties supporting Yeltsin were listed on the ballot. These coordination failures not only split the party list vote, but also meant that reformist and centrist candidates ultimately competed against one another in numerous single member districts (Belin and Orttung 1997, 57–58). In the end, no pro-presidential party gained more than 10 percent of the party list vote, and the Communists emerged on top.

---

[45] It is not just governors who performed this role. Other work has examined how elected mayors constructed political machines and put them to work for the regime (Reuter and Buckley 2015, Gel'man and Ryzhenkov 2011).

By contrast, in the 2000s, United Russia provided a single party label around which pro-regime candidates could coordinate. Furthermore, the party became instrumental as an institutional mechanism for organizing strategic withdrawals in single member district races. According to party officials in the regions, the most difficult and complicated negotiations that occur during meetings of the regional *politsovet* usually concern conflicts between two party candidates seeking to run in the same district. The Presidium of the *politsovet* resolves these conflicts by providing other career advancement opportunities, rents, and promises of future ballot access to those who agree to withdraw.[46] In turn, the party has sought to enforce these agreements by punishing defectors with expulsion.[47] Of course, conflicts over ballot access still occur and often grab headlines, but, on the whole, these measures have resulted in a level of electoral discipline that is remarkable for post-Soviet parties of power.[48] In the 43 gubernatorial elections that took place between 2012 and 2014, there were no instances of two UR candidates competing against one another. In the 60 large-city mayoral elections analyzed previously, coordination failures occurred in 7 elections, as is consistent with the impression that UR has more difficulty ensuring discipline at the local level. Yet, these numbers likely overstate the true number of coordination failures, because in some instances loyal UR candidates have been asked to serve as "technical" candidates in order to divide the opposition or to help legitimate elections by filling out the ballot when opposition candidates are barred from running. Coordination failures led to the defeat of a UR candidate in only one instance over this period (Bratsk in 2010).[49]

[46] Author's interview with Sergei Baburkin February 21, 2010, Yaroslavl. For prominent examples of potential electoral conflicts that were worked out by the United Russia leadership see "Murmanskikh edinorossov pomirila rukha Moskvy." *Kommersant* December 11, 2006, "Edinaya Rossia pomirila gubernatora s merom" *Kommersant* January 19, 2007, and "Aleksandr Uss ne idyot v gubernatory Krasnoyarskogo kraya po veleniyu partii" Dela.ru May 29, 2014. Accessed online at www.dela.ru/lenta/120217/ Some officials also claimed that the system of party primaries, introduced as an internal nomination procedure in 2009 and opened up to voters in 2013, has helped legitimate nomination decisions and thus eased conflicts over party nominations. See also "Edinaya Rossiya otbiraet kandidatov koe-kak" *Kommersant* October 30, 2009.

[47] See, for example, "Chelyabinskogo edinorossa isklyuchili iz partii." *Kommersant* October 8, 2014, "Vitse-premera Gornogo Altaya isklyuchili za nepravilnuyu agitatsiyu" RIA-Novosti. September 19, 2013. Accessed online at http://ria.ru/politics/20130919/964223233.html, December 20, 2014.

[48] Some examples of these headline-grabbing exceptions include "Itogi vyborov podvodyat Edinuyu Rossiyu" *Kommersant* May 25, 2010, and "Edinaya Rossiya razdvoilas na vyborakh" *Kommersant* August 14, 2009.

[49] A similar instance occurred in the 2009 elections for mayor of Smolensk. Eduard Kochanovskii, a UR legislator, was excluded from the party for running as an independent despite the fact that the party had nominated another candidate. In an exceptional display of irresoluteness the party allowed Kochanovskii to rejoin after the elections.

A final electoral benefit that United Russia provides the regime is organization. As noted, the party has a much larger mass following and grassroots organization than any other party in Russia. Particularly useful are the party's 82,000 (as of 2013) primary party organizations. The leadership of these PPOs – mostly politically ambitious civil servants and midlevel managers – constitute the party's activist core. At election time, these activists penetrate workplaces and civil institutions in order to facilitate agitation, voter intimidation, vote buying, and clientelist exchange. In recent years, the party has made it a priority to ensure that these activists are rewarded for their service with opportunities for political advancement. This is evidenced by the increasing representation of former PPO activists in leadership organs at higher levels in the party hierarchy.

5.3 Commitment Problems and United Russia

Russia's Leaders and United Russia

Dominant parties are institutions that help leaders and elites reap gains from mutual cooperation. This section describes how the dominant party system structures incentives to prevent the Kremlin and elites from reneging on their promises to cooperate. I begin by discussing the ways that the dominant party system functions as a commitment device for Russia's leaders.

It is perhaps best to start off by noting the limits of United Russia's role as an institutional commitment device for leaders. The ultimate commitment that Putin could have made would have been to step down as president and let a party-nominated candidate take his place. Alternatively, he could have reformed the entire political structure, perhaps by turning Russian into a parliamentary system, and put both the government and his own tenure in office under the direct control of the party collective. Or, he could have instituted reforms that elevated the party's state supervisory role, such that major policy decisions would be made within nonstate party organs and then transmitted to state organs for implementation under the watchful eye of the party. This would have approximated the Soviet system, and Putin's own actions would have been controlled by the party collective.

But Putin did not do this. As scholars have noted (Gill 2012, Isaacs and Whitmore 2014, Roberts 2012a), United Russia's party organs do not formulate the main political direction of the country and then dictate that direction to formal state institutions. In particular, nonstate party organs have not exercised manual control over the executive branch as the CPSU once did. In fact, as is often noted, President Putin did not become a formal member of the party in the 2000s (although he was party chairman in 2008–2012 and Prime Minister Medvedev since 2012 has been a party member). In fact, most high-ranking officials in the presidential administration did not become party members in the 2000s.[50]

In order to prevent the party from becoming too strong and challenging Putin, the Kremlin sought to place limits on its independent authority. From the beginning, the federal leadership maintained close, often subservient, ties with the presidential administration. Deputy Head of the Presidential Administration Vladislav Surkov, though he did not hold a formal party position, met frequently with party leaders and exercised significant control over major party decisions.[51] Even in the Duma, where United Russia has displayed the most autonomy, the work of the faction is monitored by the president's representative in the Duma. For these reasons, many of the Kremlin's commitments to party-based cooperation with elites have remained tenuous.

But two important points must be kept in mind concerning United Russia's dependence on the Kremlin. First, one should be careful not to overstate United Russia's lack of autonomy, for while it lacks total control over politics in Russia, it has been delegated significant autonomy over spoil distribution and policy making, especially in legislatures and the regions. And, second, the party state model, typified by the CPSU or the CCP in China, is an ideal type that few, even the most institutionalized, dominant party regimes approximate. For example, even Mexico under the PRI, the paradigmatic example of a dominant party regime in many scholars' eyes, does not typify the party state model. Policy direction was not formulated by party organs and transmitted to state institutions for implementation, and nonstate party organs did not exercise control over the state (e.g. Rodriguez and Ward 1994, Weldon 1997). Instead, as in Russia, the executive branch largely kept the party at arm's length, a relationship that extended to the choice of presidents. Indeed, as at least one insider account describes it (Castaneda 2000), presidential succession in Mexico was a highly personalized process in which the outgoing president selected his successor without consulting the PRI.

---

[50] One exception to this is the Department of Internal Politics. A bridge of cadres between UR and the DIP was established in the 2000s and many members of the DIP carried UR affiliations.
[51] In 2008–2012, Sergei Sobyanin, who was a party member, performed this function for Putin. Since 2012, Vyacheslav Volodin, who rose through the party ranks, has performed this role for the presidential administration.

5.3 Commitment Problems and United Russia

In other paradigmatic dominant party regimes, as well, the party was less autonomous from state leaders than often imagined. Slater (2003) describes how Malaysian Prime Minister Mahathir Mohammed personalized UMNO by packing the party with his own clients. In Taiwan, Chiang Kai-Shek sought to exert control over the KMT, so he refrained from becoming a member of the party's central leadership organs. In turn, he handpicked the party leadership and required that party cadres swear a personal oath of loyalty to the generalissimo, not the party (Dickson 1993). In Egypt and Indonesia, neither the NDP nor GOLKAR had direct control over the president or the military (Brownlee 2007, Slater 2010, Blaydes 2011) Even in the Soviet Union, the most paradigmatic party state, the general secretary often exerted immense personal control over policy direction. This was most pronounced, obviously, in the case of Stalin.

Does this mean that these dominant parties had no autonomy or institutional significance? Those who study them seem to think otherwise. Most dominant parties, like United Russia, have limited collective control over state leaders. But state leaders delegate certain tasks, such that the party regains some autonomous control over policy and spoil distribution in certain spheres. United Russia is not unusual among dominant parties in this regard. One area where this is true is in legislatures. As noted, my interviews with legislators suggest that while the executive branch's representatives in the Duma are deeply involved in the writing of some high-profile legislation, most legislation is still written by United Russia deputies. When asked whether he had to consult the presidential administration when writing his bills, Evgenii Trofimov – vice head of United Russia's Executive Committee (2002–2004) and member of the UR faction in the Fourth Duma – answered that he had "only had to do that one time. Over the course of the whole convocation, only once."[52] Although Trofimov did indicate that he thought the practice of clearing bills with the Kremlin had become more common in the Fifth Duma, other deputies emphasized that the president and prime minister's representatives in the Duma simply did not have the time and resources to follow and micromanage all the legislation being written by the United Russia faction.[53] In an interview with the author, Konstantin Kostin, head of the presidential administration's DIP in 2011–2012, agreed with this assessment, pointing out that the Kremlin delegates the task of writing most legislation to the United Russia faction.[54]

---

[52] Author's interview, June 11, 2013, Moscow.
[53] Author's interview with Vladimir Pligin, June 13, 2013, Moscow.
[54] Author's interview, June 9, 2014. Moscow.

United Russia has also been delegated significant control over the composition of party lists in Duma elections, as well as over the selection of the federal party bureaucracy, the Duma leadership, Federation Council senators, and regional governors. According to party officials familiar with the process of drawing up United Russia's lists ahead of the Duma elections, the party was responsible for creating the lists of candidates, which were then cleared with the presidential administration. As Sergei Popov noted in an interview, these consultations with the presidential administration took place, but the process of creating the list was not micromanaged by the Kremlin:

> The party leadership forms the lists. The president approves them – agrees, disagrees, asks questions, and so on. But the administration doesn't personally manage the process. How could they! Our list had hundreds of candidates. We had 5000 people participating in the primaries last year. What, is the administration going to vet all 5000?![55]

Over the course of the 2000s, the party was also increasingly delegated the task of vetting and making nominations to the Federation Council. This was most pronounced for that half of the senatorial corpus that is chosen by regional legislatures, but, over the course of the decade, UR governors increasingly felt pressured to choose party candidates for their nominees as well.[56] Governors were also vetted by the party. Between 2009 and 2012, United Russia was tasked with drawing up a list of candidates for governor. President Medvedev then chose a nominee from among those candidates. And while insider accounts suggest that the final decision was always made by Putin or Medvedev (Ivanov 2008), the party was given significant leeway over composing those lists.[57] With the restoration of direct gubernatorial elections in 2012, UR's influence over gubernatorial selection has likely only grown, since regional party organs control nominations for those contests.

The area where United Russia has been delegated the most authority, however, is in the management of regional politics. Over the course of the 2000s, the party became increasingly centralized and hierarchical. Local branches must clear many political decisions with regional branches, and regional branches must clear many political decisions with the federal leadership. Candidates for governor, mayor of regional capitals (where appointed), and regional legislative chairman, as well as the UR regional legislative faction's choice for Federation Council nominee, must all be

---

[55] Author's interview, June 8, 2012, Moscow.
[56] See "Edinaya Rossiya formiruyet Sovet Federatsii" *Kommersant* May 6, 2010.
[57] Author's anonymous interview with a former official in the presidential administration's Department for Internal Politics, June 1, 2010.

5.3 Commitment Problems and United Russia

cleared with the federal Presidium of the General Council. Most other important cadre decisions in the regions are made by the regional (or local) *politsovet* (or its Presidium) and confirmed at regional and local party conferences (held yearly), but the federal Presidium certifies the protocols of those conferences and can cancel their decisions if they are found to contradict the party charter.[58]

In turn, the party leadership in Moscow is given significant leeway to manage its relations with the regions. In my interviews with presidential administration officials and federal party leaders in Moscow, I asked about presidential administration involvement in four main areas of party work at the federal level: writing legislation, cadre politics, the conduct of election campaigns, and relations with the regions. There was universal agreement that the party leadership was delegated the most autonomy to manage relations with the regions. Indeed, as much of this book emphasizes, United Russia's most important function has been to help the Kremlin manage its cooperation with regional elites.

This impression was confirmed by interviews with regional party officials. The head of the Yaroslavl Oblast Executive Committee reported that he was on the phone every day with his region's coordinator in Moscow but that he had never spoken to anyone in the presidential administration.[59] The head of the Kirov Oblast Executive Committee expressed a similar sentiment.[60]

In many regions, regional administrations exert significant influence over party branches (e.g. Slider 2010). To the extent that governors answer directly to the Kremlin, this limits the autonomy of the party and undermines its role as an institutional commitment device. At the same time, however, most governors have been party members since the mid-2000s. In turn, governors are frequently held accountable for the performance of the party in the regions (Reuter and Robertson 2012). Indeed, it seems unlikely that United Russia's federal leadership would have wanted strong governors to be completely detached from the party, given that the party depended on strong governors to help it win elections.

Nonetheless, the dependence of United Russia on regional administrations should not be exaggerated. My interviews in the regions reveal more consultation, cooperation, and independence than some existing accounts would lead one to expect. As regards executive–legislative relations, governors have veto power, and their informal resources give them

---

[58] See sections 10 and 13 of the party charter, http://er.ru/party/rules/#10. Regional branches often bristle at this vertical hierarchy. "V 'Edinoi Rossii' zakhoteli demokratii" *Kommersant* March 22, 2012.
[59] Author's interview with Sergei Baburkin, February 21, 2010, Yaroslavl.
[60] Author's interview with German, July 29, 2008, Kirov.

significant influence over the legislative process, but their control is not complete. As the leader of United Russia's faction in the Yaroslavl Oblast Duma put it to me in 2010:

> Every bill that is developed in the regional administration is developed in a working group that includes our deputies. From there, it goes to the committee, which is controlled by United Russia deputies, and the committee usually introduces amendments... If we are developing our own bills, then, of course, we seek out experts from the apparat of the regional administration for expert evaluation, but we do the main work ourselves.[61]

Governors play an active role in crafting legislation but must take the interests of United Russia deputies into account as well. As one empirical study of political parties in the Russian regions noted: "The absence of direct links between a governor and United Russia [this quote is describing the rare case of an opposition governor] gives the governor a certain freedom of action. He is less encumbered by responsibilities set forth by the party of power, including responsibilities to take into consideration the interests of the key elite groups that make up the party ranks" (Bogatyreva 2013, 148). United Russia governors and regional party branches usually work together, and public conflict between the two is rare. This makes it difficult (and perhaps pointless) to parse the influence of one on the other. Yet, it should be noted that in several notable instances, conflictual relations have led United Russia branches to stand up to governors publicly, and in some cases, win. For example, in Irkutsk Oblast, a series of conflicts erupted during 2006–2008 between local United Russia deputies and the newly appointed governor, Alexander Tishanin, over sources of regional tax revenue.[62] The conflict came to a head when the legislature, led by the United Russia faction, refused to pass the governor's budget, overrode his veto on their own budget, and passed amendments to the regional charter that required vice governors to be confirmed by the legislative assembly.[63] Later in 2008, the governor was removed from his post. In Kirov, the region's nonpartisan governor attempted in 2014 to have his vice governor appointed as head of the regional party branch but was rebuffed by the regional party leadership, who chose one of their own as party leader.[64]

---

[61] Author's interview with Vladimir Savelev, March 1, 2010, Yaroslavl.
[62] See http://tayga.info/news/2006/11/20/~65616 and http://kommersant-irk.com/byudzhet-2008-ocherednoj-raund/
[63] See "Irkutsky gubernator osparivayet v sude zakonnost byudzheta, prinyatogo zaksobraniem." regnum.ru April 14, 2008 www.regnum.ru/news/985568.html and http://tayga.info/details/2006/05/28/~89559
[64] "Edinaya Rossiya podbiraet kirovskogo lidera." *Kommersant* November 25, 2014.

5.3 Commitment Problems and United Russia

In cadre politics, as well, the role of the regional administration is complicated. On the one hand, my respondents indicate that governors take an active role overseeing the process of drawing up party lists for regional elections.[65] Party lists are composed by the regional *politsovet* and presented to the governor for approval. They are then formally approved at the party conference. The active role played by the governor makes sense, given that governors often head the UR party list in regional elections and are held responsible for regional election results. By contrast, the regional elites I spoke with report that regional administrations rarely interfere in the process of making internal party appointments or legislative appointments. Regional branches are also left to manage local elections and local party appointments mostly on their own. As one of Eduard Rossel's former advisers on internal politics in Sverdlovsk Oblast described it in a 2008 interview:

> There are only a few of us working in this office. And we are tasked with working with all political parties and social movements. So we have to use our resources rationally. Rossel is a [UR] party member and attends all major party functions. He has influence in the party. But it is not our job [the regional department of internal politics] to duplicate United Russia's work, especially in local self-government.[66]

My interpretation of this statement is that officials in the regional administration are happy to delegate the task of managing local elections to the party.

In sum, while United Russia does not directly control the executive branch, as the CPSU once did, it has been delegated some institutional control over spoil distribution and career advancement. While Putin undoubtedly has influence over the party leadership, neither the General Council, the Higher Council, nor the Executive Committee is chosen by him.[67] By delegating to United Russia responsibility for managing patronage and careers in legislatures, the Kremlin limited its ability to gather information on how these goods should be distributed. Twice, the

---

[65] The impressions in this paragraph are drawn, in particular, from the following interviews: Andrei Krutikov, former chairman of the Yaroslavl Oblast Duma, Yaroslavl, March 4, 2010; Sergei Baburkin, head of United Russia Executive Committee in Yaroslavl Oblast, Yaroslavl, February 21, 2010; Alexander Luzin, vice chairman of Kurgan Oblast Duma, Kurgan July 24, 2008, and Aleksei Kopysov, head of the Politics Department in the Perm Executive Committee of United Russia, Perm, July 9, 2008; and Semen Mitel'man, chairman of the Economic Politics Committee, Chelyabinsk Oblast Legislative Assembly, July 5, 2007.

[66] Author's anonymous interview, July 17, 2008, Ekaterinburg.

[67] As noted in Chapter 4, these bodies, as well as the Party Chairman and the Secretary of the Presidium, are chosen by delegates the congress. Since 2012, they have been chosen in multi-candidate, intraparty elections.

Kremlin hinted that it might support a second party of power, Rodina in 2003 and Just Russia in 2007, though both times, in the end, it made clear that these parties were not to challenge the dominance of United Russia. This tied the Kremlin's hands because dismantling United Russia abruptly would leave them without a way to manage the co-optation of elites efficiently.

Of course, these hand-tying moves are not without their limitations. The Department of Internal Politics duplicates many of United Russia's functions. But the DIP simply cannot perform all the tasks that United Russia does. Although exact figures are difficult to locate, it is clear that the size of the staff in the DIP pales in comparison to the size of United Russia's organization and the DIP's abilities to gather information at the regional level remain limited. Konstantin Kostin, the former head of the DIP, explained in 2014:

> United Russia exists to manage all these tasks [the conversation at this point concerned regional and local elections]. We didn't feel like it made sense to do something that United Russia was already doing. And even if we wanted to ... the party is too large to administer by us. It has tens of thousands of branches, thousands of employees. Such a behemoth can't be controlled so easily.[68]

Another way that United Russia has made the Kremlin's commitments to cooperation with elites credible is by solving elite collective action problems. Gehlbach and Keefer (2012) argue that collectively organized elites are better able to constrain leaders and impose sanctions on them for predatory behavior. This accords with the Russian experience. The Kremlin feared nothing more in the late 1990s than to see the governors solve their collective action problems and unite against the Kremlin (e.g. Shvetsova 2003, Hale 2004). Russia's leaders encouraged divisions among regional elites and were initially hesitant to create a dominant party out of fear that prominent elites would use it as a platform to challenge the Kremlin.

By sanctioning the creation of a centralized, well-disciplined party in the early 2000s, the Kremlin gave elites the institutional tools to keep themselves united. In turn, elites could use this unity to prevent Russia's leaders from impinging on the spoil sharing bargain. And if the Kremlin were to impinge on that bargain – perhaps by purging too many elites, refusing to share rents, or passing party cadres over for promotion – then elites might use their unified position to punish Russia's leaders.

Of course, United Russia has not rebelled against the Kremlin, and there is no reason to think that it will do so in the near future. But the

---

[68] Author's interview, June 9, 2014. Kostin also confirmed for me my suspicion that the party had many more employees than the DIP.

5.3 Commitment Problems and United Russia

lack of open conflict between the Kremlin and United Russia does not prove that the latter lacks the ability to sanction Russia's leaders. The latter have shared ample spoils and career advancement opportunities with party elites, and the lack of open conflict may reflect the fact that both sides have so far remained committed to the spoil sharing bargain.

Nonetheless, certain events of the 2000s speak to the dynamics sketched previously. The potential for conflict between the Kremlin and the party was demonstrated early in the 2000s by public disagreements between Putin and party leaders about whether the government should be formed on a party basis (see Chapter 4). Since then, conflicts have periodically erupted between United Russia and the government. One of the first of these instances was the party's criticism of the implementation of the aforementioned law on social benefit monetization in 2005.[69] Party leaders feared that this unpopular reform would undermine their electoral base, a theme that has motivated many subsequent disagreements between party and the government. In 2006, United Russia harshly criticized the government for underfunding social programs in its draft of the 2007 budget bill.[70] The party demanded, and ultimately secured, additional funding for the National Projects, which United Russia sought to trumpet in the 2007 campaign. Conflicts between the two erupted again in 2010 when First Deputy Secretary of United Russia's Presidium Andrei Isayev accused Finance Minister Alexei Kudrin of "putting a stick in United Russia's spokes" by advocating an increase in the pension age.[71] In response to these conflicts, United Russia proposed the creation of special party "commissars" who would correspond to ministerial departments. According to Isayev, "Every minister should know that in the party there is a 'komissar' who is going to coordinate this work from beginning to end." In the end, this proposal remained just a proposal, and these "komissars" do not appear ever to have obtained any real influence, but the initiative and the Kremlin's wariness of it are noteworthy.[72]

Another way that Russia's leaders raised the costs of defecting from the dominant party system was by nesting their commitments to the dominant party project inside other institutional commitments. For example,

---

[69] Moscow Mayor Yurii Luzhkov was among the most vocal critics. See Makarkin, Aleksei and Tat'yana Stanova. "Edinaya Rossii: Ot partii vlasti k pravyashei partii" Politcom.ru. November 28, 2005. www.politcom.ru/article.php?id=1664

[70] "Pervaya 'obkatka.'" *Parlamentskaya Gazeta* July 5, 2006.

[71] "Partiya vlasti v poiskakh vraga naroda" *Kommersant* July 2, 2010 and "'Edinaya Rossiya' nashla antipartiinogo lidera." *Kommersant* July 7, 2010. Examples of such conflicts could also be found in the 2010s. See "Duma raskritikovala zakonproekt o bor'be s finansovymy narusheniyami." *Vedomosti* February 20, 2013.

[72] See "'Edinaya Rossiya' Obeshayet pristavit k ministram komissarov." *Izvestia* October 3, 2008, and "Edinaya Rossiya prokontroliruyet Putin." *Gazeta.ru* October 3, 2008.

fixed election cycles meant that United Russia majorities elected in one election would, at least according to the letter of the law, be stable until the next election. This stickiness was reinforced by the introduction of imperative mandate laws that prevented national and regional legislators from switching parliamentary factions.

More generally, the early and mid-2000s saw the introduction of a series of reforms that strengthened the role of political parties in the electoral process. These reforms favored the dominant party at the expense of independents and small, regional parties. The 2001 Law on Political Parties and subsequent amendments increased the barriers to entry for small and regional parties by requiring all parties to be registered in at least half of Russia's regions as well as to demonstrate membership of more than 50,000. In 2005, electoral blocs, which many regional elites had used to circumvent the ban on regional parties, were banned as well. In 2002, amendments to the Law on Voters' Rights exempted party nominated candidates from requirements to present signatures in order to register for elections. More importantly, the law mandated that at least half the seats in all elections to regional assemblies be held under proportional representation. By itself, this reform created a role for parties in regional elections and was sure to increase party penetration in the regions, but when combined with the reforms prohibiting regional parties outlined previously, this reform mandated a place for national parties in regional legislatures.[73]

The most significant of the "proparty" institutional changes was the decision in 2005 to move from a mixed to fully proportional electoral system for State Duma elections (see Moraski 2006, Smyth et al. 2007). Further dampening the prospects of small parties, new legislation also increased the barrier of representation from 5 to 7 percent. Simultaneously, the Kremlin encouraged regional legislatures to increase their electoral thresholds for the party list component to a minimum of 7 percent. With all these reforms the Kremlin sent a clear signal to elites that it was serious about investing in a single, dominant party. These changes made it more complicated for the Kremlin, at least in the short term, to dismantle the dominant party system.[74]

United Russia's grassroots organization and social support base also helped increase the costs of dismantling the party. Over the course of the 2000s, the party developed a massive organization in the regions and attracted millions of party identifiers. Shifting these supporters to a new

[73] In early 2006, the central election commission sent a "model" bill to the regions suggesting that they adopt mixed systems as well (Kynev 2006a).
[74] Chapter 9 discusses some recent changes to these rules.

5.3 Commitment Problems and United Russia

party brand – or distributing this support base efficiently among pro-regime independents – would be difficult to achieve in a short amount of time.

In addition to all this, the mere act of creating United Russia compelled Putin to make some public commitments to the dominant party system. By associating with the party, and later becoming party chairmen, he linked his name, reputation, and personal brand to the party. In doing so, he sent a signal to other elites that he was willing to accept responsibility for the party's fate. Ultimately, a dominant party is a risk pool. By jointly committing themselves to the party, both sides become hostages to the party's collective fortunes. Grave policy failures, an electoral catastrophe, a scandal, or other shocks could leave both the rulers and the elites worse off than if they had eschewed the dominant party project in the first place.

By tying himself so closely to the party, Putin raised the reputational costs of suddenly disavowing the party. Resolve is one of the traits that voters respect most in Putin. Since 1999, the Levada Center has asked voters once a year to name the traits that they like in Vladimir Putin. Between 1999 and 2013, the number one response was his "energy, *resolve*, and *decisiveness* [emphasis added]."[75] By suddenly dissociating himself from the party, Putin would risk appearing irresolute.

Finally, it is worth saying a few words about how the party helps leaders and elites monitor their commitments and thus reduces the temptation for each side to defect (e.g. Svolik 2012). In Russia, the act of being a member of a party has meaning. It indicates who is participating in the accommodative arrangement with the regime and who is not. As United Russia's first party leader, Aleksandr Bespalov, put it, "We want them [governors, bureaucrats] to join so that they don't sit on the fence, so that we know exactly who is with whom."[76] Joining the party sends a visible sign of loyalty, and rules embedded within the dominant party system – the party charter, faction charters, party directives, and norms – make it easier for actors to identify indiscipline. This likely makes Russia's leaders feel more comfortable in knowing that they are not being abused by elites. In turn, knowing that indiscipline can be identified by leaders, elites are less likely to try to abuse leaders.

In sum, Russia's leaders have not ventured to take the far-reaching steps – e.g. placing the party in direct control of executive branch institutions – that would constitute the most robust commitments to the dominant party system. At the same time, they have delegated certain

---

[75] See www.levada.ru/16-04-2014/vladimir-putin-otnoshenie-i-doverie
[76] "My ne moskalskie mordy" *Kommersant* August 6, 2002.

powers to United Russia, placed limits on their ability to micromanage key political tasks, given elites a way to defend their interests collectively, devoted reputational resources to the party, and cultivated mechanisms that facilitate monitoring. In many spheres, access to spoils and career advancement have come to depend on loyal service to the party. Party cadres rely on United Russia for the provision of these goods, such that their political survival depends on the continued existence of the party. And so, by dismantling or subverting United Russia, Russia's leaders could have risked elite defection or rebellion.[77] Thus, over the course of its development United Russia came to represent an equilibrium arrangement that was incentive compatible for the Kremlin.

Elite Commitments and United Russia

The inability of elites to commit to cooperating with leaders can be as detrimental to the fortunes of a ruling party as a leader's lack of commitment. In the paragraphs that follow, I discuss how the dominant party system in Russia functions as a commitment device for elites.

First, elites made their commitments credible by joining the party and making themselves subject to sanction by the central party leadership. Legislators who vote against the party may be excluded from the faction and, thus, deprived of access to legislative spoils. Party members who run against officially sanctioned candidates in elections may be purged from the party and deprived of access to lobbying opportunities. Mayors who support non–United Russia candidates may lose the support of United Russia copartisans in city councils. In legislatures, the existence of an imperative mandate adds weight to these commitments, for if a legislator leaves his party faction, she or he also loses the legislative seat.

Another commitment step was the move by prominent elites – especially governors and mayors – to dismantle or link their political machines to United Russia. By dismantling regional parties of power – or subsuming them into United Russia – governors in regions such as Tatarstan, Chelyabinsk, Khabarovsk, Kemerovo, and Sverdlovsk deprived themselves of autonomous political resources and thus limited their ability to defect from the party bargain. For new governors who came to power after 2004 the absence of a strong political machine in the region made their commitments to the party all the more credible.

---

[77] Indeed, when Putin experimented in 2013 with installing non-UR governors in three regions, United Russia cadres in the regions protested and in at least one case – Zabaikalskii Krai – defected against the regime. See "Zabaikal'skie edinorossi razdumali podderzhivat' vrio gubernatora" *Kommersant* May 27, 2013, and "Gubernatory ulozhili v srok" *Kommersant* June 16, 2014.

5.3 Commitment Problems and United Russia

In the 2000s, United Russia began to take over many of the functions – selecting candidates, distributing patronage, controlling legislative spoils, managing election campaigns – that gubernatorial machines had once performed. In the 1990s, many State Duma deputies were handpicked by Russian governors and elected with the backing of regional machines and local financial–industrial groups (Hale 2006). But as the 2000s wore on, governors' clients were increasingly replaced by cadres selected by United Russia. Evgenii Trofimov, who was responsible for composing United Russia's regional list for the North Caucasus in 2003, relates the following anecdote:

I remember when we were forming the lists for the 2003 elections. I went to Rostov, Kabardino-Balkaria, Karachaevo Cherkessia, Stavropol Krai, Krasnodar Krai. I remember meeting Tkachev [then-governor of Krasnodar] who was proposing one candidate and we were proposing another. I told him that we really preferred our candidate. He [Tkachev] was a party supporter at that time. And we had a serious fruitful exchange and came to an agreement. I remember how when I was in Rostov the governor wanted to put himself at the top of the regional list followed by one of his deputies and then put another one of his deputies in the third spot. I spoke with him and said: "What? You don't trust people? Why don't we put this woman, a doctor, well- trusted in the number 2 spot?" Everyone liked her. He agreed with me. That's how we formed the lists. And there weren't any questions at the Congress.[78]

Increasingly over the course of the 2000s, the machines of local notables began to be melded into United Russia. Far-reaching party reforms adopted at the Sixth Party Congress in November 2005 extended the reach of the central party organs deep into the decision making realm of regional party organizations and leaders. The federal leadership of the party gained control over (1) nominating the heads of regional party organizations, (2) proposing the candidates for speaker of the regional legislature, (3) proposing the candidate for governor, (4) choosing candidates that will represent the legislature in the Federation Council, and (5) certifying the protocols of regional party conferences.

Since then the central party leadership has become increasingly active in regional cadre politics.[79] In a number of high-profile cases the party

---

[78] Author's interview with Evgenii Trofimov, member of UR faction in Fourth Duma and vice chairman of United Russia's Executive Committee, June 11, 2013, Moscow.

[79] In 2008, party leaders announced a campaign to make regional branches even more independent of governors. In addition to making rotation of regional party functionaries mandatory, the party leadership proposed to make regional party secretaries full-time employees. The latter reform never happened, however. For more on the campaign see: "Vperyod, Kommissari." *Nezavisimaya Gazeta* April 22, 2009, "Edinaya Rossia razlubila bystrye s"ezdy" *Kommersant* July 29, 2008, and "Aleksandr Tkachev poluchil partiinuyu dolzhnost.'" *Kommersant* April 6, 2010, and "Edinaya Rossiya razliubila bystrye s'ezdy." *Kommersant* July 29, 2008.

leadership has intervened to iron out differences among regional elites over party list spots and imposed solutions if rivals could not come to agreement.[80] In other instances, the party has sent special delegations to the regions to determine who among the regional elite should face sanction for economic crises or social unrest. For example, when large-scale anti-regime protests broke out in Kaliningrad in 2009, United Russia sent a delegation of party officials to the region to determine which local party officials should be punished.[81] In the end, Sergei Bulychev, head of the regional United Russia branch and one of Governor Boos's close associates, was removed from his post. In the past, regional governors would have been in charge of managing their own political machines, but in the 2000s, United Russia began to manage many such tasks.

That these efforts to draw gubernatorial machines into the orbit of the party had some teeth is demonstrated by the extent to which they irked prominent regional governors. For example, the 2005 party reforms provoked staunch opposition from Moscow Mayor Yuri Luzhkov (Slider 2006). In June 2009, Baskhortorstan President Murtaza Rakhimov made waves by decrying the growing influence of the party: "I have just heard that United Russia needs to be independent – 'not under the paw of governors'... I am sorry, but the core of the party should be formed from below. But that doesn't seem to be the case right now. The party is being run by people who have never commanded anything more than three chickens. Is that the way it's really going to be?"[82] Such statements indicate that United Russia's expanded role in the regions was more than virtual.

5.4 Conclusion

Mikhail Gorbachev once said that United Russia is a "bad copy of the CPSU."[83] By this he likely meant that the party exhibits the centralized

---

[80] Notable cases include Pskov and Murmansk during the run-up to the March 2007 regional elections. In both regions, conflicts flared in the regional branches of the party. And in both cases party leaders from Moscow imposed a solution to the conflict. See Maria Luiza Tirmaste, "Edinaya Rossia pomirila gubernatora s merom." *Kommersant* January 19, 2007, and Elena Bilevskaya, "Murmanskikh edinorossov pomirila rukha Moskvy'" *Kommersant* December 11, 2006. Another more recent example is taken from the events surrounding the reconstitution of theVolgograd regional branch in 2014: See "23 aprelya sostoitsya konferentsiya Volgogradskogo otdeleniya Partii" United Russia Online New Feed. Accessed online: http://er.ru/news/115365/

[81] "Mitingovavshim za vsye obeshayut 'protiv vsekh'" *Kommersant* February 2, 2010, and "Kremlin, United Russia Worried After Kaliningrad Rally" *Moscow Times* February 2, 2010.

[82] "Dissident Respubliki Bashkortorstan" *Moskovskii Komsomolets* June 4, 2009.

[83] "Vopros Nedeli." *Vlast'*, August 6, 2007.

5.4 Conclusion

bureaucratic tendencies of a dominant party but eschews the clear ideological vision that was a hallmark of communist parties. While prophecies of a return to CPSU-style, single party rule have proven false in Russia, United Russia is now functioning as a dominant party institution that provides benefits to both leaders and elites. For the Kremlin, the party helps maintain elite cohesion, makes passing legislation easier, routinizes the process of making political appointments, and reduces the costs of coordinating supporters in elections. For elites, United Russia provides access to patronage and policy and reduces the uncertainty associated with securing the access to these spoils.

By delegating a range of important political tasks to United Russia – especially in legislatures and the regions – the Kremlin raised the costs of reneging on its commitments to cooperate with elites under the framework of a dominant party system. The Kremlin further strengthened its commitments by linking the maintenance of the dominant party to other institutional commitments, making public commitments to the party, giving elites the institutional tools to solve their collective action problems, and limiting investment in parallel institutions that duplicate the functions of United Russia. Elites, for their part, made their commitments credible by linking their political machines to the party and giving the central party leadership the ability to sanction them for indiscipline. These commitments have helped the two sides assure each other that the other will be a faithful partner in the dominant party system.

Furthermore, by making the rules of the accommodative arrangement clear to both sides the dominant party has made it easier for the Kremlin and elites to monitor each other's compliance. Enshrined in the dominant party system are rules – parchment or implicit – specifying what constitutes compliance on the part of both the leader (e.g. supporting party candidates in elections or privileging party cadres in legislatures) and elites (e.g. maintaining party discipline). By making it easier to identify defections, United Russia reduces the temptation of both elites and leaders to spurn their commitments and abuse the other.

However, United Russia does not exercise direct, collective control over the executive branch. In the Soviet Union, most important political decisions were made by nonstate party organs. Those decisions were then transmitted to state organs for implementation. This is not the practice in post-Soviet Russia. Most officials in the executive branch – including Putin – do not owe their positions in power to United Russia, and the executive branch sets the policy direction. This necessarily limits United Russia's independence, and, ultimately, undermines its role in the political system.

Because of this, some authors have sought to downplay United Russia's role as a political institution (e.g. Bader 2011, Gill 2012, Roberts 2012b, Isaacs and Whitmore 2014). According to some, United Russia – like other post-Soviet parties of power – is a sui generis phenomenon that should not be compared to other dominant parties (Makarenko 2011, Bader 2011, Roberts 2012b). The perspective that I offer is somewhat different. While United Russia's state-supervisory role pales in comparison to that of some of history's most highly institutionalized ruling parties, such as the Chinese Communist Party, it is something more than an institutional shell, and we can learn much about it – and about other dominant parties – by comparing it to other dominant parties.

For one thing, as this chapter has noted, the dominant party ideal envisioned by many – in which a party exercises collective and autonomous control over state institutions – is a very rare phenomenon. The institutional strength of dominant parties varies significantly among countries, but most of the world's dominant parties are like United Russia in that their collective influence over the top leadership is limited. Leaders in dominant party regimes may selectively violate the independence of the dominant party (perhaps by purging elites), even as they delegate it some authority and remain constrained by the system (e.g. see Magaloni 2008, 723–724). Most dominant parties constrain leaders (and elites) in some ways, but are still dependent on them in others. United Russia falls into this category.

It is certainly not the case that United Russia is identical to the PRI, UMNO, or PDP. No two political institutions are ever identical. But the differences among dominant parties should not prevent comparative analysis of their similarities. Analyzing the creation of United Russia with a theory of dominant party formation can improve, I hope, our understanding both of Russia's political institutions and of authoritarian institutions more generally.

There is also a tendency, I think, among many observers and scholars to understate the institutional significance of United Russia. For observers in Russia – and perhaps some scholars – I suspect that this arises out of a tendency to make implicit comparisons between Russia's political institutions and those that exist in the West. The frame of comparison is rarely other autocracies and certainly not personalist autocracies. But in comparison with many of those personalist autocracies, Russia's ruling party institutions are significant. I have argued that, over the course of the 2000s, United Russia came to function as an institution, a bundle of rules and norms that structured the behavior of leaders and elites. Putin grew to rely on United Russia to secure elite loyalty, win elections, control legislatures, and help him manage cadres. And many elites began to

5.4 Conclusion

rely on United Russia for the dependable provision of spoils and careers. By defecting from the party, elites risk loss of access to those spoils, and by dismantling the party Putin would jeopardize his ability to keep elites loyal. Thus, both sides have retained an interest in maintaining the dominant party system.

United Russia has played a key role in the maintenance of Russia's electoral authoritarian regimes, and I suspect that Putin's Russia would look very different without it. As Vladislav Surkov remarked during the height of the 2009 economic crisis: "The system is working… One party dominates and there are many minuses to this, but I am deeply convinced that there are many more pluses in this. If we had entered this turbulent zone in a more undisciplined fashion, I can assure you, the damage that the state and society would have suffered would be much greater."[84] Without United Russia, elites would be more fractious, policy making would be more difficult, and Russia's rulers would have a harder time mobilizing political support. As rulers in countries not so far from Russia have repeatedly found out, holding on to power in a country with fractious elites and weak ruling party institutions is not so easy. Without United Russia, the Putin regime might not have persisted for this long.

---

[84] Remarks by Vladislav Surkov at the Strategy 2020 Forum March 2, 2009 www.polit.ru/country/2009/03/03/surkov_text.html.

6 United Russia and Russia's Governors

Chapters 3 and 4 showed how ruling party formation in Russia has been shaped by the balance of resources between elites and the Kremlin. In Chapter 8, I examine the cross-national implications of my argument through an analysis of dominant party emergence in all non-democracies between 1945 and 2006. But before leaving the Russian case, this chapter and Chapter 7 take advantage of United Russia's recent emergence to probe deeper into the individual-level mechanisms that stand behind my argument. Herein, I seek to show that individual actors have the interests that I posit for them and act upon those interests in a fashion that is consistent with my theory and inconsistent with competing explanations.

The main argument in this book simplifies reality by positing a bilateral interaction between the leader and elites as a whole. This simplification made it easier to explicate the central features of the argument. In reality, however, "the elite" is not always a single actor. As this chapter shows, individual elites make individual decisions about investment in the dominant party.

The balance of resources between leaders and elites varies across countries, such that one can speak about "strong elites" in one setting and "weak elites" in another. This seems evident. But it is also evident that, within any given country, some elites are stronger than others. A logical implication of my theory is that when a country is moving from a situation in which elites control a preponderance of resources to one in which resources are balanced between leaders and elites, then elites weak in resources will be the first to join an emergent dominant party. They are the first elites for which it is more advantageous to cooperate in the bonds of a dominant party than it is to remain autonomous. Thus, I argue that elites with more significant stores of political, personal, and/or economic resources that are difficult for state leaders to repress or control are less likely to seek affiliation with nascent dominant parties.

This chapter tests this hypothesis with data on the timing of Russian regional executives' decisions to join United Russia. I analyze the behavior of Russian governors both because they are the most significant elite actors in post-Soviet Russia and because there is useful variation in their decisions to join the dominant party. I show that regional governors with autonomous resources delayed joining the party longer than those without such resources.

Most of the literature in comparative politics now agrees that elite cohesion is one of the fundamental underpinnings of stable authoritarian rule (Brownlee 2007, Slater 2010, Reuter and Gandhi 2011, Svolik 2012). And yet the causes of elite unity remain poorly understood. Those accounts of elite cohesion that do exist usually focus on how ruling party institutions help bind elites into a cohesive coalition (Brownlee 2007), but there are far fewer explanations for why elites would cohere in such a party in the first place. This chapter contributes to this understanding.

The chapter proceeds as follows. Section 6.1 relates my theory of dominant party formation to hypotheses about the dominant party affiliation behavior of individual elites. Section 6.2 discusses some alternative explanations of Russia's governors' dominant party affiliation behavior. Since this chapter relies on original data collected by the author, Section 6.3 offers an extended discussion of the dependent variable (governors' month of entry into United Russia). Section 6.4 lays out the research design and models. Section 6.5 discusses the results and Section 6.6 concludes.

6.1 Individual Elites, Dominant Party Affiliation, and Russia's Governors

The balance of resources between leaders and elites varies across countries. But it is also true that the strength of individual elites varies within countries. My theory of dominant party formation has implications about the behavior of individual elites.

If dominant parties emerge when resources become balanced between leaders and elites, it stands to reason that countries must transition to this set of circumstances from one in which resources are not so balanced. The balance of resources may be tilted in favor of elites, or it may be tilted in favor of leaders. Thus, dominant parties begin to emerge according to one of two scenarios:

1. They may begin to emerge as the balance of resources shifts from a strong leader toward elites.
2. They may begin to emerge as the balance of resources shifts toward leaders in countries where elites hold a preponderance of resources.

As the overall balance of resources between leaders and elites shifts toward a point where neither side holds a preponderance of these resources, individual elites will begin joining the party. Some may join at early stage, while others join later. The order in which they join depends upon the individual resources of each elite actor and whether leaders or elites as a whole control a greater share of the overall balance of resources. In scenario one, the *strongest* elites will be the first to be co-opted into the party, because they are the first with whom the leader needs to strike bargains. In this setting, weak elites may want to reach a cooperative bargain with leaders, but leaders have little reason to coopt them. By contrast, leaders do have a motive to contract with strong elites. Under this scenario, the overall balance of resources still favors the leader, but leaders have an ever-increasing need to co-opt strong elites in order to govern cost-effectively.

In scenario two, the *weakest* elites should be the first to make investments in the party because they are the first who stand to reap significant gains from cooperation with leaders. As Chapter 4 showed, the emergence of United Russia is in this category. Under such a scenario, weak elites have the least to lose in relinquishing their autonomy, but they are still strong enough that leaders need their cooperation. For stronger elites, maintaining one's own patronage networks and autonomous power bases may be preferable to contracting with the regime. Such elites can ensure their political survival and extract rents without linking their fates to the regime. But if the balance of political resources continues to shift in favor of central leaders, then the benefits of contracting with the regime will increase and these stronger elites will begin joining the party.[1] In sum, I argue that when dominant party formation is brought about by a shift in resources away from elites (i.e. toward leaders), then elites who are weaker in resources should join earlier than those stronger in resources.

In this chapter, I examine this argument with data on the dominant party affiliation behavior of Russia's governors. As Chapters 3 and 4 illustrated, Russia's governors accumulated immense formal and informal resources over the course of the 1990s. By far the most important of these elites were Russian governors. In the mid-2000s, Russia's governors suffered a severe loss of autonomy as a direct result of Putin's recentralizing efforts. Yet, as Chapters 4 and 5 show, even after Putin's reforms – and, indeed, even after Putin cancelled direct gubernatorial

---

[1] Of course, if the balance of resources between the two sides ceases to shift, then the process of gradual elite affiliation, and hence of dominant party emergence, may come to a halt. Alternatively, the balance of resources may shift so drastically and completely from elites to leaders (or vice versa) that the conditions for dominant party emergence cease to exist. Though it is theoretically possible, the stickiness of formal and informal institutions makes this an unlikely sequence of events.

elections – Russia's governors still retained expansive political resources that made it necessary for the Kremlin to co-opt them if it hoped to govern the regions cost-effectively and win elections.

In the early 2000s, the Kremlin was unwilling to invest significantly in either Unity or United Russia. In response, only the weakest governors made a formal commitment to the party. As the resource balance continued to shift in the Kremlin's favor after 2003, the Kremlin was able to offer more to governors and simultaneously chip away at their autonomy. Thus, the benefits of joining United Russia rose and the costs fell. As time went on and the resource balance continued to shift toward the Kremlin, more and more governors found themselves ready to commit. In turn, as more and more governors (and other elites) demonstrated their willingness to commit to the nascent dominant party, the Kremlin ventured its own commitments.

If we assume, as I think it is safe to do, that the balance of resources was shifting in favor of the Kremlin over the course of the decade, then the preceding framework predicts that the first governors to join United Russia should have been those with the least robust resource endowments, while those with larger endowments of resources should have waited longer. Hence, I examine the following hypothesis:

> H1: Governors with significant endowments of political and economic resources will postpone joining United Russia longer than those without such resources.

6.2 Alternative Explanations

There are at least two alternative predictions about the relationship between resource ownership and the decision to join United Russia. The first is that there should be no systematic relationship, because governors were simply forced to join United Russia. If the Kremlin could simply form a dominant party whenever it pleased, then there should be no systematic relationship between the resources elites control and their entry into the party.

A second alternative prediction about the relationship between resources and governors' decisions to join is that governors who are strong in resources join the party early. Indeed, a handful of Russia's "strongest" governors were among the founders of the party. Tatarstan President Mintimer Shaimiyev, Bashkortostan President Murtaza Rakhimov, and Moscow Mayor Yuri Luzhkov, leaders of the OVR coalition since 1999, were among the nominal founders of the party, though as I argue later, the actual date of their accession to the party is a matter of dispute. One of the benefits that the Kremlin receives through investment in United Russia is votes. Therefore, if the agency of governors played no role, then the Kremlin might enlist the strongest governors first in order to mobilize the most votes. One could also speculate that the strongest governors would join the party first in order to gain control of the party apparatus and secure privileged positions in it. This chapter tests whether these alternative predictions are superior to the one I have offered.

6.3 The Dependent Variable: Governors' Decisions to Join UR

The dependent variable in this analysis is the number of months it took for a governor to join United Russia after March 2003. Data on the timing of Russia's governors' decisions to join UR were collected by the author from the United Russia Web site and online news sources. United Russia publicizes the accession of high-ranking officials to the party, so most governors' entry into the party is documented on the site. With data missing on six governors, this amounts to 121 governors serving at some time during this period.[2] These data provide information on the month in which each of Russia's governors joined UR. It is shown in full in the Online Appendix to this book.

I code a governor as joining the party when he/she formally accepts a party card as a full-fledged member (*chlen partii*). I do not count the following as indicators of membership unless, of course, they are accompanied by formal party membership: heading the United Russia party list in regional or federal elections, accepting the party's support in gubernatorial elections, or professing support for UR candidates in elections. Also, I do not count party supporters (*storonniki*) as members.

Party membership is a more credible signal of commitment than these other steps. Joining the party requires the governor to give up other party affiliations (e.g. becoming a *storonnik* does not). Entry into the party is widely reported in the news media, making it difficult for the governor to deny his membership. Other possible indicators permit governors significant leeway in making provisional commitments. In the 1990s, governors frequently supported more than one party or accepted the support of multiple parties in elections. Party membership, thus, represents a

---

[2] Data on party affiliation date back to 2001, but only a handful of governors (five, to be exact) were in any way affiliated with the party prior to March 2003, and several of these governors appeared not to be actual party members until some time later. Thus, the analyses in this chapter begin on March 2003. All models were also run using data stretching back to December 2001 with the same results. The data end in November 2007, when all but five governors had joined.

6.3 The Dependent Variable: Governors' Decisions to Join UR

conscious decision to signal one's commitment that goes above and beyond other indicators of party support. In itself, the act of joining the party is not likely to incur heavy costs, aside from the public signal it sends, but it is the most practical proxy for other costly commitments that are likely to accompany membership such as only supporting party candidates in elections and relinquishing some control over the nomination of personnel and candidates. Surely, there are more valid indicators of commitment to the party that could be gleaned from detailed case studies, but party membership is perhaps the most reliable measure that is also sufficiently valid.

A particularly difficult hurdle in deciding whether a governor is a member of United Russia is presented by the Higher Council (*Vyshii Sovet*). Before 2005, governors were prohibited by law from belonging to any political party, though press reports and the party's own Web site report that dozens of governors nonetheless became members (*chleny*) of the party in 2003 and 2004. United Russia leaders created the Higher Council as a parallel advisory council where governors could sit without being party members. Only in November 2005, at the Fifth Party Congress, did United Russia leaders amend the party charter to stipulate that all newly initiated members of the Higher Council be party members. This Higher Council is separate from the central decision-making structures of the party, the General Council and its Presidium, and there are no provisions in the party's charter for when it should meet. Sources close to the party confirm that the Higher Council is not "a governing body" (Ivanov 2008, 81). As one high-ranking party official put it to me, "Membership in the Higher Council is more an honor than a privilege." The problem is that some governors chose to join the Higher Council and only later chose to join the party formally, while others joined the Higher Council and, to the best of my knowledge, never formally joined the party.[3] This problem is made even more acute by those governors who joined the Higher Council (but not the party) only to flout party discipline. For example, Kemerovo Governor Aman Tuleev was a member of the party's Higher Council (but not a member) in 2003 and on United Russia's Duma party list, but he ran his own list of candidates, Sluzhu Kuzbassu (I Serve the Kuzbass), in the oblast regional election of the same year (Slider 2006). By the time the region held regional elections again in October 2008, however, Tuleev had become a party

---

[3] So, for example, Orel Governor Yegor Stroyev joined the party's Higher Council in March 2003, but then received his party membership card in November 2005. "Egor Stroyev zavyazal s bespartiinost'yu" *Kommersant* Voronezh November 26, 2005. Accessed online at www.ancentr.ru/data/media/arch_media_1948.html on November 20, 2007.

member and threw his full support behind the United Russia list, helping it secure 35 of 36 seats in the regional assembly.

For the reasons indicated, I do not count joining the Higher Council as joining the party unless a governor joined the Higher Council after November 2005 (when the party charter was amended to require party membership for Higher Council members). Sixteen governors joined the Higher Council before being party members (mostly in 2003). Four governors later joined formally, so I code them as joining on the date they accepted their party card. For the other 12, I code them as joining the party when they are first documented as serving on the party's Political Council (*Politsovet*) in their region. According to the party's charter, party membership is required to serve on the *politsovet*. Most United Russia governors hold posts in the regional *politsovet* since that is the primary political organ of the party in the regions. Official membership in this organ indicates a clear signal of commitment to party activities and association with the party. To ensure the robustness of my results, I also report results where governors who join the Higher Council are coded as party members from that time.

Three governors, the former Moscow Mayor Yurii Luzhkov, former Tatarstan president Mintimer Shaimiyev, and former Bashkortostan president Murtaza Rakhimov, present potential problems for the coding scheme. These three governors, who were among the party's founders and who were once widely viewed as among Russia's most influential regional executives, appear to have never formally accepted formal party nomination, though they were members of the party Higher Council since the beginning. More significantly, none of these three figures ever served on the *politsovet* in his region. Instead, these governors' role in the party appears more akin to the symbolic leadership post that Putin holds than it does to the leading cadre positions that most governors occupy.

One way to approach this problem is to code these governors as never joining the party. But this might understate their commitment to the party. On the other end of the spectrum, coding them as joining from the beginning denies the arm's length relationship they appear to have developed with the party by not participating in regional leadership organs and denying themselves the title "party member."[4] Thus, in the baseline models, I omit these governors from analysis. For robustness, I also present several other models that code these three governors as joining when they joined the Higher Council and in November 2005 when the party charter was amended to require party membership for all Higher

---

[4] For another example, see "'Edinaya Rossiya' potrebuyet obysnenii ot Rakhimova" *Kommersant* June 5, 2009.

6.3 The Dependent Variable: Governors' Decisions to Join UR

Council members. I also present results for when these governors never join the party. As we will see, these changes have only a minor effect on one substantive variable, length of tenure in office, for which these governors are significant outliers.[5]

Figure 4.1 (in the previous chapter) presents the number of governors who were members of United Russia in each month from March 2003 until November 2007. In the 1990s, Russia's governors affiliated with various parties of power and regional political blocs, but, with the exception of the Communist Party of the Russian Federation (KPRF), they very rarely became full-fledged members of any party. The situation was no different in 1999, when the governors faced severe coordination dilemmas in deciding which party to support ahead of the 1999–2000 election cycle (Shvetsova 2003). Yet even in 1999, very few governors actually "joined" Unity or OVR. With United Russia, this situation began to change, though, as the figure shows, only slowly.

An implicit assumption in some of the literature on Russia's emerging authoritarian regime is that the Kremlin forced all governors to join United Russia, paying little heed to their political resources, which were expropriated for use by the party. Such a view would lead to the prediction that Russia's governors were coerced into joining United Russia en masse. But descriptive data on the governor's dominant party affiliation patterns cast some doubt on this perspective.

Though United Russia was tapped as the sole bearer of the Kremlin standard in the December 2003 parliamentary elections, governors were not forced to join en masse at this time. In addition, as Figure 4.1 shows, there was no discernible rush to join the party. Though many governors agreed to be placed on the UR party lists for the December 2003 Duma elections (27 in fact), only 15 governors had formally joined the party by that time.

Another common misconception is that most of Russia's governors joined the party immediately after Putin's proposal to cancel gubernatorial elections was passed into law in September 2004, implying that Russia's governors were essentially forced into joining the party. This proposition seems intuitive. With no independent electoral mandate, governors appeared wholly dependent on the Kremlin after 2004 and were required to curry favor with the president in order to secure reappointment. In fact, in September 2004, the number of governors in the

---

[5] The fact that these governors became connected with the party so early despite their immense resources might be explained by the fact that they were able to achieve more than the usual benefits of party membership. The chance to be among the top party leadership made the benefits of joining much higher for this handful of governors.

party was only 23, and while 11 governors did join by January 2005, this was still far short of a majority. It is true that the pace of governors' joining the party slightly increased in the fall of 2004, but as the figure shows, this was only a minor deviation from the linear trend. In fact, by far the largest increase in governor membership occurred in the fall of 2005, just after the Kremlin floated the idea of giving the largest party in regional parliaments the right to nominate candidates for regional executive posts.[6] The proportion of Russia's governors who were party members reached 50 percent only in October 2005. The party continued to grow at a steady pace in 2006, so that 67 governors were members by the end of the year. In 2007, the pace of joining slowed, and by November of that year, when the analysis ends, all but 5 of Russia's governors had joined.

Another intuitive expectation that this figure disproves is that governors joined at an increasing rate as other governors joined United Russia. The intuition here would be that governors developed stronger beliefs about the future role of the party in distributing rents as the number of "peer governors" joined. Such a phenomenon would be represented in the figure by a curve of *increasing* slope rather than by the constant upward linear trend depicted. The figure shows little evidence of a classical tipping point, which would be represented by a substantial increase in the rate of joining followed by a tapering off as the critical mass was surpassed (an S-shaped pattern). Part of the reason for this is surely that, unlike legislators, Russia's governors lack an institutional lobbying forum where majorities or supermajorities matter. Instead, as oil prices increased, real incomes grew, and the transitional uncertainties waned over this period, the Kremlin was able to offer more to Russia's governors, and they were in a better position to commit to the party. The reason why some governors joined early and others later is explained in this chapter.

At a time of great uncertainty about the future of United Russia, some governors were casting their lot with United Russia while others were opting to remain independent. With the benefit of hindsight, it may seem that some joined while others merely postponed, but United Russia's future as a dominant party was by no means certain in this period. And while the time span (five years) covered may seem short in historical terms, it is a very long time in the political careers of these governors.

---

[6] "Strana Sovetov 'Edinoi Rossii' Gazeta.ru." October 3, 2005. This move may be interpreted as coercive, sending a signal to governors that they were to come under the further control of the Kremlin, or it may be seen as an institutional carrot granting the party (in which governors played a central role) more institutional authority over personnel. Kynev (2006, 6) notes the ambiguity over whether this should be considered a carrot or stick.

6.4 Independent Variables: The Governors' Resources

The primary hypothesis tested in this chapter is that governors who had significant stores of autonomous resources postponed joining United Russia. Measuring those resources is the challenge I discuss in this section. For ease of exposition, I divide the resources that governors have at their disposal into several categories: inherited political resources, economic resources, administrative /geographic resources, and ethnic resources.

Inherited Political Resources

In an extensive study of the determinants of governors' political machines in the 1990s, Henry Hale (2003) shows how the legacies of the transition gave governors the ability to build strong political machines. The most direct way to tap this observation and translate it into governor-specific terms is to measure the length of tenure of governors. Thus, governors who have enjoyed longer tenures in office are likely to have had the time to develop strong political machines and extensive clientelist networks and will be more likely to postpone joining United Russia. This variable, called *Tenure*, is the number of years that a governor has been in office. Similarly, large electoral mandates may be both the cause and consequence of strong political machines, so the margin of the governor's most recent electoral victory is tapped. This variable is called *Electoral margin*.

Economic Resources

Governors in post-Soviet Russia have been able to tap the economic resources in their region to pursue political gain. The ability to exert influence and distribute patronage has depended heavily on their ability to control regional economies. Henry Hale (2003) has argued that the complexity of a region's economy translates into the strength of the governor's political machine. Single-industry or "single-company" regions are likely to generate strong competition between the governor and that enterprise or sector. But since the region is dependent on that enterprise or sector, governors have neither the incentive nor the resources to subdue their economic opponent. When the economy is diversified, on the other hand, governors could more effectively exploit collective action problems among economic actors and had both motive and opportunity to create complex patronage networks that relied on divide and rule tactics. Diversified economies place the governor in a strong position to mediate interests and play kingmaker. On the other hand, concentrated economies give the governor few resources with which to oppose a unified elite, thereby weakening his machine.

A second reason that diversified economies translate into a resource for governors is related to the expropriability of those resources. Greene (2007) argues that levels of party dominance depend largely on the state's control of the economy. When mobile, inexprobriable assets fuel a region's economy, the Kremlin's threat of taxation and predation is less credible. Therefore, governors in these regions will be less likely to relinquish autonomy over those rent flows and link their fates to the Kremlin's party. Highly concentrated economies are more likely to be built on immobile assets – i.e. resource extraction or heavy manufacturing.[7] Single-sector regions are thus more vulnerable to taxation and control, and the governor's political machine is vulnerable from the bottom up. The more complex the regional economy, then the more complex the political machine of the governor and the more costly it would be for the Kremlin to govern a region cost-effectively without keeping the machine intact. Governors who preside over diversified regional economies are thus more likely to leverage this resource against party affiliation.

To tap the concentration of the economy, I employ several variables. The first, *Industrial concentration*, is a Herfindahl index of the proportion of GRP (Gross Regional Product) composed of the main industrial and extractive sectors of the economy in 2005.[8] This index ranges from 0 to 1, with larger values indicating greater concentration and lower values indicating more diversification. Governors in regions with concentrated economies should join United Russia earlier. To ease interpretation, this variable is rescaled to range between 0 and 100.

Two other economic variables are also included. First, GRP per capita is included, *GRP/Capita*. Hale (2000) finds that, during the transition, wealthy regions were more likely to make declarations of sovereignty, because, as he argues, they have more to lose from exploitation by other regions and are presumably more viable as separate states. This is no doubt true, but as noted in my discussion of a region's population size, the analysis at hand assumes that threats of secession or even autonomy grabs were off the table by 2003–2007, so it becomes more difficult to envision a relationship between wealth and a governor's machine. Finally, I include the share of a region's budget revenues that federal subventions

---

[7] For a comparable use of economic diversification measures as a proxy for asset mobility see Boix 2003.

[8] *Industrial y Concentration* = $\sum_{i=1}^{N} s_i^2$, where *s* is the share of GRP composed of the ith industrial sector. This was calculated from data in Regiony Rossii (2007) Goskomstat Rossii, Moscow. All economic variables are gleaned from the Region Rossii volumes.

constituted, *Federal transfers*. Presumably, governors in regions that are more "dependent" on the center should be more inclined to join United Russia. However, *Federal transfers* is, in large part, a proxy for GRP per capita and governors, as noted, in wealthy regions may not be any more or less inclined to join UR.

Ethnic Resources

Soviet nationalities policy codified ethnic diversity in the form of state-administrative divisions. During the transition and early 1990s, Russia's ethnic republics were among the leaders in making declarations of sovereignty and securing writs of autonomous authority. Throughout the 1990s, these leaders leveraged on their ability to mobilize nationalist/ethnic opposition in order to accrue greater autonomy from the center and build strong political machines. Moreover, the "ethnic minority social networks" inherited from the Soviet federal system and bolstered during the transition provided a ready-made basis for strong political machines (Hale 1998, 2000). And most importantly for this analysis, with the disappearance of the CPSU, the organization of these networks became highly personalized and informally complex, making the governors who headed ethnic regions more indispensable and less likely to join UR.

I employ several indicators of political ethnicity. The first is the percentage of a region's population that is ethnically Russian, *Percent Russian*. Since Muslim regions exhibited more separatist activism in the 1990s and were more likely than Buddhist, Christian, or shamanist regions to be headed by members of the titular ethnic group, I include a dummy variable for Muslim ethnic republics, *Muslim*.

Geographic and Administrative Resources

Russian rulers since Peter the Great have invested enormous energy into controlling their vassals across the country's expansive territory. This continues to be true. As a legislator in Nenets Autonomous Okrug said about federal proposals to reform local election rules in October 2008, "We are located in the far north. It takes a long time for the Federal winds of change to blow our way."[9] Governors in far-flung regions may be less likely to join United Russia, so I include each region's logged distance from Moscow, *Distance*. Second, republics may have accrued the administrative capacity in the 1990s to resist federal incursions and

[9] "Edinuyu Rossiyu Ogradili Bar'erom" *Kommersant* November 12, 2008.

governors in these regions may postpone joining UR longer. So I include a dummy variable, *Republic*, coded 1 if a region is a republic and 0 if not.

Controls

I also include a set of controls. First, to control for factors that may make the region's population more ideologically disposed to United Russia and, therefore, give the governor some impetus to join the party in order to please his former constituents, I include the share of the vote received by Unity in 1999, *Unity Vote*. I use Unity's vote share in 1999 as opposed to the UR vote share in 2003 or 2007, in order to ensure that the vote share is not endogenous to the governor's dominant party affiliation. Second, a casual look at the raw data reveals that KPRF governors waited longer to join United Russia. One could be inclined to count this as a resource, but since it is a choice, I describe it here as a control. KPRF governors postponed joining the party longer, and I include a dummy variable, *KPRF Governor*, coded 1 if the governor is or was a member of the KPRF. Last, I include a region's unemployment rate in 2003.

I also include a variable to test for the bandwagon process noted previously. As more elites join the party, the opportunity costs of remaining outside the party logroll could become higher. *Number of Governors Joined* is simply a count of the number of governors who have joined the party at time t. To test whether this hypothesis exhibits a tipping dynamic, such that the impact of the 41st governor joining on the propensity of other governors' joining is higher than the marginal impact of the 8th governor joining, we will want to square this term – without its constituent linear term if we expect the relationship to be monotonic, as we do. Finally, I included a temporal dummy variable, *Cancel gubernatorial elections*, that captures the September 2004 decision to cancel gubernatorial elections. This variable is coded 1 in September, October, and November 2004.

Statistical Method

This study examines the relationship between resource endowments and the timing of Russian governors' decisions to join UR. Event history models are ideally suited to analyze data of this nature. These models take as their dependent variable the amount of time that some object is in a state before it experiences some event. In these data, joining United Russia is the event. Much has been written about these models and they are now common in applied political science, so I will not belabor their technical details here (cf. Box-Steffensmeier and Jones 2004).

One of the most divisive issues in survival analysis is the choice of how to characterize the nature of the baseline hazard rate.[10] Political methodologists have rightly warned that the underlying nature of the hazard rate is highly sensitive to included (and omitted) covariates (Box-Steffensmeier and Jones 2004). Without strong theory to guide assumptions about the true underlying hazard (and the full range of appropriate covariates), some argue for semiparametric approaches, such as the Cox proportional hazards model, which make no assumptions about the shape of the underlying hazard rate.

A pitfall of the Cox model, however, lies in how semiparametric models use the information contained in the data. Semiparametric models compare subjects at risk to other subjects that are still at risk (Box-Steffensmeier and Jones 2004). For this reason, semiparametric models require a great deal of data points with which to compare subjects at risk. When subjects experience the event, their information is lost as a reference point for other subjects still at risk.

Such comparative estimates are not necessary for parametric models. Parametric models estimate probabilities of what occurs to the subject given what is known about the subject (the covariates) during its time at risk (Cleves, Gould, and Gutierrez 2004). In short, fewer data are required for a well-specified parametric model to produce efficient estimates. Parametric models can produce more precise estimates of covariate effects when the underlying hazard rate is specified correctly (Collett 1994, Box-Steffensmeier and Jones 2004, 21).

Given the small size of the data set used here, I employ a parametric Weibull that assumes a monotonically increasing or decreasing (or flat) baseline hazard. The Akaike information criterion, based on the log likelihood and the number of parameters in the model, was used to rule out other parametric models that allow for nonmonotonic hazards. The results of these tests showed the Weibull had the best fit with the data.[11]

6.5 Results

The results of the models are shown in Table 6.1. The full model with controls is in the first column. The reduced model, shown in the second column, excludes nonsignificant controls and nonsignificant substantive variables that are inducing collinearity. The substantive quantities of

---

[10] The hazard rate is the rate at which subjects end at time t, given that they have survived until time t. The baseline hazard rate is that which is not directly modeled by covariates included in the model.

[11] Cox models reveal similar results for all models, though, for the reasons discussed here, the standard errors are larger for some variables.

Table 6.1 *Weibull model estimates of governor's hazard of joining United Russia*

Variables	Coefficients				
	Model 1	Model 2	Model 3	Model 4	Model 5
Inherited political resources					
Tenure	0.915**	0.939*	0.958	0.939*	0.962
	(0.035)	(0.031)	(0.030)	(0.032)	(0.031)
Electoral margin	0.992	0.987**	0.992*	0.987**	0.989**
	(0.006)	(0.005)	(0.005)	(0.005)	(0.005)
Population in region	1.000				
	(0.000)				
Economic Resources					
Federal transfers	0.547				
	(0.566)				
Services share	0.206				
	(0.393)				
Export share	0.945				
	(0.067)				
Industrial concentration	1.049**	1.054**	1.042**	1.054**	1.046**
	(0.014)	(0.013)	(0.012)	(0.013)	(0.013)
GRP/capita	0.997	0.997*	0.998	0.997*	0.998
	(0.002)	(0.002)	(0.002)	(0.002)	(0.002)
Ethnic resources					
Percent Russian	1.029*	1.027**	1.022**	1.027**	1.022**
	(0.016)	(0.007)	(0.007)	(0.007)	(0.007)
Muslim region	0.529				
	(0.439)				
Territorial resources					
Distance	0.886				
	(0.104)				
Republic	1.221				
	(0.676)				
Dynamics and Kremlin signals					
Number of governors Joined	1.050**	1.048**	1.046**	1.047**	1.049**
	(0.010)	(0.010)	(0.008)	(0.010)	(0.010)
Cancellation of gubernatorial elections	2.732**	2.832**	2.368**	2.790**	2.718**
	(0.845)	(0.869)	(0.722)	(0.857)	(0.831)
		Controls			
KPRF governor	0.250**	0.292**	0.288**	0.293**	0.270**
	(0.134)	(0.153)	(0.150)	(0.153)	(0.141)

6.5 Results

Table 6.1 (*continued*)

Variables	Coefficients				
	Model 1	Model 2	Model 3	Model 4	Model 5
Unity vote	1.026	1.025**	1.012	1.025**	1.017
	(0.017)	(0.011)	(0.012)	(0.011)	(0.012)
Unemployment	1.045*				
	(0.027)				
Shape parameter P	0.729	0.770	0.550	0.776	0.765
	(0.179)	(0.184)	(0.104)	(0.186)	(0.184)
Log likelihood	−61.560	−66.403	−102.739	−66.222	−67.365
Number of subjects	117	118	118	118	118
Failures	82	83	88	83	86
Time at risk	2665	2684	2332	2687	2615

Notes: Entries are hazard ratios with standard errors in parentheses.
* $p < 0.1$, ** $p < 0.05$

interest discussed later are taken from this model. The results show hazard ratios and their standard errors.[12] Models 3, 4, and 5 are robustness checks using the variables in Model 2 to check the robustness of results across different codings of the dependent variable introduced earlier and discussed in further detail later.

In the model with all variables and controls, we see that *Tenure* and *Electoral margin* have the expected effect though only *Tenure* is statistically significant. In the reduced model, both are significant. The size of the effects is substantial. To make this hazard ratio more interpretable, consider the change in the hazard of a governor joining UR as his margin of victory in the most recent election goes from the 25th percentile in the data (12 percent margin) to the 75th percentile (58 percent margin). The probability that this governor joins United Russia in any given month would decrease by 52 percent relative to the baseline hazard. Results on *Tenure* are similar. Decreasing *Tenure* from eight years (the 75th percentile in the data) to one year (the 25th percentile) increases the probability of joining 42 percent. This difference is depicted in Figure 5.1, which

---

[12] Hazard ratios provide an easily interpretable exposition of event history results. Hazard ratios should be interpreted relative to a baseline of 1, such that a hazard ratio of 1 means that the particular variable has no effect on the likelihood a governor joins. A hazard ratio of 2 means that a 1-unit change in the variable doubles the baseline probability that a governor will join the party in a given month. A hazard ratio of .75 indicates that a 1-unit change in the variable decreases the hazard of a governor joining by 25 percent.

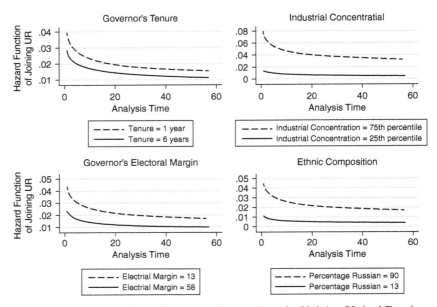

Figure 6.1 Effect of key variables on hazard of joining United Russia.

shows differences in the hazard rates (the propensity of a governor to join) for governors at the 25th and 75th percentiles of the given independent variable.

Few of the variables measuring economic resources are significant with the notable exception of *Industrial concentration*. In such a small data set, collinearity plagues the inclusion of all these variables but *Industrial concentration* stands out.[13] In fact, the effect of *Industrial concentration* is large, robust, and in the expected direction. Governors in regions with diversified economies are less likely to join the party early. This is a key finding. Recalling that *Industrial concentration* is rescaled to range between 0 and 100, Figure 6.1 shows the difference in the hazards of joining for two levels of industrial concentration.

These two illustrative levels were chosen to be roughly equivalent to the 25th and 75th percentiles of *Industrial concentration*, though for clarity's sake I chose to make examples of two well-known regions: Chelyabinsk and Irkutsk. The former, with its heavy dependence on steel production and related heavy industry, has a more concentrated economy than Irkutsk, with its well-developed light and heavy manufacturing sectors as

---

[13] Models that use broader measures such as sectoral concentration also display a large and significant effect.

6.5 Results

well as natural resource extraction.[14] *Federal transfers* appears to have no demonstrable effect. *GRP/capita* is close to significance in Model 1 and attains significance in some later models, such that governors of wealthy regions were more likely to postpone joining, though the substantive effect is quite small.

Governors of ethnic regions are also more likely to postpone joining the party. *Percent Russian* and *Muslim* are highly collinear, however, and either of the variables on its own is significant, but likelihood ratio tests confirm a better model fit when only *Percent Russian* is included. A single percentage increase in the proportion of a region's population that is ethnically Russian increases the hazard of a governor's joining by more than 2 percent, a significant result.

Distance is in the expected direction, such that governors in far-flung regions are more likely to postpone joining, though this effect appears insignificant. Also, when one controls for the ethnic resources outlined previously, republican administrative status has no independent effect on the propensity of governors to join United Russia. *Republic* is highly collinear with *Percent Russian*, but AIC tests suggest that the model with *Percent Russian* is the better fit.

As expected, former KPRF governors have a lower hazard of joining. They are less likely to join UR early and the effect is substantial. In addition, the higher the percentage of the vote received by Unity in the 1999 Duma elections in the region, the more likely the governor is to join United Russia early.

Number of governors joined is significant in its linear form. In analyses not shown here, I also tried the square term, with and without the linear term, to test for tipping dynamics, but this does not improve model fit. This result must be taken with a large grain of salt, however. The number of governors joining the party is almost perfectly collinear with time and with the baseline hazard. In the models shown here, the shape parameter p is less than 1, indicating a declining baseline hazard of party affiliation. However, if one removes *Number of Governors Joined* from the analysis, this shape parameter indicates a steeply increasing baseline hazard. If it is true that the resources of the Kremlin increase monotonically across time, as I argue, then this result is unproblematic and we are free to conclude that there is no contagious process in which governors use the behavior of other governors in deciding whether or not to join. If, on the other hand, the resources of the Kremlin are unchanged across time,

---

[14] Two other possible proxies for economic concentration are the share of services in GRP, *ServicesShare*, and the share of exports in GRP, *ExportsShare*. Both are in the predicted direction but neither is statistically significant.

then the entire baseline hazard could be determined by peer membership dynamics. Without more data, we cannot adjudicate between these two alternatives.

Last, governors were more likely to join in the wake of the Kremlin's decision to cancel gubernatorial elections in the fall of 2004. That more governors joined after Putin cancelled direct gubernatorial elections is not surprising, but what may be surprising in light of conventional wisdom is that not all governors joined at this point. In fact, the enduring significance of other variables is testament to the fact that many governors still commanded bargaining leverage vis-à-vis the Kremlin even after 2004.

Robustness Checks

Model 3 presents the results of models in which those governors who joined the Higher Council prior to joining the party are coded as joining the party from the date on which they joined the Higher Council. Model 4 uses the same rules for coding party membership applied in the baseline model, but adheres to a strict interpretation of those rules by coding Shaimiyev, Luzhkov, and Rakhimov as never joining the party. Model 5 codes these three governors as joining the party in November 2005, when the party changed its charter to require party membership for Higher Council members. The results on the controls, *Industrial concentration*, *Electoral margin*, and *Percent Russian*, remain robust across these specifications. Only the statistical significance of *Tenure* appears to dip slightly below statistical significance. This is understandable given that these three governors are significant outliers for their length of tenure in office.

6.6 Conclusion

One of the main arguments advanced in this book is that the emergence of dominant parties depends on the incentives of elites to join such parties. When elites, as a group, are too strong in resources to commit to a party, a dominant party is unlikely to emerge. As the balance of resources shifts toward leaders, however, the benefits of joining may come to outweigh the costs. The first to join should be those weakest in resources, while those stronger in resources postpone joining.

Using data on the timing of Russia's governors' decisions to join United Russia, this chapter examined this hypothesis. The data indicate that Russia's governors were not forced to join United Russia all at once. Instead, they joined incrementally over a period of five years. As the

6.6 Conclusion

Kremlin became stronger vis-à-vis the regions in the early to mid-2000s, more governors opted to join the party. The first to join were those weak in resources, while those with access to significant political resources that could be leveraged against dominant party affiliation postponed joining.

In particular, governors in regions with more concentrated economies were significantly more likely to join United Russia early. Governors who presided over diversified regional economies are more likely to be in control of complex patronage machines that could be deployed as an autonomous political resource. Governors in such regions postponed joining. Second, long-serving governors and those who had dominated elections in their regions were more hesitant to join the party. Third, leaders of ethnic regions were also more likely to postpone joining the party. These leaders sat atop ethnically based clientelist networks that provided the governor with important political resources.

These results provide evidence for the proposition that governors with autonomous resources were less likely to join United Russia. The Kremlin was unable to force certain governors to join, at least at first. These governors controlled political machines that could ensure their political survival without linking their fates to the center. These findings demonstrate that elites have interests in retaining their own autonomy and act on those interests. This suggests that dominant parties will not emerge when elites have autonomous political resources that give them incentives to eschew commitment to the party.

7 Economic Elites and Dominant Party Affiliation

According to the theory advanced in this book, dominant parties are more likely to emerge when neither elites nor leaders hold a preponderance of political resources. As noted in Chapter 6, this argument has implications about the individual behavior of elites. In a setting where leaders are becoming stronger relative to elites, we would expect to observe that elites with significant stores of political and economic resources will be less likely to join the nascent dominant party. In Chapter 6, I examined this hypothesis and demonstrated that Russian governors strong in such resources were more reluctant to join United Russia. In this chapter, I extend the analysis of dominant party affiliation to economic elites who hold seats in Russia's regional legislatures.

Almost half of Russian regional legislators are directors of firms in the region, and most of the major firms in a region are usually represented in the regional legislature. Thus, this analysis provides a way to assess the dominant party affiliation calculus of Russia's business elite. I argue that legislators who work in sectors of the economy that are more vulnerable to state pressure lack the autonomous resources that allow them to eschew United Russia faction membership. This leads to four hypotheses: First, deputies who represent businesses that are state owned will be more likely to join the ruling party. Second, those who represent businesses whose primary assets are immobile and thus easy to tax or regulate (e.g. natural resource extraction, heavy industry, and mining) should be more likely to join United Russia. Third, deputies whose businesses are more affected by regulatory and state procurement policies should be more likely to join United Russia. Finally, because businesses that are large are easier to monitor, regulate, and tax, deputies who represent large companies should be more likely to join United Russia.

This chapter contributes to testing the theory laid forth in this book because it demonstrates the operation of one of the key causal mechanisms that I have put forward. If individual elites strong in resources are more reluctant to join an emergent dominant party, then we have additional reason to believe that the process of dominant party formation is dependent, at least in part, on elite incentives to invest in a dominant party.

Beyond the theory in this book, this chapter also has broader implications for how scholars understand the political economy of regime transition. Various authors have argued that democracy is more likely to emerge in market economies (e.g. Lindblom 1977). McMann (2006) argues that economic autonomy from the state (i.e. employment in the private sector) provides citizens with the freedom to engage in political activity without fear of political reprisal. Greene (2010) has argued that a large public sector provides authoritarian incumbents with ample patronage resources, while a small public sector limits those opportunities. Arriola (2012) has illustrated how financial liberalization made it easier for opposition forces in Africa to gain access to the capital necessary to fund their opposition to the regime.

My approach also holds to the notion that large public economies entrench authoritarian rule, but I offer another causal mechanism for this relationship. Large public economies undermine democracy because they make economic *elites* reliant on the state.[1] This vulnerability to repression, sanction, taxation, and regulation increases their incentives to remain politically loyal to the regime.

The theory and findings in this chapter also demonstrate how the structure of a country's economy affects its prospects for democratization. A core finding of the economic literature on democratization is that countries with economies characterized by immobile assets – i.e. land, large factories, natural resources, and the like – are less likely to democratize. Since assets that are difficult to relocate are especially vulnerable to taxation, some argue that holders of immobile assets will be more likely to subvert democratization because they fear that the poor will demand redistribution in the wake of free and fair elections (Boix 2003, Acemoglu and Robinson 2006). Scholars who study the effects of natural resources on politics take another view, arguing that natural resources generate rent revenues, which allow autocrats to buy public support (Ross 2001). At the same time, much of the neo-institutional literature on authoritarianism takes the view that because dictators who have access to resource rents can buy social support, they do not invest in the institutions that could make their rule robust to challenges (Smith 2005, Gandhi 2008).

---

[1] Thus, this perspective is similar to Radnitz's (2010) account of how post-Soviet countries that engaged in large-scale privatization saw the rise of powerful capitalist classes whose interests sometimes led them to challenge the regime.

My account embraces this ambivalence about the role of resource revenues, focusing on a different mechanism by which resource rents can affect a country's prospects for democratization. On the one hand, natural resource rents may reduce incentives for leaders to co-opt elites and build dominant party institutions. This is true when leaders are strong relative to elites. On the other hand, when leaders are in a vulnerable position vis-à-vis elites, a natural resource–based economy can make the regime more robust. Because elites that own or control natural resource firms are more dependent on the state, the presence of natural resources makes key economic elites loyal to the ruling party, thus reducing the potential for elite schisms. This is the environment that prevailed during the construction of United Russia in the early 2000s and it is the environment that is analyzed in this chapter.

This chapter also has important implications for how scholars think about Russian political institutions in the Putin era. My approach suggests that the commodity price boom, which transformed the Russian economy, strengthened Putin's hand. It did so not just because it allowed Putin to buy social support or because it spurred a decade of sustained economic growth, but also because it expanded the role of the natural resource sector in the economy and made the business community more dependent on the state.

The rest of this chapter proceeds as follows. The next section discusses the data that are used to test the hypotheses. This data are from an original database that contains information on both the legislative faction membership and occupational backgrounds of 1,958 deputies in 53 Russian regional legislatures in 1999–2005. Section 7.2 discusses the research design for testing the hypotheses. Section 7.3 discusses the results of the analysis and Section 7.4 concludes.

7.1 The Dependent Variable: Regional Legislators

Why should an analysis of dominant party affiliation behavior look at regional legislators? First, the composition of a regional legislature is a vivid cross section of the most important elite groups and actors in a region. This is especially true of business elites. The most prominent figures in the regional economic elite – directors of the largest industrial and agricultural enterprises, representatives of large federally owned corporations, and directors of major hospitals and research institutes – are all likely to be members of (or have representatives in) their region's legislature. In my sample of regional legislators in the early and mid-2000s (discussed later), 55 percent of all lawmakers were employed full time in business. And this number surely underestimates the total number

7.1 The Dependent Variable: Regional Legislators

of business-affiliated deputies, for it only includes those deputies whose full-time place of employment (as listed in official biographies) is in business. It excludes "professional politicians" (14 percent), many of whom are likely to have started in business or to have financial interests. Of those deputies who represent business, 82 percent are the general director, chairman of the board of directors, or president of their companies. The representation of important economic interests in regional parliaments sets these legislatures apart from Soviet legislatures, where representation was based on class quotas and key economic interests were absent (Vanneman 1977).

Indeed, a plausible defense could be mounted for treating businesses, rather than individual deputies, as the unit of analysis in regional legislatures. In my sample of 1,958 deputies in 43 regions, there are 70 separate instances of multiple deputies representing a single enterprise or group within a legislature, and in only 12 cases did the delegation split between joining and not joining United Russia. Thus, dominant party affiliation decisions may be made at the enterprise level as much as they are made at the individual level. Thus, examining the party affiliation behavior of regional deputies affords a simultaneous glimpse into the party affiliation behavior of economic elites.

A second reason for examining Russian regional legislatures is practical. Given that the hypotheses in this chapter make predictions about when elites join United Russia, we require an arena where data on partisan affiliations are available. While many members of the elite carry partisan affiliations, information on those affiliations is not public and is difficult to gather. For legislators, the matter is simplified by the fact that legislative factions make plain each deputy's partisan loyalties. Finally, regional legislatures provide a much larger number of potential observations than the State Duma.

To analyze the relationship between resources and dominant party affiliation I have assembled a dataset that contains the legislative faction membership of 1,958 deputies in 53 convocations of 44 Russian regional legislatures elected between 1999 and 2005.[2] The early 2000s was a formative time in United Russia's history and an optimal period in which to test the implications of my theory of dominant party formation. During this period United Russia's dominance was on the rise and the Kremlin's commitment to it was deepening, but the future of the party was still far from certain. Thus, this period provides a brief window into the key moment when elites were making substantive decisions about their party affiliations.

---

[2] Table 7.1 provides a list of the convocations.

Conducting the analysis in an earlier time would be inappropriate for this was a period when exceedingly few deputies were members of any faction, let alone United Russia. In the 1990s, Russian regional elections were overwhelmingly nonpartisan affairs. Golosov (2003) shows that only 14 percent of regional deputies elected in the third regional electoral cycle (1999–2003) were party nominees.[3] Party labels rarely carried over into legislative organization. Indeed, prior to 2003, many Russian regions explicitly banned the formation of formal legislative factions in their legislatures.

In December 2003, legislation took effect that required all regions to elect at least 50 percent of their chambers with proportional representation. Prior to this reform, nearly all regions elected their deputies in single member districts (SMDs). With increasing Kremlin investments in United Russia and the move to mixed electoral systems after 2003, regional legislatures began changing their charters to permit factions, and legislators began forming groups at a faster rate. In most legislatures, factions formed before new elections were held. Glubotskii and Kynev (2003) find that, by mid-2003, more than 50 percent of regional deputies were members of a legislative party or group.

In most regions, the largest legislative faction was United Russia. In my sample, 32 percent of deputies in 2003 and 2004 were members of United Russia factions. In 2005, that proportion was 47 percent. By late 2007, all but five regional legislatures had United Russia majorities. Thus, the sheer dominance of United Russia after early 2006 makes those elections less useful for studying the decisions of elites to join United Russia. With almost all SMD deputies seeking United Russia affiliation, there would be less interesting variance to analyze – especially for a study of dominant party emergence. In sum, the period 2000–2006 covers the entire span from the founding of United Russia up until the point at which it became so dominant that there is little usable variation in elite affiliation strategies.

The analysis focuses on SMD deputies with the exception of the data for Kirov Oblast, where legislators were elected in two member districts in 2001. Thirty-three of the convocations in the sample were elected purely in SMDs before the 2003 electoral reform. Twenty were elected after the electoral reform under mixed systems, and 1, Krasnoyarsk, was elected in 2001 via a mixed system. For Krasnoyarsk and the 23 post-2003 convocations, I focus only on the party affiliation decisions of SMD deputies.

---

[3] This was actually less than the percentage of party nominees (21 percent) elected in elections held between 1995 and 1999.

7.1 The Dependent Variable: Regional Legislators

For the elections occurring prior to the electoral reform, there is no choice but to focus the analysis on SMD deputies. For elections occurring under mixed systems, I focus only on SMD deputies, for several reasons. Most importantly, party list deputies enter the chamber with an existing party affiliation. My research design is set up to analyze the behavior of previously unaffiliated deputies, and while some deputies elected on opposition party lists defected to United Russia factions in 2004 and 2005, the most significant migrations into United Russia (and other parties, for that matter) were by previously unaffiliated SMD deputies.[4] Thus, SMD deputies both are a more appropriate unit of analysis and exhibit more interesting variation.

The year of analysis is the first year for which data are available on the faction composition of that convocation. As noted, almost all deputies in elections prior to December 2003 were elected as independents. Between 2001 and 2007, party factions were created in most of these legislatures. In all such cases, a United Russia faction emerged. Some deputies joined this faction, while others remained independent or joined opposition factions. I analyze variation in the decisions of deputies to join the dominant party faction when it is first established. For example, regional elections were held in Murmansk Oblast in 2001 in single member districts. All deputies were independents and served as such until May 2003. At that time, three factions were created, including a United Russia faction. For Murmansk, I analyze variation in the dominant party affiliation behavior of deputies in May 2003, when the new factions were created. For elections after 2003, I also analyze variation in faction affiliation on the date when factions formed, but this usually occurred immediately after elections were held.

Table 7.1 shows the percentage of SMD deputies in a region who were United Russia members at the time of analysis. Many of these figures appear low for a dominant party, but it is important to remember that these numbers reflect the percentage of deputies who joined early in the party's existence just as it was becoming dominant.

Data on the faction composition of legislatures were collected from the archived Web sites of regional legislatures, where available. Since this information is archived for only a small handful of legislatures (most provide only the current faction composition of the legislatures), I gathered

---

[4] In my sample, there is no instance of a United Russia party list deputy leaving the party faction and remaining in the legislature (i.e. some leave upon death, illness, or transfer to another position). Analyses of party defections in other post-Soviet legislatures have shown that party switching is much higher among SMD deputies (Herron 2002, Thames and Edwards 2006).

Table 7.1 *Convocations used in analysis*

Region	Year convocation elected	Year of analysis	Percentage of deputies in UR
North Ossetia	1999	2001	11
Vladimir obl	2000	2001	29
Kostroma obl	2000	2002	45
Yaroslavl	2000	2002	41
Arkhangelskaya obl	2000	2002	33
Kaliningradskaya obl	2000	2001	48
Kurgan	2000	2002	30
Yamalo-N	2000	2003	48
Chita obl	2000	2003	21
Agin-Buryat AO	2000	2003	69
Sakhalinskaya_obl	2000	2002	25
Moscow city	2001	2003	54
Murmanskaya obl	2001	2002	38
Adygei Repub	2001	2003	30
Stavropol kr	2001	2002	40
Kirov	2001	2003	53
Perm	2001	2002	59
Samara	2001	2002	48
Tyumen	2001	2002	68
Krasnoyarsk	2001	2002	38
Novosibirsk	2001	2003	36
Tomsk oblast	2001	2003	55
Amurskaya obl	2001	2002	17
Smolensk obl	2002	2002	53
Karelia	2002	2003	27
Pskov	2002	2003	25
St. Petersburg	2002	2002	30
Chuvashia	2002	2002	38
Nizhegorodskaya	2002	2003	50
Yakutiya	2002	2002	46
North Ossetia	2003	2003	40
Udmurtia	2003	2003	68
Ulyanovsk	2003	2004	50
Yaroslavl	2004	2004	48
Arkhangelsk	2004	2004	64
Karachaev-Ch	2004	2004	66
Tatarstan	2004	2004	78
Kurgan	2004	2004	86
Khakassiya	2004	2004	44
Irkutsk obla	2004	2004	57
Chita Obl	2004	2004	25
Sakhalinskaya_obl	2004	2004	58
Belgorod	2005	2005	77
Voronezh	2005	2005	91

Table 7.1 (*continued*)

Region	Year convocation elected	Year of analysis	Percentage of deputies in UR
Kostroma	2005	2005	50
Ryazan	2005	2005	44
Tambov obl	2005	2005	84
Tver obl	2005	2005	86
Yamalo Nenetsk	2005	2005	70
Chelyabinsk	2005	2005	93
Novosibirsk	2005	2005	83
Khabarovskii krai	2005	2005	92
Amurskaya obl	2005	2005	38
Magadan	2005	2005	88

much of the data in person (or via telephone and fax) from the *apparat* of various legislative assemblies. These data were collected on research trips to the regions in the summers of 2008 and 2009. The raw data contain the faction membership of deputies and their biographical information.

Faction membership is an imperfect proxy for commitment to the dominant party. A more accurate indicator would be formal party membership or, better still, a detailed analysis of each legislator's financial contributions to the party, his voting record, and behavior during elections. Unfortunately, such data are not publicly available. Nonetheless, faction membership is likely to be a necessary (but not sufficient) condition for party membership. Very few party members are likely to forgo membership in the faction, but many nonparty members are likely to participate in the faction. Nonetheless, my interviews with regional parliamentary deputies indicate that United Russia factions have placed very strict restraints on their members' voting behavior. Most indicated the presence of near-perfect voting discipline. This indicates that joining the United Russia faction necessitates the relinquishing of legislative autonomy and is a useful proxy for commitment to the party.

7.2 Resource Ownership and United Russia Faction Membership

There are few studies of elite party affiliation in the Putin era. Using surveys of firm directors from the 1990s, Frye (2003, 2006) finds that older directors, those in state enterprises, and those with a stagnant or shrinking workforce are less likely to vote for promarket parties. Also focusing on the 1990s, Hale (2006) finds that Duma candidates supported by gubernatorial political machines and those supported by financial industrial groups are more likely to eschew partisan affiliation during elections. Smyth (2006) reaches a similar conclusion, arguing that candidates who own businesses are less likely to join parties because their business structures provide the financial and organizational resources that parties would otherwise provide.

The approach pursued in this chapter is similar to that in the studies cited but differs in several important ways. In contrast to Frye (2003, 2006), but in line with Smyth (2006) and Hale (2006), this study focuses on the actual party affiliation behavior of elites, not on their voting behavior. As I have argued, the imperatives of political survival under authoritarianism often lead elites to join parties for reasons that have little relation to their personal ideological preferences. In contrast to Hale and Smyth, this study focuses not just on the binary decision to accept any partisan affiliation, but on the specific decision to join the dominant party. Thus, I also examine why deputies chose to join United Russia rather than an opposition party. Finally, in contrast to existing work that focuses on the fragmented political space of the 1990s, I emphasize the party affiliation decisions of elites under an emergent dominant party regime.

In line with existing accounts, I argue that elites value partisan affiliation because parties provide access to organizational resources and a brand that may help them be elected. However, as noted in Chapter 2, my account also stresses other benefits that are specific to affiliation with the ruling party, such as access to spoils and reduced uncertainty about the provision of those spoils. I also share the existing literature's emphasis on autonomy as a goal pursued by politicians. Loss of political autonomy is the major cost associated with accepting a partisan affiliation. But in my account, politicians value not only autonomy from partisan organizations during elections, but also autonomy from state control.

The primary hypothesis examined in this chapter is that deputies who had significant autonomous resources were more reluctant to join United Russia. The resources that matter for this analysis are those that allowed deputies to leverage their personal political machines, clientelist networks, and economic autonomy against inducements to join the regime party. Elites value autonomy highly, for it is synonymous with the pursuit of self-interest. Autonomy provides political elites with the freedom to pursue their self-interest, should their interests conflict with those of others who would seek to limit their autonomy (i.e. the Kremlin or a powerful governor). Those who have autonomous resources that are sufficient to ensure their political survival independent of the state

Table 7.2 *Professions of regional deputies*

Professions	Percentage of Sample
Business	55
Full-time legislator	14
Budget sphere	11
Municipal government	5
Social organization	5
Academia	4
Other/worker	3
Regional executive branch	2
Journalist	2
Military	1

are more likely to have resisted joining United Russia. In the sections that follow, I describe how the autonomous resources of many deputies depend on the nature of their business affiliations. As Table 7.2 indicates, more than half of deputies report a business affiliation as their primary place of work.

McMann (2006) has argued that economic autonomy (i.e. employment in the private sector) provides citizens with the freedom to engage in political activity without fear of political reprisal. Here I take a similar stance: economic autonomy permits deputies to maintain their political autonomy. Those factors that reduce the economic autonomy of businessperson deputies will increase their incentives to join United Russia factions.

I argue that two related factors affect the economic autonomy of businessmen. First is the extent to which their enterprise is vulnerable to state pressure, taxation, and/or sanction. The second is the extent to which contact with the state (e.g. obtaining permits, securing subsidies, achieving favorable regulations) is required for conducting business. Such firms are state dependent.

One straightforward determinant of state dependence is ownership structure. State-owned firms are easier to tax and control (Gehlbach 2006, Tedds 2010). Though all firms are vulnerable to political interference, state firms are decidedly more so. This leads to the following hypothesis:

> H1: Deputies from private sector enterprises will be less likely to join United Russia.

A second determinant of state dependence is sector. Firms engaged in natural resource extraction, heavy industry (refining, metallurgy, and

Table 7.3 *Logistic regression estimates for effect of sector on likelihood of being visited by tax authorities*

Variables	(1)
Manufacturing sector	0.609**
	(0.099)
Size of enterprise	0.068**
	(0.016)
Constant	−0.359**
	(0.124)
Observations	2793

Notes: Standard errors in parentheses. Manufacturing sector is compared to services sector.
* $p < 0.1$, ** $p < 0.05$
Source: EBRD–World Bank Business Environment and Enterprise Performance Survey (BEEPS)

heavy machinery), and agriculture are likely to be more state dependent than firms engaged in light industry, trade, and services. Firms in these sectors are characterized by immobile assets and, thus, are more vulnerable to taxation and predation (e.g. Boix 2003). Tax avoidance has been a major problem for the post-communist Russian state (Yakovlev 2001, Gehlbach 2006, Easter 2012). The authorities have reacted by crafting a revenue extraction system based on taxing firms, and in particular, large firms in asset-immobile sectors that find it difficult to hide or reroute their revenues (Easter 2012). Indeed, asset immobility leaves firms in these sectors vulnerable not only to taxation but also to regulation and coercion.

This expectation is partially validated by the EBRD–World Bank Business Environment and Enterprise Performance Survey (BEEPS) of 9,000 firms in post-communist and southern Europe. This survey includes a question that asks whether an enterprise has been visited by the tax authorities in the last year. I use this item from the 2005 wave to determine whether firms in the manufacturing sector engage with the tax authorities more than service sector firms. The results in Table 7.3 show that, in the post-communist region, even when controlling for the size of the firm (as measured by their total sales), firms in the manufacturing sector are 15 percent more likely than service/trading sector firms to be visited by the tax authorities.

> H2: Deputies in firms characterized by immobile assets will be more likely to join United Russia.

The sector of a deputy's firm is also important because it determines how the business interfaces with the state. Some firms, such as those in the defense industry and in construction, rely heavily on state contracts for their business. Firms in some sectors are also more likely to have to sell their goods through government bottlenecks or are ensconced in production chains that link to state-controlled bottlenecks. Firms in the natural resource sector, mining, and metallurgy often fall into this category. In addition, while all firms must endure a certain amount of state regulation to conduct business, some engage in business activity that makes them intrinsically subject to additional rules and regulations. This is especially true of the construction industry, which must contract with the state to secure building permits and successfully reach deals with municipal utilities. This weakens their economic autonomy.

> H3: Deputies in firms whose business activities depend on contact with the state will be more likely to join United Russia

Another determinant of state dependence is firm size. Larger firms are easier to tax and more vulnerable to predation (Easter 2012). Table 7.3 confirms this. This leads to the fourth hypothesis.

> H4: Deputies from larger firms will be more likely to join United Russia.

7.3 Models and Results

The first dependent variable I analyze is a dummy variable equal to 1 if the deputy joins the United Russia faction and 0 if the deputy is not. The key independent variables are a series of binary indicators that describe features of the deputy's occupation at time of election. Data on the occupations of deputies were taken from the deputy's official biographies and, where applicable, from the Russian Central Election Commission. The deputy's occupation was then coded across several professional categories. For businessperson deputies, data on the ownership structure, sector, and yearly revenue of the enterprise were collected for the author by SKRIN Ltd., a private market analysis firm in Moscow that has access to Goskomstat registries of balance sheet information for all enterprises in Russia.[5]

---

[5] I classify businessperson deputies as those in upper management. Usually, they are directors. Workers and middle managers are not classified as businessperson deputies. Such legislators (3 percent of the sample) are given their own professional category in the full model. Many of these legislators are from the KPRF, which maintains the Communist tradition of class-based representation and sometimes selects workers as legislative candidates.

Given the dichotomous dependent variable, I use binary logit models.[6] To account for unmodeled time effects that influence the propensity of all deputies to join United Russia, I include biannual fixed effects.[7] Table 7.4 shows the results. Model 1 includes both businessperson deputies and nonbusinessperson deputies in the analysis.

The results are largely consistent with the hypotheses. Hypothesis 1 is supported, as deputies in the private sector are, on average, 9 percentage points less likely to join United Russia. Turning to the sectoral hypotheses, the table shows that deputies in asset-specific sectors – *Oil/Gas, Heavy Industry, Mining/Timber* – are more likely to join UR. Thus, as predicted, deputies in sectors that are vulnerable to taxation, regulation, and predation are more likely to join the ruling party. Table 7.5 shows the descriptive breakdown of UR faction membership among employment sectors.

One point to note about the tables is that deputies in business are, on the whole, more likely to join United Russia than nonbusiness deputies. This stands at odds with some of the literature on party affiliation in post-Soviet Russia, which argues that business affiliations provide candidates with substitute resources that allow them to eschew partisan affiliation (Smyth 2006, Hale 2006). These results are a reminder about the benefits of affiliating with the dominant party. For businessperson deputies, affiliating with United Russia gains access to lobbying influence that is essential for their business. Journalists, social activists, academics, and the like, have fewer lobbying goals. To be sure, some categories of nonbusiness deputies are especially dependent on the state, and as such, are more likely to seek UR affiliation in order to protect or further their careers. Thus, we see that deputies who work in the *BudgetSphere* are more likely than the average deputy to join United Russia.

Separating Hypothesis 3 from Hypothesis 2 is not straightforward because most asset-specific sectors are also sectors whose business activities are intertwined with the state. One important exception is the *Construction* sector, which is not asset specific, but whose business activities are closely intertwined with the state. The results show that deputies in the *Construction* sector are more likely than any other type of deputy to join UR. This indicates support for Hypothesis 3.

---

[6] I do not use fixed effect use because, in six regions, the dependent variable would not vary in the businessperson-only models, because all businessperson deputies are UR members. In addition, several important control variables do not vary across regions.

[7] Using year-fixed effects needlessly drops a handful of post-2005 observations where UR membership does not vary among businesspersons. Nonetheless, results are robust to using both yearly fixed effects and a time trend.

7.3 Models and Results 235

Table 7.4 *Logit models of dominant party affiliation*

	Model 1	Model 2	Model 3	Model 4	Model 5
Private enterprise	−0.09**	−0.09**	−0.07*	−0.05	−0.07**
	(0.037)	(0.039)	(0.036)	(0.035)	(0.35)
Oil/gas	0.22**	0.09	0.08	0.04	0.04
	(0.063)	(0.058)	(0.056)	(0.059)	(0.06)
Heavy industry	0.25**	0.13**	0.10*	0.07	0.84*
	(0.077)	(0.054)	(0.052)	(0.050)	(0.48)
Mining/timber	0.23**	0.11	0.11	0.07	0.54
	(0.106)	(0.075)	(0.079)	(0.074)	(0.64)
Utilities/energy	0.01	−0.12	−0.08	−0.14*	−0.14*
	(0.082)	(0.081)	(0.081)	(0.080)	(0.78)
Transportation	0.04	−0.08	−0.13**	−0.11	−0.09
	(0.072)	(0.066)	(0.065)	(0.067)	(0.07)
Construction	0.31**	0.17**	0.16**	0.18**	0.18**
	(0.071)	(0.069)	(0.066)	(0.066)	(0.06)
Agriculture	0.02	−0.10*	−0.10**	−0.07	−0.07
	(0.074)	(0.053)	(0.048)	(0.048)	(0.05)
Services	0.14**	0.02	0.03	0.05	0.03
	(0.054)	(0.045)	(0.052)	(0.050)	(0.04)
Light industry	0.12**				
	(0.055)				
Executive branch	0.03				
	(0.117)				
Social organization	0.02				
	(0.065)				
Budget sphere	0.13**				
	(0.049)				
Military	−0.04				
	(0.170)				
Municipal government	0.08				
	(0.065)				
Journalism	−0.12				
	(0.095)				
Other/worker	−0.07				
	(0.074)				
Academia	0.02				
	(0.098)				
Incumbent	0.01	0.06			
	(0.031)	(0.040)			
Moscow based company	0.16**	0.16**	0.08	0.09	0.07
	(0.079)	(0.077)	(0.084)	(0.084)	(0.08)
Press freedom	0.05*	0.05	0.04	0.04	0.05
	(0.031)	(0.039)	(0.043)	(0.042)	(0.04)
Percentage Russian	−0.00	−0.00	−0.00	−0.00	−0.00
	(0.001)	(0.001)	(0.001)	(0.001)	(0.001)

(*continued*)

Table 7.4 (continued)

	Model 1	Model 2	Model 3	Model 4	Model 5
Governor member	0.12**	0.15**	0.16**	0.16**	0.15**
	(0.044)	(0.056)	(0.064)	(0.064)	(0.06)
Revenue			0.00		
			(0.000)		
Log revenue				0.02**	0.02**
				(0.007)	(0.007)
Time fixed effects	Yes	Yes	Yes	Yes	Yes
Observations	1,653	892	780	780	926

Notes: Cell entries contain average marginal effects. Standard errors, clustered on region, in parentheses. Baseline category for occupational dummies in Model 1 is *ProfessionalLegislator*. Baseline category for occupational dummies in Models 2 and 3 is *Light Industry*
* $p < 0.1$, ** $p < 0.05$

Table 7.5 *Sector employment and United Russia faction membership*

Business sectors	Percentage in UR	Nonbusiness sectors	Percentage in UR
Construction	66**	Budget sphere	52**
Heavy industry	63**	Executive branch	47
Oil/gas	61*	Professional legislator	43
Mining/timber	60	Social organization	43
Utilities/energy	46	Municipal government	42
Services	50	Academia	41
Transportation	49	Military	40
Light industry	47	Journalist	28*
Agriculture	34*	Other	27**

Notes: Stars indicate categories that are statistically different from average in business and nonbusiness sectors, respectively
* $p < 0.1$, ** $p < 0.05$

Overall, the results on the sectoral dummies indicate support for the notion that the dependence of a firm on the state, whether due to asset immobility or the necessity of interaction with the authorities, increases the chances that deputies affiliated with that firm will join UR. But several caveats and exceptions are worth noting. One potentially intriguing finding in this table is that deputies from the utilities/energy sector are not any more or less likely to join United Russia. Until very recently almost all utilities were state owned and thus dependent on the state.

7.3 Models and Results

Simultaneously, however, it is important to remember that the Russian electricity monopoly RAO–Unified Energy Systems was headed until its dissolution by a moderate opposition figure, Anatoly Chubais. Indeed, a look at the data reveals that almost all deputies representing RAO–UES affiliates in the regions eschewed joining United Russia and most were members of SPS, Chubais's political party. This finding highlights the importance of personal connections and informal clientelist networks. Despite their dependence on the state, these deputies could rely on a powerful liberal patron who was not affiliated with United Russia.

Another intriguing result is that the directors of collective farms (the vast majority of those deputies employed in the agricultural sector) were not more likely to join the United Russia faction in their regions. In fact, as Models 2–5, they may even have been less likely to join UR. Given that agricultural land is an immobile asset, this finding is puzzling in light of the preceding discussion. However, it is important to remember the political dimension of deputies' decisions as well. As Henry Hale (2003) has shown, collective farm directors have at their disposal very powerful political machines, resources that can be leveraged against dependence on United Russia. It is also possible that collective farm directors are inherently more leftist in their ideology (or their constituents are more leftist), making it more difficult for them to join a center-Right ruling party. This finding also aligns empirically with the initial difficulties that United Russia faced in consolidating its position in rural organs of local self-government.

The results on the control variables are also of note. In particular, the positive and significant coefficient on *MoscowBasedBusiness* indicates that deputies from Moscow-based businesses – i.e. businesses with headquarters in Moscow that have branches in the regions – are more likely to join UR. This suggests that geographic distance increases the autonomy of enterprises from centralized political control.

In addition, deputies are more likely to join UR when the regional governor is already a member, as the positive and significant coefficient on *GovernorMember* indicates. This is not surprising given the importance of the regional executive branch in regional politics. If the governor is a member of UR, legislators have added incentives to demonstrate their loyalty by joining.

The other control variables exert no effect on the probability of a deputy's joining United Russia. *Incumbent* deputies are not more likely to join. An alternative hypothesis about deputies' decisions to join UR is coercion. One might conjecture that deputies will feel more compelled to join UR in regions that are less liberal or where political repression is more common. One proxy for this is level of *PressFreedom* in the region, but we see here that it has no effect on the propensity of deputies in a region to join UR. Another proxy is ethnicity. Russia's ethnic regions are, as a rule, more autocratic. But again, the percentage of Russians living in a region has no effect on the propensity of deputies to join UR.

Some of the asset-mobile sectors, such as *Services*, are statistically significant in Model 1. But this is due to the fact that the reference category in Model 1 is the nonbusinessperson category, *ProfessionalLegislator*. In Model 2, I restrict the analysis to businessperson deputies and use *LightIndustry* as the reference category. Here we see that deputies in asset-immobile sectors and sectors that conduct business with the state are much more likely to join UR. For example, deputies in *HeavyIndustry* are 13 percentage points more likely to join UR than deputies in *Light Industry*. Deputies in *Construction* are 16 percentage points more likely to join UR. However, the coefficient on *Oil/Gas* and *Mining/Timber* falls short of statistical significance. I discuss the insignificance of the former in more detail later.

Hypothesis 4 was not tested in Models 1 and 2 because data on the size of firms – as measured by their revenue – are missing for a large part of the sample. In Model 3, I include the firm's revenue as a predictor.[8] There is some support for Hypothesis 4 – the coefficient on *Revenue* is positive – but the coefficient falls slightly short of statistical significance ($p = .114$). Since *Revenue* is highly negatively skewed and contains a number of outliers (i.e. very large companies such as Russian Railways or Gazprom), it makes sense to transform the variable. Model 4, therefore, uses the natural log of revenue as a measure of firm size. The coefficient is positive and statistically significant. Increasing *FirmSize* from the 10th to the 90th percentile increases the probability of a deputy's joining UR by 16 percentage points.[9] In this model Private Enterprise ($p = .157$), Heavy Industry ($p = .163$), and Mining/Timber ($p = .361$) lose statistical significance. This occurs for two reasons. First, firm size is correlated with both ownership structure and asset specificity. Second, revenue is missing for a sizable portion of the sample so the sample size drops considerably in Models 3 and 4. This is a problem not only for statistical efficiency, but also because *Revenue* is not missing at random. It is more likely to be missing for smaller firms, firms that are not publicly traded, and firms in certain sectors. This has the potential to bias results. To address this, I use multiple imputation to estimate and replace

---

[8] As discussed later, *Revenue* is missing for a sizable portion of the sample. In order to conserve sample size, I exclude *Incumbent* – a variable that is also missing for some observations – from models that include *Revenue* as a predictor.
[9] Results are similar using a square root transformation.

7.3 Models and Results

missing values of *Log Revenue*. Specifically, I use multiple imputation with chained equations with 50 imputations (using the mi impute chained routine in STATA 14).[10] Results are similar using the multivariate normal algorithm. Model 5 shows the results of models that impute missing values on *Log Revenue*. *Log Revenue* remains statistically significant and positive. *Private Enterprise* and *Heavy Industry* return to statistical significance. *Mining/Timber* remains positive but does not return to statistical significance and *Oil/Gas* remains positive but statistically insignificant.

Table 7.5 models the decision to join UR as a binary one: join the dominant party or remain outside it. But deputies who remain outside UR have two distinct options. They can remain independent of any party, a very common choice in post-communist Russia, or they can join another party faction. Indeed, one potential concern with the preceding models is that I am conflating the choice to join UR with the choice to join any party, such that my results speak to the general calculus of party affiliation and not the more specific calculus of dominant party affiliation. Thus, we would like to examine how the dependence of deputies' enterprises on the states affects their decisions to join United Russia versus some other political party.

One way to achieve this is to model the affiliation decision as a trichotomous dependent variable and model affiliation decision with an unordered choice model, such as a multinomial logit. Another option is to create separate dependent variables and estimate separate models. In order to make substantive results comparable with previous results, I choose the latter strategy. Table 7.6 shows the results of six binary logit models. In the first three columns the dependent variable is equal to 1 if the deputy joined UR and 0 if the deputy joined another party faction. Thus, this model examines how covariates affect the decision to join UR as opposed to another opposition party. In the last three columns of Table 7.6, the dependent variable is 1 if the deputy joins UR and 0 if the deputy remains independent of any party faction.[11] Models 3 and 6 impute missing values on *Log Revenue*.

The results indicate that the main results are not driven simply by the decision to join a political party. As the results in Models 1–3 indicate, the same factors that made deputies more likely to join UR in Table 7.4 also increase their likelihood of choosing UR over another party. In fact,

---

[10] The imputation model contained all the right-hand-side covariates in Model 4 as well as the dependent variable in Model 4 and region dummies. Estimating this model as an OLS with the observed data gives an R-squared of .52. The imputation model converged easily.
[11] Results are substantively and statistically similar using a multinomial logit model. However, the multinomial logit estimates are more efficient, with lower standard errors.

Table 7.6 *Differentiating between party affiliation strategies*

	DV: 1 = join UR, 0 = join another faction			DV: 1 = join UR, 0 = remain independent		
	Model 1	Model 2	Model 3	Model 4	Model 5	Model 6
Private enterprise	−0.06	−0.08**	−0.07*	−0.09*	−0.07	−0.06
	(0.041)	(0.036)	(0.037)	(0.052)	(0.051)	(0.049)
Oil/gas	0.25**	0.16**	0.12	0.16**	0.02	−0.02
	(0.113)	(0.081)	(0.078)	(0.059)	(0.050)	(0.050)
Heavy industry	0.21*	0.13**	0.10	0.22**	0.07	0.03
	(0.121)	(0.064)	(0.062)	(0.064)	(0.059)	(0.054)
Mining/timber	0.26**	0.18**	0.13*	0.15	0.01	−0.03
	(0.109)	(0.079)	(0.071)	(0.103)	(0.067)	(0.062)
Utilities/energy	−0.04	−0.10	−0.13*	0.07	−0.07	−0.08
	(0.098)	(0.074)	(0.071)	(0.086)	(0.086)	(0.094)
Transportation	0.15	0.07	0.05	−0.04	−0.17**	−0.18**
	(0.098)	(0.088)	(0.084)	(0.067)	(0.062)	(0.060)
Construction	0.19**	0.10	0.11*	0.36**	0.19**	0.20**
	(0.090)	(0.066)	(0.062)	(0.102)	(0.078)	(0.076)
Agriculture	−0.05	−0.12**	−0.09	0.09	−0.06	−0.05
	(0.078)	(0.055)	(0.056)	(0.071)	(0.054)	(0.049)
Services	0.10	0.03	0.05	0.16**	−0.00	0.01
	(0.066)	(0.045)	(0.044)	(0.060)	(0.048)	(0.047)
Light industry	0.07			0.14**		
	(0.069)			(0.063)		
Executive branch	0.03			0.03		
	(0.129)			(0.117)		
Social organization	−0.01			0.07		
	(0.047)			(0.094)		
Budget sphere	0.13**			0.10*		
	(0.058)			(0.051)		
Military	−0.05			0.03		
	(0.191)			(0.156)		
Municipal government	0.15**			0.02		
	(0.073)			(0.064)		
Journalism	−0.10			−0.09		
	(0.101)			(0.095)		
Other/worker	−0.05			−0.07		
	(0.076)			(0.072)		
Academia	0.04			0.02		
	(0.121)			(0.083)		
Incumbent	−0.01	0.03		0.03	0.06	
	(0.027)	(0.032)		(0.036)	(0.041)	
Moscow based company	0.07	0.05	−0.03	0.20**	0.20**	0.13
	(0.079)	(0.073)	(0.064)	(0.091)	(0.083)	(0.092)

7.3 Models and Results 241

Table 7.6 (*continued*)

	DV: 1 = join UR, 0 = join another faction			DV: 1 = join UR, 0 = remain independent		
	Model 1	Model 2	Model 3	Model 4	Model 5	Model 6
Press freedom	0.02	0.01	0.01	0.07*	0.07	0.07*
	(0.034)	(0.040)	(0.040)	(0.039)	(0.046)	(0.045)
Percentage Russian	−0.00*	−0.00	−0.00	0.00	−0.00	−0.00
	(0.001)	(0.001)	(0.001)	(0.001)	(0.001)	(0.001)
Governor member	0.21**	0.26**	0.27**	0.02	0.03	0.03
	(0.050)	(0.064)	(0.062)	(0.059)	(0.069)	(0.070)
Log revenue			0.02**			0.01*
			(0.005)			(0.008)
Time fixed effects	Yes	Yes	Yes	Yes	Yes	Yes
Observations	1,214	686	707	1,282	701	717

Notes: Cell entries contain average marginal effects. Standard errors, clustered on region, in parentheses. Baseline category for occupational dummies in Model 1 and Model 4 is ProfessionalLegislator. Baseline category for occupational dummies in all other models is Light Industry
* $p < 0.1$, **$p < 0.05$

several of the sectoral variables – including *Oil/Gas* and *Mining/Timber* – have larger positive coefficients in these models than in Table 7.4. The coefficients on these variables are statistically significant in Models 1 and 2 and fall just short of statistical significance in Model 3 ($p = .133$ and $p = .127$, respectively). By contrast, the marginal effect of these variables is much lower in Models 5 and 6. In general, results on the sectoral variables of interest are stronger in Models 1–3. Deputies in asset-specific sectors appear particularly unlikely to join party factions that are not UR. Deputies in the construction sector, however, appear more likely to choose UR over remaining independent than they are to choose UR over another party. But the coefficients are positive and statistically significant in both sets of models.

The coefficient on *Private Enterprise* remains positive in all models, but it drops slightly below conventional statistical significance levels in some models. In general, standard errors are much higher in these models because splitting the dependent variable results in a lower number of observations in each model. There do not appear to be major differences in the effect of this variable between Models 1–3 and Models 4–6. Finally, the size of the firm has a positive and statistically significant effect in both sets of models. Deputies in larger firms are more likely to choose UR over another party, and they are more likely to choose UR over remaining independent.

Overall, Hypotheses 1, 3, and 4 are well supported and there is suggestive evidence in favor of Hypothesis 2. Across multiple specifications, it was found that deputies in the private business sector were less likely to join UR factions. Deputies from smaller firms were also clearly less likely to join UR. The sectoral hypotheses require more careful interpretation. It is clear in all statistical specifications that deputies in the *Construction* sector, whose businesses must interact frequently with the government, are more likely to join UR. In addition, deputies in asset-specific sectors – *Oil/Gas, Heavy Industry*, and *Mining/Timber* – are more likely than the average deputy to join UR. But companies in these sectors are also large, and once we include a measure of firm size in the models, *Oil/Gas* and *Mining/Timber* lose statistical significance. Thus, we are unable to conclude definitively that deputies in these sectors eschew UR affiliation because of the nature of the sector – it could be due to the size of the enterprise. However, the coefficient on *Heavy Industry* remains statistically significant even when controlling for firm size. This suggests that asset mobility does play some role.

7.4 Discussion and Conclusion

This chapter has used evidence from Russia to contribute to our understanding of dominant party origins. Dominant parties sometimes do not emerge because elites cannot commit themselves to such a party. This was the case in Russia in the 1990s and early 2000s. This chapter examined in more detail the claim that elites make their dominant party affiliation decisions on the basis of the resources available to them. Those with autonomous resources cannot commit themselves to joining the party, while those lacking in such resources can. If individual elites strong in resources are more reluctant to join an emergent dominant party, then we have additional reason to believe that the process of dominant party formation is dependent, at least in part, on elite commitment.

Using data on the faction membership of Russian regional legislators, this chapter provided evidence for this proposition. The primary finding was that those employed in state-dependent enterprises were more likely to affiliate with United Russia. Deputies who were dependent on the state for their livelihood were more likely to join the party. Among businessperson deputies, those in the state sector were more likely to join, as were deputies in large firms, which, by virtue of their size, are easier to tax and pressure. The multivariate analysis also reveals that deputies from more asset immobile sectors (heavy industry, in particular) are

7.4 Discussion and Conclusion

more likely to have joined United Russia than those engaged in industries such as services, trade, and light manufacturing. Deputies in asset immobile sectors know that their firm is vulnerable to state pressure, so they have less autonomy. I also found that deputies in the construction sector were more likely to join UR, as firms in that sector must maintain good relations with the state in order to win state contracts and secure permits.

The findings in this chapter provide new insight into the link between economic liberalization and democracy. In line with several recent works (McMann 2006, Greene 2010, Radnitz 2010, Arriola 2012), this chapter argues that economic liberalization can lead to democracy. But in contrast to these works, the approach in this chapter focuses on how economic liberalization frees economic elites from state dependence and undermines the construction of a ruling party.

This chapter also contributes to debates about how the nature of economic assets in a country affects democratization. Some of the most influential recent studies of democratization argue that holders of immobile economic assets subvert democratization because they fear that free and fair elections will lead to redistribution (Boix 2003, Acemoglu and Robinson 2006). Scholars of the natural resource curse point to a different causal mechanism, arguing that natural resources revenues allow autocrats to buy public quiescence (Ross 2001).

My account focuses on a different way that resource rents can affect a country's prospects for democratization. When leaders are in a vulnerable position vis-à-vis elites, a natural resource–based economy can strengthen the regime by ensuring the loyalty of key economic elites. Because elites who own or control natural resource companies are more dependent on the state, natural resource rents make elites loyal to the ruling party, thus reducing the potential for elite schisms.

Finally, with respect to Russian politics, the findings in this chapter also provide insight into the relationship of business to United Russia. Regional legislators join United Russia to lobby for their interests. Deputies from business can secure privileges and rents for their enterprises. In the 1990s and early 2000s, these deputies achieved these goals via ad hoc deals with governors and federal ministries. Today this process has been institutionalized within the United Russia factions of regional legislatures. Managing this patronage is one of the party's major functions at the regional level.

8 Dominant Party Emergence around the World

In previous chapters, I have illustrated how the interests and resources of Russian leaders and elites affected the process of dominant party formation (and nonformation) in that country. This chapter extends testing of the book's main argument to the cross-national setting. Can we find evidence that dominant party emergence in other non-democracies has been affected by the balance of resources between leaders and elites, as it was Russia? This chapter uses data on dominant party emergence in all the world's non-democracies between 1945 and 2006 to examine this question. The main hypothesis that I examine is the curvilinear hypothesis discussed in Chapter 2 and illustrated in Figure 1.4. Specifically, I expect that dominant parties will be unlikely to emerge when leaders are strong in resources. Under such conditions, leaders' incentives to seek the cooperation of elites are few, and they are tempted to defect from any bargain with elites that would limit their freedom of maneuver. Credible commitments are not feasible. But I also expect that dominant parties will be unlikely when elites are very strong in resources. When elites are strong relative to leaders, they can achieve many of their political goals on their own, so they have strong incentives to defect from any agreement that would require them to relinquish autonomy. Thus, dominant party formation should be most likely when resources are balanced between leaders and elites in a country.

The chapter unfolds as follows. In Section 8.1, I discuss an original, minimalist coding of dominant parties in non-democracies that I use as the dependent variable in the analysis. In Section 8.2, I tackle the difficult task of developing a cross-national, quantitative measure of elite and leader strength. Sections 8.3 and 8.4 discuss the statistical models used and their results. In Section 8.5, I discuss the findings. Although the measures of leader and elite strength are noisy, and should be treated with caution, the statistical models appear to indicate that dominant parties are most likely to emerge when resources of leaders and elites are balanced.

Table 8.1 *Conceptual map of party organization under autocracy*

Is there a dominant party?	Are opposition parties allowed to compete in elections?	
	Yes	No
Yes	Regimes with a hegemonic party (Malaysia 1969–, Zimbabwe 1979–, Cambodia 1998–, Nigeria 1999–2015)	Regimes with a single party (Turkmenistan 1991–2013, Soviet Union 1917–1991, Burma 1962–1988, Kenya 1968–1992)
No	Multiparty autocracies without a dominant party (Morocco 1977–, Belarus 1994–, Ukraine 1999–2004, Pakistan 1999–2008)	No-party regimes (Saudi Arabia 1932–, Myanmar 1988–2010, Chile 1973–1989)

8.1 Dependent Variable

In this section, I describe three coding rules used in developing an original data set of dominant parties around the world since 1946 that is used to test hypotheses about their emergence. As discussed in Chapter 1, I define a dominant party as a political institution that has a leading role in determining access to many important political offices, shares powers over policy making and patronage distribution, and uses privileged access to state resources to maintain its position in power. As noted, this definition subsumes both hegemonic parties – i.e. dominant parties in electoral authoritarian regimes – and single party regimes – i.e. regimes in which only one party is legal. Table 8.1 makes this conceptual distinction and provides examples. It also demonstrates that the set of negative cases (i.e. the nonemergence of dominant parties) includes both regimes where no parties exist and multiparty autocracies where the regime does not invest in a single dominant party but rather relies on shifting coalitions of allied parties and independents to pass legislation. In fact, contrary to some perceptions, almost half of electoral authoritarian regimes lack a dominant party.

The last part of my definition means that dominant parties occur in non-democracies. This leads to the first rule used in coding dominant parties. *Rule 1: The regime must be no-democratic.*

To identify nondemocratic regimes, I use the Polity IV classification of regimes and exclude all countries with a combined Polity score higher than 7. I use Polity's ordinal measure of regime type rather than dichotomous, retrospective codings of regime type, such as those employed by Przeworski et al. (2000), because ordinal measures permit inclusion of hybrid regimes, which are ultimately coded as democratic by Przeworski et al. We know in retrospect that regime alternation occurred in these countries, but it is within the realm of possibility that a dominant party could have formed there. Removing such cases from the analysis would constitute a form of selection bias, as they are regimes in which institutional forms were sufficiently fluid that the emergence of a dominant party was possible.

With a sample of non-democracies, the next task is to code a set of dominant parties within that class of regimes. Dominant parties must exercise some influence over cadres, policy, and the distribution of spoils. Thus, I omit regimes that do not have a legislature, since legislatures are the primary arenas for parties to exercise their influence, even in autocracies (Gandhi 2008). When a single party exists without a legislature, then I assume that the party is likely to be window dressing for a group of supporters who share in the patrimonial dividends of dictatorship.

Of course, in addition to the legislature, there must be a strong regime party. I argue that a legislature with a party that controls more than 50 percent of seats marks a reasonable dividing line between those rulers who have invested in organized institutions of bureaucratic co-optation and those who seek to buy off supporters and/or compete with opponents on an ad hoc basis. The 50 percent cutoff point is thus intended to capture not only the party's electoral dominance, but its degree of influence. There are likely to be few instances when a dictator permits a legislature and a majority party to form without ceding the party any influence or authority.

Thus, this operationalization maximizes reliability by positing clear, replicable coding rules, while minimizing error by positing meaningful institutional criteria. Additionally, it permits the inclusion of recently emerged and short-lived dominant parties, where extant operationalizations do not. Yet, the 50 percent figure is not arbitrary. A lower figure is clearly unwarranted since that would mean that the dominant party controls less than a majority of seats in the legislative chamber and could not, without securing other parties' support, pass its own bills or control the legislative appointments. On the other hand, a higher figure would be too restrictive, for it would eliminate dominant party regimes that operated in the presence of strong, but divided opposition parties. For example, the PRI secured 52 percent of seats in the Mexican election of 1988 and continued to rule Mexico for another decade. KANU in Kenya

8.1 Dependent Variable

received 50 percent and 51 percent of the seats in the 1992 and 1997 elections, respectively. During this period, both parties resided comfortably within the set of dominant party regimes that are widely recognized by general comparativists and area studies scholars alike. Thus, the second rule for classifying dominant party regimes is the following: *Rule 2: The party, or its legislative arm, must control more than 50 percent of seats in the primary legislative chamber.*

A third rule is that the party must truly be unequivocally affiliated with the dictator or regime leader. This rule is not often used, for it would entail a dictatorship that permits an opposition or nonaligned force to hold a majority in the legislature. *Rule 3: The party must be affiliated directly with the regime leader(s).*

Finally, I also exclude from analysis the eight Soviet-maintained communist regimes of Eastern Europe and the Soviet-maintained Communist Party in Mongolia.

Note that, unlike Greene (2010), I avoid using a durability criterion to operationalize dominant party emergence. While the strength of party institutions and party duration may often be correlated, strong dominant parties may be short-lived for reasons that are unrelated to their organizational capacity, just as organizationally weak dominant parties may survive for long periods in spite of their institutional weakness. In other words, party strength and party duration are different concepts. This is not to mention the fact that using a duration criterion would disallow analysis of the scores of dominant parties that have emerged recently in the past few decades.

The operationalization of dominant parties presented here is designed for the purposes of this study. The other prominent classification of ruling parties in authoritarian regimes is Geddes's (1999) well-known typology of authoritarian regime types. In order for a regime to be classified as a "single party regime" under Geddes's typology, it must meet several subjectively coded criteria that attempt to tap the origins and institutional autonomy of these parties. This typology was designed to characterize regime ideal types and as such conflates several aspects of authoritarian politics that are not mutually exclusive. My purposes are different. This study is interested in the emergence of dominant parties. That some dominant parties wield more institutional autonomy than others is no doubt true, but since this study investigates the origins of dominant parties rather than the emergence of regimes that exemplify the "single party regime ideal," a minimal operationalization is more appropriate. Such an operationalization permits inclusion of all instances of dominant party formation, regardless of whether the current leader comes to power after the party is created, whether the party holds a total monopoly on all leadership recruitment, or whether it is long-lived.[1]

The other main virtue of the measure used here is its reliability, a trait that it shares with other minimalist codings of authoritarian institutions in the literature (e.g. Gandhi 2008, Svolik 2012) As Chapter 5 indicated, there are sharp divisions, even among country experts, about how authoritarian institutions operate in individual countries. This division compromises the reliability, and perhaps even the validity, of subjectively coded cross-national measures.

The Online Appendix contains a list of the 128 dominant parties identified by these rules that have existed at some time from 1946 to 2006. As the appendix discusses in more detail, dominant parties have existed consistently in about half of all non-democracies since 1946. In the immediate postwar period, dominant parties were rare, but they became more common in the early 1960s as many nascent postcolonial democracies shed free elections and adopted authoritarian modes of governance, often with the backing of a dominant party. In 1980, 53 regimes in the world, excluding Soviet controlled Eastern Europe, were backed by a dominant party. By 2006, that number had fallen back to 40, but dominant parties still existed in 46 percent of all authoritarian regimes, a higher proportion than in 1980. Indeed, the proportion of the world's authoritarian regimes that have dominant parties is now the highest since the end of the Cold War.

The early 1960s witnessed the most instances of dominant party emergence in history. During this decade more than 40 dominant parties emerged. Malaysia's UMNO, Ivory Coast's Democratic Party of Cote d'Ivoire (PDCI), Botswana's BDP, Kenya's KANU, and Algeria's FLN are prominent examples of dominant parties that emerged in the early and mid-1960s. The next wave of dominant party emergence began in the 1990s and continues through the present. In this wave, hegemonic parties emerged in many "failed" Third Wave democracies (e.g. the PDP in Nigeria, the CPP in Cambodia, the FLN in Algeria, OTAN in Kazakhstan, and the Rwandan Patriotic Front in Rwanda).

Dominant parties may exist only for a short period until they are dislodged by coups, lose autocratic elections, are disbanded by regime leaders, or collapse internally. Others persist for decades. The median

---

[1] Indeed, one of the several criteria that Geddes uses to identify single party regimes is that the party preexisted the current leader. This criterion is not appropriate for the current analysis, since I am also interested in when leaders will invest in creating such parties. In any case, as I show later, results are robust to using Geddes's coding of single party regimes.

duration of a dominant party is 14 years. Twenty-five percent of parties survived for less than 7 years and 25 percent survived for more than 28 years. Well-known examples of long-lived dominant parties abound, including the Mexican PRI, the CPSU in the Soviet Union, the True Whig Party in Liberia, and the KMT in Taiwan. Examples of short-lived dominant parties include the CUG in Georgia, the Bangladesh National Party (BNP) in Bangladesh, Cambio 90 in Peru, and the DP in Turkey.

Using these data, I construct the dependent variable, which is equal to 1 in a nondemocratic country-year after 1945 when a dominant party emerged and 0 in a country-year after 1945 without a dominant party.[2] Descriptive statistics on the dependent variable and all other variables are presented in the Supplemental Appendix.

8.2 Independent Variables

The main independent variables in this analysis are leader strength and elite strength. Both must be taken into consideration because the strength of one is always relative to the resources of the other. The challenge of operationalizing elite strength is harder. I address it first.

Both between and within countries there is always variation in the extent to which elites hold or have access to some actual or latent base of resources that is autonomous from the regime. Elites are powerful to the extent that they control these resources. As noted, such resources might include, but are not limited to, autonomous control over clientelist networks, de facto or de jure regional autonomy, hard-to-tax economic assets, positions of traditional authority, and the individual-specific ability to mobilize citizens.

---

[2] This operationalization encompasses several different paths to dominant party emergence. Most notably, it combines instances when the regime chooses to create a dominant party "from scratch" with those instances when some elements of party organization predate the regime. The latter form of dominant party emergence includes many revolutionary and anticolonial dominant parties. My theory is somewhat better suited to explaining the first type of dominant party emergence. Although some of the best-known dominant parties of the 20th century started as revolutionary or anticolonial parties, they represent just 37 percent of the 128 dominant parties analyzed here (see Chapter 2). And for obvious reasons, almost no parties that have emerged (or will emerge) since the end of the Cold War were anticolonial or revolutionary parties. Nonetheless, I think that the present argument can offer some insights into the reasons that leaders and elites remain committed to institutionalizing a dominant party as a key feature of the regime at the moment when the regime is constituted. After all, leaders and elites retain significant agency in such transitional periods, and the decision to retain (or jettison) a dominant party at those crucial junctures is clearly a conscious one. If my argument does not apply to these cases, then including them in the dependent variable should make it harder to find results that support my hypothesis. At the same time, including them allows us to see whether the present argument can help further understanding of those cases as well.

In this cross-national analysis, I treat the strength of elites as a country-specific factor. This does not mean that elites necessarily contract with the leader as a single actor, but rather that we can identify countries where elites, as a whole, are strong vis-à-vis rulers and countries where elites, as a whole, are weak vis-à-vis rulers.

Measuring the strength of elites across countries is a challenge. Despite its importance as a concept in comparative politics, there are no existing cross-national measures of elite strength. An ideal measure of aggregate elite resources would be able to tap the myriad ways that elites have exerted independent political influence (vis-à-vis leaders) in societies through the ages. It would identify the characteristics of a polity that abet the construction of strong, elite-led clientelist networks and political machines. Thus, one problem with the construction of a measure of elite strength is the inherent breadth of the concept. A second challenge is endogeneity. For the resources belonging to elites to have meaning, it must be costly or difficult for regime leaders to expropriate these resources systematically.

My approach to these problems is to proxy for elite strength by constructing a scale of the historical and demographic factors that are most closely associated with the concept of elite strength sketched previously. A good place to start in constructing this scale is to look at how power historically has been dispersed across the geographic space of a polity. Indeed, many of the conflicts that have defined politics in the developing world over the past century have been center–periphery conflicts. As state leaders have attempted to exert control over society, time and again they have been stymied in their efforts by regional elites (e.g. Migdal 1988, Herbst 2000).

A key indicator of regional elite strength, I argue, is a country's history of political decentralization. Granting state administrative authority to regional elites may be a reflection of their power, or state administrative autonomy may give elites the resources to build strong local political machines.

Using data from the Comparative Constitutions Project (Elkins, Ginsburg, and Melton 2009), I have constructed a scale of political decentralization that is based on the constitutional powers granted to regional and local governments in all non-democracies since 1946.[3] The

---

[3] The data on the federalism subcomponents were provided to the author by the Comparative Constitutions Project in 2009. Several other sources, including Daniel Treisman's data set on decentralization (www.sscnet.ucla.edu/polisci/faculty/treisman/Pages/unpublishedpapers.html), Peaslee (1974), and Blaustein and Flanz (2007), were used to make some corrections to the CCP data where mistakes were evident. In some cases, I consulted the constitution itself to make determinations.

8.2 Independent Variables

scale receives a score of 1 if there are no local or provincial governments mentioned in the constitution for a given year or local government chief executives are appointed by the center. It receives a score of 2 if local governments are elected *or* provincial governments are mentioned in the constitution. It receives a score of 3 if provincial governments are mentioned *and* local governments are elected. It receives a score of 4 if all of these conditions are met, subnational chief executives exist, and the constitution gives provincial government significant policy autonomy *or* the provincial government is elected.[4] This produces a 4-point scale of past political decentralization. I call this variable *Political Decentralization*.

Political Decentralization is a highly reliable measure, but its validity is limited in many developing countries. While recent work has shown that formal institutions constrain actors even in authoritarian regimes, the extent to which formal institutions reflect the informal distribution of power is, nonetheless, usually more limited in developing countries. Therefore, I have chosen to supplement *Political Decentralization* with two other proxies for the geographic dispersion of elite resources. These two additional proxies are meant to identify cases in which regional elites have the potential to develop strong political machines but, for whatever reason, power has not been formally decentralized.

The first supplemental measure is the dispersion of human population within a country. Regional elites are more likely to have the tools necessary to build strong political machines when much of a country's population is spread across its territory and far from areas that are easy to control by state leaders, often the capital city (see Herbst 2000). This is especially true when this population is spread across major urban centers that contain significant portions of a country's economic output. As a matter of historical fact, most states in the developing world have, at one time or another, lacked the material and infrastructural resources to exert social control across their territory. To the extent that it requires more infrastructure and financial resources to implement state authority across large distances, countries with dispersed populations generate greater opportunities for regional elites to construct local machines. Also, as observers from Madison onward have noted, countries with dispersed populations are more likely to exhibit diversities of attitude, geography, and custom. This diversity may give regional strongmen more opportunity for fortifying their own local legitimacy at the expense of a faraway ruler.

---

[4] Provincial governments are deemed to have significant policy autonomy when they have the power to tax and/or they are the residual lawmakers in areas not covered by federal law. These determinations are made using the CCP data.

Thus, I supplement my scale of regionalism with a measure of the geographic dispersion of human settlement. This scale combines information on how far citizens live from the capital with information on the overall fragmentation of human settlement in a country. It is constructed with GIS data from the Gridded Population of the World Project at the Earth Institute of Columbia University. This geocoded data set provides information on the latitude and longitude of all human settlements in the world as well as their population.

My scale of population dispersion is calculated in the following manner: the distance of each human settlement from the capital city is multiplied by its share of the total population as of 1990. These totals are then summed up for the entire country. The measure can be thought of as the dispersion per capita (DPC) in the country, or the average distance of each citizen from the capital city.[5] Formally the measure is calculated as $DPC = \sum_i P_i D_i$, where P is settlement i's share of the country's population, and D is the distance of that settlement from the country's capital. This continuous measure provides a good proxy for the dispersion of human population because it taps both a country's size and the dispersion of settlement within its borders. For example, a country such as Saudi Arabia is large, but its population is concentrated in only a few locations. Therefore, DPC penalizes Saudi Arabia's size for the fact that its population is concentrated. On the other hand, Vietnam is not a particularly large country, but its population is spread across many different population points. DPC rewards Vietnam for this dispersion, while also taking into account its modest geographic size.

One significant flaw of this measure is it does not take into account the fragmentation of human settlement outside the capital city. For example, in Saudi Arabia, a sizable proportion of the population is located *outside* Riyadh, but this population is concentrated in only a handful of centers. Thus, I weight DPC by a modified Herfindahl index that measures the effective number of human settlements in the country.[6] This weight

---

[5] This measure is similar in construction to Hill and Gaddy's (2003) "temperature per capita" metric, a measure used for summarizing the population-weighted average temperature for a country.

[6] More specifically, this variable is constructed by first calculating the "effective number of population points" in the country (1 divided by the Herfindahl index). Since this variable is heavily skewed, I then take the natural log of that value. I then create the weights by dividing the log of each country's "effective number of population points" by the log of the effective number of population points in the country with the largest effective number of population points (South Africa). Thus, this creates a weight that describes each country's relative level of population dispersion.

8.2 Independent Variables

decreases the value of DPC for countries such as Saudi Arabia and increases it for countries such as Vietnam. Finally, I take the natural log of DPC and transform it into a 4-point scale for ease of inclusion in the broader scale of elite strength. I call this variable *Population Dispersion*.

A final component of the elite strength scale is geographically concentrated ethnic minorities. Some of the strongest elite political machines in non-democracies tend to be ethnically based (e.g. Lemarchand 1972, Hale 2006). Ethnic leaders leverage their ability to mobilize nationalist or ethnic opposition in order to accrue greater autonomy from the center and build strong political machines. Indeed, ethnic minority social networks can provide a ready-made basis for strong political machines.

One could simply tap ethnic diversity as a measure of regional elite strength. The difficulty with this is that not all ethnic divisions can provide a strong basis for elite political machines. Groups whose populations are dispersed throughout the country are harder to mobilize. Regionally based groups are much more likely to provide bases for strong political machines. To acknowledge this fact, I start with data on ethnic groups provided by Fearon (2003). I then use the group concentration index developed by the Minorities at Risk (MAR) project to exclude those groups that are "widely dispersed" or constitute only a minority in one region (GROUPCON < 2 in the MAR data). The excluded groups are "subsumed" into the plurality ethnic group of the country and a Herfindahl index of ethnic diversity is then computed, as has become standard in the literature.

In other words, this measure weights the traditional ethnic fragmentation measure by the extent to which ethnic minorities are concentrated in specific geographic regions. This measure ranges between 0 and 1, but for the purposes of inclusion in the broader scale of elite strength, I rescale the measure to range from 1 to 4 at equal intervals, with 4 indicating higher levels of regional ethnic diversity. I call this variable *Concentrated Ethnic Divisions*.

To construct a scale of elite strength, the three components of the scale (histories of political decentralization, population dispersion, and regional ethnic fragmentation) are added together to create a scale that ranges from 3 to 12. A score of 12 indicates maximally strong elites. I call this measure *Elite Strength*.

One might object that this measure is vulnerable to aggregation bias, since all of its three components may be related. To be sure, studies of federalism in *democracies* have related a country's size and its ethnic diversity to the maintenance of federalism (Treisman 2002). I do not deny such a relationship in democracies but only note that my additive scale is constructed precisely because I believe that decentralization is sometimes not reflected in the institutional forms of authoritarian regimes. Thus, I expect a relatively low correlation between these two measures for my sample of authoritarian regimes. Second, the measure of regional ethnic diversity is added precisely to account for the many African countries that are not particularly large, but contain a great diversity of ethnic groups that provide strong bases for the cultivation of regionalized tribalism and bossism. Therefore, I do not expect a strong correlation between *Population Dispersion* and *Concentrated Ethnic Divisions*. Table III in the appendix shows the correlations among components of this measure, which are all low.

Leaders are strong to the extent that they are able to use their political power to make political appointments, secure favored policies, and ensure social cooperation without relying on the favor of other prominent elites. But these resources must be exogenous. That is, the measure of leader strength I employ here must not depend on the strength of elites. I argue that resource rents and economic growth do an adequate job of capturing this concept. Nontax revenues give leaders easy access to funds and can be used to buy social cooperation and enrich supporters. As most of the literature has done, I focus on per capita revenues from fuel and mineral income. Specifically, I use the natural log of a country's total income (in 2007 dollars) from natural resources divided by population.[7] These data are taken from Haber and Menaldo (2011). This variable is called *Log Rents*. For inclusion in the elite strength scale, I rescale the variable into a 4-point scale where 1 is the lowest level (bottom 25 percent of the data) of *Log Rents* and 4 is the highest (top 25 percent of the data).[8]

All leaders, including authoritarian ones, find it difficult to rule without any mass support. Leaders who enjoy strong economic growth curry more favor among citizens and have more rents to distribute to mass supporters (see Haggard and Kaufman 1996, Magaloni 2006, Treisman 2011). As studies of economic voting show, voters are more likely to blame national leaders for economic performance than they are to blame legislators and local officials (Stein 1990, Samuels 2004). Furthermore leaders find it easier to retain the loyalty of elites when economic performance is good (Reuter and Gandhi 2011). This puts them in a strong position. Therefore, I take economic growth as a measure of leaders'

---

[7] I then rescale the measure to run from 0 to 18.4 by adding 7.1 in order to remove the negative numbers induced by taking the natural log of fractions.
[8] The Haber–Menaldo data are missing for a handful of nondemocratic country-years. For these observations, I used data on oil and mineral exports from the World Bank World Development Indicators, where available. This is done for 84 observations.

8.2 Independent Variables

strength vis-à-vis elites.[9] I take four-year moving averages of lagged economic growth using data from the World Bank, Penn World Tables, and Angus Maddison's *The World Economy: Historical Statistics*. In order to integrate this into a broader measure of leader strength, I then scale these four-year moving averages into a 4-point scale ranging from 1 to 4 that separates the continuous measure at equal intervals. Four represents the highest four-year averages of economic growth.

The two components of the scale (*Resource Rents* and *Economic Growth*) are added together to create a scale of leaders' strength that ranges from 2 to 8. A score of 8 indicates maximally strong leaders. I call this measure *Leader Strength*.

In addition to the variables listed, I include several analytic controls that tap competing explanations of dominant party emergence. First, I include the Polity IV measure of regime type; second, GDP per capita; and finally, two variables that are intended to capture the difficult-to-measure concept of "social opposition." The first, used by Gandhi (2008) to measure the same concept, is a 3-point scale that measures the number of political parties that the current regime confronts when it rises to power: zero, one, or more than one. Regimes that confront existing parties upon ascending to power confront situations in which some segments of society have the ready-made capability to organize. This may be either a cause or consequence of the latent level of social opposition.[10]

This measure is not without its flaws, however. In particular, it does not adequately capture variation among those regimes that inherited more than one party – the majority of the sample. Second, it does not measure the extent to which latent social opposition is actualized against the regime. To tap this notion, I exploit data on antigovernment demonstrations, strikes, and riots from Banks Cross National Time Series Data Archive. This variable counts the number of these events in a year and sums them to make an index called *Social Opposition*.

As several authors have suggested (e.g. Huntington 1968, Levitsky and Way 2012), dominant parties may be more likely to emerge in times of violent crisis, so I include a binary variable equal to 1 if there is a *Civil War* in the country for a given year. I also control for whether the regime is *Parliamentary* or presidential, and for whether a *Multiparty Election* is held in a given year. Finally, I include a series of region dummies,

---

[9] Another advantage of including economic growth as part of this scale is that it helps tap variation in the strength of leaders for that large subset of countries with few natural resources.

[10] Note that this is not the lagged value of the dependent variable in this analysis, but rather a "regime-specific" lag (Gandhi 2008).

colonial dummies, period dummies, and a binary variable equal to 1 if a country has ever had a dominant party in the past, called *Previous Dominant Party*.

8.3 Modeling Strategy

The unit of analysis is the country-year, and the dependent variable is a binary variable equal to 1 in years with a dominant party and 0 in years without. My interest is in the emergence of dominant parties, so dominant party country-years drop from the analysis after the year in which a dominant party emerges.[11] The analysis runs from 1946 to 2006, such that dominant parties emerging prior to 1946 (e.g. the CPSU) are not included. The data structure is binary time-series, cross-sectional (BTSCS) of the type described by Beck, Katz, and Tucker (1998). To control for time dependence in the data, I include a cubic polynomial (time, time-squared, and time-cubed) of the number of years until a dominant party emerges (Carter and Signorino 2010). Since the outcome of interest is binary, I use probit models throughout.

One way of testing the argument is by creating a single variable that captures the balance of resources between elites and leaders, and modeling it in a curvilinear fashion to see whether the probability of dominant party emergence is highest when resources are balanced. Unfortunately, the scale resulting from such a transformation does not lend itself to easy interpretation. Moreover, this approach does not permit analysis of the asymmetric effects of leader and elite strength (Berry, Golder, and Milton 2012). A better approach, which captures the curvilinear nature of my hypothesis and permits analysis of the symmetrical, contingent hypothesis, is to interact the two scales and look at the resultant conditional marginal effects. Predicted probabilities from the model still permit direct examination of the curvilinear argument in Figure 8.1, but using these interaction terms also allows us to see whether the effect of *Elite Strength* on dominant party emergence changes across values of *Leader Strength and* vice versa. It also allows us to examine how different types of resource balances affect the likelihood of dominant party emergence.[12]

---

[11] In the appendix, I also model the determinants of dominant party *existence*, where all dominant party country-years are left in. Results are similar, though slightly weaker. But since the factors that make a dominant party persist may differ from the factors that lead to the creation of a dominant party, I focus here on dominant party formation.
[12] In any case, results are similar from models where the two scales are aggregated into a single scale that captures the balance of strength between leaders and elites.

According to the argument, an increase in *Elite Strength* should have a negative effect on dominant party emergence when leaders are weak, and a positive effect when leaders are strong. In the former case, increasing *Elite Strength* will add to the imbalance in resources between leaders and elites, which should reduce the likelihood of dominant party emergence. By contrast, when leaders are strong, increasing *Elite Strength* moves resources more into balance, which should increase the probability of dominant party emergence. And following the same logic, an increase in *Leader Strength* should have a negative effect on the probability of dominant party emergence when elites are weak, but a positive effect when elites are strong.

8.4 Results

Table 8.2 presents the results. Before including the measures of *Elite* and *Leader* strength, I first estimate a set of baseline models that examine the effect of key competing explanations and analytic controls. Several positive findings of note are that dominant parties are less likely to emerge in wealthy countries, in more competitive non-democracies, and in years when dominant multiparty elections are held. Consistent with existing work (Smith 2005, Gandhi 2008), dominant parties are more likely to emerge in those countries that have inherited more political parties, which stands as a measure of the potential for organized opposition. Among the region dummies, dominant parties are most likely to emerge in Sub-Saharan Africa, as well as in Eastern Europe and the former Soviet Union.[13] Dominant parties are also more likely to emerge in former Portuguese and Spanish colonies.[14] The cubic polynomial of time indicates nonmonotonic hazards: the probability of a dominant party emerging initially grows in each year without a dominant party until about 7 years, and then, the probability begins to drop again after 26 years.

Some interesting negative findings also stand out. For example, some previous work has argued that dictators who have access to significant rent revenues can use those rents to buy the cooperation of elites and/or society and, therefore, have less need to make institutional concessions to elites and/or society (e.g. Gandhi 2008, Boix and Svolik 2013). According to this perspective, authoritarian institutions should be less likely when dictators control significant resource rents. And yet, as Model 1 shows, *Log Rents* appears to have no linear negative effect on

---

[13] The base category for these dummies is South America.
[14] The base category for these dummies is countries that were never colonized.

Table 8.2 *Determinants of dominant party emergence*

	Model 1	Model 2	Model 3	Model 4	Model 5	Model 6
Elite strength				−0.017***	−0.011***	
				(0.006)	(0.004)	
Leader strength				−0.029***	−0.012*	
				(0.010)	(0.007)	
Elite strength × leader strength				0.004***	0.002**	
				(0.001)	(0.001)	
Log rents	0.001	0.000	0.001			−0.004***
	(0.001)	(0.002)	(0.001)			(0.002)
Population dispersion			0.009*			
			(0.005)			
Political decentralization			0.001			−0.023***
			(0.004)			(0.007)
Concentrated ethnic diversity			−0.008*			
			(0.005)			
Lagged GDP growth scale			−0.004			
			(0.003)			
GDP per capita	−0.008	−0.006	−0.005	−0.005	0.002	−0.010*
	(0.005)	(0.005)	(0.006)	(0.006)	(0.004)	(0.005)
Inherited parties	0.014***	0.007	0.012**	0.010*	0.009**	0.012**
	(0.005)	(0.010)	(0.005)	(0.005)	(0.004)	(0.005)
Polity	−0.002***	−0.002***	−0.002**	−0.002**	0.000	−0.002***
	(0.001)	(0.001)	(0.001)	(0.001)	(0.001)	(0.001)
Civil war	−0.005	−0.006	−0.009	−0.007	0.007	−0.006
	(0.011)	(0.011)	(0.011)	(0.011)	(0.007)	(0.011)
Parliamentary	−0.013	−0.025*	−0.018	−0.016	0.002	−0.014
	(0.012)	(0.013)	(0.013)	(0.012)	(0.008)	(0.012)
Previous dominant party	0.001	0.003	0.000	0.002	0.004	−0.002
	(0.009)	(0.009)	(0.010)	(0.009)	(0.006)	(0.009)
Multiparty election	0.071***	0.070***	0.068***	0.071***	−0.003	0.071***
	(0.009)	(0.009)	(0.009)	(0.009)	(0.008)	(0.009)
Former British colony	0.016	0.014	0.018	0.020	0.011	0.013
	(0.015)	(0.016)	(0.016)	(0.016)	(0.014)	(0.015)
Former Spanish colony	0.048*	0.072**	0.071	0.072**	0.142	0.049*
	(0.028)	(0.034)	(0.034)	(0.035)	(4.32)	(0.028)
Former French colony	0.028*	0.030*	0.033*	0.036**	−0.003	0.035**
	(0.016)	(0.017)	(0.017)	(0.017)	(0.012)	(0.016)
Former Portuguese colony	0.051**	0.056**	0.062**	0.056**	0.033*	0.078***
	(0.024)	(0.024)	(0.025)	(0.024)	(0.004)	(0.025)

8.4 Results

Table 8.2 (*continued*)

	Model 1	Model 2	Model 3	Model 4	Model 5	Model 6
Other former colony	0.010 (0.019)	0.006 (0.019)	0.008 (0.020)	0.015 (0.020)	0.014 (0.018)	0.013 (0.019)
Time	−0.015*** (0.004)	−0.013*** (0.004)	−0.014*** (0.004)	−0.014*** (0.004)	−0.013*** (0.003)	−0.016*** (0.004)
Time2	0.001*** (0.000)	0.001*** (0.000)	0.001*** (0.000)	0.001*** (0.000)	0.001*** (0.000)	0.001*** (0.000)
Time3	−0.000*** (0.000)	−0.000** (0.000)	−0.000*** (0.000)	−0.000** (0.000)	−0.000** (0.000)	−0.000*** (0.000)
Social opposition		0.000 (0.002)				
Inherited parties × Log rents		0.001 (0.001)				
Political decentralization × Log rents						0.003*** (0.001)
Region dummies	Y	Y	Y	Y	Y	Y
Period dummies	Y	Y	Y	Y	Y	Y
Observations	2,685	2,603	2,523	2,523	2,803	2,650

dominant party emergence. Nor are dominant parties more likely to emerge during times of civil strife as the insignificant coefficient on *Civil War* indicates.

In Model 2, I investigate whether the effect of social opposition and rents is multiplicative: i.e. dominant parties are most likely in the face of strong social opposition *and* limited access to rents (see Smith 2005). Thus, I interact *Log Rents* with *InheritedParties*. The coefficient on the interaction term is insignificant. An examination of conditional coefficients indicates that 1) the impact of neither is conditional on the other, and 2) the predicted probability of dominant party emergence is not higher when social opposition is higher and resource rents are low. This model also includes a measure of actualized opposition to the regime in the form of strikes, demonstrations, and riots. The insignificant coefficient on *Social Opposition* indicates that this type of social opposition has little effect on dominant party emergence.

Model 3 is the same as Model 1 but includes the components of the scale used to construct *Leader Strength* and *Elite Strength*. On their own, the components of the scale are not strong and consistent predictors of dominant party emergence. Model 4 presents the full model that tests my interactive hypotheses. I include *Elite Strength*, *Leader Strength*, and their interaction. The statistically significant coefficient on *Elite Strength* × *LeaderStrength* indicates that these two variables modify one another's effects in some way, but by just looking at the coefficients in the main results we cannot determine the nature of that modification (Brambor, Clark, and Golder 2006). It is necessary to look at the conditional marginal effects of *Elite* and *Leader Strength* as they change across values of the other.

The upper left panel of Figure 8.2 displays the conditional average marginal effect of *Elite Strength* across the range of values on *Leader Strength*. The figure is consistent with my hypotheses. When leaders are weak (*Leader Strength* less than 5), the effect of a 1-unit increase in *Elite Strength* is to reduce the probability of dominant party emergence. When *Leader Strength* is high, with a value of 7, for example, a 1-unit increase in *Elite Strength* increases the probability of dominant party emergence by almost 2 percentage points. This effect is quite sizable, considering that the baseline probability of a dominant party's emerging in any given country-year is 3.8 percent. Thus, in this example, a 1-unit increase in *Elite Strength* translates into nearly a 50 percent increase in the probability of a dominant party when *Leader Strength* is high. On the other hand, when *Leader Strength* is low, with a value of 3, for example, a 1-unit increase in *Elite Strength* decreases the probability of dominant party emergence by 1.5 percentage points, a 39 percent reduction over the baseline probability of dominant party emergence. In sum, any change in *Elite* Strength that moves the distribution of resources into greater balance increases the probability of dominant party formation, while any change that makes elites stronger relative to leaders decreases the probability of dominant party emergence.

The upper right panel of Figure 8.2 displays the flip side of the interactive hypothesis: the effect of *Leader Strength* on dominant party emergence as values of *Elite Strength* change. This figure is also consistent with the argument. *Leader Strength* appears to increase the probability that a dominant party will form when elites become strong (*Elite Strength* greater than 7). When elites are very weak, the effect of a 1-unit increase in *Leader Strength* is to decrease the probability that a dominant party will form. In sum, any change in the balance of resources between leaders and elites that creates a more equitable balance between these two sides increases the probability of dominant party emergence, while changes in *Elite* and *Leader Strength* that make one side stronger than the other decrease the probability of dominant party emergence. These results suggest that dominant parties are unlikely to emerge when

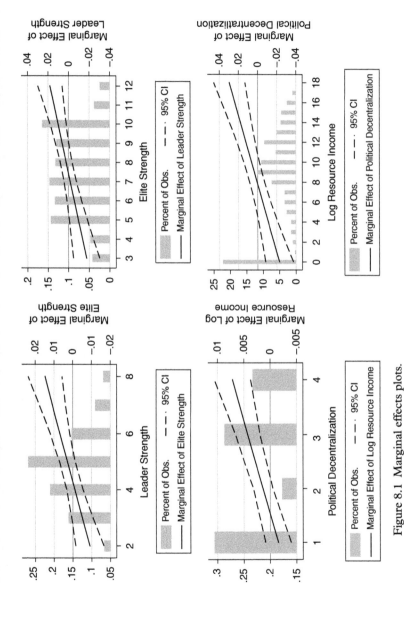

Figure 8.1 Marginal effects plots.

Note: Left *y*-axis in all plots depicts percentage of observations. Right *y*-axis is the average marginal effect for a given variable; thus, these figures indicate the change in the $\Pr(y=1)$ associated with a 1-unit increase in the variable listed on the right *y*-axis, across values of the modifying variables (*x*-axis).

Table 8.3 *Predicted probability of dominant party emergence*

Elites' strength	Leader strength		
	2	5	8
4	.071 [0.025–0.13] (Rwanda 1975)	0.031 [0.016–0.046]	0.012 [0.000–0.026] (Qatar)
8	0.030 [0.018–0.042]	0.040 [0.032–0.047] (Ivory Coast 1960)	0.053 [0.028–0.078]
11	0.014 [0.002–0.013] (Brazil 1985)	0.048 [0.032–0.064]	0.129 [0.053–0.205] (Nigeria 1999)
Political decentralization	Log rents scale		
	0	9	17
1	0.053 [0.028–0.078] (Senegal 1960)	0.037 [0.024–0.051]	0.027 [0.007–0.047] (Libya)
2	0.029 [0.018–0.040]	0.040 [0.031–0.049]	0.052 [0.027–0.076]
3	0.015 [0.007–0.024]	0.042 [0.034–0.051] (Yugoslavia 1992)	0.093 [0.055–0.131]
4	0.007 [0.001–0.014]	0.046 [0.031–0.060]	0.155 [0.079–0.231]
	(Comoros)		(Russia 2003)

Note: Cell entries are average predicted probabilities; 95 percent confidence intervals in brackets. Countries in brackets are examples of those that have the given values.

leaders are very strong relative to elites or when elites are very strong relative to leaders.

Another way of viewing these substantive results is to look at the predicted probability of dominant party emergence given different levels of *Elite Strength* and *Leader Strength*. The upper panel of Table 8.3 displays these average predicted probabilities, along with examples of the type of countries that fit into each category in the data.

The probability of dominant party emergence in any given year when both leaders and elites are strong is .13. When compared to the baseline probability of .039, this indicates that dominant parties are more than four times as likely to emerge when both leaders and elites are strong. By contrast, when elites are very weak and leaders very strong, then dominant parties are very unlikely to emerge: the predicted probability is .012. The same is true when elites are very strong and leaders are very weak: the predicted probability is .014. Thus, as Figure 8.2 makes clear, these predicted probabilities bear out the curvilinear hypothesis discussed earlier.

8.4 Results

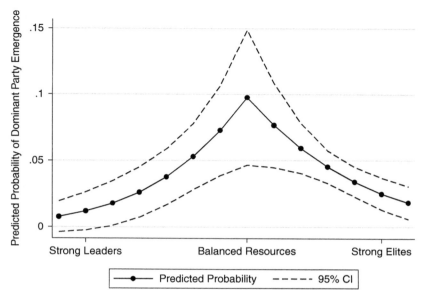

Figure 8.2 Predicted probability of dominant party emergence across various distributions of resources between leaders and elites.

Note: This "'balance'" of resources represented by this figure is one in which both leaders and elites are "strong" (Elite Strength = 10, Leader Strength = 8). This is the value that produces the peak in the figure. The point on the far left of the scale corresponds to Leader Strength = 8 and Elite Strength = 3. The point to the far right of the figure corresponds to Elite Strength = 10 and Leader Strength = 2. Logically, such a figure could be constructed for any other balance of resources (e.g. when parity is achieved because both are "weak" in resources). As Table 8.3 indicates and I have confirmed, the curvilinearity shown above here is preserved in any such alternative depictions. Note also that the right-skewedness in the figure is due to the fact that Elite Strength is scaled differently than Leader Strength.

Dominant parties are also more likely when resources are balanced between weak elites and weak leaders or between somewhat strong elites and somewhat strong leaders, though the probability of dominant party emergence is not as high in those categories as it is when both sides are strong. This discrepancy is intriguing and deserves further study. Nonetheless, it is still true that dominant parties are more likely to emerge when resources are balanced between "weak" leaders and "weak" elites than they are when one side is disproportionately strong.

Model 5 is a robustness check that uses the qualitative coding of authoritarian regime type developed by Geddes (2003) for the dependent variable. Specifically, the dependent variable is equal to 1 in years when a single party regime or any hybrid regime type that includes single party elements (e.g. Personal/Single Party) begins and 0 otherwise. As with the other models, dominant party country-years drop after the year in which a dominant party emerges. The results are consistent with the other models; dominant parties, as defined by Geddes, are most likely to emerge when resources are balanced between leaders and elites, and least likely when one side is demonstrably stronger than the other.

One drawback of *Elite Strength* and *Leader Strength* is that their aggregate values mask the underlying multidimensionality that go into their construction. Previously, I have defended these scales on substantive grounds, but nonetheless, as a robustness check, Model 6 takes the components of *Elite Strength* and *Leader Strength* that most closely tap the background concepts and interacts them, rather than interacting the full composite scales. Thus, I interact *Log Rents*, a good proxy for leader resources, and *Political Decentralization*, the element of elite strength that most closely maps the background concept of regional elite resources. The results of this model are consistent with models including the full scales. As the lower right panel in Figure 8.1 shows, a 1-unit increase in the scale of *Political Decentralization* increases the probability of dominant party emergence by 3 percentage points (almost doubling it) when leaders are rich in resource rents. This is because, under this condition, a 1-unit increase moves resources more into balance between the two sides. Conversely, when leaders have no resource rents, a 1-unit increase in the scale of *Political Decentralization* decreases the probability of dominant party emergence by ~2.5 percentage points, which is more than a 60 percent reduction from the baseline probability of dominant party emergence. The lower left panel in Figure 8.1 tells a similar story with the symmetric marginal effects; a 1-unit increase in *Log Rents* increases the probability of dominant party emergence when *Political Decentralization* is high but decreases it when *Political Decentralization* is low.[15]

Finally, the predicted probabilities in the lower panel of Table 8.3 paint the same picture; the predicted probability of dominant party emergence is highest (.157) when *Political Decentralization* and *Log Rents* are both high and, thus, balanced. Thus, when using these more direct proxies of leader and elite strength, we reach the same findings as before: dominant parties are most likely to emerge when resources are balanced between

---

[15] *Marginal Effects* are smaller in this panel, because *Log Rents* is scaled in smaller units (0–18).

leaders and elites and less likely when either side is disproportionately strong relative to the other.

8.5 Discussion and Conclusion

The evidence presented in this chapter suggests that dominant parties are most likely to form when political resources in a country are balanced between leaders and elites. While I do find, as previous authors do, evidence that dominant parties form in response to pressures from forces in society, the findings suggest that the process of dominant party formation also involves relations between leaders and elites. When elites are strong in resources, such as local political autonomy and clientelist networks, and leaders are weak in resources, dominant parties are unlikely to emerge. In addition, when leaders are made strong by a growing economy and natural resource revenues, and elites are weak in resources, dominant parties are unlikely to emerge. But when resources are balanced between leaders and elites, dominant parties are most likely to emerge.

This chapter also helps us identify the conditions under which resource rents undermine authoritarian rule. When elites are weak, natural resource wealth will lead leaders to eschew institution building, which, in turn, may weaken the regime in the long term (e.g. Gandhi and Przeworski 2007). Under this scenario, resource rents can make authoritarian regimes more vulnerable to collapse, as others in the literature have suggested (Haber and Menaldo 2011). And yet, we also found that if elites are strong, then natural resource wealth may make it more likely that dictators (and elites) will invest in a dominant party, which, in turn, may extend the regime's life span. Thus, resource rents are not always associated with weak authoritarian institutions and can bolster authoritarian rule, as much of the literature suggests (Ross 2001, Smith 2004).

The analysis also has important limitations, however. Making causal inferences on the basis of cross-national regressions is always difficult. The correlations revealed here are suggestive of the causal story that I have sketched, but endogeneity problems abound in analyses such as this. I have made efforts to alleviate concerns about the most obvious endogeneity problems, but one can never be sure that unobserved factors are not biasing the results. I am encouraged, however, by the fact that these results are consistent with the case studies in previous chapters.

In addition, the measures of elite and leader resources that I have developed are noisy. For this reason as well, we should be cautious about the findings. At the same time, the noisiness of these measures should increase standard errors and make insignificant results more likely. So it is encouraging that significant results were obtained.

Finally, I have focused here on the origins of dominant parties, but the findings beg important questions about the duration of dominant parties. I suspect that some of the same factors that lead dominant parties to emerge can also help explain their persistence, but it may also be that dominant parties persist for other reasons. This seems likely given that parties themselves become actors in their own right after they are formed. Surely the institutional features of the party must matter a great deal. This is an area for future research.

9 Conclusion

9.1 Summary

This book began with a puzzle: if dominant parties stabilize authoritarian regimes, then why do only some leaders build them? In an attempt to answer this question, I developed an argument for why dominant parties emerge (and fail to emerge) when and where they do. I began by observing that the key actors in many authoritarian regimes were leaders, on the one hand, and elites, on the other. I then noted that these actors faced a set of commitment problems. Leaders want to make sure that elites will be loyal, a goal they might achieve by promising to channel spoils to elites in a dependable, routine fashion. But leaders have no way to make those promises credible. Elites, for their part, want dependable access to the spoils distributed by leaders, a goal that they could achieve if leaders knew that elites would remain loyal. But elites find it difficult to pledge their loyalty to leaders credibly.

Mutual investment in a third-party institution could help solve this commitment problem. In particular, a dominant party system, with its mechanisms for distributing spoils in a rule-governed manner, could make these commitments credible. But it seemed clear that this approach, on its own, could not explain dominant party emergence. Instead, it was only a functionalist exposition of the benefits that dominant parties could provide. After all, leaders and elites in any country could conceivably invest in a dominant party institution and solve their commitment problem. Why didn't they? Here I felt compelled to look at the incentives of actors to seek cooperation with the other side. I noted that when leaders are very strong relative to elites their incentives to seek cooperation with elites are few, and they are tempted to defect from any bargain with elites that would limit their freedom of maneuver. Therefore, strong leaders are hesitant to invest in a dominant party.

But there are also times when leaders simply cannot construct a dominant party because elites are too strong. When elites are strong in autonomous resources, they value cooperation with leaders less. Thus, when elites are strong, they are hesitant to link their fates to a centralized dominant party.

Hence, in contrast to existing work, I have argued that the likelihood of dominant party emergence depends not just on the calculations of leaders, but also on the calculations and strength of other elites. Dominant parties only emerge when elites are strong enough that leaders need to co-opt them, but not so strong that they themselves are loath to link their fates to a dominant party.

The book examined this argument across six empirical chapters. No single piece of evidence was definitive, but by examining multiple streams of evidence, I have tried to convince readers that the argument holds weight. In Chapters 3 and 4, I compared the nonemergence of a strong ruling party in 1990s era Russia with the emergence of a dominant party under Putin after 2001. In the 1990s, Russia's regional elites built strong political machines and were reluctant to relinquish their autonomy to a centralized ruling party. Recognizing that these elites were not dependable allies, the Kremlin undermined its own parties of power in order to preclude wasting effort and resources on them.

Circumstances changed in the early 2000s, however. The Kremlin was now in a stronger bargaining position because of increased revenues from hydrocarbon sales, sustained economic growth, and Putin's popularity. Thus, for elites, the benefits of cooperation had increased considerably. But at the same time, the Kremlin still needed to co-opt Russia's elites because the latter sat atop strong political machines that made them powerful purveyors of political stability. Thus, the Kremlin sanctioned the creation of United Russia, a dominant party that would channel resources and careers to elites. In turn, elites tied their fates to the dominant party.

Chapter 5 examined how that dominant party worked in the 2000s. In particular, I showed how the dominant party system benefits both the Kremlin and elites, and how the two sides have made commitments to that system. Because of these benefits and commitments, both sides developed an interest in the preservation of the system. The Kremlin came to depend on United Russia for electoral support and the maintenance of elite cohesion. Meanwhile, many elites began to rely on United Russia for the provision of spoils, especially in legislatures. The Kremlin did not want to provoke elite discord by dismantling the party, and elites did not want to jeopardize their access to spoils by defecting.

While United Russia did not exercise direct collective control over Putin in the 2000s, it was something more than an institutional shell. It served as a bundle of rules, norms, and agreements that structured the incentives of each side to cooperate. The party provided an institutional

9.1 Summary

framework for the distribution of spoils among regime supporters, especially in legislatures. And as a disciplined party, it has helped the regime maintain elite cohesion, thus becoming a key pillar of regime stability in Putin era Russia.

Since one of the primary innovations of this study was to introduce elites into the equation of dominant party formation, I also wanted to delve deeper into their choices in order to elucidate some of the key causal mechanisms in my argument. I endeavored to show, at the individual level, that elites invest in dominant parties when the benefits of cooperation with state leaders outweigh the costs of relinquishing their own autonomous resources. To do this, I needed a setting where variation in elite dominant party affiliation decisions could be observed. What was needed was an emergent dominant party, which elites were gradually joining. Russia in the early 2000s was a perfect setting for this. My framework suggested that when the balance of power is shifting from elites to leaders, then those elites weakest in resources should be the first to join the party. With fewer autonomous resources, they have less to lose by linking their fates to the dominant party. In Chapters 6 and 7, I showed this to be case. Specifically, governors who sat atop strong political machines joined United Russia later than those without such resources. Moreover, regional businessmen who headed firms that were dependent on the state joined United Russia earlier than those who headed firms that were autonomous from the state. Thus, Russia's governors and regional legislators chose when to join on the basis of calculations about the costs and benefits of relinquishing their autonomous resources to a dominant party. Those with more such resources were less likely to link their fates to United Russia. These findings lend credence, I think, to a theory of dominant party formation that is predicated on the incentives of elites to join a dominant party.

The main empirical focus of this book was Russia, and it is my hope that the insights drawn from the close examination of this case may illuminate other cases of dominant party emergence. But in order to probe the generalizability of my argument directly, I also attempted to analyze how the balance of resources between leaders and elites affected the likelihood of dominant party emergence in a global sample of non-democracies. Recognizing significant data limitations, I introduced, in Chapter 8, a scale of regional elite strength based on (1) historical patterns of political decentralization, (2) the dispersion of population across a country's territory, and (3) regionally concentrated ethnic minorities. Leaders, I argued, were strong relative to elites when (1) they ruled in the presence of strong economic growth and/or (2) they controlled access to natural resource revenues. I found evidence that dominant parties are most likely to emerge when resources are balanced between the two sides.

Many factors influence dominant party formation, and I suffer no illusion that mine is the only explanation. Existing social explanations are also important (e.g. Huntington 1970, Smith 2005). I also noted that my argument was of less utility for explaining dominant party origins when elements of the party organization predate the regime, as is the case in many revolutionary regimes. At the same time, my theory improves our understanding of why dominant parties do and do not emerge in many countries around the world. For instance, it can help us understand why dominant parties have emerged in a number of resource rich countries – e.g. Russia, Angola, Venezuela, Kazakhstan, and Nigeria – even though some existing explanations predict that resource rich dictators would undermine regime institutions. Resource wealth may facilitate the construction of a dominant party if it tips the balance of resources toward leaders and gives strong elites an incentive to seek cooperation with the regime. This implies that authoritarian institutions can exist in resource rich regimes. At the same time, as existing explanations predict, resource wealth may make dominant parties less likely if elites are weak. In this case, leaders need less cooperation with elites and will be reluctant to invest in a dominant party.

In addition, my explanation helps us understand why leaders in countries with unruly regional elites have been unable to build strong regime parties. Thus, for example, it might help explain why Brazilian President Getulio Vargas was unable to consolidate a single dominant party during either the Estado Novo period or the postwar electoral period. It also may help explain why Nigeria's military rulers never built a ruling party in the 1980s or early 1990s. In Ukraine, it sheds light on why both Leonid Kuchma and Viktor Yaunkovych governed with shifting coalitions of weak pro-regime parties, rather than constructing a dominant party. In each of these cases, regime leaders were confronted by powerful regional barons and oligarchs who did not want to be under the thumb of a centralized ruling party.

Some of the theoretical arguments developed in this book could also shed light on the process of party formation in democracies. After all, leaders and elites in all regimes would like to reap gains from cooperation, and parties can help. Moreover, all politicians want autonomy and parties are a restriction on autonomy. Thus, there are similar dynamics at play. But several conditions make this theory less applicable in democratic settings. First, non-democracies are typically characterized by a much higher level of institutional fluidity, such that the party system can be restructured at will by leaders and elites. In established democracies, politicians are much more constrained by existing political parties, voter attachments, social organizations, and institutional rules. I suspect that explanations for one-party dominance in democracies will have more relation to social factors and electoral competition (e.g. Pempel 1990, Scheiner 2006).

I also think that my argument is better suited to explaining the creation of dominant parties than it is to explaining the duration of dominant parties. Once a dominant party is created, the party institution changes the incentive structures of actors and may even change the relevant actors themselves. Moreover, once a party is established, variations in opposition strategy and the determinants of social support become important factors (e.g. Greene 2007, Magaloni 2006).

Nonetheless, since almost all dominant party regimes have a leader – a first among equals at least – and elites play an important role in all autocratic politics, I think that insights about dominant party duration can be gleaned from the commitment framework developed in this book. Indeed, my theory does not predict that dominant parties, once formed, will remain forever stable. A given set of dominant party institutions makes cooperation an equilibrium for a given distribution of resources between leaders and elites. Exogenous changes (e.g. a drop in oil prices, an economic crisis, the death of a leader, or a scandal) may alter that balance of resources to such an extent that existing institutions are no longer sufficient to solve the commitment problem. This is one way that dominant party institutions may break down in a fashion that is not only consistent with, but, in fact, predicted by my theory. I suspect that the design of dominant party institutions will play a major role in determining the long-term stability of these regimes. Future work could profit by looking at how variation in the institutional structure of dominant parties affects their ability to solve the commitment problem and, thus, remain stable.

9.2 A New Era? United Russia after the 2011–2012 Elections

Much of this book has focused on the *emergence* of United Russia as a dominant party. And while my argument is not designed to explain the evolution of United Russia, the theoretical framework in this book also sheds some light on recent developments in Russia's party system, including both moves to weaken United Russia and steps taken to preserve it.

In early 2011, the popularity ratings of both Putin and United Russia began to slip. The share of the electorate prepared to vote for United Russia declined from just above 60 percent at the end of 2010 to 51 percent in December 2011. Putin's approval rating, meanwhile, dropped from 79 percent at the end of 2010 to 63 percent at the end of 2011.[1] In a bid to expand its electorate ahead of the 2011–2012 election season, the Kremlin created, in May 2011, the All-Russian People's Front (ONF), an umbrella organization of political parties, social movements, and trade unions. United Russia formed the core of the ONF, and much of its top leadership was drawn from the party, but the front also included nongovernmental organizations that were not a part of UR. According to Putin, the main goal of the ONF was to provide United Russia with "new ideas, new suggestions, and new faces."[2] In a move that angered many long-standing UR cadres, nonpartisan ONF members were allowed to run on UR lists.[3]

At United Russia's September 2011 congress, Putin announced that he would be running for president in March 2012. Putin also stated that, if elected, he would propose Medvedev as prime minister and suggested that Medvedev head the United Russia list for the 2011 elections. In addition to setting the stage for Putin's return to the Kremlin, the announcement transformed United Russia's Duma campaign, placing both Putin and Medvedev at its center.

Nevertheless, UR's ratings continued to drop through the summer and fall. A prominent blogger and anticorruption activist, Alexei Navalny, criticized United Russia relentlessly, labeling it a "party of thieves and swindlers" (*partiya zhulikov i vorov*), a moniker that quickly gained currency on the Internet. While few Russians knew who Navalny was, widespread dissatisfaction with United Russia among members of the liberal elite and in the blogosphere stained the party's image.

In December 2011, the party turned in a disappointing performance, capturing only 49.5 percent of the vote and a bare majority in the Duma. Moreover, as became clear soon after Election Day, considerable fraud had been required to obtain that vote total. In response to the fraud, thousands took to the streets. The protests, which swelled in Moscow to almost 100,000, were the largest in Russia since the collapse of the Soviet Union.

Fearing that the scandal-tainted party might damage his image, Putin decided to keep a safe distance from it during the presidential campaign. Although he was officially nominated by UR, the party's brand was noticeably absent on most campaign materials and UR did not organize

---

[1] Levada Center Omnibus Surveys. Various years.
[2] See "Why Putin Created the All-Russia People's Front" *Moscow Times*. May 11, 2011.
[3] However, nonpartisan ONF members had a hard time securing high spots on the list, and in the end, only about one-fifth of United Russia's legislative faction were from the ONF. See "Front protiv peremen" *Gazeta.ru*. August 24, 2011.

9.2 A New Era? United Russia after the 2011–2012 Elections

events for Putin. After securing victory in the March 2012 presidential elections, Putin announced in April that he would be stepping down as chairman of the party. Putin justified his decision as the continuation of a recent Russian political tradition: "It has become common practice for us that the president is an 'above-party' figure. The Constitution does not prohibit the President from being a member of a party, but in the spirit of our political traditions, the President should be a consolidating figure for all political forces, for all citizens of the country."[4] But it was clear to most that Putin wanted to distance himself from the party's tarnished image.[5]

Putin did not disavow the party, however, noting that he would continue "not only to cooperate with, but also to work closely with" UR and that he expected the party to maintain its "leadership" in the party system.[6] In May, Putin spoke once again at the party congress and proposed that UR select Medvedev to replace him as party chairman. In October 2013, Putin again attended United Russia's conference but limited his participation to a one-hour meeting with the heads of primary cells and did not address the delegates.

Putin's moves to distance himself from United Russia prompted speculation in 2012–2013 that the party might be disbanded or replaced by the ONF.[7] But UR did not collapse. In both the 2012 and 2013 regional elections, the party performed better than expected, achieving vote and seat totals on par with the late 2000s (see Figure 4.2). And as the data in Chapter 5 show, significant defections from the party did not materialize. Moreover, the regime has continued to privilege United Russia members when making appointments. Eighty-one percent of the governors appointed (or elected) between 2012 and 2015 were party members.

Putin, while distancing himself from UR in front of the electorate, was keen to give signals to the *elite* that UR would not be discarded. Answering a question about the future of the party during a meeting with political scientists in February 2012, Putin stated:

United Russia as the basis of the State Duma is absolutely necessary… If [during the crisis] we had not had the ability to make legislative decisions quickly,

---

[4] The stenogram of the meeting where Putin made his announcement can be found on United Russia's Web site: http://er.ru/news/82334/.
[5] Another blow for the party occurred when several high-ranking officials in the presidential administration, including First Deputy Chief of Staff Vyacheslav Volodin and DIP head Oleg Morozov, froze their membership in the party. See "Kreml' sformiruyet kadrovyi reserv iz oppositsii" *Izvestiya* March 18, 2013.
[6] Ibid.
[7] "Election Lebedinnaya Pesnya Edinoi Rossii: kakova strategii vlasti na predstoyashikh vyborakh" Forbes.ru June 18, 2013. "Elections Show the End of One-Party System" *Moscow Times*. August 26, 2013.

we would not got through the crisis with such minimal losses. At that time we needed to make legislative decisions, of course professionally, but without chatter, without politicizing things. With United Russia's help we did this. Such a key, unified political force is need in this Duma as well.[8]

Months later, at a meeting of the ONF, Putin sought to dispel rumors that the UR faction would be disbanded or reconstituted on the basis of the ONF: "We need to maintain the unity of the United Russia faction in the State Duma, because this is what will give us the possibility to legislate in a normal regime. In parliament there is one leading political force – that is a guarantee that the legislative process will continue and move forward in a positive direction."[9]

Even though Putin was no longer chairman, party leaders continued to link the party to him, referring to him as the party's "founder and moral leader."[10] And after 2012, Putin continued to meet with party leaders behind closed doors and stage public events with UR primary participants.[11] Thus, the regime sought to reassure UR cadres that its commitment to spoil sharing with the party remained strong.

Other members of the inner circle sent similar signals. Medvedev, for instance, took an active role in party affairs. Unlike Putin, he became a party member, and since becoming chairman he has regularly presided over party functions, has met with party leaders at his residence, and often lectures at party training events.[12] Kremlin ideologues and party leaders meanwhile set out on a public relations campaign to dispel rumors that United Russia was going to be discarded.[13]

Meanwhile, the party continued the party building initiatives that it had begun before the 2011 elections. In particular, it sought to expand its organizational reach at the local level. By December 2013 it held 180,000 of the 250,000 municipal council seats in Russia. Of Russia's 22,755 municipal district heads, 17,383 were UR members. In June 2012, the party created a permanent "party school" to train cadres in

---

[8] Stenogram of Prime Minister Vladimir Putin's Meeting with Political Scientists. February 6, 2012. Accessed online: http://premier.gov.ru/events/news/18008/.
[9] Report on Putin's Meeting with Coordinating Council of All-Russia People's Front. April 3, 2012. Accessed online at http://er.ru/news/80101/
[10] See "Pyat' Mifov o Edinoi Rossii" *Nezavisimaya Gazeta*. December 2, 2013.
[11] See "Putin Provyol Zakrytuyu Vstrechu c Rukovodtsvom 'Edinoi Rossii'" RBK Daily. October 1, 2015 and "Vladimir Putin postoyal za partiyu" *Kommersant.* April 21, 2016.
[12] See "Prem'er-lektor 'Edinoi Rossii'" *Gazeta.ru.* March 27, 2013, "Prem'er i edinorossii sverili plany" *Kommersant* April 30, 2013, and "Dmitry Medvedev prizval 'edinorossov' ne stesnyat'sya svoyei partii" *Kommersant* June 9, 2012.
[13] For example, see Stenogram of Radio Program "Polny Albats: Chto Proiskhodit s Edinoi Rossii" April 1, 2013. Accessed online www.echo.msk.ru/programs/albac/1043194-echo/.

9.2 A New Era? United Russia after the 2011–2012 Elections

the regions.[14] And in September 2014, the party instituted a reform requiring the heads of party executive committees in the regions to be full-time employees.[15]

The ONF's role, meanwhile, changed little between 2011 and 2016. It remained a broad-based front with United Russia at its core. It did not register as a political party, form legislative factions, or obtain the right to nominate candidates. In order to gain ballot access, ONF members must participate in United Russia's party primaries.[16]

The ONF was created as an attempt by the Kremlin to broaden and supplement the electoral appeal of United Russia. It sought to co-opt that part of the electorate that was supportive of Putin, but not United Russia. This is reflected in the front's focus on social organizations. According to ONF officials themselves, the front is intended to be "free of bureaucrats at all levels, in order to preserve its 'popular roots.'"[17] The co-optation and management of elites have remained within UR's purview.

The events described in the preceding pages are understandable in light of the commitment framework put forward in this book. United Russia's level of institutionalization reached its peak in 2010. But Putin had grown too strong, too fast over the course of the 2000s, and, as a result, the investments that the Kremlin had made in the dominant party system were not sufficient to prevent it from reneging on some of those commitments when the party's image was tarnished during the 2011–2012 election campaign. In particular, because United Russia did not exercise collective control over the executive branch, the party could not prevent the Kremlin from distancing itself when the party's rating dropped.

At the same time, Putin was unable and unwilling to jettison United Russia. The momentum behind 10 years of dominant party building was strong. Putin and other Kremlin leaders had made public commitments to the party that were difficult to rescind, and the Kremlin, lacking an alternative organization if UR was disbanded, relied on United Russia's organization to help it win elections. But even more importantly, United Russia had come to play a key role as a guarantor of elite cohesion. The dominant party helps the regime manage legislatures and contain elite discord. Discarding the party abruptly would have led to elite defections

---

[14] "'Edinaya Rossiya' reshila sozdat' partiinuyu shkolu" *Lenta.ru* June 1, 2012.
[15] "'Edinaya Rossiya'" vyyavlyayet sovmestitelei" *Kommersant* October 13, 2014.
[16] Between 2011 and 2016, UR gradually developed a primary system for choosing candidates. ONF members are allowed to run in those contests, but UR candidates usually win. See "Partii ne poidut v Gosdumu edinym 'Frontom'" *Kommersant.* July 29, 2015.
[17] "'Obsherossiskii Front' Vzyal Nizkii Start" *Kommersant* April 29, 2013.

and possibly even revolt. Ultimately, Putin had to send signals to the elite that he was sticking by United Russia, while searching for ways to win extra votes. Without signals from Putin that United Russia would continue to receive his support, elites surely would have defected. Thus, Putin was unwilling to turn the ONF into a political party.

As of this writing, United Russia remains Russia's dominant party. On the heels of the 2014 Ukraine crisis, patriotic sentiment rose sharply in Russia, leading to a meteoric rise in the popularity of both Putin and United Russia. At the same time, a precipitous drop in oil prices, combined with Western sanctions, has left Russia in its worst recession since the 1990s. The consequences for Russia's dominant party regime remain uncertain. It is possible that the recession will lead to an even sharper drop in United Russia's popularity than was seen in 2011–2012, potentially leading the Kremlin to take the risky step of abandoning United Russia or reconstituting the ruling party on the basis of the ONF. While the Kremlin still seems unable to renege on its commitments to UR at this time, the creation of the ONF as a contingency plan has made it easier to imagine that those commitments could be broken.

Alternatively, the recession may weaken Putin and strengthen regional elites. Such a dynamic might be exacerbated by recent institutional reforms that have given more autonomy to regional elites. In response to the protest movement's calls for political liberalization, direct gubernatorial elections were reintroduced in 2012. And in 2014, the Duma reformed its own electoral rules, reverting to the mixed electoral system (250 members elected on party lists and 250 members elected in single member districts) that it had used from 1993 to 2007. Since the SMD component favors large parties, the move was clearly aimed at boosting UR's seat totals.[18]

Direct elections may make governors harder to control and the SMD component will give governors more influence over Duma deputies.

---

[18] In the early 2000s, the main electoral challenge for United Russia arose from powerful independents (and their gubernatorial patrons). In the Duma, Russia's parties of power always had problems enforcing discipline on their SMD members. Thus, while building a dominant party, it made sense to eliminate the SMD portion of the ballot (e.g. see Smyth et al 2007). But once United Russia became established as a dominant party and the machines of regional elites became integrated into the party, it made sense to revert to a mixed system. As Diaz-Cayeros and Magaloni (2001) note, mixed electoral systems are advantageous for ruling parties because the SMD component "disproportionately rewards existing majorities," while the party list component gives opposition parties a disincentive to coordinate. Indeed, as Chapter 4 noted, United Russia's performance in the SMD portion of the ballot for regional elections improved dramatically over the course of the 2000s, such that by 2014, it was routinely winning 90 percent of those seats.

This, combined with a stagnant economy, could realign the balance of resources to where it was in the mid-2000s and call forth new commitments to the dominant party system. Alternatively, Putin may be so weakened by the recession that the balance of resources will come to resemble what it looked like in the 1990s, and regional elites may begin defecting from the regime.

At this point, United Russia seems capable of containing such defections, but a large exogenous shock could change the situation. The difficulty for regime leaders in Russia, or, it seems, in any electoral authoritarian regime, is that while the regime benefits from giving regional elites the autonomy to craft their own political machines, which can be used to help the regime win elections, elites can become difficult to control if they have too much autonomy.

The future of the ONF, meanwhile, is still unclear. It is possible that it could one day obtain some organizational structure of its own and eventually replace UR. But, as noted, such a strategy would entail grave risks for the ruling elite and only seems possible in a political crisis. Alternatively, United Russia could be superficially rebranded as the ONF. Such precedents exist in other autocracies. In 2012, the ruling party of Togo, the Rally of the Togolese People, was disbanded and reconstituted as the Union for the Republic. In Venezuela, Hugo Chavez transformed the ruling Fifth Republic Movement into a new ruling party, the United Socialist Party of Venezuela, in 2007. In Egypt, Sadat dissolved the Arab Socialist Union in 1977 and reconstituted the ruling party – with mostly the same members – as the National Democratic Party in 1978.

The most likely scenario is that the ONF will retain its role as a coalition of different groups with United Russia maintaining a dominant role at its center. Such national fronts are common in dominant party regimes, especially in the communist world. For example, the Chinese Communist Party is the central player in the United Front, a grouping of legally permitted parties in China. In Poland, the Front of National Unity served as the pro-regime coalition, with the Polish United Workers' Party at its center. In noncommunist countries, such arrangements exist as well. In Malaysia, the Barisian National Alliance has been in power since 1957, with UMNO, the ruling party, as its lead coalition partner. Russia's leadership is undoubtedly familiar with these arrangements, especially those in the former communist bloc.

9.3 Dominant Parties and Regime Breakdown

This study also has implications for several related research agendas. First, and perhaps most importantly, understanding dominant party origins provides insight into why some countries democratize, but others do not. If dominant parties extend the life span of authoritarian regimes, then understanding where those institutions get their start will help us better understand a country's prospects for democracy. In particular, this study can help make sense of regime trajectories after the "Third Wave." While many regimes that experienced political transition during the 1990s went on to democratize, many others backslid into electoral authoritarianism (e.g. Carothers 2002, Diamond 2002, Balzer 2003, Schedler 2006). In today's world, these electoral authoritarian regimes are by far the most common type of autocracy (Howard and Roessler 2006, Miller 2014), and recent work has suggested that such regimes are more stable when they have a strong ruling party (Levitsky and Way 2010). If this is the case, then the present study has the potential to advance the field by elucidating the factors that contribute to the emergence of strong ruling parties.

Previous studies have emphasized that some authoritarian leaders are unable to consolidate their rule because "the state is too weak and the government too fragmented" (Way 2002, 2005). This seems right, but as an explanation for authoritarian instability, it approximates the outcome that it seeks to explain. One way to improve such explanations is to identify the factors that make the state weak and government fragmented. In this regard, I have emphasized the importance of regional elites and the factors that make them strong.

This study offers a similar contribution to those works that emphasize "elite cohesion" as a factor influencing the longevity of authoritarian regimes (O'Donnell, Schmitter and Whitehead 1986, Przeworski 1991, Brownlee 2007). Some have argued that party institutions can help sustain elite cohesion in hard times (Haggard and Kaufman 1995, Geddes 2003, Brownlee 2007). This study provides us with a clearer view of the factors that make "elite cohesion" within the bonds of the party achievable.[19]

This study also improves our ability to identify the causal relationship between dominant parties and regime stability. One major problem in the new institutionalism is determining whether institutions exert an independent effect on outcomes that is separate from the circumstances that bring them into being. As Przeworski puts it, the danger is that "conditions shape institutions and institutions only transmit the causal effects of those conditions" (2004, 527).

In the case of dominant parties, we cannot know for certain whether dominant party institutions stabilize authoritarian regimes or whether

[19] See Slater (2010) for another perspective on this.

the conditions that generate dominant party institutions stabilize authoritarian regimes (e.g. Pepinsky 2014). What is needed in order to improve causal claims is an empirically robust explanation for dominant party emergence. Such an explanation will give us a fighting chance at sweeping out the effects of initial conditions when we analyze the effects of dominant parties.

9.4 Implications for Russian Politics

In this study, I have tried to draw the literature on Russian politics into a dialogue with the latest literature on authoritarian institutions. In the 1990s, scholars of Russian politics fruitfully engaged with disciplinary arguments about institution building, party development, voting behavior, and a range of other topics related to democratization. But as Russia has become more autocratic since 2000, Russia scholars have been slow to incorporate insights from the neo-institutional literature on authoritarianism. Similarly, that literature has largely missed out on the data and perspective that the countries of the former Soviet Union can offer. I hope that this work will inspire other scholars of Russian politics to engage with this literature and bring the Russian case to bear on theories of modern authoritarian politics.

Consistent with this approach, I take authoritarian institutions in Russia seriously. Just as scholars a generation ago were wrong to dismiss autocratic institutions as mere "window dressing," students of contemporary Russian politics would be wrong to dismiss Russia's political institutions out of hand. Elections allow the Kremlin to gather information on elites and society (Reuter and Robertson 2012). Legislatures facilitate the sharing of spoils and help defuse social opposition (Remington 2008, Reuter and Robertson 2015, Szakonyi 2015). Systemic opposition parties help the regime co-opt opposition forces (March 2009). And, as this book has shown, United Russia helps the regime win social support and manage relations with key elites.

Russia is too complex a society to be ruled by force and patrimony alone. Russia's presidents require cooperation from governors, oligarchs, opinion leaders, deputies, bureaucrats, and business elites. Putin needed Russia's elites, just as they needed him. This, it seems, is a recurring theme in Russian political history. Writing about clientelism in 16th century Russia, the historian Daniel Orlovsky draws a conclusion about Peter the Great that sounds familiar to observers of contemporary Russia:

It is now clear that Peter the Great did less to transform the "deep structures" of Russian institutional and political life than has been commonly thought. Peter, as would be the case with Lenin some 200 years later, was in large measure prisoner of inherited social and institutional determinants, despite the enormous personal and moral authority at his disposal. (1980, 183)

At first glance, Russia's autocrats appear to wield absolute power, but closer inspection often reveals that they are constrained by the social fabric that surrounds them.[20]

Achieving cohesive majorities among elite groups was a top priority for Putin. And while fraud, repression, coercion, and patronage are indeed tools that the regime employs to maintain control, elite cohesion is an intermediate factor that makes authoritarian rule possible. United Russia institutionalized this elite cohesion and made the regime more stable as a result. Speaking at United Russia's 2012 party congress, then–Ukrainian Prime Minister Nikolai Azarov enviously praised United Russia for "bringing stability to Russia."[21] As he stated, "You should cherish stability as you would your beloved and not let anything harm her. Our country has felt all the sad consequences of political instability." In Ukraine, neither Kuchma nor Yanukovych was able to rope Ukraine's unruly oligarchs and elites into a disciplined dominant party, and Yanukovych suffered the consequences on more than one occasion. Russia, on the other hand, has thus far avoided the "colored revolutions" that its leaders fear so much.

Many accounts, especially popular ones, treat Russia as a personalist autocracy or highlight the importance of informal institutions in post-Soviet politics (e.g. Wilson 2005, Ledeneva 2006, Judah 2014, Baturo and Elkink 2016). Are such perspectives incommensurable with the one that I have offered? I do not believe so. It is no doubt true that informal institutions play a prominent role in Russian politics. And it is also true that President Putin's authority is, in part, based on charismatic and personalist appeals. But it is also important to maintain a comparative perspective. In Haile Selassie's Ethiopia, the emperor personally appointed every postmaster and police constable in the country and was accountable only to God. Putin's Russia does not approach this level of personalism. When one looks closely at its political institutions, it becomes clear that Russia is much less personalist than most regimes that are usually classed as "personalist."[22] It should not be classed in the same category as personalist dictatorships such as Gaddafi's Libya,

[20] See Voslensky (1984) for a discussion of this under Stalin.
[21] "Azarov posovetoval rossiyanam berech' stabil'nost' 'kak zenitsu oka'" *UNIAN.net* May 26, 2012 Accessed online: www.unian.net/politics/654613-azarov-posovetoval-rossiyanam-berech-stabilnost-kak-zenitsu-oka.html.
[22] Indeed, these impressions are confirmed by recent studies that measure personalism using observable indicators. Using a Bayesian measurement model, Gandhi et al. (2014)

9.4 Implications for Russian Politics

Bokassa's Central African Empire, Franco's Spain, Mobutu's Zaire, Saddam Hussein's Iraq, or Idi Amin's Uganda, as some popular accounts would have us believe.

I suspect that the prevalence of such exaggerations has something to do with Russia's history and geographic location. Given its cultural and spatial proximity to the Western world, Russia's political institutions are often compared to those that exist in Western democracies.[23] Such comparisons fuel perceptions that Russia is not a "normal" country, when, in fact, careful comparative analyses reveal that Russia's economic and political institutions function about as well as those in other middle-income countries (see Shleifer and Treisman 2005).

The perspective endorsed in this book does not seek to suggest that informal institutions do not matter in Russia or that all political exchange is governed by formal rules. Rather, I simply hold to the view that Russia's authoritarian institutions have some significant effects on important political outcomes. They perform a role similar to the role that such institutions perform in other non-democratic countries. In this way, my account shares common ground with recent work that sees meaning in Russia's formal political processes (e.g. Sakwa 2011, Hale 2014, Gel'man 2008, Smyth et al 2007, Greene 2014, Remington 2014).

---

find that Russia was the 11th *least* personalist regime of 100 regimes with personalist characteristics identified by Geddes et al. (2014).

[23] This is all the more true since Russia flirted with democracy in the 1990s and its political institutions were analyzed using conceptual frameworks designed for the study of democracies.

References

Aburamoto, Mari. 2010. "Who Takes Care of the Residents? United Russia and the Regions Facing the Monetization of L'goty." *Acta Slavica Iaponica*, 28: 101–115.
Acemoglu, Daron, and James A. Robinson. 2006. *The Economic Origins of Dictatorship and Democracy*. Cambridge: Cambridge University Press.
Aldrich, John Herbert. 1995. *Why Parties? The Origin and Transformation of Political Parties in America*. Chicago: University of Chicago Press.
Alina-Pisano, Jessica. 2010. "Social Contracts and Authoritarian Projects in the Post-Soviet Space: The Use of Administrative Resource." *Communist and Post-Communist Studies*, 43(4): 373–382.
Almond, Gabriel. 2006. "Introduction: A Functional Approach to Comparative Politics," in Almond, Gabriel and James Coleman, eds., *The Politics of Developing Areas*. Princeton: Princeton University Press.
Ames, Barry. 1970. "Bases of Support for Mexico's Dominant Party." *American Political Science Review*, 64(1): 153–167.
Andrews, Josephine. 2002. *When Majorities Fail: The Russian Parliament, 1990–1993*. Cambridge: Cambridge University Press.
Apter, David Ernest. 1965. *The Politics of Modernization*. Chicago: University of Chicago Press.
Arriola, Leonardo Rafael. 2012. *Multiethnic Coalitions in Africa: Business Financing of Opposition Election Campaigns*. New York: Cambridge University Press.
Åslund, Anders. 1995. *How Russia Became a Market Economy*. Washington, DC: Brookings Institution.
  2007. *How Capitalism Was Built: The Transformation of Central and Eastern Europe, Russia, and Central Asia*. Cambridge: Cambridge University Press.
Axelrod, Robert M. 1984. *The Evolution of Cooperation*. New York: Basic.
Bader, Max. 2011. "Hegemonic Political Parties in Post-Soviet Eurasia: Towards Party-Based Authoritarianism." *Communist and Post-Communist Studies*, 44(3): 189–197.
Baland, Jean-Marie, and James A. Robinson. 2008. "Land and Power: Theory and Evidence from Chile." *American Economic Review*, 98(5): 1737–1765.
Balzer, Harley. 2003. "Managed Pluralism: Vladimir Putin's Emerging Regime." *Post-Soviet Affairs*, 19(3): 189–227.
Barnett, A. Doak. 1968. *Cadres, Bureaucracy, and Political Power in Communist China*. New York: Columbia University Press.

Bates, Robert H. 1988. "Contra Contractarianism: Some Reflections on the New Institutionalism." *Politics and Society*, 16(2–3): 387–401.

Bates, Robert H., Avner Greif, Margaret Levi, Jean-Laurent Rosenthal, and Barry Weingast. 1998. *Analytic Narratives*. Princeton, NJ: Princeton University Press.

Baturin, Yuri M., A. L. Il'in, V. F. Kadatskii, V. V. Kostikov, M. A. Krasnov, A. Y. Lifshits, K. V. Nikiforov, L. G. Pikhoya, and Georgi A. Satarov. 2001. *Epokha Yel'tsina: ocherki politicheskoi istorii*. Moscow: Vagrius.

Baturo, Alexander, and Johan Elkink. 2016. "Dynamics of Regime Personalization and Patron-Client Networks in Russia, 1999–2014." *Post-Soviet Affairs*, 32(1).

Bayart, Jean Francois. 1989. *The State in Africa: The Politics of the Belly*. London: Longman.

Beck, Nathaniel, Jonathan Katz, and Richard Tucker. 1998. "Taking Time Seriously: Time-Series-Cross-Section Analysis with a Binary Dependent Variable." *American Journal of Political Science*, 42(4): 1260–1288.

Belin, Laura, and Orttung, Robert W. 1997. *The Russian Parliamentary Elections of 1995: The Battle for the Duma*. Armonk, NY: M. E. Sharpe.

Belonuchkin, Grigorii. 1997. "Sootnoshenie politicheskikh cil v Sovete Federatsii." *Panorama 39*. Available online at: http://www.panorama.ru/gazeta/p39sf.html

Berry, William D., Matt Golder, and Daniel Milton. 2012. "Improving Tests of Theories Positing Interaction." *Journal of Politics*, 74(3): 653–671.

Bienen, Henry. 1978. *Armies and Parties in Africa*. New York: Africana.

Blaustein, Albert, and Gilbert Flanz. 2007. *Constitutions of Countries of the World*. Dobbs Ferry, NY: Oceana.

Blaydes, Lisa. 2011. *Elections and Distributive Politics in Mubarak's Egypt*. New York: Cambridge University Press.

Bogatyreva, Lyudmila. 2013. *Politicheskiye partii v sisteme v otnoshenii "tsentr-regiony" v 2000-e gg (na primere TsFO)*. Ph.D. Dissertation. Moscow State University.

Boix, Carles. 2003. *Democracy and Redistribution*. Cambridge: Cambridge University Press.

Boix, Carles, and Milan Svolik. 2013. "The Foundations of Limited Authoritarian Government: Institutions and Power-Sharing in Dictatorships." *Journal of Politics*, 75(2): 300–316.

Box-Steffensmeier, Janet M., and Bradford S. Jones. 2004 *Event-History Modeling: A Guide for Social Scientists*. Cambridge: Cambridge University Press.

Brambor, Thomas, William Roberts Clark, and Matt Golder. 2006. "Understanding Interaction Models: Improving Empirical Analyses." *Political Analysis*, 14(1): 63–82.

Brownlee, Jason. 2007. *Authoritarianism in an Age of Democratization*. Cambridge: Cambridge University Press.

Brudny, Yitzhak M. 1993. "The Dynamics of 'Democratic Russia', 1990–1993." *Post-Soviet Affairs*, 9(2): 141–170.

Brudny, Yitzhak. 1996. "In Pursuit of the Russian Presidency: Why and How Yeltsin Won the 1996 Presidential Election." *Communist and Post-Communist Studies*, 30(3): 255–275.

References

Buckley, Noah, Timothy Frye, Guzel Garifullina, and Ora John Reuter. 2014. "The Political Economy of Russian Gubernatorial Election and Appointment." *Europe-Asia Studies*, 66(8): 1213–1233.

Bueno de Mesquita, Bruce, and Alastair Smith, Randolph Siverson, and James D. Morrow. 2003. *The Logic of Political Survival*. Cambridge, MA: MIT Press.

Bunce, Valerie. 2003. "Rethinking Recent Democratization: Lessons from the Post-Communist Experience." *World Politics*, 55(2): 167–192.

Burns, John P., ed. 1989. *The Chinese Communist Party's Nomenklatura System: A Documentary Study of Party Control and Leadership Selection, 1979–1984*. Armonk, NY: M. E. Sharpe.

Burton, Michael, Richard Gunther, and John Higley. 1992. "Introduction: Elite Transformations and Democratic Regimes," in Higley, John, and Richard Gunther, eds., *Elites and Democratic Consolidation in Latin America and Southern Europe*. Cambridge: Cambridge University Press, 1–37.

Cappelli, Ottorino. 1988. "Changing Leadership Perspectives on Centre-Periphery Relations," in Lane, David Stuart, ed., *Elites and Political Power in the USSR*. Aldershot, UK: Elgar, 245–266.

Carothers, Thomas. 2002. "The End of the Transition Paradigm." *Journal of Democracy*, 13(2): 5–21.

Carter, David B., and Curtis S. Signorino. 2010. "Back to the Future: Modeling Time Dependence in Binary Data." *Political Analysis*, 18(3): 271–292.

Castaneda, Jorge G. 2000. *Perpetuating Power: How Mexican Presidents Were Chosen*. New York: New Press.

Chaisty, Paul. 2006. *Legislative Politics and Economic Power in Russia*. Basingstoke, UK: Palgrave Macmillan.

   2013. "The Preponderance and Effects of Sectoral Ties in the State Duma." *Europe-Asia Studies*, 65(4): 717–736.

Chubb, Judith. 1982. *Patronage, Power and Poverty in Southern Italy: A Tale of Two Cities*. Cambridge: Cambridge University Press.

Clapham, Christopher S. 1982. "The Politics of Failure: Clientelism, Political Instability and National Integration in Liberia and Sierra Leone," in Clapham, Christopher S., ed., *Private Patronage and Public Power: Political Clientelism and the Modern State*. London: Frances Pinter, 76–92.

Cleves, Mario A., William W. Gould, and Roberto G. Gutierrez. 2004. *An Introduction to Survival Analysis Using Stata*, rev. ed. College Station, TX: Stata Press.

Coleman, James Smoot, and Carl Gustav Rosberg. 1966. *Political Parties and National Integration in Tropical Africa*. Berkeley: University of California Press.

Collett, David. 1994. *Modelling Survival Data in Medical Research*. London: Chapman.

Colton, Timothy. 1998. "Introduction: The 1993 Election and the New Russian Politics," in Colton, Timothy, and Jerry Hough, eds., *Growing Pains: Russian Democracy and the Elections of 1993*. Washington, DC: Brookings Institution.

   2008. *Yeltsin: A Life*. New York: Basic.

Colton, Timothy, and Henry E. Hale. 2009. "The Putin Vote: Presidential Electorates in a Hybrid Regime." *Slavic Review*, 68(3): 473–503.

Colton, Timothy, and Jerry Hough, eds. 1998. *Growing Pains: Russian Democracy and the Elections of 1993*. Washington, DC: Brookings Institution.

Cox, Gary W. 1997. *Making Votes Count: Strategic Coordination in the World's Electoral Systems*. Cambridge: Cambridge University Press. *Systems*.

Cox, Gary W., and Scott Morgenstern. 2002. "Epilogue: Latin America's Reactive Assemblies and Proactive Presidents," in Morgenstern, Scott, and Benito Nacif, eds., *Legislative Politics in Latin America*. Cambridge: Cambridge University Press, 446–468.

Dahl, Robert. 1961. *Who Governs? Democracy and Power in an American City*. New Haven, CT: Yale University Press.

Daniels, Robert Vincent. 1960. *The Conscience of the Revolution: Communist Opposition in Soviet Russia*. Cambridge, MA: Harvard University Press.

1971. "Soviet Politics since Khrushchev," in Strong, John W., ed., *The Soviet Union under Brezhnev and Kosygin: The Transition Years*. New York: Van Nostrand Reinhold, 16–25.

D'Anieri, Paul. 2007. *Understanding Ukrainian Politics: Power, Politics, and Institutional Design*. Armonk, NY: M. E. Sharpe.

Diamond, Larry Jay. 2002. "Elections without Democracy: Thinking about Hybrid Regimes." *Journal of Democracy*, 13(2): 21–35.

Diaz-Cayeros, Alberto, and Beatriz Magaloni. 2001. "Party Dominance and the Logic of Electoral Design in Mexico's Transition to Democracy." *Journal of Theoretical Politics*, 13(3): 271–293.

Dickson, Bruce. 1993. "The Lessons of Defeat: The Reorganization of the Kuomintang on Taiwan, 1950–92" *The China Quarterly*, 133: 56–84.

Duncan Baretta, Silvio R., and John Markoff. 1987. "Brazil's *Abertura*: A Transition from What to What?" in Malloy, James M., and Mitchell A. Seligson, eds., *Authoritarians and Democrats: The Politics of Regime Transition in Latin America*. Pittsburgh: University of Pittsburgh Press, 43–65.

Easter, Gerald. 2012. *Capital, Coercion, and Post-Communist States*. Ithaca, NY: Cornell University Press.

Eckstein, Harry. 1975. "Case Studies and Theory in Political Science," in Greenstein, Fred I., and Nelson W. Polsby, eds., *Political Science. Vol. 7. Scope and Theory. Handbook of Political Science*. Reading, MA: Addison-Wesley, 94–137.

Elkins, Zachary, Thomas Ginsburg, and James Melton. 2009. *The Endurance of National Constitutions*. New York: Cambridge University Press.

Elster, Jon. 1979. *Ulysses and the Sirens: Studies in Rationality and Irrationality*. Cambridge: Cambridge University Press.

1998. "A Plea for Mechanisms," in Hedström, Peter, and Richard Swedberg, eds., *Social Mechanisms: An Analytical Approach to Social Theory*. Cambridge: Cambridge University Press, 45–73.

Fainsod, Merle. 1953. *How Russia Is Ruled*. Cambridge, MA: Harvard University Press.

Fearon, James. 1995. "Rationalist Explanations for War." *International Organization*, 49(3): 379–414.

1997. "Signaling Foreign Policy Interests: Tying Hands versus Sinking Costs." *Journal of Conflict Resolution*, 41(1): 68–90.

2003. "Ethnic and Cultural Diversity by Country." *Journal of Economic Growth*, 8(2): 195–222.

Finer, Samuel. 1967. "The One-Party Regimes in Africa: Reconsiderations." *Government and Opposition*, 2(4): 491–509.
Fish, Steven. 2005. *Democracy Derailed in Russia: The Failure of Open Politics*. New York: Cambridge University Press.
Fish, M. Steven and Matthew Kroenig. 2009. *The Handbook of National Legislatures: A Global Survey*. New York: Camridge.
Frye, Timothy. 2003. "Markets, Democracy, and New Private Business in Russia." *Post-Soviet Affairs*, 19(1): 24–45.
  2004. "Credible Commitment and Property Rights: Evidence from Russia." *American Political Science Review*, 98(3): 453–466.
  2006. "Ownership, Voting, and Job Creation in Russia." *European Journal of Political Economy*, 22(2): 452–471.
  2010. *Building States and Markets after Communism: The Perils of Polarized Democracy*. New York: Cambridge University Press.
Frye, Timothy, Ora John Reuter, and David Szakonyi. 2014. "Political Machines at Work: Voter Mobilization and Electoral Mobilization in the Workplace." *World Politics*, 66(2): 195–228.
Gandhi, Jennifer. 2008. *Political Institutions under Dictatorship*. New York: Cambridge University Press.
Gandhi, Jennifer, and Adam Przeworski. 2006. "Cooperation, Cooptation, and Rebellion under Dictatorships." *Economics and Politics*, 18(1): 1–26.
  2007. "Authoritarian Institutions and the Survival of Autocrats." *Comparative Political Studies*, 40(11): 1279–1301.
Geddes, Barbara. 1999a. "Authoritarian Breakdown: Empirical Test of a Game Theoretic Argument." Working Paper. Prepared for the Annual Meeting of the American Political Science Association.
  1999b. "What Do We Know about Democratization after Twenty Years?" *Annual Review of Political Science*, 2: 115–144.
  2003. *Paradigms and Sand Castles: Theory Building and Research Design in Comparative Politics*. Ann Arbor: University of Michigan Press.
Geddes, Barbara, and John Zaller. 1989. "Sources of Popular Support for Authoritarian Regimes." *American Journal of Political Science*, 33(2): 319–347.
Geddes, Barbara, Joseph Wright, and Erica Frantz. 2014. "Autocratic Breakdown and Regime Transitions: A New Data Set." *British Journal of Political Science*. 12(2): 313–331.
Geertz, Clifford. 1965. *The Social History of an Indonesian Town*. Cambridge, MA: MIT Press.
Gehlbach, Scott. 2006. "The Consequences of Collective Action: An Incomplete Contracts Approach." *American Journal of Political Science*, 50(3): 802–823.
Gehlbach, Scott, and Philip Keefer. 2012. "Private Investment and the Institutionalization of Collective Action in Autocracies: Ruling Parties and Legislatures." *Journal of Politics*, 74(2): 621–635.
Gel'man, Vladimir. 2006. "From "Feckless Pluralism" to "Dominant Power Politics?' The Transformation of Russia's Party System." *Democratization*, 13(4): 545–561.
  2008. "Party Politics in Russia: From Competition to Hierarchy." *Europe-Asia Studies*, 60(6): 913–930.

References

Gel'man, Vladimir and Sergei Ryzhenkov. 2011. "Local Regimes, Sub-National Governance and the 'Power Vertical' in Contemporary Russia." *Europe-Asia Studies*, 63 (3): 449–465.

Gerring, John. 2007. "Is There a (Viable) Crucial Case Method?" *Comparative Political Studies*, 40(3): 231–253.

Gill, Graeme. 2012. "The Decline of a Dominant Party and the Destabilization of Electoral Authoritarianism?" *Post-Soviet Affairs*, 28(2): 449–471.

Glubotskii, Alexander, and Alexander Kynev. 2003. "Partiinaya sostavlayuschaya zakondatel'nykh sobranii rossisskikh regionov." *Polis*, (6): 71–87.

Golosov, Grigorii V. 1997. "Russian Political Parties and the 'Bosses': Evidence from the 1994 Provincial Elections in Western Siberia." *Party Politics*, 3(1): 5–21.

  1999. "Political Parties in the 1993–1996 Elections," in Gel'man, Vladimir, and Grigorii V. Golosov, eds., *Elections in Russia, 1993–1996: Analyses, Documents and Data*. Berlin: Edition Sigma, 99.

  2000. "Gubernatorii i partiinaya politika." *Pro et Contra*, 5(1): 96–108.

  2002. "Party Support or Personal Resources? Factors of Success in the Plurality Portion of the 1999 National Legislative Elections in Russia." *Communist and Post-Communist Studies*, 35(1): 23–38.

  2003. *Political Parties in the Regions of Russia*. Boulder, CO: Lynne Rienner.

  2011. "Russia's Regional Legislative Elections, 2003–2007: Authoritarianism Incorporated." *Europe-Asia Studies*, 63(3): 397–414.

Goode, John Paul. 2007. "The Puzzle of Putin's Gubernatorial Appointments." *Europe-Asia Studies*, 59(3): 365–399.

Greene, Kenneth F. 2007. *Why Dominant Parties Lose: Mexico's Democratization in Comparative Perspective*. Cambridge: Cambridge University Press.

  2010. "The Political Economy of Authoritarian Single Party Dominance." *Comparative Political Studies*, 43(7): 807–834.

Greene, Samuel A, 2014. *Moscow in Movement: Power and Opposition in Putin's Russia*. Palo Alto, CA: Stanford University Press.

Greif, Avner. 1992. "Institutions and International Trade: Lessons from the Commercial Revolution." *American Economic Review*, 82(2): 128–133.

Greif, Avner, Paul Milgrom, and Barry Weingast. 1994. "Coordination, Commitment, and Enforcement: The Case of the Merchant Guild." *Journal of Political Economy*, 102(4): 745–776.

Haber, Stephen, and Victor Menaldo. 2011. "Do Natural Resources Fuel Authoritarianism? A Reappraisal of the Resource Curse." *American Political Science Review*, 105(1): 1–26.

Haggard, Stephan, and Robert R. Kaufman. 1996. *The Political Economy of Democratic Transitions*. Princeton, NJ: Princeton University Press.

Hagopian, Frances. 1996. *Traditional Politics and Regime Change in Brazil*. Cambridge: Cambridge University Press.

Hale, Henry E. 1998. "Bashkortostan: The Logic of Ethnic Machine Politics and Democratic Consolidation," in Colton, Timothy, and Jerry Hough, eds., *Growing Pains: Russian Democracy and the Elections of 1993*. Washington, DC: Brookings Institution, 539–636.

  2000. "The Parade of Sovereignties: Testing Theories of Secession in the Soviet Setting." *British Journal of Political Science*, 30(1): 31–56.

2003. "Explaining Machine Politics in Russia's Regions: Economy, Ethnicity, and Legacy." *Post-Soviet Affairs.* 19(3): 228–263.

2004a. "The Origins of United Russia and the Putin Presidency: The Role of Contingency in Party-System Development." *Demokratizatsiya: The Journal of Post-Soviet Democratization,* 12(2): 169–194.

2004b. "Party Development in a Federal System: The Impact of Putin's Reforms," in Reddaway, Peter, and Robert W. Orttung, eds., *The Dynamics of Russian Politics: Putin's Reform of Federal-Regional Relations,* Vol. II. Lanham, MD: Rowman & Littlefield, 179–212.

2006. *Why Not Parties in Russia? Democracy, Federalism, and the State.* Cambridge: Cambridge University Press.

Hale, Henry, and Timothy Colton. 2009. "Russians and the Putin-Medvedev 'Tandemocracy'" NCEEER Working Paper.

2013. "Putin's Uneasy Return: The 2012 Russian Election Studies Survey" NCEEER Working Paper.

Hale, Henry. 2014. *Patronal Politics: Eurasian Regime Dynamics in Comparative Perspective.* New York: Cambridge University Press.

Hall, Peter A., and Rosemary C. R. Taylor. 1996. "Political Science and the Three New Institutionalisms." *Political Studies,* 44: 936–957.

Harasmyiw, Bohdan. 1984. *Political Elite Recruitment in the Soviet Union.* New York: St. Martin's Press.

Haspel, Moshe, Thomas F. Remington, and Steven S. Smith. 2006. "Lawmaking and Decree Making in the Russian Federation: Time, Space, and Rules in Russian National Policymaking." *Post-Soviet Affairs,* 22(3): 249–275.

Hellman, Joel. 1998. "Winners Take All: The Politics of Partial Reform." *World Politics,* 50(2): 203–234.

Herbst, Jeffrey. 2000. *States and Power in Africa: Comparative Lessons in Authority and Control.* Princeton, NJ: Princeton University Press.

Herron, Erik S. 2002. "Causes and Consequences of Fluid Faction Membership in Ukraine." *Europe-Asia Studies,* 54(4): 625–639.

Hesli, Vicki L., and William M. Reisinger, eds., 2003. *The 1999–2000 Elections in Russia: Their Impact and Legacy.* Cambridge: Cambridge University Press.

Hicken, Allen. 2011. "Clientelism." *Annual Review of Political Science,* 14: 289–310.

Hill, Fiona, and Clifford Gaddy. 2003. *The Siberian Curse: How Communist Planners Left Russia Out in the Cold.* Washington, DC: Brookings Institution.

Hill, Ronald J., and Peter John Frank. 1981. *The Soviet Communist Party.* London: Allen & Unwin.

Hough, Jerry F. 1969. *The Soviet Prefects: The Local Party Organs in Industrial Decision-Making.* Cambridge, MA: Harvard University Press.

1997. *Democratization and Revolution in the USSR, 1985–1991.* Washington, DC: Brookings Institution.

1998. "The Failure of Party Formation and the Future of Russian Democracy," in Colton, Timothy J., and Jerry F. Hough, eds., *Growing Pains: Russian Democracy and the Election of 1993.* Washington, DC: Brookings Institution, 669–712.

2001. *The Logic of Economic Reform in Russia, 1991–1998.* Washington, DC: Brookings Institution.

Hough, Jerry F., and Merle Fainsod. 1979. *How the Soviet Union Is Governed.* Cambridge, MA: Harvard University Press.

Howard, Marc Morjé, and Philip G. Roessler. 2006. "Liberalizing Electoral Outcomes in Competitive Authoritarian Regimes." *American Journal of Political Science*, 50(2): 365–381.

Huntington, Samuel P. 1968. *Political Order in Changing Societies.* New Haven, CT: Yale University Press.

1970. "Social and Institutional Dynamics of One-Party Systems," in Huntington, Samuel P., and Clement Henry Moore, eds., *Authoritarian Politics in Modern Society: The Dynamics of Established One-Party Systems.* New York: Basic, 3–47.

Huntington, Samuel P., and Clement Henry Moore. 1970. *Authoritarian Politics in Modern Society: The Dynamics of Established One-Party Systems.* New York: Basic.

Huskey, Eugene. 2001. "Overcoming the Yeltsin Legacy: Vladimir Putin and Russian Political Reform," in Brown, Archie, ed., *Contemporary Russian Politics: A Reader.* Oxford: Oxford University Press, 82–98.

Isaacs, Rico, and Sarah Whitmore. 2014. "The Limited Agency and Life-Cycles of Personalized Dominant Parties in the Post-Soviet Space: The Cases of United Russia and Nur Otan." *Democratization*, 21(4): 699–721.

Ivanov, Vitalii. 2008. *Partiya Putina: Istoriya Edinoi Rossii.* Moscow: Europa.

2013. *Glava Sub'ektov Rossisskoi Federatsii: Pravovaya i Politicheskaya Istoriya Instituta.* Moscow: Praksis.

Johnson, Juliet. 1997. "Russia's Emerging Financial-Industrial Groups." *Post-Soviet Affairs*, 13(4): 333–365.

2000. *A Fistful of Rubles: The Rise and Fall of the Russian Banking System.* Ithaca, NY: Cornell, University Press.

Judah, Ben. 2014. *Fragile Empire: How Russia Fell in and out of Love with Vladimir Putin.* Ne Haven, CT: Yale University Press.

Kalyvas, Stathis N. 1999. "The Decay and Breakdown of Communist One-Party Systems." *Annual Review of Political Science*, 2: 323–343.

Kalyvas, Stathis. 2000. "Commitment Problems in Emerging Democracies: The Case of Religious Parties." *Comparative Politics*, 32(4): 379–399.

Kern, Robert W. 1973, ed. *The Caciques: Oligarchical Politics and the System of Caciquismo in the Luso-Hispanic World.* Albuquerque: University of New Mexico Press.

Kern, Robert, and Ronald Dolkart. 1973. "Introduction," in Kern, Robert, ed., *The Caciques: Oligarchical Politics and the System of Caciquismo in the Luso-Hispanic World.* Albuquerque: University of New Mexico Press.

Khenkin, Sergei. 1996. "Partiya Vlasti: rossisskii variant." *Pro et Contra*, 1(1): 32–45.

Kim, Woosang, and James D. Morrow. 1992. "When Do Power Shifts Lead to War?" *American Journal of Political Science*, 36(4): 896–922.

Kitschelt, Herbert. 2000. "Formation of Party Cleavages in Post-Communist Democracies." *Party Politics*, 1(4): 447–472.

2003. "Accounting for Postcommunist Regime Diversity: What Counts as a Good Cause?" in Ekiert, Grzegorz, and Stephen E. Hanson, eds.,

Capitalism and Democracy in Central and Eastern Europe: Assessing the Legacy of Communist Rule. Cambridge: Cambridge University Press, 49–86.

Knight, Alan. 1992. "Mexico's Elite Settlement: Conjecture and Consequences," in Higley, John, and Richard Gunther, eds., *Elites and Democratic Consolidation in Latin America and Southern Europe.* Cambridge: Cambridge University Press, 113–145.

Koter, Dominika. 2013. "King Makers: Local Leaders and Ethnic Politics in Africa." *World Politics,* 65(2): 187–232.

Kryshtanovskaya, Olga, and Stephen White. 2003. "Putin's Militocracy." *Post-Soviet Affairs,* 19(4): 289–306.

Kullberg, Judith S. 1998. "Preserving the Radical Stronghold: The Election in Moscow," in Colton, Timothy J., and Jerry F. Hough, eds., *Growing Pains: Russian Democracy and the Elections of 1993.* Washington, DC: Brookings Institution, 311–348.

Kynev, Aleksandr V. 2006. "Politicheskii Partii v Rossiskikh Regionakh: vzglyad cherez prizmu regional'nyi izbiratel'noi reformy." *Polis,* (6): 145–160.

Lapalombara, Joseph, and Weiner, Myron, eds., 1963. *Political Parties and Political Development.* Princeton, NJ: Princeton University Press.

Lapidus, Gail, and Edward Walker. 1995. "Nationalism, Regionalism, and Federalism: Dilemmas of State-Building in Post-Communist Russia," in Lapidus, Gail, ed., *The New Russia: Troubled Transformation.* Boulder, CO: Westview.

Lapina, Natalya, and Alla Chirikova. 1999. *Regional'nye elity v RF: Modeli povedeniia i politicheskie orientatsii.* Moscow: Institut nauchnoi informatsii po obshchestvennym naukam.

   2000. *Strategii regional'nykh elit: ekonomika, modeli vlasti, politicheskii vybor.* Moscow: Institut nauchnoi informatsii po obshchestvennym naukam.

   2002. *Regiony-Lidery: Ekonomika i politicheskaia dinamika.* Moscow: Izdatel'stvo Instituta sotsiologii RAN.

Laver, Michael, and Kenneth A. Shepsle. 1990. "Coalitions and Cabinet Government." *American Political Science Review,* 84(3): 873–890.

Ledeneva, Alena. 2006. *How Russia Really Works: The Informal Practices That Shaped Post-Soviet Politics and Business.* Ithaca, NY: Cornell University Press.

Lemarchand, René. 1972. "Political Clientelism and Ethnicity in Tropical Africa: Competing Solidarities in Nation-Building." *American Political Science Review,* 66(1): 68–90.

Levitsky, Steven, and Lucan Way. 2002. "The Rise of Competitive Authoritarianism." *Journal of Democracy,* 13(2): 51–65.

   2010. *Competitive Authoritarianism: Hybrid Regimes after the Cold War.* Cambridge: Cambridge University Press.

   2012. "Beyond Patronage: Violent Struggle, Ruling Party Cohesion, and Authoritarian Durability." *Perspectives on Politics,* 10(4): 869–889.

Lindblom, Charles Edward. 1977. *Politics and Markets: The World's Political-Economic Systems.* New York: Basic.

Luong, Pauline Jones, and Erika Weinthal. 2004. "Contra Coercion: Russian Tax Reform, Exogenous Shocks, and Negotiated Institutional Change." *American Political Science Review,* 98(1): 139–152.

Lussier, Danielle. 2002. "The Role of Russia's Governors in the 1999–2000 Federal Elections," in Ross, Cameron, ed., *Regional Politics in Russia*. Manchester, UK: Manchester University Press, 57–76.

Lust-Okar, Ellen. 2006. *"Elections under Authoritarianism: Preliminary Lessons from Jordan."* Democratization, 13(3): 456–471.

Lyubimov, Nikolai. 2005. "Nulevoye Chteniye Zakonoproektov Kak Instrument Soglasovaniya Interesov." *Predstavitelnaya Vlast – 21 во век: zakonodatelstvo, kommentarii, problem*, (1): 3–4.

Magaloni, Beatriz. 2006. *Voting for Autocracy: Hegemonic Party Survival and Its Demise in Mexico*. New York: Cambridge University Press.

2008. "Credible Power-Sharing and the Longevity of Authoritarian Rule." *Comparative Political Studies*, 41(4–5): 715–741.

Magaloni, Beatriz, and Ruth Kricheli. 2010. "Political Order and One-Party Rule." *Annual Review of Political Science*, 13: 123–143.

Mainwaring, Scott. 1999. *Rethinking Party Systems in the Third Wave of Democratization*. Stanford, CA: Stanford University Press.

Makarenko, Boris. 1998. "Gubernatorskiy Partii Vlasti kak novyi obshestvennyi phenomenon." *Politiya*, 1(7): 50–58.

2011. "Post-Sovetskaya Partiya Vlasti: 'Edinaya Rossiya' v sravnitelnom contekste." *Polis*, (1): 42–65.

Makarkin, Aleksei. 1999. "Gubernatorskiye Partii," in McFaul, Michael, Nikolai Petrov, and Andrei Ryabov, eds., *Rossiya Nakanunye Dumskikh Vyborov 1999 goda*. Moscow: Moscow Carnegie Center.

Makhortov, Evgenii. 2008. "Lobbism in TsFO: Analiz, Monitoring, Informatsia." Special Issue of Lobbying.ru. www.lobbying.ru/docs/bouklette_s.pdf. December 30, 2014.

March, Luke. 2009. "Managing Opposition in a Hybrid Regime: Just Russia and Parastatal Opposition." *Slavic Review*, 68(3): 504–527.

Markov, Sergei. 1999. "The Kremlin's Last Gasp: How the New Unity Bloc Can Make or Break the Family's–And the Country's–Future." *Russian Election Watch*, 3(1).

Marples, David R. 2007. *The Lukashenko Phenomenon: Elections, Propaganda, and the Foundations of Political Authority in Belarus*. Trondheim, Norway: Trondheim Program on East European Cultures and Societies.

Matsuzato, Kimitaka. 2001. "From Ethno-Bonapartism to Centralized Caciquismo: Characteristics and Origins of the Tatarstan Political Regime, 1990–2000." *Journal of Communist Studies and Transition Politics*, 17(4): 43–77.

McFaul, Michael. 1997. *Russia's 1996 Presidential Election: The End of Polarized Politics*. Stanford, CA: Hoover Institution Press.

1998. "Russia's Choice: The Perils of Revolutionary Democracy," in Colton, Timothy J., and Jerry F. Hough, eds., *Growing Pains: Russian Democracy and the Elections of 1993*. Washington, DC: Brookings Institution, 115–140.

2001. *Russia's Unfinished Revolution: Political Change from Gorbachev to Putin*. Ithaca, NY: Cornell University Press.

McFaul, Michael, Nikolai Petrov, and Andrey Ryabov. 1999. *Primer on Russia's 1999 Elections*. Washington, DC: Carnegie Endowment for International Peace.

McFaul, Michael, and Timothy J. Colton. 2003. *Popular Choice and Managed Democracy: The Russian Elections of 1999 and 2000*. Washington, DC: Brookings Institution.

McFaul, Michael, and Sergei Markov. 1993. *The Troubled Birth of Russian Democracy: Parties, Personalities, and Programs*. Stanford, CA: Hoover Institution.

McFaul, Michael, and Nikolai Petrov, eds., 1998. *Politicheskii Almanakh Rossii 1997*. Moscow: Moscow Carnegie Center.

McMann, Kelly M. 2006. *Economic Autonomy and Democracy: Hybrid Regimes in Russia and Kyrgyzstan*. Cambridge: Cambridge University Press.

Migdal, Joel. 1988. *Strong Societies and Weak States: State-Society Relations and State Capabilities in the Third World*. Princeton, NJ: Princeton University Press.

Milgrom, Paul, Douglas North, and Barry Weingast. 1990. "The Role of Institutions in the Revival of Trade: The Law Merchant, Private Judges, and the Champagne Fairs." *Economic and Politics*, 2(1): 1–23.

Miller, Michael. 2015. "Democratic Pieces: Autocratic Elections and Democratic Development Since 1815" *British Journal of Political Science* 45(3): 501–530.

Moe, Terry M. 1990. "Political Institutions: The Neglected Side of the Story." *Journal of Law, Economics, and Organization*, 6:213–253.

Moraski, Bryon. 2006. *Elections by Design: Parties and Patronage in Russia's Regions*. Dekalb, IL: Northern Illinois University Press.

Moser, Robert G. 2011. *Unexpected Outcomes: Electoral Systems, Political Parties, and Representation in Russia*. Pittsburgh: University of Pittsburg Press.

Myagkov, Mikhail. 2003. "The 1999 Duma Election in Russia: A Step toward Democracy or the Elites' Game?" in Hesli, Vicki L., and William Reisinger, eds., *The 1999–2000 Elections in Russia: Their Impact and Legacy*. Cambridge: Cambridge University Press, 142–162.

Myagkov, Mikhail G., and D. Roderick Kiewet. 1996. "Czar Rule in the Russian Congress of Peoples' Deputies?" *Legislative Studies Quarterly*, 21(1): 5–40.

Myerson, Roger. 2008. "The Autocrat's Credibility Problem and the Foundations of the Constitutional State." *American Political Science Review*, 102(1): 125–139.

North, Douglas C., and Barry R. Weingast. 1989. "Constitutions and Commitment: The Evolution of Institutions Governing Public Choice in Seventeenth-Century England." *Journal of Economic History*, 49(4): 803–832.

North, Douglass. 1993. "Institutions and Credible Commitment." *Journal of Institutional and Theoretical Economics*. 149(1): 11–23.

O'Donnell, Guillermo, Philippe C. Schmitter, and Laurence Whitehead. 1986. *Transitions from Authoritarian Rule*. Baltimore: Johns Hopkins University Press.

Olson, Mancur. 1993. "Dictatorship, Democracy, and Development." *American Political Science Review*, 87(3): 567–576.

Orlovsky, Daniel. 1980. "Political Clientelism in Russia: the Historical Perspective," in Rigby, T. H. and Bogdan Harasymyiw, eds., *Leadership Selection and Patron-Client Relations in the USSR and Yugoslavia*. London: George Allen and Unwin, 174–199

Orttung, Robert W. 2004. "Business and Politics in the Russian Regions." *Problems of Post-Communism*, 51(2): 48–60.

Ostrom, Elinor. 1990. *Governing the Commons: The Evolution of Institutions for Collective Action*. Cambridge: Cambridge University Press.

Panov, Petr. 2008. "Vybory v Rossii: Institutsional'naya Perspektiva" *Polis*, 5, 99–112.

Peaslee, A. J. 1974. *Constitutions of Nations*. 4th ed. Berlin: Springer.

Pempel, T. J., ed. 1990. *Uncommon Democracies: The One-Party Dominant Regimes*. Ithaca, NY: Cornell University Press.

Pepinsky, Thomas. 2014. "The Institutional Turn in Comparative Authoritarianism" *British Journal of Political Science*, 44(3): 631–653.

Petrov, Nikolai. 2003. "Russia's Party of Power Takes Shape." *Russia and Eurasia Review*, 2(16).

Petrov, Nikolai, and Aleksei Makarkin. 1999. "Unity(Medved)," in McFaul, Michael, Nikolai Petrov, and Andrei Ryabov, eds., *Primer on Russia's 1999 Duma Elections*. Washington, DC: Carnegie Endowment for International Peace.

Powell, John Duncan. 1970. "Peasant Society and Clientelist Politics." *American Political Science Review*, 64(2): 411–425.

Powell, Robert. 2006. "War as a Commitment Problem." *International Organization*, 60(1): 169–203.

Przeworski, Adam. 1991. *Democracy and the Market: Political and Economic Reforms in Eastern Europe and Latin America*. Cambridge: Cambridge University Press.

    2004. "Institutions Matter?" *Government and Opposition*, 39(4): 527–540.

Przeworski, Adam, Michael Alvarez, Jose Antonio Cheibub, and Fernando Limongi. 2000. *Democracy and Development: Political Institutions and Well-Being in the World, 1950–1990*. New York: Cambridge University Press.

Radnitz, Scott. 2010. *Weapons of the Wealthy: Predatory Regimes and Elite-Led Protests in Central Asia*. Ithaca, NY: Cornell University Press.

Reisinger, W. M., and Moraski, B. J. 2013. "Deference or Governance? A Survival Analysis of Russia's Governors Under Presidential Control." in Reisinger, William ed., *Russia's Regions and Comparative Subnational Politics* New York: Routledge.

Remington, Thomas F. 1988. *The Truth of Authority: Ideology and Communication in the Soviet Union*. Pittsburgh: University of Pittsburgh Press.

    2001. *The Russian Parliament: Institutional Evolution in a Transitional Regime*. New Haven, CT: Yale University Press.

    2006. "Presidential Support in the Russian State Duma." *Legislative Studies Quarterly*, 31(1): 5–32.

    2008. "Patronage and the Party of Power: President-Parliament Relations under Vladimir Putin." *Europe-Asia Studies*, 60(6): 959–987.

    2010. "Accounting for Regime Differences in the Russian Regions: Historical and Structural Influences." Working Paper. Atlanta: Emory University.

    2014. *Presidential Decrees in Russia: A Comparative Perspective*. New York: Cambridge.

Remington, Thomas F., Steven S. Smith, D. Roderick Kiewiet, and Moshe Haspel. 1994. "Transitional Institutions and Parliamentary Alignments in Russia,

1990–1993," in Remington, Thomas F., ed., *Parliaments in Transition: The New Legislative Politics in the Former USSR and Eastern Europe.* Boulder, CO: Westview, 159–180.

Reuter, Ora John. 2010. "The Politics of Dominant Party Formation: United Russia and Russia's Governors." *Europe-Asia Studies,* 62(2): 293–327.

2013. "Regional Patrons and Hegemonic Party Electoral Performance." *Post-Soviet Affairs,* 29(2): 101–135.

Reuter, Ora John, and Jennifer Gandhi. 2011. "Economic Performance and Elite Defection from Hegemonic Parties." *British Journal of Political Science,* 41(1): 83–110.

Reuter, Ora John, and Thomas Remington. 2009. "Dominant Party Regimes and the Commitment Problem: The Case of United Russia." *Comparative Political Studies,* 42(4): 501–526.

Reuter, Ora John, and Graeme Robertson. 2012. "Sub-National Appointments in Authoritarian Regimes: Evidence from Russia." *Journal of Politics,* 74(4): 1023–1037

2015. "Legislatures, Cooptation, and Social Protest in Contemporary Authoritarian Regimes." *Journal of Politics,* 77(1): 235–248

Reuter, Ora John, and Rostislav Turovsky. 2014. "Dominant Party Rule and Legislative Leadership in Authoritarian Regimes." *Party Politics,* 20(5): 663–674.

Rigby, Thomas Henry. 1981. "Early Provincial Cliques and the Rise of Stalin." *Soviet Studies,* 33(1): 3–28.

Rigby, Thomas Henry, and Bohdan, Harasymiw, eds. 1980. *Leadership Selection and Patron-Client Relations in the USSR and Yugoslavia.* London: Allen and Unwin.

Roberts, Sean P. 2012a. *Putin's United Russia Party.* Abingdon, UK: Routledge.

2012b. "United Russia and the Dominant-Party Framework: Understanding the Russian Party of Power in Comparative Perspective." *East European Politics,* 28(3): 225–240.

Rodden, Jonathan. 2009. "Back to the Future: Endogenous Institutions and Comparative Politics," in Lichbach, Mark Irving, and Alan S. Zuckerman, eds., *Comparative Politics: Rationality, Culture, and Structure,* 2nd ed. Cambridge: Cambridge University Press, 333–357.

Rodriguez, Victoria E., and Peter M. Ward. 1994. "Disentangling the PRI from the Government in Mexico." *Mexican Studies,* 10(1): 163–186.

Ross, Cameron. 2005. "Federalism and Electoral Authoritarianism under Putin." *Demokratizatsiya: The Journal of Post-Soviet Democratization,* 13(3): 347–372.

Ross, Michael. 2001. "Does Oil Hinder Democracy?" *World Politics,* 53(3): 325–361.

Rothchild, Donald. 1985. "State-Ethnic Relations in Middle Africa," in Carter, Gwendolen Margaret, and Patrick O. O'Meara, eds., *African Independence: The First 25 Years.* Bloomington: Indiana University Press, 71–96.

Ryabov, Andrei. 2006. "'Poka ne nachalos': ot partii vlasti k pravyashei partii." *Apologiya,* (8).

Sakwa, Richard. 1995. "The Russian *Elections* of December *1993.*" *Europe-Asia Studies,* 47(2): 195–227.

2003. "Elections and National Integration in Russia," in Hesli, Vicki L., and M. William Reisinger, eds., *The 1999–2000 Elections in Russia: Their Impact and Legacy*. Cambridge: Cambridge, 121–141.
2011. *The Crisis of Russian Democracy: The Dual State, Factionalism and the Medvedev Succession*. New York: Cambridge.
Samuels, David. 2004. "Presidentialism and Accountability for the Economy in Comparative Perspective." *American Political Science Review* 98(3): 425–436.
Samuels, David, and Fernando Luiz Abrucio. 2000. "Federalism and Democratic Transitions: The 'New' Politics of the Governors in Brazil." *Journal of Federalism*, 30(2): 43–61.
Sanchez-Cuenca, Ignacio. 1998. "Institutional Commitments and Democracy." *European Journal of Sociology*, 39(1): 78–109.
Sartori, Giovani. 1976. *Parties and Party Systems: A Framework for Analysis*. Cambridge: Cambridge University Press.
Schachter, Ruth. 1961 "Single-Party Systems in West Africa." *American Political Science Review*, 55(2): 294–307.
Schapiro, Leonard Bertram. 1964. *The Communist Party of the Soviet Union*. New York: Vintage.
Schedler, Andreas, ed., 2006. *Electoral Authoritarianism: The Dynamics of Unfree Competition*. Boulder, CO: Lynne Rienner.
Scheiner, Ethan. 2006. *Democracy without Competition in Japan: Opposition Failure in a One-Party Dominant State*. Cambridge: Cambridge University Press.
Schelling, Thomas C. 1960. *The Strategy of Conflict*. Cambridge, MA: Harvard University Press.
Schmidt, Steffen. 1980. "Patrons, Brokers, and Clients: Party Linkages in the Colombian System," in Lawson, Kay, ed., *Political Parties and Linkage*. New Haven, CT: Yale University Press, 266–288.
Schurmann, Franz. 1968. *Ideology and Organization in Communist China*, 2nd ed. Los Angeles: University of California Press.
Schwartz, Thomas. 1986. The Logic of Collective Choice. New York: Columbia University Press.
Scott, James. 1972. "Patron-Client Politics and Political Change in Southeast Asia." *American Political Science Review*, 66(1): 91–113.
Service, Robert. 1979. *The Bolshevik Party in Revolution: A Study in Organisational Change, 1917–23*. London: Macmillan.
Sharafutdinova, Gulnaz. 2013. "Getting the 'Dough' and Saving the Machine: Lessons from Tatarstan." *Demokratizatsiya: The Journal of Post-Soviet Democratization*, 21(4): 507–530.
Shefter, Martin. 1994. *Political Parties and the State: The American Historical Experience*. Princeton, NJ: Princeton University Press.
Shepsle, Kenneth. 1991. "Discretion, Institutions, and the Problem of Government Commitment," in Bordieu, Pierre, and James Samuel Coleman, eds., *Social Theory for a Changing Society*. Boulder, CO: Westview, 245–263.
Shepsle, Kenneth, and Barry Weingast. 1981. "Structure-Induced Equilibrium and Legislative Choice." *Public Choice*, 37(3): 503–519.
Shleifer, Andrei, and Daniel Treisman. 2001. *Without a Map: Political Tactics and Economic Reform in Russia*. Cambridge, MA: MIT Press.

2005. "A Normal Country: Russia after Communism." *Journal of Economic Perspectives*, 19(1): 151–174.
Shugart, Matthew. 1998. "The Inverse Relationship between Party Strength and Executive Strength: A Theory of Politicians' Constitutional Choices." *British Journal of Political Science*, 28(1): 1–29.
Shvetsova, Olga. 2003. "Resolving the Problem of Preelection Coordination: The 1999 Parliamentary Election as an Elite Presidential Primary," in Hesli, Vicki L., and William M. Reisinger, eds., *The 1999–2000 Elections in Russia: Their Impact and Legacy*. Cambridge: Cambridge University Press, 213–231.
Sidel, John. 1999. *Capital, Coercion, and Crime: Bossism in the Philippines*. Stanford, CA: Stanford University Press.
Slater, Dan. 2003. "Iron Cage in an Iron Fist: Authoritarian Institutions and the Personalization of Power in Malaysia." *Comparative Politics*, 36(1): 81–101.
  2010. *Ordering Power: Contentious Politics and Authoritarian Leviathans in Southeast Asia*. Cambridge: Cambridge University Press.
Slider, Darrell. 1994. "Federalism, Discord and Accommodation: Intergovernmental Relations in Post-Soviet Russia," in Friedgut, Theodore H., and Jeffrey W. Hahn, eds., *Local Power and Post-Soviet Politics*. Armonk, NY: M. E. Sharpe, 239–269.
  1996. "Elections to Russia's Regional Assemblies." *Post-Soviet Affairs*, 12(3): 243–264.
  1997. "Russia's Market-Distorting Federalism." *Post-Soviet Geography and Economics*, 38(8): 445–460.
  2001. "Russia's Governors and Party Formation," in Brown, Archie, ed., *Contemporary Russian Politics: A Reader*. Oxford: Oxford University Press, 224–234.
  2005. "Politics in the Regions," in Gitelman, Zvi, Stephen White, and Richard Sakwa, eds., *Developments in Russian Politics*, 6th ed. Houndmills, UK: Palgrave Macmillan, 168–185.
  2006. "United Russia and Russia's Governors: The Path to a One Party System." Working Paper. Presented at the American Association for the Advancement of Slavic Studies National Convention.
  2010. "How United Is United Russia? Regional Sources of Intra-Party Conflict." *Journal of Communist Studies and Transition Politics*, 26(2): 257–275.
Smith, Benjamin. 2004. "Oil Wealth and Regime Survival in the Developing World, 1960–1999." *American Journal of Political Science*, 48(2): 232–246.
  2005. "Life of the Party: The Origins of Regime Breakdown and Persistence under Single-Party Rule." *World Politics*, 57(3): 421–451.
Smith, Peter H. 1979. *Labyrinths of Power: Political Recruitment in Twentieth-Century Mexico*. Princeton, NJ: Princeton University Press.
Smith, Steven S., and Thomas F. Remington. 2001. *The Politics of Institutional Choice: The Formation of the Russian State Duma*. Princeton, NJ: Princeton University Press.
Smyth, Regina. 2002. "Building State Capacity from the Inside Out: Parties of Power and the Success of the President's Reform Agenda in Russia." *Politics and Society*, 30(4): 555–578.

2006. *Candidate Strategies and Electoral Competition in the Russian Federation: Democracy without Foundation.* New York: Cambridge University Press.

Smyth, Regina, Anna Lowry, and Brandon Wilkening. 2007 "Engineering Victory: Institutional Reform, Informal Institutions and the Formation of a Dominant Party Regime in the Russian Federation." *Post-Soviet Affairs*, 23(2): 118–137.

Sobyanin, Alexander. 1994. "Political Cleavages among the Russian Deputies," in Remington, Thomas F., ed., *Parliaments in Transition: The New Legislative Politics in the Former USSR and Eastern Europe.* Boulder, CO: Westview, 181–215.

Solnick Steven. 1998. "Gubernatorial Elections in Russia 1996–1997." *Post-Soviet Affairs*, 14(1): 48–80.

Solnick, Steven. 2000. "Is the Center Too Weak or Too Strong in the Russian Federation?" in Sperling, Valerie, ed., *Building the Russian State.* Boulder, CO: Westview, 123–157.

Starodubtsev, Andrei. 2009. "Regionalniye interesy v Rossiskom parlamente: deputaty-odnomandatniki kak byudzhetnyi lobbisty." *Politea*, 53(2): 90–101.

Stasavage, David. 2002. "Credible Commitment in Early Modern Europe: North and Weingast Revisisted." *Journal of Law, Economics, and Organization*, 18(1): 155–186.

Stein, Robert. 1990. "Economic Voting for Governor and U.S. Senator: The Electoral Consequences of Federalism." *Journal of Politics* 52(1): 29–53.

Stokes, Susan C. 2005. "Perverse Accountability: A Formal Model of Machine Politics with Evidence from Argentina." *American Political Science Review*, 99(3): 315–325.

Stoner-Weiss, Kathryn. 1997. *Local Heroes: The Political Economy of Russian Regional Governance.* Princeton, NJ: Princeton University Press.

1999. "Central Weakness and Provincial Autonomy: Observations on the Devolution Process in Russia." *Post-Soviet Affairs*, 15(1): 87–106.

Svolik, Milan W. 2012. *The Politics of Authoritarian Rule.* Cambridge: Cambridge University Press.

Szakonyi, David. 2015. "Renting Higher Office: The Participation of Economic Elites in Political Institutions" Working Paper. New York: Columbia University.

Taylor, Brian. 2011. *State-Building in Putin's Russia: Policing and Coercion after Communism.* Cambridge: Cambridge University Press.

Tedds, Lindsay M. 2010. "Keeping It off the Books: An Empirical Investigation of the Firms that Engage in Tax Evasion." *Applied Economics*, 42(19): 2459–2473.

Thames, Frank C., and Martin S. Edwards. 2006. "Differentiating Mixed-Member Electoral Systems: Mixed-Member Majoritarian and Mixed-Member Proportional Systems and Government Expenditures." *Comparative Political Studies*, 40(7): 905–927.

Titkov, Alexei. 2007. "Krizis Naznacheniyi." *Pro et Contra*, 11(4–5), 90–103.

Tolstykh, Pavel. 2007. *GR: Praktikum po lobbizmu v Rossii.* Moscow: Al'pina Biznes Buks.

Treisman, Daniel. 1999. *After the Deluge: Regional Crises and Political Consolidation in Russia.* Ann Arbor: University of Michigan Press.

2002. "Defining and Measuring Decentralization: A Global Perspective." Working Paper. University of California, Los Angeles.

2011. "Presidential Popularity in a Hybrid Regime: Russia under Yeltsin and Putin." *American Journal of Political Science*, 55(3): 590–609.

Troxel, Tiffany A. 2003. *Parliamentary Power in Russia, 1994–2001: A New Era.* Houndmills, UK: Palgrave-MacMillan

Truex, Rory. 2014. "Returns to Office in a Rubber Stamp Parliament." *American Political Science Review*, 108(2): 235–261.

Tsebelis, George. 1990. *Nested Games: Rational Choice in Comparative Politics.* Berkeley: University of California Press.

Turovsky, Rostislav. 2002. "Gubernatory i Oligarkhi: Istoriya Otnoshenii," in Turovsky, Rostislav, ed., *Politika v Regionakh: Gubernatory i Gruppy Vliyaniya.* Moscow: Center for Political Technologies.

2009. "Praktiki Naznacheniya gubernatorov: Inertsiya i radicalismv politike tsentra" *Politiya*. 53(2): 72–89.

2012. "The Rise and Fall of Oppositional Governors in Russia." Working Paper. Moscow: Higher School of Economics.

Urban, Michael E. 1989. *An Algebra of Soviet Power: Elite Circulation in the Belorussian Republic, 1966–86.* Cambridge: Cambridge University Press.

Urban, Michael. 1994. "December 1993 as a Replication of Late-Soviet Electoral Practices." *Post-Soviet Affairs*, 10(2): 127–158.

Van Dam, Nikolaos. 1979. *The Struggle for Power in Syria: Sectarianism, Regionalism, and Tribalism in Politics, 1961–1978.* London: Croom Helm.

Van de Walle, Nicolas. 2006. "Tipping Games: When Do Opposition Parties Coalesce?" in Schedler, Andreas, ed., *Electoral Authoritarianism: The Dynamics of Unfree Competition.* Boulder, CO: Lynne Rienner, 77–92.

Vanneman, Peter. 1977. *The Supreme Soviet: Politics and the Legislative Process in the Soviet Political System.* Durham, NC: Duke University Press.

Voslensky, Mikhail. 1984. *Nomenklatura: Anatomy of the Soviet Ruling Class.* London: Bodley Head.

Way, Lucan. 2002. "Pluralism by Default in Moldova." *Journal of Democracy*, 13(4): 127–141.

2005. "Authoritarian State Building and the Sources of Regime Competitiveness in the Fourth Wave: The Cases of Belarus, Moldova, Russia, and Ukraine." *World Politics*, 57(2): 231–261.

2008. "The Evolution of Authoritarian Organization in Russia under Yeltsin and Putin" Working paper. Kellogg Institution for International Studies.

Weiner, Myron. 1967. *Party Building in a New Nation: The Indian National Congress.* Chicago: University of Chicago Press.

Weingast, Barry. 1993. "Constitutions as Governance Structures: The Political Foundations of Secure Markets." *Journal of Institutional and Theoretical Economics.* 149(1): 286–311.

Weldon, Jeffrey. 1997. "The Political Sources of Presidencialismo in Mexico," in Mainwaring, Scott, and Matthew Soberg Shugart, eds., *Presidentialism and Democracy in Latin America.* Cambridge: Cambridge University Press, 225–258.

White, Stephen. 1979. *Political Culture and Soviet Politics.* London: Macmillan.

2011. "Elections Russian-Style." *Europe-Asia Studies*, 63(4): 531–556.

Whitmore, Sarah. 2010. "Parliamentary Oversight in Putin's Neo-Patrimonial State." *Europe-Asia Studies*, 62(6): 999–1025.
Wilson, Andrew. 2005. *Virtual Politics: Faking Democracy in the Post-Soviet World*. New Haven, CT: Yale University Press.
Wilson, Kenneth. 2006. "Party-System Development under Putin." *Post-Soviet Affairs*, 22(4): 314–348.
Wright, Joseph. 2008. "Do Authoritarian Institutions Constrain? How Legislatures Affect Economic Growth and Investment." *American Journal of Political Science*, 52(2): 322–343.
Wright, Joseph and Abel Escriba-Folch. 2012. "Authoritarian Institutions and Regime Survival: Transitions to Democracy and Subsequent Autocracy." *British Journal of Political Science*, 42(2): 283–309.
Yakovlev, Andrei. 2001. "Black Cash Tax Evasion in Russia: Its Forms, Incentives, and Consequences at Firm Level." *Europe-Asia Studies*, 53(1): 33–55.
Zolberg, Aristide R. 1966. *Creating Political Order: The Party-States of West Africa*. Chicago, Rand McNally.
Zubarevich, Natalya. 2005. *Krupnyy Biznes v Regionakh Rossii: Territorialniye Strategii Razvitiya i Sotsialniye Interesy*. Moscow: Pomatur.

Index

Abramovich, Roman, 110n3, 129–31
Aburamoto, Mari, 154–55
administrative resources
  of gubernatorial elites, 213–14, 215–20
  political decentralization and strength of, 249–56
  of Russian regional elites, 87, 99–101, 102–4, 198–99
Africa
  dominant party emergence in, 257–65
  election outcomes in, 52
  elite party structures in, 45
  ethnic diversity and elite strength in, 253–54
  financial liberalization and regime opposition in, 222–24
  postcolonial dominant parties in, 14, 34
African National Congress (ANC), 5
Agrarian Party (Russia), 90–91
Aldrich, John, 35–37, 47, 51–52
All-Russian Coordinating Council (OKS), 93–95, 112–14
All Russian Party "Unity and Fatherland." *See* United Russia Party
All Russia (Vsya Rossii) movement, 109, 110, 112–14, 123–24
All-Russian Peoples Front (ONF), emergence of, 271–77
anti-colonial liberation movements, dominant party origins in, 46
"Apatit" company, 154–55
Arab Socialist Union, 277
ARENA party (Brazil), 45
Arriola, Leonardo Rafael, 222–24
Artyukh, Evgenii, 182n44
Assad regime, 7–8
asset-mobile sectors, party affiliation in, 238
audience costs for leaders, 62n8

authoritarian regimes
  agreements with elites, monitoring of, 63
  benefits of United Russia Party dominance for, 159–60
  breakdown of, 277–79
  commitment credibility and, 49
  democratic characteristics of, 1–4
  democratization and, 37–39
  dominant party as stabilizers of, 4–9, 10–13, 37–39, 277–79
  future in Russia for, 279–81
  Geddes' typology of, 247–48
  global patterns in party organization by, 245–49
  liberal non-democracies, lack of dominant parties in, 257–65
  limits of dominant parties in, 1–4
  parties established by, 46
  in post-Soviet Russia, 32–35
  presidential succession in Mexico, 186
  rent distribution (rent-seeking) in, 257–65
  United Russia Party as commitment device for, 185–96
autonomous resources
  of business elites, 222–24, 229–33
  credible commitments and, 60
  in dominant party regimes, 187, 242–43, 265–66, 267–71
  elite commitment problems and, 67–70
  extent of leaders and elites control of, 249–56
  of gubernatorial elites in Russia, 204–5, 211–15
  of Russian regional elites, 83–89, 99–104, 116–21, 137–46, 148
Ayatskov, Dmitry, 104–5
Azarov, Nikolai, 280

301

302 Index

Ba'ath party, 7–8
Baburkin, Sergei, 166–67
balance of power and resources
  dominant party emergence and, 23–24, 202, 256–57, 265–66
  individual and gubernatorial elite party affiliation and, 203–5
  institutional solutions to commitment and, 65–66
  maximization of dominant party likelihood and, 70–73
  probability of dominant party emergence and, 262–65
bandwagon process, gubernatorial elite party affiliation and, 214
banking institutions
  business elites control of, 100n30
  Our Home is Russia party and, 92–93
Barisian National alliance, 277
Belarus, authoritarian regime in, 2
Berozovsky, Boris, 103, 110n3, 111
Bespalov, Alexander, 124–25, 126, 195–96
Bienen, Henry, 11, 45
Bogatyreva, Lyudmila, 166–67
Bogomolov, Valerii, 126, 133–34, 140–41
Bolshevism
  intraparty conflicts in, 46n6
  power seizure by, 13
Botswana, dominant party in, 5
Botswanan Democratic Party (BDP), 5, 17
Brazil
  authoritarian regime in, 2
  elite control of resources in, 69–70
  elite influence on election outcomes in, 52
  factionalism in parties of, 270
Brownlee, Jason, 6, 12–13, 17–18
Brudny, Yitzhak, 102
Bulychev, Sergei, 198
Burbulis, Gennady, 77, 79, 82
business elites
  dominant party affiliation of, 222–43
  economic conditions and power of, 99–101
  in Egypt, parliamentary clashes with, 162n7
  executive branch influence on, 164–66
  gubernatorial economic control and, 211–13, 215–20
  models of party affiliation of, 233–42
  Our Home is Russia party and, 92–93, 95
  penetration of Russian parliaments by, 163–64
  in regional legislatures, 101n31, 224–29, 237–38
  resource ownership and membership in United Russia Party, 229–33
  United Russia Party and, 129–31, 150, 153–55, 267–71
  Yeltsin's reelection campaign and role of, 102–4

Cambodian People's Party (CPP), 89f1.2
capitalist class, emergence in post-Soviet countries of, 223n1
Castaneda, Jorge G., 32
causality
  dominant party research and, 39–41
  endogeneity in neo-institutionalist research and, 37–39
  global patterns in dominant party emergence and, 265–66
  proliferation of dominant parties and, 14
  quantitative analyses of, 41
Center for the Study of Business-State Interactions, 160–68
center-periphery, strength of elites and leaders and outcomes of, 249–56
Chaisty, Paul, 163
Chavez, Hugo, 277
Chechnya conflict, Russian political division over, 92–93
Chemezov, Viktor, 129–31
Chernetsky, Arkady, 94n18
Chernomyrdin, Viktor, 89–90, 94–95, 104–5
Chiang Kai-Shek, 187
Chinese Communist Party (CCP), 46, 277
Chirikova, Alia, 153–54
Christian Democratic Party (Italy), 4–5
Chubais, Anatoly, 79, 234–37
Citizens Union of Georgia (CUG), 7–8
civil war, dominant party emergence in, 255, 257–65
clientelist networks
  of business elites, 234–37
  commitment credibility and, 49
  democratic regimes, dominant parties and, 5
  dominant party emergence in Russia and, 4
  as gubernatorial resource, 211
  Putin's regime and, 34–35
  of Russian regional elites, 83–89, 99–101
  strength of elites and leaders over, 249–56
  United Russia Party and, 135, 136, 143–46, 151–52

Index

collective action problems
  dominant parties and, 21
  of elites, 44n3, 62
  gubernatorial economic control and, 211–13
  political parties and, 35–37
  United Russia Party management of, 192–93
Colorado Party, 7–8
Colton, Timothy, 82–83
commitment framework
  balanced resources and maximization of dominant party likelihood, 70–73
  dominant party emergence and, 17–18, 58–65, 271
  elite commitment problems, 47–48, 55–58, 63–64, 67–70, 105–6, 196–98
  institutional constraints on dominant party emergence and, 65–66
  leader's commitment problems, 50–55, 60–63, 66–67, 105–6, 185–96
  political parties and, 47–48
  problems of, 17–18, 19–24
  of Russian gubernatorial elites to United Russia Party, 206–10
  severity of problems with, 66–67
  solutions to problems in, 58–73
  two-sided commitment problem, dominant party formation and, 48–58
  United Russia Party and, 30–32, 154–58, 185–98
commodity prices
  in post-Soviet growth of, 137–39, 142–43, 224
  Russian central economy and role of, 99
common pool resource issues, commitment credibility and, 49
Communist Party of the Russian Federation (KPRF), 93–95, 111
  cooptation and rent distribution by regional legislatures and, 163
  gubernatorial membership in, 209, 214, 215–20
Communist Party of the Soviet Union (CPSU), 9
  constitutional support for, 60
  demise of, 24–26
  evolution of, 13
  legacy of, 40–41, 83–89, 96–99
  origins of, 46
  United Russia Party compared with, 159–60
communist systems
  dominant parties in, 10–13

Comparative Constitutions Project, 250–51
Congress Party (India), 5
cost-benefit exchange, leadership and elite commitment and, 107–8
court systems, in autocratic regimes, 1–4
credibility
  balanced resources and increase of, 70–73
  for dominant parties, 21, 63–64, 267–71
  of elite commitments, 63–64
  leader's credible commitments, 60–63
  repeated play for enhancement of, 58–65
  two-sided commitment problem and, 48–58
  for United Russia party, 30–32
crisis conditions, dominant party emergence in, 255, 257–65
Cuba, single party regime in, 9
Cuban Communist Party, 46
cultural institutions, United Russia Party dominance in, 131–32

decentralized political institutions
  probability of dominant party emergence and, 262–65
  strength of elites and leaders and, 249–56
decree-making presidential powers, limits in Russia on, 176–79
delegation of decision-making, leader's credible commitments and, 60–63
democracies, dominant party formation in, 270–71
Democratic Party (DP) (Turkey), 7–8
Democratic Party of Russia, 77–78, 80–81
Democratic Party of Turkmenistan, 9
democratic regimes, dominant party characteristics in, 5
Democratic Russia movement, 74–79
  elections of 1993 and, 79
democratization
  dominant parties and, 37–39
  economic liberalization and, 242–43
  failure in First Russian Republic of, 74–79
  failure of Third Wave democracies, dominant party emergence and, 248–49
  regime breakdown and, 248–49, 277–79
Department for Internal Politics (DIP) (Russia), 132–34, 164–65, 186n50, 191–92
Deripaska, Oleg, 129–31

303

Desalegnhas, Hailemariam, 89f1.2
developing countries
  dominant parties in, 10–13
  political decentralization assessment in, 249–56
dispersion per capita measurements (DPC), population dispersion and, 251–53
distance indicator, geographic resources of gubernatorial elites, 213–14, 215–20
distributional theories of institutions, 65–66
dominant parties. *See also* political parties
  actors in formation of, overview, 42–58
  authoritarian survival and formation of, 10–13
  autocratic regime structure and, 1–4
  barriers to formation of, 2–3
  business elites affiliation with, 222–43
  characteristics of, 4–9
  commitment problems of, 58–65
  democratization and, 37–39
  determinants in emergence of, 257–65
  elite commitment credibility and, 63–64
  elite role in creation of, 44n3, 242–43
  EliteStrengthXLeaderStrength coefficient and emergence of, 257–65
  emergence of, 13–16, 65–73
  global patterns in emergence of, 89f1.2, 244
  independent authority of, 61–62
  independent funding for, 60
  individual and gubernatorial elite affiliation and, 203–5
  institutional evolution in nascent systems, 72–73
  institutions of, 58–65
  international comparisons of, 200–1
  leader's credible commitments and, 60–63
  logit models of affiliation, 234
  modeling emergence of, 256–57
  modeling existence of, 256n11
  mutual investment in, 2–3
  new institutionalism and, 35–37
  predicted probability of emergence of, 262–65
  proportion of regimes with, 1–4, 248–49
  qualitative studies of outcomes for, 12–13
  regime breakdown and, 277–79
  replacement of leader with candidate from, 61
  research methodology concerning, 39–41
  revolutionary organizations and origins of, 46
  rules and norms of, 64–65
  society-based explanations for, 44–47
  stabilization of regimes by, 4–9, 10–13, 37–39, 277–79
  summary of research on, 267–71
  terminology used for, 9
  theories on formation of, 42–73
  two-sided commitment problem and formation of, 48–58
  United Russia Party as example of, 159–201
  Unity Party case study and, 108–23
Duma
  business elite penetration of, 163–64, 224–29
  cooptation and rent distribution and, 163
  declining United Russia Party majority in, 272, 274
  in First Russian Republic, 74–79
  legislation passed from 2007-2010 by, 164–66
  logrolling procedures in, 160–68
  loyalty to United Russia Party in, incentives for, 170–71
  party lists for elections to, United Russia Party control of, 188
  presidential monitoring of, 186
  proportional electoral system for, 193–95
  Putin's bargains with, 176–77
  Putin's cooptation of, 1–4, 145
  regional elite autonomy and, 58–59, 149–50
  United Russia Party influence on, 30–32, 127–29, 152–53, 187
durability of dominant parties, 7–8, 247, 248–49
  global patterns in, 265–66
Dyachenko, Tatyana, 110n3

Earth Institute of Columbia University, 252
Eastern Europe, dominant party emergence in, 257–65
EBRD-World Bank Business Environment and Enterprise Performance Survey (BEEPS), 232–33
economic conditions
  autonomous resources of regional elites and, 116–21
  democratization and liberalization of, 242–43

Index

gubernatorial control over, 211–13, 215–20
Kremlin power linked to, 129–31, 141–42
large public economies and authoritarian rule, 222–24
leadership strength and, 254–56
political institutions and, 49
privatization initiatives in Russia and, 87
regional elites and impact of, 83–89, 99–101, 148–49
United Russia Party rise linked to, 142–43
economic elites. *See* business elites
Edinstvo (Unity) bloc, 109, 110–11, 122
Egypt
dominant party-leadership commitment problems in, 187
NDP influence in, 6
parliamentary clashes with business elites in, 162n7
electoral authoritarian regimes, emergence of, 277–79
Eliseev, Evgenii, 171–72
elites. *See also* regional elites
agency of, 67–70
autonomous resources of, 67–70, 267–71
balance of resources and cooperation with leaders, 70–73, 256–57, 265–66
career advancement of, 55
cohesion of, 5, 11–12, 16–19, 44n3, 203
collective action problems of, 44n3, 62, 192–93
commitment problems for, 55–58, 66–67
costs of cooperation and incentives to renege by, 54–55, 56–57, 198–99
definition of, 16, 42–43
democratization and endogenization of, 37–39
dominant parties and role of, 19–24, 41, 42–58, 242–43, 267–71
duration of authoritarian regimes and cohesion of, 277–79
electoral politics and, 52
incentives for party affiliation, 44
independent authority of, 61–62
individual elites, Russia's governors and, 203–5
leaders' cooperation with, 2–3, 45–46, 50–53, 55–56, 63
leadership strength separate from strength of, 254–56

maximization of gains and cooperation of, 70–73
measurements of strength of, 41
modeling of strength of, 256–57
policy influence of, 56
political parties and commitment of, 47–48
population dispersion and strength of, 251–53
reduction of transaction costs through cooperation of, 56
regime breakdown and cohesion of, 37–39
routinzed political appointment of, 53
schisms among, as threat to leaders, 50–51
society-based theories of dominant party origins and, 44–47
spoils distribution and, 12, 56
strength of, 249–65
support for regimes and role of, 47
United Russia Party cooptation of, 176–85
United Russia Party example of, 28, 32–35
endogeneity
global patterns in dominant party emergence and, 265–66
in leader-elite relationships, 37–39, 138n50
of resources strength of elites and leaders linked to, 249–56
Ethiopia, Haile Selassie's regime in, 280–81
Ethiopian People's Democratic Revolutionary Front (EPRDF), 89f1.2
ethnic minorities
elite strength and concentration of, 253
gubernatorial ethnic resources and, 213, 215–20
Russian regional elites and, 85, 101–2
event history model, of gubernatorial party affiliation, 214–20
Executive Branch, United Russia party influence over appointments in, 171–72
exogenous factors, in leader-elite power distribution, 43n2, 138n50

Fatherland (Nur-OTAN) (Kazakhstan), 7–8, 17, 45
Fatherland-All Russia (OVR) party
formation of, 110
Kremlin relations with, 112–14, 122

Index

Fatherland-All Russia (OVR) party (*cont.*)
   Putin and, 110–11
   Unity Party merger with, 112, 123–24, 139, 146–47
Fearon, James, 62n8, 253
federal government in Russia (Kremlin)
   autonomous resources of regional elites *vs.*, 116–21
   gubernatorial elites and, 209, 215–20
   lack of support for Our Home party from, 95–99, 104–5, 108, 121–23
   limits on United Russian Party by, 185–96
   non-partisan structure of, 132–34
   regional elites and, 85–87, 108–9, 112–14, 188–92
   transfers of wealth and, 212–13, 215–20
   United Russia Party and, 137–46, 176–85, 198–99
   Unity Party and, 112–14
federal transfers, gubernatorial economic resources and, 212–13
Federation Council (Russia), 90–91, 166–67
   elections to, United Russia Party control of, 188
   legislative activity of, 164–66
   loyalty to United Russia Party and appointments to, 171–72
   political independence of, 93–95
   Putin's restructuring of, 137–46
   regional elite power and, 101–2
   United Russia Party membership and, 126–27
Federation Treaty (Russia), 86
Feith, Herbert, 52
Fifth Republic Movement (Venezuela), 277
Filatov, Sergei, 93–95, 97–99
financial industrial groups, 99–101, 103
First Russian Republic (1990-1993), absence of ruling party in, 74–79
500 days program (Russia), 80–81
"For Our Native Ural" party, 148n73
fraudulent vote totals, United Russia Party results and, 272
free-riding, commitment credibility and, 49
Front of National Unity (Poland), 277
Frye, Timothy, 52, 229–33

Gabuniya, Georgii, 104–5
Gadaffi, Muammar, 2, 280–81
Gaidar, Yegor, 79, 82–83, 87, 92–93
game theory, commitment credibility and, 50
Gandhi, Jennifer, 12, 15–16, 45, 179–83, 255

Gattarov, Ruslan, 171–72
Gazprom, 92–93
Geddes, Barbara, 37–39, 247–48
Geertz, Clifford, 52
Gehlbach, Scott, 62, 192–93
General People's Congress (GPC) (Yemen), 89f1.2
Georgia, 'colored' revolution in, 34–35
Glorious Revolution, 66
GOLKAR party (Indonesia), 187
Golosov, Grigorii V., 87, 103, 226
Gorbachev, Mikhail, 85–87, 198–99
Goskomstat registries, 233
governors
   appointment of, United Russia Party influence in, 172–73
   autonomous resources of, 204–5, 211–15
   business elites and, 237–38
   coercion of, to join United Russia, 150–53, 209–10
   collective action problems of, 192–93
   controls as resource for, 214
   defections from United Russia Party, 179–83
   economic resources of, 211–13, 215–20
   election outcomes for, 101–2, 139–40, 172–73, 188–92, 196–98, 211, 215–20
   ethnic resources of, 213, 215–20
   federal government relations with, 188–92, 204–5
   geographic and administrative resources of, 213–14, 215–20
   Higher Council (*Vyshii Soviet*) membership for, 206–10
   individual elites in Russia and, 203–5
   inherited political resources of, 211, 215–20
   legislative clashes with, 162
   membership status in United Russia Party of, 206–10
   party affiliations of, 114–15, 204–5, 209
   peer pressure among, concerning United Russia party membership, 210
   political machines of, 183–85
   Putin's electoral reforms concerning, 204–5, 209–10
   statistical analysis of party affiliation and resource endowment, 214–20
   tenure of, 211
   United Russia Party and, 127–29, 136–37, 172–73, 196–98, 206–10, 267–71
Govorun, Oleg, 132n39

Index

Greene, Kenneth E., 222–24, 247
Gridded Population of the World Project, 252
Grief, Avner, 58–59
Gromov, Boris, 90–91
GRP per capita variable, gubernatorial economic resources and, 212–13, 215–20
Gryzlov, Boris, 126, 127, 133–34
Gusinsky, Vladimir, 103
Guyana, dominant party regime in, 5
Guzhvin, Anatolii, 115n8

Haber-Menaldo data, 254n8
Hagopian, Frances, 52
Haile Selassie, 280–81
Hale, Henry, 48, 65–66, 103–4, 211–13, 229–33, 237
hazard rate, statistical analysis of gubernatorial party affiliation and, 214–20
hegemonic parties, dominant parties *vs.*, 89f1.2
Herfindahl index, 212, 251–53
Higher Council *(Vyshii Soviet)*, 206–10
Hough, Jerry, 84
Huntington, Samuel P., 14–15, 64

Igummov, Gennady, 104
immobile assets
  business elites with, 222–24, 229–33, 238
  in economic resources of gubernatorial elites, 211–13
imperative mandate laws, introduction in Russia of, 193–95
India, dominant party regime in, 5
Indonesia
  dominant party-leadership commitment problems in, 187
  election outcomes in, 52
industrial concentration, gubernatorial economic resources and, 212, 215–20
infrastructure projects, United Russia Party spoils distribution through, 167–68
institutional nesting, leader's credible commitments and, 60
Iran Novin party, 45
Isayev, Andrei, 170–71, 192–93
Italy, dominant parties in, 4–5
Ivan Rybkin Bloc, 90–91, 95–99
Ivlev, Leonid, 132n39

Japan, dominant parties in, 4–5
Jatiya Party (Bangladesh), 45

Jordan, parliamentary clashes with business elites in, 162n7
judicial independence, commitment credibility problems and role of, 58–59
Just Russia party, 191–92

Kalmykov, Yurii, 81
Kazakov, Aleksandr, 93–95
Keefer, Philip, 62, 192–93
Kenya African National Union (KANU), 7–8, 9, 246–47
Kenyatta, Uhuru, 7–8
Kerimov, Suleiman, 129–31
Khasbulatov, Ruslan, 75–76
Kochanovskii, Eduard, 184n49
Kokov, Valery, 104–5
Kolsk Metallurgical Company, 154–55
Kostin, Andrei, 129–31
Kostin, Konstantin, 164–65, 187
Kozak, Dmitrii, 146n71, 172n24
Kozyrev, Andrei, 79
KPRF. *See* Communist Party of the Russian Federation (KPRF)
Krashennikov, Pavel, 152–53
Kuchma, Leonid, 2, 176, 280
Kudrin, Alexei, 179n41, 192–93
Kuomintang (KMT), 7–8, 187

Laos, single party regime in, 9
Lapina, Natalya, 153–54
large companies, party affiliation of, 222–24, 232–33
Latin America
  dominant party emergence in, 257–65
  elite influence on voting behavior in, 52
Law on Political Parties (Russia), 193–95
Law on Voters' Rights (Russia), 193–95
leadership in authoritarian regimes. *See also* regime leaders
  balance of resources and cooperation with elites, 70–73, 256–57, 265–66
  benefits for elites from, 50–53, 55–56
  breakdown of, 277–79
  commitment problems for, 50–55, 66–67
  costs of cooperation and incentives to renege in, 54–55, 56–57, 198–99
  credible commitments in, 60–63
  dominant parties and, 12–13, 19–24, 267–71
  dominant party affiliation of, 42–58, 247
  elites commitment to, 2–3, 67–70
  elite strength independent from, 254–56
  equilibrium constraints on, 18
  future in Russia for, 279–81

Index

leadership in authoritarian regimes (*cont.*)
  global patterns of party dominance and characteristics of, 245–49
  modeling of strength of, 256–57
  parallel party organizations and, 59–60
  population dispersion and strength of, 251–53
  PRI in Mexico and, 32
  pro-regime candidates, election outcomes and coordination of, 53
  regime typology and, 255
  relinquishing authority to parties by, 61–62
  rent distribution (rent-seeking) by, 257–65
  replacement of, 61
  reputation mechanisms for credibility enhancement, 62
  routinization of political appointments by, 53
  strength of, 249–57
  United Russia Party and, 26–32
legislative branch. *See also* Duma; parliamentary institutions
  career advancement opportunities in, United Party influence and, 168–73
  collective action problems in, 36n14
  cooptation and rent distribution in Russia by, 163
  cross-national measures strength of, 163
  defections from United Russia Party in, 179–83, 224–29
  economic elites in regional legislatures, 222–29
  in First Russian Republic, 74–79
  global patterns of party dominance and presence of, 245–49
  governors' power concerning, 188–92
  leader's control of, 51–52
  logrolling procedures in Russian Duma, 160–68
  political parties, 47
  Putin's cooptation of, 1–4, 145
  regional legislative autonomy, 58–59, 149–50
  United Russia Party influence on, 30–32, 127–29, 152–53, 176–79, 187, 196–98
  voting discipline of United Russia in regional legislatures, 177–78
Levitsky, Steven, 12–13
Liberal Democratic Party (LDP) (Japan), 4–5
Liberal Democratic Party of Russia (LDPR), 79–80

liberal non-democracies, lack of dominant parties in, 257–65
Libya, authoritarian regime in, 2
lobbying efforts of United Russia Party, 166–67
local governments
  coordination of elections for, 184n49
  defections from United Russia Party and, 179–83
  influence on elites of, 152–53
  legislative-governor clashes and, 162
  logrolling in local and regional parliaments, United Russia Party role in, 161–62
  political decentralization and strength of, 249–56
  political machines of, 183–85
  United Russia Party dominance in, 131–32, 135, 274–75
LogoVaz group, 103
Lukashenko, Aleksandr, 2
Luzhkov, Yurii
  business elites and, 140–41
  commitment problems for, 198
  political machines and, 109, 110, 146–47
  post-Soviet politics and, 94–95
  Russia's Choice Party and, 81
  United Russia Party and, 25, 124–25, 179n41, 205–6, 208–9
Lysytsin, Anatoly, 114–15, 148, 166–67

Maddison, Angus, 255
Magaloni, Beatriz, 18, 59–60
Makarenko, Boris, 94
Malaysia, dominant party rule in, 187, 277
Markov, Sergei, 115n8
mayors
  coordination of elections of, 184n49
  defections from United Russia Party and, 179–83
  dominant party influence on, 152–53
  legislative-governor clashes and, 162
  logrolling in local parliaments, United Russia Party role in, 161–62
  political machines of, 183–85
  United Russia Party influence over, 131–32, 135, 196–98
McFaul, Michael, 115n8
McMann, Kelly M., 222–24
media
  business elites control of, 100n30
  Russian regional elites control of, 87
  United Russia Party dominance in, 131–32, 153–54

Index

Medinsky, Vladimir, 171–72
Medvedev, Dmitry
  candidates list selections and, 188
  Federation Council and, 171–72
  Presidential Administration and, 136–37
  Putin and, 26–32, 271–77
  United Russia Party and, 89f1.2, 185–86
Melik'yan, Gennadii, 81
Mexico
  opposition parties in, 246–47
  patron-client ties in, 32
  policy brokerage in, 186
  "presidencialismo" period in, 176–77
Mezhregionalnnoy Dvizheniye ("Edinstvo") (Interregional Movement "Unity"). *See* Unity Party (Russia)
Migdal, Joel, 16, 34
Milgrom, Paul, 58–59
Miller, Alexei, 129–31
Milosevic, Slobodan, 7–8
modernization
  dominant party origins and, 14–15
  postcolonial proliferation of dominant parties in Africa and, 14
Mohammed, Mahathir, 187
Moiseev, Boris, 153–54
Molodaya Gvardia (Youth Guard), 170–71
monetization of social benefits
  business elites role in, 140–41
  government-United Russia Party conflict over, 192–93
  United Russia Party cohesion over, 176–77
Morozov, Oleg, 136–37, 171–72, 273n5
Most Group, 103
Motherland party (Russia), 142–43
Movement for Democratic Reforms (Russia), 77–78
Mozambique Liberation Front (FRELIMO), 46
Mubarak, Gemal, 6
multiparty elections, lack of dominant parties in years with, 257–65
Murashev, Arkadii, 79
Muslim indicator, gubernatorial ethnic resources and, 213, 215–20

Namibia, dominant party regime in, 5
national agenda, dominant parties' influence on, 6
National Democratic Party (NDP) (Egypt), 1, 6, 89f1.2, 187, 277
National Liberation Front (FLN) (Algeria), 9

National Projects of United Russia Party, 136, 142–43, 167–68, 192–93
National Resistance Movement (NRM) (Uganda), 1
natural resources
  dominant party emergence and role of, 270
  leadership strength and revenues from, 254–56
  party affiliation of business elites in, 229–33
  political impact of, 222–24, 242–43
Navalny, Alexei, 272, 275–76
Neverov, Sergei, 170–71
new institutionalism
  dominant party analysis in, 11–12, 35–37, 277–79
  endogeneity in research of, 37–39
  on post-Soviet Russia, 32–35
Nigeria, absence of dominant parties in, 1, 7–8, 17, 45, 200–1, 270
nomenklatura system in Soviet Union, 5, 10–13, 53
nomination procedures
  Russian electoral coordination and, 184n46
  Russian legislation concerning, 193–95
North, Doublas C., 58–59, 66
North Korea, single party regime in, 9

oil prices
  decline in, 17
  Kremlin-elite relations and, 2–3, 107–8, 116–23
  lack of Our Home party support and, 96–99
  leader's commitment, 54–55
  Putin's ascendancy and, 17, 40–41
  United Russia party and, 24–26, 129–31, 141–42
Orlovsky, Daniel, 279–80
OTAN. *See* Fatherland (Nur-OTAN) (Kazakhstan)
Otechestvo (Fatherland) movement (Russia), 109, 110
"Our Home is Our City" movement (Russia), 94n18
Our Home is Russia (NDR) party, 24–26, 74
  commitment problems and failure of, 105–6
  electoral losses of, 90–91
  failure of, 89–105
  formation of, 89–90

310   Index

Our Home is Russia (NDR) party (*cont.*)
   Kremlin lack of support for, 95–99, 104–5, 121–23
   national elites and, 92–93, 104–5
   presidential and regional neglect of, 92
   regional elites lack of support for, 92, 93–95, 99–105
   rump status of, 108

parliamentary institutions
   commitment problems and, 66
   cross-national measures strength of, 163
   independence of, 58–59
   regional parliaments, business elites in, 224–29
   United Russia Party control of, 169–70
Parliamentary Powers Index, 163
Partido Revolucionario Institucional (PRI), 1, 7–8
   as dominant party, 200–1
   elite circulation and, 10–13
   factors in dominance of, 13
   hegemony of, 89f1.2
   opposition to, 246–47
   patron-client ties and, 32
   policy direction controlled by, 186
   "presidencialismo" period and discipline of, 176–77
Party for Russian Unity and Accord (PRES), 80–81, 88, 92–93
Party of Life (Russia), 142–43
Party Projects of United Russia Party, 167–68, 170–71
party-state model in communist regimes, 186
party substitutes, in electoral campaigns, 48
patron-client ties
   Mexican PRI and, 10–13, 32
   proliferation of dominant parties and, 14
   Putin's development of, 112–14
   in Russia, 30–32
   United Russia Party influence on, 135, 136–37, 160–68, 183–85
Pempel, T. J., 4–5
Penn World Tables, 255
People's Democratic party (PDP) (Nigeria), 1, 7–8, 17, 45, 200–1
People's National Congress (PNC) (Guyana), 5
People's Party (Russia), 142–43
People's Republic of China
   dominant party rule in, 277
   parliamentary clashes with business elites in, 162n7
   single party regime in, 9

Percent Russian indicator, gubernatorial ethnic resources and, 213, 215–20
personalism, future of authoritarian regimes and role of, 279–81
Philippines
   elite control of resources in, 69–70
   political bosses in, 52
Platov, Vladimir, 114
Pligin, Vladimir, 165
Poland, dominant party rule in, 277
Polish United Worker's Party, 277
political appointments
   avoidance of term limits through, 150–53
   costs of cooperation and incentives to renege, 54–55
   delegation of elite control over, 63–64
   elected officials as, 146n70
   routinzation of, 53
political decentralization
   probability of dominant party emergence and, 262–65
   strength of elites and leaders and, 249–56
political machines
   autonomous resources of, 116–21
   in collectivized agriculture, 237
   economic resources controlled by, 211–13
   elite dismantling of, 63–64
   in ethnic regions, 85, 99
   ethnic resources of, 213, 253
   geographic and administrative resources for, 213–14
   as gubernatorial inherited political resources, 211
   Our Home Party neglected by, 92
   in post-Soviet Russian politics, 80–81, 84–85
   Putin's cooptation of, 143–46
   of regional elites, 87, 108–9, 115–16, 141–42, 155–58
   strength of elites and leaders over, 249–56
   United Russian Party cooptation of, 183–85, 196–98
political parties. *See also* dominant parties
   in autocratic regimes, 1–4
   commitment problem and formation of, 65–66
   elite commitment and formation of, 47–48
   First Russian Republic and absence of, 76–78
   new institutionalist theory and, 35–37

Index

Our Home is Russia party, 89–105
in post-Soviet Russia, 48
Russian legislative reforms concerning, 193–95
Russian regional parties, 115n8
Russia's Choice party, failure of, 79–89
Yeltsin's initiatives for creation of, 89–90
politsovet (political councils).
  business elites and, 131–32
  conflicts within, 183–85
  delegation of authority to, by United Russia Party, 188–92
  gubernatorial membership in, 208
  local elites and, 135
  mobility and turnover in, 170–71
  regional governors in, 95
  regional *politsovets*, 166–67
  United Russia Party organization and role of, 133–34
Popov, Gavril, 77–78, 80–81
Popov, Sergei, 122, 139–40
popularity of regime leaders
  dominant party investment and, 45n5
  Putin's popularity decline and, 271–77
Popular Movement for the Liberation of Angola (MPLA), 46
population dispersion, strength of elites and leaders and, 251–53
power-sharing
  balance of resources and, 23–24, 70–73
  by elites and leaders, 23–24, 42–43, 45–46
  First Russian Republic manipulation of, 75–76
  regime survival and, 7–8
  regional elites and, 84–85
  strength of elites and leaders linked to, 249–56
  by United Russia party, 25
Presidential Administration (Russia)
  absence of party affiliation in, 185–86
  declining United Russia Party influence in, 273n5
  dominance of legislative process by, 162
  Duma list of candidates and, 188
  regional elite relations with, 188–92
  United Russia Party and, 132–34, 136–46, 172–73, 182–83, 187
Primakov, Yevgenii, 25, 110, 111
primary party organization (PPOs), 185
prisoner's dilemma, commitment credibility and, 49–50
private sector, party affiliation of business elites in, 229–33, 234

privatization
  business elites and, 222–24
  demise of dominant parties and, 13–16
  Russian regional elites' power over, 87, 99–101
proportional electoral system, Russian shift to, 145, 193–95
Przeworski, Adam, 12, 245–46, 277–79
public sector
  party affiliation of business elites in, 229–33, 234–37
  patronage resources in, 222–24
Putin, Vladimir
  declining popularity of, 271–77
  defections from regime of, 179–83, 195–96
  dominant parties and, 40–41
  Duma negotiations of, 176–77
  economic conditions and rise of, 137–46
  election as president, 111
  gubernatorial elites and electoral reforms of, 204–5, 209–10
  limits on United Russia imposed by, 185–96
  party coalition building and, 112–14
  public approval of, 142–43
  regional elites and, 4, 17, 24–26, 34, 107–8, 116–23
  United Russia Party and, 89f1.2, 26–32, 124–25, 127, 136, 152, 192–93, 195, 199–200
  Yeltsin and, 110–11

qualitative analysis
  dominant parties and democratization outcomes, 12–13
  dominant party emergence and, 41

Rakhimov, Murtaza
  commitment problems of, 198
  federal government and, 112–14, 146–47
  Russia's Choice Party and, 81
  United Russia Party and, 124–25, 205–6, 208–9
Rally of the Togolese People, 277
RAO-Unified Energy Systems, 234–37
rational choice theory
  dominant party analysis and, 35–37
  political party formation and, 47
regime leaders
  agreements with elites, monitoring of, 63
  balance of resources and cooperation with elites, 70–73

312 Index

regime leaders (*cont.*)
  benefits for elites from, 50–53, 55–56
  commitment problems for, 50–55, 66–67
  costs of cooperation and incentives to renege, 54–55, 56–57, 198–99
  credible commitments of, 49, 60–63
  defined, 42
  dominant party emergence and, 42–58, 247, 267–71
  failure of, 277–79
  generating support and winning elections, 52
  global patterns of party dominance and characteristics of, 245–49
  modeling of strength of, 256–57
  parallel party organizations for, 59–60
  population dispersion and strength of, 251–53
  preexisting party constraints on, 46
  presidential succession in Mexico, 186
  regional elites and, 43–44
  relinquishing authority to parties by, 61–62
  rent distribution (rent-seeking) by, 257–65
  replacement of, 61
  reputation mechanisms for credibility enhancement, 62
  routinzation of political appointments by, 53
  strength of, 249–65
  United Russia Party benefits for, 176–96
regional elites. *See also* business elites; elites; ethnic regions; gubernatorial elites; national elites
  access to policy and spoils through United Russia Party, 160–68
  autonomy of, 83–89, 108–9, 149–50
  benefits of United Russia Party for, 160–75
  business elites and, 101n31, 237–38
  career advancement through United Russia Party for, 168–73
  coercion of, to join United Russia, 150–53
  collective action problems of, 192–93
  commitment problems in Russia of, 105–6
  definition of, 42–43
  discipline of, under United Russia Party, 154–55
  dominant party emergence and, 4, 40–41, 74, 123, 267–71
  in early post-Soviet Russia, 24–26, 40–41
  economic conditions in Russia and, 83–89, 99–101
  electoral politics and, 102–4, 109–10, 183–85, 188–92
  ethnic minorities and strength of, 253
  federal government in Russia and, 85–87, 108–9, 112–14, 123, 137–46
  in First Russian Republic, 74–79
  lack of party affiliation in Russia of, 89–90
  leaders' ties with, 37, 43–44
  legislative-governor relations, 162, 188–92
  lobbying activities of, 166–67
  logrolling in local and regional parliaments by, 161–62
  multiple political affiliations of, 114–15
  Our Home Party and, 92, 93–95, 99–105
  political decentralization and strength of, 249–56
  political machines of, 109, 183–85
  population dispersion and strength of, 251–53
  professions of regional deputies, 231
  purges by United Russia Party of, 170–71, 177–78
  Putin and, 111, 137–46
  regional legislatures, economic elites in, 222–29
  regional parties and movements and, 115n8, 115–16
  Russia's Choice party failure and, 80–81
  uncertainty reduced by United Russian Party for, 168–73
  United Russia Party and, 26–32, 123–37, 139–40, 146–55, 188–92, 196–98
  Unity Party of Russia and, 111–12, 114–21
  voting discipline in regional legislatures, 177–78
  Yeltsin and, 83–89, 102–4, 108–9
Remington, Thomas, 161–62, 163
rent distribution (rent-seeking)
  costs of cooperation and incentives to renege, 54–55
  democratization and, 222–24, 242–43
  dominant parties and, 17, 257–65
  leadership strength and, 254–56
  Our Home is Russia party and lack of, 96–99
  by Russian regional elites, 89, 163
  United Russia Party role in, 161–62

Index

Reuter, Ora John, 52, 163, 172, 179–83
revolutionary organizations
  dominant party emergence and role of, 270
  dominant party origins in, 46
Reznik, Vladislav, 151
Robertson, Graeme, 163, 172
Rodina party, 191–92
Roizman, Evgenii, 182n44
roll-call voting, institution of compulsory voting, 177–78
Rossel, Eduard, 93–95, 148n73, 151
ruling parties, in autocratic regimes, 1–4
Russian Congress of People's Deputies, 74–79, 85–87
Russian Federation, Russia regional elites and legacy of, 85–87
Russian Movement for Democratic Reforms, 80–81
Russian Union of Industrialists and Entrepreneurs, 129–31
Russia's Choice party
  Chechnya conflict and, 92–93
  failure of, 79–89, 105–6
  formation of, 79
  loss of power by, 89–90
Rwandan Patriotic Front (FPR), 7–8
Ryabov, Andrei, 115n8
Rybkin, Ivan, 89–90

Sadat, Anwar, 277
Sanchez-Cuenca, Ignacio, 22, 49
Scott, James, 52
Shabdurasulov, Igor, 110n3
Shaimiev, Mintimer, 205–6
  Kremlin and, 146–47
  political machines and, 109, 141
  post-Soviet politics and, 94n17, 94–95
  United Russia Party and, 124–25, 208–9
Shakhrai, Sergei, 80–81, 83–90, 92–93
Shevardnadze, Eduard, 7–8
Shoigu, Sergei, 110–11
Shokhin, Alexander, 81, 104–5, 108
Shvetsova, Olga, 109–10, 111
Sidel, John, 52
single member districts (SMDs)
  business elites in, 150
  challenges to United Russia Party from, 276n18
  election of legislators from, 224–29
  Our Home is Russia party and, 90–91, 95–99
  political machines in, 87
  Putin's coalitions with, 112–14

Russian party coalitions in, 123–24
Russia's Choice Party and, 79–80, 81
United Russian party influence on, 127–29, 140–41, 145, 149, 154–55
Unity Party presence in, 115, 115n10
single parties
  as dominant parties, 9
  modernization and evolution of, 14–15
  regimes characterized as, 247–48
Sizov, Aleksander, 166–67
SKRIN Ltd., 233
Slider, Darrell, 103
Sluzhu Kuzbassu (I Serve the Kuzbass) movement, 148, 207–8
Smith, Benjamin, 15–16, 45
Smyth, Regina, 37, 48, 65–66, 145, 229–33
Sobchak, Anatolii, 80–81
Sobyanin, Sergei, 124–25, 136–37, 146–47, 172n25, 186n51
social benefits, monetization of
  business elites role in, 140–41
  government-United Russia Party conflict over, 192–93
  United Russia Party cohesion over, 176–77
Social Democrats (Sweden), 4–5
Socialist party of Yugoslavia, 7–8
social opposition
  defections from United Russia Party as, 179–83, 224–29
  dominant parties' influence on division of, 6
  inherited political resources and emergence of, 257–65
  strength of leaders in relation to, 255
society-based variables in dominant party origins, 44–47
South Africa, dominant party in, 5
Southwest Africa People's Organization (SWAPO), 5
Soviet Congress of People's Deputies, competitive elections for, 74–79
Soviet Union
  collapse of, 24–26, 75
  party-state structure in, 187
  Russia regional elites and institutional legacy of, 85–87
"Soyuz Pravykh Sil" (Union of Right Forces) party, 112–14
Special Purpose Programs, 167–68
spoils distribution
  costs of cooperation and incentives to renege, 54–55

spoils distribution (*cont.*)
  delegation of elite control over, 63–64, 191–92
  elite commitment and, 12, 18, 61–62
  independence of dominant parties concerning, 59–60
  logrolling of legislation and, 51–52
  loyalty to leaders and, 50–51
  routinzed political appointments and, 53
  security of elite access to, 56, 191–92
  United Russia Party role in, 28–32, 160–68, 186, 191–92
Stable Russia group, 92–93
Stalin, Joseph, 187
Stankevich, Sergei, 81
state-affiliated businesses
  economic elites from, 222–24
  party affiliation in, 229–33, 234–37
Stroev, Egor, 88, 94–95, 207n3
Strossner, Alfredo, 7–8
subnational elites. *See* regional elites
Sumin, Petr, 94n17
Surkov, Vladislav, 110n3, 124–25, 136–37, 139, 144–45, 186
Svolik, Milan W., 23n6
Sweden, dominant parties in, 4–5
Szakonyi, David, 52

Taiwan, dominant party-leadership commitment problems in, 187
Tanganyika Africa National Union (TANU), 11, 46
tax avoidance, in post-Soviet Russia, 232–33
tax policy
  commitment problems and establishment of, 66
  immobile assets and, 222–24
temperature per capita metric, 252n5
The World Economy: Historical Statistics, 255
third-party institutions
  absence in dictatorships of, 2–3
  commitment of political parties and, 47
  commitment problems of dominant parties and, 58–59
  dominant parties and role of, 267–71
  Russian party development and, 103–4
Third Wave regimes, democratization and dominant party emergence in, 248–49, 277–79
Tishanin, Alexander, 190
Titov, Konstantin, 109, 112–14, 150–53
Tkhakushnov, Aslan, 146n71, 172n24
Togo, dominant party emergence in, 277

transaction costs in politics
  elite cooperation and reduction of, 56
  pro-regime candidates, coordination of linked to, 53
  United Russia Party reduction of, 30–32
Transformation of the Urals Party, 94n17
Travkin, Nikolai, 77–78, 80–81
Trofimov, Evgenii, 187, 197
True Whig Party (Liberia), 45
Tuleev, Aman, 109, 148, 207–8
Turchak, Andrei, 172
Turkmenistan, single party regime in, 9
Turovsky, Rostislav, 169–70
two-sided commitment problem
  dominant party formation and, 48–58
  independence of dominant parties and, 59–60
  summary of, 58

Ukraine
  authoritarian regime in, 2
  'colored' revolution in, 34–35
  dominant party influence in, 176
  Russian dominant party cohesion and crisis in, 276
  uncertainty, United Russia Party dominance and reduction of, 154–55, 168–73
uncommon democracies, 4–5
Union for the Republic (Togo), 277
"United Election Days" (Russia), 145–46
United Front (China), 277
United Malays National Organization (UMNO), 1, 89fl.2, 187, 200–1, 277
United Russia Party, 1
  access to policy and spoils and, 160–68
  accommodative arrangements and membership rules in, 168–73
  approval ratings for, 135–36
  autonomous resources of, 183–85, 186
  benefit to authoritarian regime of, 159–60
  benefits of membership in, 150–53, 160–75
  business elites and, 129–31, 150, 153–54
  career advancement opportunities and, 168–73
  cell organizations in, 135
  coalition building by, 123–24
  coercion to join, for regional and gubernatorial elites, 150–53, 209–10
  collective action problems managed by, 192–93

commitment problems and, 30–32,
154–58, 185–98
current organizational structure
of, 133–34
declining popularity of, 271–77
defections from, 179–83, 193–96,
224–29, 276–77
as dominant party, 89f1.2, 26–32,
39–40, 198–201, 267–71
Duma coalition, 176–77
electoral benefits of membership
in, 173–75
electoral reforms and strengthening
of, 146
electoral success and mobilization of
popular support by, 183–85
evolution from 2001-2010 of, 123–55
executive branch influence on, 164–66
future challenges after 2011-2012
elections, 271–77
grassroots organization by, 185
gubernatorial elites and, 127–29,
136–37, 172–73, 196–98,
206–10, 214–15
Kremlin and, 137–46, 176–85
leadership commitment and role
of, 185–96
lobbying activities of, 166–67
logit models of party affiliation, 234
membership statistics for, 126–27
natural resources affect on loyalty
to, 222–24
origins of, 4, 24–26
party brand of, 150–53
popularity of, 173–75
purges in regional branches by, 170–71
Putin's association with, 107–8, 195
"Putin's Plan" platform of, 136
regime stability and, 32–35
regional elites and, 26–32, 45, 123–37,
139–40, 146–55, 196–98
regional legislative dominance of,
125–26, 127–29, 139–40, 224–29
resource ownership and membership
in, 229–33
Russian governors' support for,
127–29, 136–37
statistical analysis of gubernatorial
affiliation with, 214–20
uncertainty reduction by,
154–55, 168–73
vote mobilization in support of, 47
United Socialist Party of Venezuela, 277
United States, political party
formation in, 47

Unity and Progress movement,
94n17, 107–8
Unity Party (Russia)
decline in regional elections of,
123–24
electoral success of, 111
evolution in 1999-2001 of,
24–26, 108–12
founding of, 110–11
Kremlin relations with, 112–14,
116–21
OVR merger with, 112, 123–24,
139, 146–47
regional elites and, 111–12,
114–21, 214
United Russia party and, 123
universities, United Russia Party
dominance in, 131–32
Ural Rebirth party, 94n17
Urlashov, Evgenii, 182n44

Vargas, Getulio, 2
Vekselberg, Viktor, 129–31
Venezuela, dominant party rule in, 277
Vietnam, single party regime in, 9
Volodin, Vyacheslav
Executive branch and, 171–72
in Presidential Administration, 136–37,
186n51
Putin and, 152
regional elites and, 170–71
United Russia Party and, 133–34, 141,
273n5
Voloshin, Alexander, 110n3
Vorob'ev, Andrei, 154–55
Vorobyov, Andrei, 172
vote mobilization
candidates' personal vote resources
and, 48
elite role in, 47, 214
registration procedures for elections
and, 173–75
United Russia Party role in,
183–85, 205–6
voter expectations
dominant parties' influence on, 6
leaders' strength and, 254–56
Vozrozhdeniye (Revival) movement, 109

Way, Lucan, 12–13
wealthy countries, lack of dominant parties
in, 257–65
Weibull test, statistical analysis of
gubernatorial party affiliation
and, 214–20

Weingast, Barry, 58–59, 66
Weldon, Jeffrey, 176–77
within-case analyses, dominant party emergence and, 40–41
World Bank Development Indicators, 254n8

Yakovlev, Vladimir, 109
Yakunin, Vladimir, 129–31
Yanukovych, Viktor, 280
Yarovaya, Irina, 170–71
Yavlinsky, Grigory, 80–81, 83–89
Yeltsin, Boris, 17
  failing health of, 108–9
  failure of Russia's Choice party and, 79–89
  Fatherland-All Russia (OVR) party and, 110
  as First Russian Republic leader, 74–79
  leadership weaknesses of, 83–89
  Our Home is Russia party and, 92, 95–99, 104–5, 121–23
  political motivations of, 82–83
  reelection campaign of, 102–4
  regional elites and, 74, 85–87
  Russia's Choice opposition to, 89–90
  undermining of parties by, 4, 105–6
  United Russia Party and, 24–26
Yumashev, Valentin, 110n3

Zelawi, Menes, 89f1.2
'zero-reading' logrolling policy, 160–68
Zheleznyak, Sergei, 170–71
Zhirinovsky, Vladimir, 79–80
Zyuganov, Gennady, 102

For EU product safety concerns, contact us at Calle de José Abascal, 56-1°,
28003 Madrid, Spain or eugpsr@cambridge.org.

www.ingramcontent.com/pod-product-compliance
Ingram Content Group UK Ltd.
Pitfield, Milton Keynes, MK11 3LW, UK
UKHW020353060825
461487UK00008B/640